AF580756

New and Revised Edition

INVESTING FOR YOUR FUTURE

How to make your money grow to give you financial independence before and after retirement

Prepared by

J. K. Lasser Tax Institute

and

Sam Shulsky

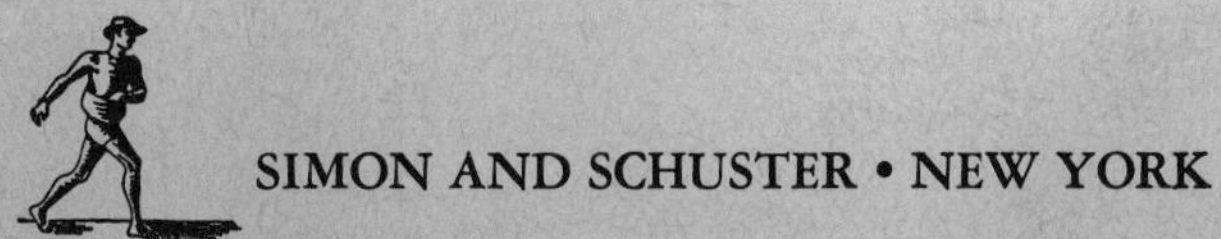

SIMON AND SCHUSTER • NEW YORK

SBN 671-21410-1

PUBLISHED BY SIMON AND SCHUSTER
ROCKEFELLER CENTER, 630 FIFTH AVENUE
NEW YORK, NEW YORK 10020
LIBRARY OF CONGRESS CATALOG CARD NUMBER: 67-13454
MANUFACTURED IN THE UNITED STATES OF AMERICA

Contents

Introduction

A BOOK on investments ideally should be so written as to set forth rules of action which apply long term even though securities values change not only from year to year and month to month, but actually from day to day and minute to minute.

Such a book, then, should obviously concentrate its message on investment truths which can stand up under all variations of financial and economic climate; must help prepare the reader to face, in fact, ever-changing economic "weather."

In the last decade alone, the country has gone through recessions and recoveries, a series of international crises and dollar devaluation. There have been political upheavals—both at home and abroad—the horrifying assassination of a President, several sharp reversals in stock market thinking.

The "cold war"—the seemingly interminable conflict between the world's two major political and social philosophies—remains very much with us and continues perhaps as the dominant influence not only on our internal economic behavior but also on our international posture in both diplomacy and commerce. The amount of "coolness" in this "war" has waxed and waned. Late in 1962—during the confrontation of this country and the Soviet Union over the buildup of missile strength in Cuba—it seemed only hours away from a shooting war. That crisis was resolved, only to be replaced by others in the Middle East, within the Communist bloc itself and among the emerging nations of Africa. In every case Communist influence served to keep the international pot boiling.

Then, too, the rise of Red China to full Communist partnership (if not, in fact, to leadership in its antagonism toward the West) brought even more serious crises in Southeast Asia.

Despite the "winding down" of the war in Vietnam, it remains in the forefront of factors influencing domestic politics and economics. It would be naive to believe that even a "solution" of this particular problem would bring true peace, since it is to the Communists' advantage to "fish in troubled waters" and thus to frustrate any attempt by our government to set a long-term constructive economic and political course, either at home or abroad.

Whether tension eases or rises, the investor—indeed, every citizen—must face up to the realization that short of actual, all-out war which could easily mean the end of modern civilization, the "cold war" (like the poor) will always be with us.

There will be sporadic outbreaks of fighting in various areas, always, of course, suiting the Communist book. There will undoubtedly be further intermittent crises over trouble-spots in Asia and Africa. There will be all the incidents which a dictatorship requires to make political capital—for both foreign and domestic consumption. It is not a pleasant prospect—but we must consider it a part of our life for the foreseeable future.

Its effect on our investment world, of course, is primarily inflationary. We must continue to spend abnormal portions of our gross national product on nonproductive weapons, research for new weapons and other military pursuits. We will most likely continue some foreign aid designed to help backward countries and to keep them out of the Communist camp. All the while, of course, we will have to continue to expand domestic government services to meet the demands of our own people.

It's a safe bet, therefore, that despite all the patriotic demands for a "sound dollar" and a balanced budget which will be made in the halls of government, we shall continue to have inflation and annual deficits—at Federal, state and city levels.

The dollar's purchasing power must, therefore, be expected to continue its downward course.

In 1968 alone, it lost an average 4.7 per cent of its purchasing strength; in 1970, 7.1 per cent; in 1971, 5 per cent; and in many specific areas of expenditure, it lost much more. This means that a substantial part of his savings for the future is in the form of equities, of tangible things which can be expected to go up in price as the dollar declines in value.

Whether these equities should be real estate or rare books and fine paintings, instead of common shares, is a decision which must be left to the individual investor, and must depend upon his knowledge of these specific fields. The one irrefutable argument in favor of corporate securities is that the layman gets management along with the investment.

There is no guaranty, of course, that the prices of these equities will, day by day or year by year, offset the decline in the dollar's purchasing power. But history has proved —as will be borne out later—that over the long term, equity securities as an investment medium have done well in protecting the investor against inflation.

We will continue to have fluctuations in individual security prices and in entire stock markets in the future as we have in the past. Sometimes price changes will reflect intra-corporate and intra-market influences. Sometimes they will be influenced by political events in far-off and hitherto little known lands. A cardinal rule of the investment market is almost constant change. All we can hope to do here is to set down rules which will help investors cope with the various seasons of the stock market.

Volumes have been written on investments. No single volume can claim it sets forth the perfect retirement plan for each and every planner. And no such claim is made for this book. Nor is any specific, single medium of investment set forth as the royal road to riches. For there is none. But the attempt has been made to outline various procedures which may be adapted, with only minor variations, to many different types of planners and situations. Statistical data, based on reliable sources and checked as carefully as humanly possible, is current to March 1, 1972. It is the hope of the publisher that because of changing economic and market conditions, revised editions of this work will be issued from time to time for those using it as a guide to investing for the future.

—Lee Gray
J. K. Lasser Tax Institute

Preface

IT IS only in comparatively recent times that the ordinary citizen has with confidence become the architect of his financial fortunes.

For centuries the urban citizen of modest means based his hopes for economic security on his children, mainly upon his sons. The farmer relied chiefly on land and the sons and daughters to work it when he himself could no longer plow and harvest.

But in the last couple of centuries currency became more than a medium of current exchange. Media appeared—banks, corporations, government bonds—which could be used by everyday citizens as building blocks for their future security. And only within this century has the ownership of corporate securities become so widespread that the N.Y. Stock Exchange now can reasonably urge the public to "own your share of American business." In a capitalist society we have learned that money can work for you as well as muscle and brain.

Today the dollar is not only a medium of exchange by which one converts his labor into the things he wants now, but a medium of purchasing a share in the nation's industrial growth and thus a device for storing up future earning and buying power.

Thus, it has become a medium for sharing in the future.

Of all man's endeavors, his efforts to peer into the future have been the least rewarding. Yet the future remains man's greatest concern.

How long will he live? In what state of health? With what amount of comfort?

This volume is no adventure in the occult. It does not presume to help one foretell the future.

But given certain basic assumptions, it will attempt to answer at least some of the financial questions which loom up in every man's future. It will attempt to outline the various methods by which a person, using dollars available today, can reasonably hope to enjoy their fruits tomorrow. It will outline methods by which a dollar earned and put by in the '70s of the twentieth century can reasonably be expected to benefit its saver when he calls upon it—whether to buy a home ten years hence, to finance a college education for his children fifteen years from now, or to pay the costs of comfortable retirement in the twenty-first century.

Today's dollar is counted as 100 cents—capable of buying, for example, roughly, three quarts of milk, or three loaves of bread. In a world being constantly altered by international rivalry, scientific adventure and drastic social changes, the prudent man will seek to invest his dollars so that they will not only be safe and generate more dollars but will also buy him at least as much milk and bread when he calls on them for support as they did when he earned them and put them aside for his future.

This may seem to be a modest goal, indeed—especially when contrasted with the flood of "you can't miss" and "get-rich-quick" schemes being offered on every hand.

We don't happen to have any such formula at hand. Nor do we think there is any. "If wishes were horses, beggars might ride." And if a sure-fire formula for amassing a fortune overnight were to be had for the price of a book, there would be little point for anyone who could read in working a 40-hour week.

To sum up: This volume is dedicated to help you accumulate dollars and put them to work for your future with all the care one can reasonably expect in the risky task of peering into the unknown.

1 How Best to Put Your Dollars to Work Today

A dollar has powers in two time zones—The present and the future. It can be immediately used for satisfying present needs: food, clothing, shelter; for acquiring both necessities and luxuries. Or it may be set aside to insure satisfaction of these and other needs in your future.

Setting aside dollars is difficult for two reasons:

It requires the denial of certain definite, current, tangible wants for the sake of a more comfortable future.

It requires difficult decisions as to where and how the dollars are to be kept.

For many persons, saving itself presents almost insurmountable difficulties. This is a problem we must all cope with in our own way—although certain ideas outlined later in this volume will aim at making the task easier.

The chief concern of this book, however, is how best to select the medium which will do the most for your dollars—during the years you are setting them aside, and later, during the years you hope to enjoy the fruits of your thrift.

Once you have diverted them from current spending, there are various media for placing dollars.

They can be physically hidden away, as currency. The sugar bowl, coffee tin, under-the-mattress hiding places common in yesteryears are now, fortunately, little used. They left hidden money vulnerable to fire, theft, erosion by inflation. And they deprived it of its ability to earn current income, and to grow.

Assume, for a moment, that you wanted to set up the simplest of retirement plans. Theoretically, you could provide for your retirement by sinking a strongbox in your cellar floor and putting $100 a week into it. At the end of thirty years you could quit work and begin taking $100 a week out of the box for the next thirty years.

You would thus have a successful retirement program—provided:

Your home wasn't burglarized or destroyed by fire at any time in the sixty years; you didn't need the interest your money could have earned; you could live on the $100 a week when you retired; *and* died before your thirty-year cache ran out.

Assuming all these ifs, you would have probably the simplest retirement program ever put into execution. But no fact of our lives today is that simple—and certainly not the problems of personal finance.

Dollars may also be preserved as dollars in savings accounts, in government or corporate bonds, in various life insurance and endowment programs.

These prime and necessary forms of investment serve to preserve the number of dollars—in many cases with the sum guaranteed by the government or one of its agencies—as well as to augment their number by accumulation of interest. One or more of these forms of savings should be included in the long-term investment program of every prudent person.

These investment media boast many advantages:

1. *Absolute Safety of the Number of Dollars.* Investments of up to $20,000 in savings accounts and certificates of deposit may be insured by either the Federal Deposit Insurance Corp. or the Federal Savings and Loan Insurance Corp., both agencies of the U.S. Government. In the more than thirty-five years since these agencies have been set up there has been no loss to savers in insured institutions.

All U.S. Government bonds, whether of the negotiable Treasury bill, note or certificate type held to maturity or of the E, H and "freedom shares" savings issues, are likewise guaranteed by the Government.

Life insurance annuity programs—sold either by commercial life insurance companies or by charitable or religious institutions—are likewise protected by state superintendents of insurance via reinsurance with other companies (but only in cases where the company or institution is licensed to operate in that state).

Corporate bonds are also available as a medium for investing dollars, yielding a fixed number of dollars of income annually and the return of the loan by maturity date. These bonds are not insured, but triple-A quality bonds of some of our larger and older industrial and utility corporations are often rated in the same investment class with government issues.

2. *Convenience of Investment.* Money may be placed in savings accounts in person or by mail. Government savings bonds may be purchased via "painless" payroll deduction programs or by simply stepping into the nearest bank.

Treasury and corporate bonds may be purchased at

brokerage firms or at commercial banks for comparatively low commission fees.

The mere mention that you are interested in any form of insurance program will bring a salesman to your door.

3. *Liquidity.* Dollars may be drawn from savings accounts on demand. Government savings bonds are easily redeemable at one's own bank or at any Federal Reserve bank. Most Treasury and high-grade corporate bonds may be sold on a moment's notice. Insurance funds are not liquid, becoming available only under the terms of the contract, although other emergency options may be obtained.

But there are two significant disadvantages in saving dollars as dollars:

1. *Lack of Inflation Protection.* Whenever a dollar price is put on an investment, as in the case of U.S. Treasury or corporate bonds, savings bonds, saving accounts or annuities, the very assurance as to the repayment of that number of dollars also becomes a factor limiting their future value. The emphasis is always on the investment and safekeeping of a specific number of dollars. There is no commitment as to the buying power or value of the dollars repaid—merely their number. Funds saved in terms of dollars lose purchasing power in periods of inflation. Funds withdrawn twenty years hence may have only a fraction of the purchasing power they possessed when put in. The program has dollar constancy but no fixed purchasing-power value, no protection against inflation.

2. *Lack of Opportunity for Capital Growth.* Savings provide no opportunity to keep step with the growth of the national economy. Business does have its ups and downs. But over the long term usually involved in retirement planning, we can count on an average 3 per cent annual growth in the overall economy and in the value of corporate ownership.

Thus, while savings institutions rate high from the point of view of safety and convenience, their usefulness as *exclusive media* for lifetime investment is severely limited by the fact that they offer absolutely no defense against the very real possibility that a pair of work shoes in 1990 may cost $50. Freezing *all your dollars* today to prepare for paying such prices years hence would be foolhardy indeed.

Even so, some investment in dollars is a necessary part of every prudent investment program. Though the investment shows no increase in number of dollars, it does provide assurance of the availability of a specified number of dollars in case of emergency, thus making possible certain fiscal planning, and insuring the advantage of consumer credit.

Life insurance protection is another medium which is a "must" in every prudent man's financial program even though it fails to meet all the requirements of a well-rounded investment plan.

Its principal disadvantage is that, as in the case of the previously discussed savings media, it is a contract for the return of *a certain number of dollars* irrespective of the purchasing power of those dollars in the years you get them. In other words, it, too, ignores the possibilities of inflation.

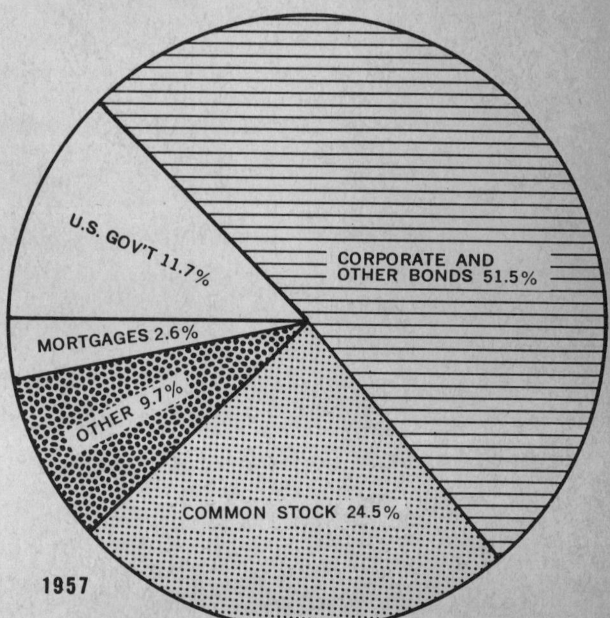

DISTRIBUTION OF ASSETS
Private Pension Funds

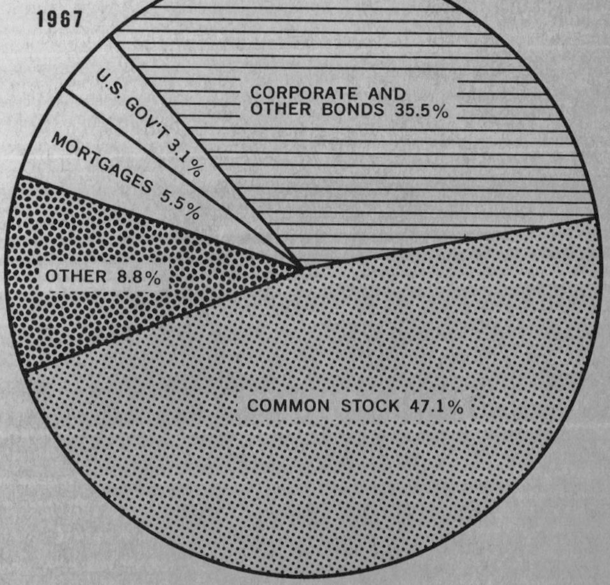

The charts show how common stocks are playing an increasingly dominant role in pension funds because of their effectiveness in providing income and capital growth possibilities in order to combat inflation and to provide larger retirement benefits.

Although this book is intended mainly for the guidance of the average individual investor, it is interesting to note that common stocks have gained increasing acceptance among the large multi-million-dollar investment institutions: insurance companies, corporate and private pension funds, educational institutions, trust funds and savings banks.

These are among the most conservative of investors who, in generations past, were content to leave the bulk of their funds in "gilt-edge" bonds. However, inflation has left its impression on these funds too—even the insurance companies, which basically are committed mainly to obligations expressed in terms of dollars.

As a result, these funds have steadily increased their participation in the common share market to the point where it is now estimated that more than a fourth of all the stocks listed on the New York Stock Exchange are now held by these "institutional" investors.

The following table shows the remarkable growth in this form of equity investment over the last quarter century. Figures are for the year end and are expressed in billions of dollars:

Type of Institution	*1949*	*1956*	*1960*	*1965*	*1968*	*1969*	*1970*	*1971*
Insurance Companies:								
Life	$1.1	$2.3	$3.2	$ 6.3	$ 9.6	$10.2	$11.7	$15.2
Non-Life	1.7	4.5	6.0	10.1	12.8	11.7	12.2	15.5
Noninsured Pension Funds:								
Corporate	0.5	5.3	13.5	33.9	51.0	52.4	57.2	72.2
Other Private	**	0.4	0.8	2.0	3.1	3.1	3.5	4.8
State & Local Government	**	0.2	0.4	2.1	5.2	6.2	8.2	12.3
Nonprofit Institutions:								
College & University Endownments	1.1	2.4	2.9	5.9	6.7	6.7	6.9	7.8
Foundations	1.1	4.1	5.3	12.4	14.0	12.1	12.2	14.9
Other	1.0	3.1	4.4	7.7	9.8	8.9	9.0	10.1
Common Trust Funds	**	1.0	1.4	3.2	4.3	4.1	4.1	4.6
Mutual Savings Banks	0.2	0.2	0.2	0.5	0.9	1.0	1.2	1.4
Market Value of All NYSE-Listed Stock	$76.3	$219.2	$307.0	$537.5	$692.3	$629.5	$636.4	$741.8
Estimated % Held by Institutional Investors	12.7%	15.8%	17.8%	22.1%	24.1%	25.4%	26.6%	28.3%

** Less than $50 million.

A LESSON FROM THE PAST

If you want to see this dramatically illustrated, hunt up some thirty-year-old magazine and look for the insurance advertisements which urged its then readers to plan for happy retirement via "a $100 a month annuity contract."

The picture often showed a contented gray-haired couple at the seashore or on their boat—every care in the world banished, thanks to a $25 weekly annuity check! But if you had bought such a contract then, how much yachting would you be doing today on $25 a week? Today's ads—thanks to 20/20 hindsight—have raised the ante to $400 to $500 *a month!* If you buy such a contract today—and pin all your hopes on it—you are gambling that living costs twenty or thirty years hence will be no higher than today's. And that's a foolish bet.

Interestingly enough, some of the insurance companies which have always stressed—and justifiably—the safety of their fixed-dollar income annuities are today selling variable annuity contracts. These contracts are based on stock investments and thus resemble another form of mutual fund—to be discussed later. Without arguing the merits of their plan, it is significant that one of the staunchest strongholds of the fixed-dollar contract has now come to realize that a dollar may be worth only fifty cents or less in purchasing power thirty years hence.

Yet it must be repeated again and again: Any insurance offering some form of annuity has the one incalculable advantage that *no one has ever outlived his retirement income.*

The safety and comfort thus assured makes an annuity especially attractive to those who are old enough to get a generous income from their capital (age is the principal determinant in annuity yields) or who have other sources of income protecting them against inflation.

If you buy an annuity contract the insurance company will pay you only a certain number of dollars, but it will pay them as long as you live. This represents a guaranteed *lifetime* payment of at least some purchasing power which *no other form of investment can offer.* It is a guaranty which definitely places *some* form of annuity insurance in the retirement program of every prudent person.

It should be stressed however that precisely because of the continuing inflation we must take into account, the terms of an annuity contract should be set as late in life as possible. A young man of 25 who now signs up for an annuity contract to begin paying him a monthly income at age 65 is, in effect, locking his retirement budget–beginning in the year 2012–to today's living costs. This, history has shown over and over again, is a 100 per cent error.

Anyone short of retirement age should direct all his investing toward building capital and not commit himself to a retirement contract until the eve of retirement or even later, if retirement is early enough to give him a life expectation of 15 or 20 or more years. He thus not only extends his period of striving for more capital, but gets a better annuity return by starting his contract at a later age and, by the same token, reduces the number of years he may reasonably expect to have to cope with inflation.

Both insurance protection and annuities are most important media for our dollars, since the first creates a protective estate with the payment of the very first premium dollar and the second assures *some* income for life.

For this reason an entire chapter is devoted later to these media.

INVESTMENT MEDIA–VARIABLE DOLLARS

So far in this chapter we have been concerned with the various investment media which can provide safety of principal and a predetermined return of a fixed number of dollars.

If government decree could assure us that today's dollar would remain the standard in purchasing power for the next half century, we would need be concerned with nothing more than the task of putting aside enough dollars in a bank or in bonds, or contracting for them via an insurance program, to enable us to meet future needs and live comfortably in retirement at a standard of living we could now foresee.

But there is no such government decree, nor even any assurance that any government which could guarantee such rigidity in prices would be worth living with. A fifty-year fixed price for bread and shoes might turn out to be a high price indeed, in terms of liberties yielded to make such rigidity possible.

To the contrary, our economic history indicates strongly that the prices of things we need are in a long-term climb. And the best way to meet these steadily rising prices is to put aside not dollars but *things* which dollars buy, things which themselves go up in value and yield, and which at any time in the future can be measured by or even converted into the then existing dollars. Such an investment means simply that instead of putting aside $10,000 in money, you acquire $10,000 worth of "real" property with the expectation that when you call upon it in the future you will be able to reconvert your investment principal into cash of an amount which will have the same purchasing power as the $10,000 originally invested ten, twenty or forty years before. Or that the income derived from your investment will have the same purchasing power that income from the original $10,000 did at the time it was invested.

SELECTED CHARACTERISTICS
OF INDIVIDUAL SHAREOWNERS

(in thousands)

	1956	1959	1962	1965	1970
AGE					
Under 21	n.a.	197	450	1,280	2,221
21-34	2,230	2,444	2,390	2,626	4,500
35-44	1,240	2,064	3,528	4,216	5,801
45-54	1,700	2,800	4,519	4,752	7,556
55-64	2,020	2,666	3,202	3,549	6,084
65 and Over	1,090	2,113	2,617	3,347	4,330
EDUCATION					
3 Years High School or Less	1,570	2,804	3,007	3,106	3,566
4 Years High School	2,750	3,130	4,828	5,344	8,697
1-3 Years College	1,540	2,587	3,284	4,012	5,867
4 Years College or More	2,420	3,566	5,137	6,028	9,999
OCCUPATION					
Professional & Technical	1,010	1,934	2,682	3,136	6,320
Clerical & Sales	1,490	1,801	2,959	2,903	4,415
Managers & Proprietors	1,140	1,982	2,276	2,330	3,981
Craftsmen & Foremen	520	580	927	924	1,377
Operatives & Laborers	140	411	439	647	849
Service Workers	430	326	423	414	622
Farmers & Farm Laborers	230	73	65	64	170
Housewives, Retired Persons, & Nonemployed Adults	3,320	4,000	5,462	8,072	10,320
INCOME					
Under $5,000	3,195	3,575	3,074	3,183	2,577
$ 5,000-$ 9,999		5,921	7,551	7,592	6,233
$10,000-$14,999	5,285	1,769	3,258	5,199	9,001
$15,000-$24,999		700	2,021	2,649	8,272
$25,000 & Over		319	802	1,147	4,437

Note: Table excludes shareowners not classified by characteristics.
N.A.–Not Available.

Value of Dollar At 2.5% Annual Inflation Rate	
Today	100¢
In 5 Years	88.1¢
In 10 Years	77.7¢
In 15 Years	68.5¢

SAVING PURCHASING POWER

An investment in "real" property, in other words, is an attempt to set aside not an actual number of dollars, but to store up a *purchasing power* which will be equal to or greater than the purchasing power of the money when it was originally invested.

What are these investments? They are, basically, investments in which you assume the position of an owner rather than the creditor which you become when you accumulate savings, bond holdings, insurance.

In what way may an investor become an owner?

He may acquire real estate–single or multiple family dwellings, commercial property, vacant land, farms.

He may buy rare works of art or collectors' items–paintings, fine tapestries, rare books and stamps, diamonds and other precious stones, antiques–in the hope that his money will thus grow.

He may buy into a business–a chain of gasoline stations, nationwide supermarkets or shoe retailers, or automobile manufacturers, or railroads, or public utilities, or banks, or hotels, or airlines.

The latter, in essence, is what he is doing when he buys common shares. He is buying a small part of a large business.

All these forms of equity investment have their advantages and disadvantages.

The investor who buys a Rembrandt in the hope of future profit must, first of all, have a lot of money. Second, he must know something about art. Third, he must have the means of caring for his work of art until he can dispose of it; and, finally, he must not require any current income from his investment until he sells the painting. The same is true of investments in rare books, antiques, diamonds, etc., etc.

Purchase of a home for personal use is, of course, only a limited investment. It will, naturally, yield a place to live (after payment of taxes, maintenance and repairs), but it is generally not income-producing, and in some ways is a disservice in that it ties up large amounts of capital, tends to cut down a wage-earner's mobility, leaves living costs at the mercy of local taxing agencies.

There are many types of real estate, however, that may be bought both for capital appreciation and for production of income.

Apartment buildings, commercial properties, farms–all bought at the right price–have yielded many investors handsome returns in capital gain, steady income, tax relief.

But their purchase requires large amounts of capital, extreme caution and a thorough knowledge of real estate management. Unless the amounts invested are sufficiently large to warrant the employment of a professional realty management firm, you must assume the burden yourself. Obviously, if there is a shortage of housing–as there has been the last thirty years–the owner's risk is considerably lightened. No tenant in his right mind is going to antagonize the landlord.

But in a free country shortages of everything–including housing–tend to be filled in time, and even to go beyond that to become "over-filled." Then the roles are reversed, the tenant is in the driver's seat and the landlord must become the supplicant. There are few tasks more distasteful for the inexperienced, or the unprepared, than maintaining someone else's home and collecting rents in a period of prolonged housing surplus.

There remains the possibility of handing over the task of management to a professional. As mentioned before, this implies that the investment must be of sufficient size to warrant paying a management fee and still have some income left over for the investor.

But let's assume that instead of putting $25,000 into a two-family dwelling in a big city you put $25,000 into the common stock of some hotel worth $1,000,000. You now own 25/1,000th of the property or 2½ per cent and can

Highlights of Six NYSE Shareowner Surveys

	1952	*1956*	*1959*	*1962*	*1965*	*1970*
No. of Individual Shareowners (Thous.)	6,490	8,630	12,490	17,010	20,120	30,850
No. Owning Shares Listed on NYSE (Thous.)	n.a.	6,880	8,510	11,015	12,430	18,290
Adult Shareowner Incidence in Population	1 in 16	1 in 12	1 in 8	1 in 6	1 in 6	1 in 4
Median Household Income	$7,100	$6,200	$7,000	$8,600	$9,500	$13,500
No. of Shareowners with Household Income:						
Under $10,000 (Thous.)	n.a.	n.a.	9,496	10,625	10,775	8,810
$10,000 & over (Thous.)	n.a.	n.a.	2,788	6,081	8,995	21,710
No. of Adult Female Shareowners (Thous.)	3,140	4,260	6,347	8,291	9,430	14,290
No. of Adult Male Shareowners (Thous.)	3,210	4,020	5,740	7,965	9,060	14,340
Average Age	51	48	49	48	49	48

n.a. not available.

expect that proportion of the net income after payment of all the expenses of operating the enterprise.

Exactly the same thing is true when you invest in any corporation. Your stock certificate represents a fixed percentage of the business—its plant, machinery, patents, raw material, inventory, sales organization, accumulated profits or deficits, its potential, its research—even a share in a process which will some day be invented in its laboratories by a young boy who is now in grade school. And, above all, a percentage of its management. In other words, you get a part of the business for your money, with the *management built in!* In fact, you *are* in business.

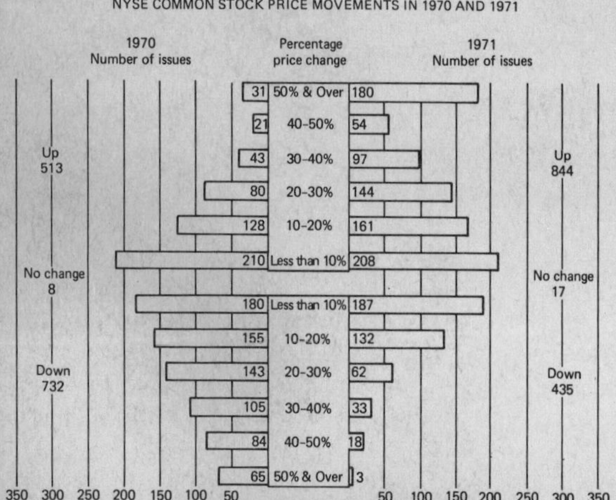

The unsophisticated investor may be influenced one way or the other by the report "The market is rising" or "The market is falling." But the professional investor, while taking these facts into consideration, will by no means allow them to dictate his investment decisions. He knows that the old saying, "It's not a stock market, but a market of stocks," although a well-worn cliché, is nevertheless true. The years 1970 and 1971 were turbulent ones for the stock market, but, as this New York Stock Exchange chart proves, the market doesn't move as a unit. In 1971, as in previous years, there was wide diversity in common stock price movements. While many investors found the year disappointing, 180 issues soared more than 50 per cent in value. And, in all, 844 issues rose while 435 lost ground. In 1970 the losers exceeded the gainers by 732 to 513.

An investor putting his money into a going business via purchase of a stock certificate is really saying to the management:

"Here is a part of my savings. I'll want it back in ten, twenty, or forty years, and when I do I expect my share of the business, if I want to sell out, will give me at least the *purchasing power* that I can get from my money today. Or—if I want to remain an owner—that the dividends this investment will produce will buy me at least as much food, clothing, shelter as this amount of money can buy me today."

Over the years, U.S. industry has managed to do such a job even though its record has been subject to short-term fluctuations. (See Chapter 2, "How Common Stocks Help Combat Inflation.")

This ability has won constantly widening acceptance of common stocks in the average American's investment program.

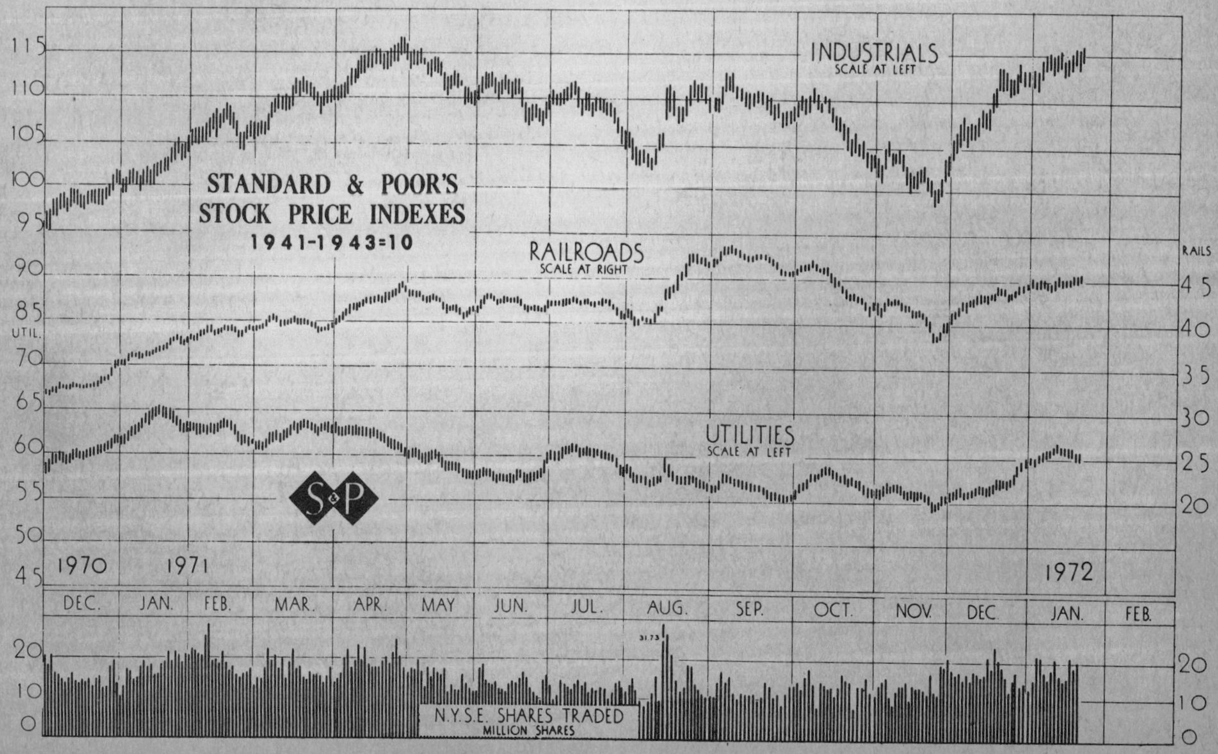

According to the latest study by the New York Stock Exchange, our shareowner population has reached the the record 31 million mark—a 53 per cent gain in 5 years and almost a fivefold increase since 1952, when the first NYSE shareownership survey was undertaken. Thus, in 1970 about one in every four adult Americans was a stockholder against one in every sixteen in 1952.

These 31 million stockholders were part owners of some 10,000 publicly owned corporations and investment companies which had some 36 billion shares of stock outstanding. The estimated market value of all that stock topped $1 trillion at the time of the study, or about $440 billion higher than in 1965.

The 53 per cent surge in shareownership since 1965 far outstripped gains in U.S. population, which increased 6 per cent in the interval. Shareowner increases, however, appeared closely related to advances in disposable personal income, which was up 54 per cent in the same period.

Other findings of the 1970 study were: Owners of shares listed on the exchange totaled 18.3 million, a 47 per cent increase over the 12.4 million in 1965. Male shareowners outnumbered female shareowners slightly for the first time since 1952.

The Middle Atlantic region had the largest shareowner population of the nation's nine regions—20.4 per cent of the total. The fastest growing region was the East South Central region—up 86 per cent since 1965.

Shareowner incomes moved sharply upward. A total of 47 per cent had family incomes between $10,000 and $20,000 a year, compared with 37 per cent in 1965—although the majority had family incomes under $15,000 a year.

Truly, it is no longer realistic to assume that stock ownership is restricted to the "wealthy."

The realization of common stocks' ability to cope with changes in the value of the dollar also has penetrated our most conservative investment circles. Harvard University—with the largest collegiate endowment fund—at one time depended heavily upon triple-A bonds for its investment income. In 1932, only 12 per cent of its funds were in common shares. In recent years it has been around 60 per cent. Other large college funds have followed the same trend and placed up to 86 per cent of their investment funds in common shares.

Large institutions, as well as individuals, have discovered in the last two decades of inflation that investments in business, via stock purchases, have proved the leavening agents which keep investments flexible enough to cope with expenses to come.

For the man who is investing his money today in order to provide for capital gain and his living expenses ten, twenty, or forty years hence, this single feature of flexibility is alone worth the price of admission.

SOME QUESTIONS AND ANSWERS

Q. *What is the difference between 5% earned on savings and dividends from a high-yield stock, such as Standard Oil of N.J., for example?*

A. If you put $3,000 into a savings account you will receive interest at whatever rate the bank or savings and loan pays, generally on a quarterly basis. If you draw out that interest (which, of course, is taxable income) your capital will remain at $3,000. Assuming your bank or savings and loan is insured by the FDIC or the FSLIC (or, in a very few instances, good state insurance programs) you need have no qualms about your capital.

If you put about the same amount into Jersey common, you will receive about the same return in dividends. This income is also taxable (except that the first $100 of total dividends received by an investor is excluded from taxable income).

Your investment may go up or down in market value. Over the last ten years, it could have climbed as high as $3,800 and dropped as low as $2,400. The dividend has risen steadily.

Q. *I notice you took a retired reader to task for having accumulated $75,000, all in savings and none in securities. You ignore his statement that he was conservative in handling his excess earnings. Evidently he was not*

NYSE COMPOSITE INDEX MAJOR MOVEMENTS (1967-1971)

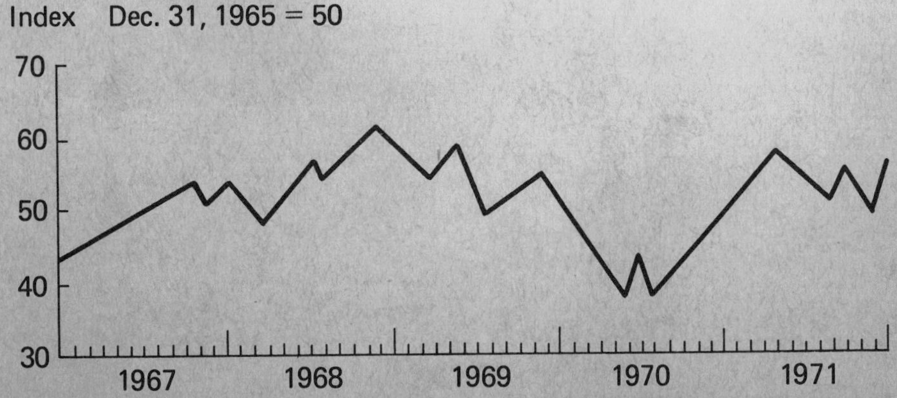

brave enough to indulge in any form of speculation, no matter how conservative. . . . So you send him a list of income-type stocks. Do you really believe that he would find any peace of mind now if he were to switch to securities? . . . What about annuities? In my opinion they far outweigh the chances of gain in securities. You do refer to annuities occasionally, but with tongue in cheek.

A. First, let's get rid of that "tongue in cheek" business. The dictionary defines this as "with insincerity, irony or whimsical exaggeration." Sir–I don't fool around with other people's money.

Fact of the matter is that I frequently suggest the purchase of annuities–both in the column and outside–by people:

[1] who are old enough not to have to worry too much about years of inflation ahead; or [2] whose age will get them an income from annuities generous enough to allow for inflation during their normal life expectancy; or [3] who have other inflation hedges (real estate, equity securities, well-heeled children).

In these, and in other instances, annuities are a prime source of retirement. And I'm not talking with "tongue in cheek."

As to the peace of mind of the reader in question:

What you have so blithely overlooked is that this reader sought me out and complained that he feels he has been hurt by accumulating only dollars and is now worried about his inability to cope with inflation from here on. So his peace of mind is not for us to debate.

He's already declared he's worried. He's the one asking for inflation-hedge advice. He is the one who says now that his "conservative" handling of his surplus funds during his working lifetime has left him uneasy. Not I. (And since when is the accumulation of dollars which steadily lose purchasing power, or reliance upon a fixed dollar income, any more "conservative" than reliance upon high-grade equity securities? If you want to be blunt about it, neither is "conservative," if by that term you mean "100% safe.")

To sum up: Annuities do have their place, a very important place, in retirement financing. The full answer on whether they should be used, and to what extent, can be arrived at only by taking age, resources, individual needs into consideration and then comparing the annuity's ability to meet the problem with that of other forms of investment. (See Chapter 20 on annuities.)

Q. *I've read your column for years. It seems that people who write you have substantial means. My problem is different. My husband and I both work. He will have a pension of about $50 a week. Currently I'm paying off a loan and putting the balance of my salary into the bank. We now have $800 saved. Is there any way we can invest so as to increase our retirement income? Some people talk about taking flyers, but I don't believe in them.*

A. I certainly don't think much of the idea for two people nearing retirement with only $800 in the bank. "Flyers" are for people who have money to lose.

I'd vote to build that bank account to at least two to three times the present amount (and, of course, to pay off that loan) before you start buying stocks for retirement income. When you do get ready, you can begin to accumulate sound stocks via a monthly investment plan or mutual funds. Until then I'd concentrate on strengthening your cash position. (And you'd be surprised at the number of letters setting forth financial positions much less affluent than yours.)

Q. *I am in my mid-20s, supporting a family of four on a $10,000 income. I'm willing to risk one half my $7,000 savings in securities. I understand some of the technical functioning of the exchange, but can't identify many of the companies by their market symbols.*

A. I'd say that's about as much of a handicap to successful trading or investing as not knowing the maker of the gear system in your car is a handicap to your driving.

A fluent knowledge of symbols is required of floor traders, clerks, brokers, and is much valued by amateur traders who spend their days in boardrooms mesmerized by the flickering figures.

Just make sure you know the company you want to invest in and don't worry about the tape symbol for its stock.

Q. *How do you compare stocks and mutuals with savings and loan deposits? Where are the best rates of interest available? We are down anywhere from 14 to 31 points on stocks we bought on our broker's recommendations. I am looking mainly for income and a moderate capital gain.*

A. Stocks (whether owned directly or via a mutual fund investment) represent part ownership of a business.

A savings and loan account represents dollars you've placed with an institution. In a way, they are on loan at interest and you are a creditor of the institution. There is all the difference between the two of OWNING part of a business venture and being OWED money.

Banks and savings and loans pay you interest for the use of your money. All they promise is the payment of that interest and the return of the exact number of dollars when you request it. There can be no hope of capital gain, except by adding interest.

When you go into business anything can happen. You might double or treble your money, or lose all or part of it–as you seem to have done.

Savings institutions today are paying either side of 5% in interest. Common stocks pay anywhere from zero to 5 and even a bit more. Good quality utility bonds yield around 7¼-7½%. Higher than that I won't go.

Q. *My husband and I are in our early 50s. We know nothing about stocks, so a few weeks ago I called on a reputable brokerage firm in my city for advice. I got the impression I needed at least $20,000 to start. We would like to invest a certain amount monthly.*

A. I think you got the wrong impression.

That $20,000-minimum bit is, of course, ridiculous. You can invest in common stocks listed on the N.Y.

Stock Exchange at a rate as low as $40 every three months. You can invest as low as $10 a month in some mutual funds. It's quite possible that the firm you visited is not interested in small accounts, and that's its business. But even in a medium-size city such as yours there are other firms that would be interested in your business.

If one lives in a small town which doesn't have a single broker he can always get a list of stock exchange member firms in surrounding cities and financial centers by simply writing to the N.Y. Stock Exchange, Dept. SU, Box 252, New York City 10005, and he can get a list of mutual funds from The Investment Company Institute, 1775 K Street N.W., Washington D.C. 20006.

Q. *We are in our mid-50s, in the process of selling our home. We are going to buy a trailer and look for a retirement area. We will have about $20,000 available, which will be needed to either buy or build another home. Where is the best place to put this money for income and, if possible, capital gain?*

A. If it is likely you may have to turn to this money within six months or a year, I can't suggest any place other than insured savings accounts. You can't expect the same money to bring you a good income, a capital gain and also be available at full strength at a moment's notice.

If you buy bonds you may have to sell out at a loss if interest rates start back up again. If you buy common shares you may be in a market downdraft just at the moment you find the house you want and need the money.

I see no alternative since you have no idea whether this money must come out of the investment in six months, a year, two years, or whatever.

Q. *I have about $10,000 in savings which I may not use for at least 10 years. Should I try to invest it? Try for more income?*

A. I would think so if, as I assume, you plan to retire in about 10 years and will then have to meet still higher living costs.

The emphasis should be on capital growth, not on getting a fraction of a percentage point more income.

Q. *Over the last several years we've been buying blue chip stocks but find that our savings accounts have done more for us than has the stock market. We are 46.*

A. The last few years have not been too rewarding for many old-line blue chip stocks. However, at 46, you can't set an investment course for the remainder of your life based only on the market experience of the last few years.

Unless you feel U.S. industry is finished as an aggressive force, you have to go along with the long-time growth theory which has proved correct over decades.

Q. *We earn about $18,000 a year, home paid for, and hold shares in two mutual funds. Should I borrow $5,500 at 6 per cent against my savings bank passbook and invest it? And in what?*

A. If you put the money into 7½ per cent bonds, you would gain 1½ per cent (82.50) a year – before taxes. Call it $50 clear profit. I can't see going into debt for $5,500 (acquiring a bond which can fluctuate in price against a debt which is fixed) for the sake of a $50 annual profit.

If you put the $5,500 into growth stocks in the hope of capital gain, you will, of course, receive far less in dividends than the interest you will have to pay the bank. And the question of whether you will ultimately get back more or less than the $5,500 so invested is in the lap of the gods. You'd have to feel very strong about a stock before you borrow $5,500 to buy it.

Q. *I have a math class I am trying to motivate. The pupils are members of upper middle income families and, it seems to me, will most likely at some time in their lives be involved with investments. And that means knowing math. What would you suggest?*

A. Let me start by saying I endorse your sentiments 100 per cent. Our educational system stresses–correctly, of course–a sound mind in a sound body, but seems to ignore finance as though the capitalist system under which we live were something to be ashamed of.

We attempt to set standards–again quite correctly–for helping the young pupil achieve a well-rounded life, but turn our backs on finance, even though 99 per cent of all grownups must come to grips with this problem for many, many more years than they will remember some obscure historical date or will remain interested in making the point after touchdown.

Certainly, high school years are not too early for introduction and understanding of some of the financial rules under which we must live for the rest of our lives. And where these studies have been overlooked, we find people who still can't figure the interest they are paying on a loan who can't figure the income they are receiving from a security and who, worse luck, are prey to every fast-talking salesman.

I would start by typing some of the math into investment situations. One source of information is the $1 investment kit offered by the New York Stock Exchange, 11 Wall Street, New York City 10005.

Secondly, any large nearby brokerage firm ought to be willing to supply you with some copies of the Standard & Poor's, Moody and Fitch stock and bond guides, as well as some of the Standard & Poor's "yellow sheets" which discuss, briefly, the status of a corporation–earnings, dividends, capitalization, type of industry, etc. etc.

Many teachers who have written me have also built interest by "investing on paper" exercises–that is, allotting each pupil "$10,000" with which to invest or speculate. Some have devoted a portion of their math time to an investment club (again, "on paper") so that pupils can get a chance to present their ideas on an investment or speculative issue.

Assuming that most of your class are college-bound and, therefore, should enjoy higher income during their working years, see if you can also generate interest in budgeting which would allow funds for investment. And never,

never overlook the income tax bite. Young professionals never seem adequately prepared for the fact that Uncle Sam is going to be their silent partner for their lifetime.

Q. *We are in our mid-50s, with two sons, one ready for college and one 14. Is it too late for us to begin an investment program?*

A. It is NEVER too late to put your money to work. Since time is an important ingredient of any capital-building program, it obviously would have been better to have begun in your mid-20s, or mid 30s or mid-40s. But that's all water over the dam and the only sensible approach now is to determine "where do we stand at this moment, and where do we go from here?"

If you are thinking of building capital for retirement 10 years off you will, naturally, have to play it closer to the vest than if you were 20 or 30 years younger. But you still should be "in the game."

You might invest in mutual funds, and directly in quality common shares—either in occasional bites of $500, $1,000 or so or, in a "monthly" investment plan requiring as little as $40 every third month in Stock Exchange-listed issues. Even though you are stationed overseas, either plan should be convenient. Decide whether you want to "pick 'em" yourself or turn the job over to a mutual fund management.

Q. *I want to retire. Most of my money is in 6% savings certificates. Is there a safer way to handle this cash for safe income?*

A. If by "safe" you mean keeping your dollars intact, and if these savings certificates are in amounts low enough ($20,000 or less) to be fully insured by the FDIC or FSLIC, then there is no "safer" method.

You can get 7½ per cent from top-quality bonds, but these will fluctuate in market price—although there is not much doubt that you will receive the $75 per $1,000 invested every year you hold the bond.

Q. *I'm a doctor, on salary, now able to put aside $100 to $150 a month for long-term growth, but want the right to withdraw the capital without any problem should a better investing opportunity or an emergency arise.*

A. There's no problem here, once we clarify the phrase "withdraw the capital." Any securities investment can be "cashed in" any time you like. But you must understand very clearly that with the exception of an insured savings account there is no guarantee that you will get out the exact number of dollars you put in. You might get the same, more, or less. Your obvious course is to invest in common shares—either directly through a monthly investment plan or indirectly via a growth-type mutual fund. If you want to be able to reverse the outward flow of money at any time, you clearly don't want a contractual mutual fund plan, since termination before the end of the 10- or 12½-year program would entail loss of commissions prepaid at the very start. However, you don't have to buy mutual fund shares on a contractual basis.

Q. *We are in our 30s, with two children. We began investing in stocks in 1969 and now my wife argues we would have done better had we put everything into savings.*

A. She's probably right. But that's using 20-20 hindsight. You came into the market just at the start of a long slide in prices, especially in the speculative stocks you chose. I don't think that proves very much, at least not for a young man with at least 30 years of working and investing ahead of him. I don't see where you have much alternative to taking this risk.

2 How Common Stocks Help Combat Inflation

If you could get hold of the household accounts book your grandmother kept around the beginning of the century you would find she paid about five cents for a loaf of bread and about as much for a quart of milk.

Your mother will tell you that when she went shopping before the start of World War II, she paid about double those prices.

Today's young housewife must be prepared to pay at least six times what her grandmother did for the same staples.

The oft-heard expression is: It's a changing world.

But in the field of shopping, the changes are all one way; toward higher prices.

The climb may be expressed in pennies in everyday items.

Or it may be expressed in the additional ten-dollar bill needed to buy approximately the same suit of clothes.

Or in the several hundred dollars more needed to buy another car.

Or in the thousands more needed to buy a home.

It is only the naive person who is surprised by rising prices.

With perhaps the single important exception of the Great Depression of the early thirties, rising prices (or declining purchasing power of the dollar) have been the rule throughout this century. This is inflation. And in recent years it has become more virulent than ever before.

Since the start of World War II alone, the cost of principal items of food, clothing and shelter have risen more than 175 per cent. Since the end of the Korean war, there has been a rise of 50 per cent, and in the last decade alone the advance has been more than 35 per cent. In the last half-dozen years alone, the Vietnam conflict has helped boost the cost of living about 25 per cent.

Percentages are only figures. But every adult can draw his own conclusions based on what he paid for a car ten years ago and what he pays today; on the trend in movie prices, restaurant meals, shoes, vacations.

Use any statistic you like—the U.S. dollar has been losing strength for years, and continues to lose buying power at the rate of 1½ to 3 per cent a year—in "good" years. In 1971 alone it was about 5 per cent, an improvement on the 7.1 per cent inflation of 1970.

That's inflation.

A "little inflation"—and ours is small when compared with the spectacular devaluation of currency in most European and Asian and South American nations—is sometimes argued as being of little consequence, as being "only natural" in a growing economy, not unlike growing pains in a teen-age youngster. Further, that segment of the population which lives on a hand-to-mouth basis and has no dollars left over to be depreciated feels it is of no concern. In fact, inflation is here often thought of as a form of "Robin Hood" since it devalues accumulated dollars of the "rich" and helps the "poor" pay their debts in cheaper dollars.

This is far from the truth. For there are few in this country, at any economic level, who do not have some stake in their future in the form of dollars—life insurance, pensions, social security. (A $250 a month retirement pension, for example, represents the income from a $50,000 fund. Any weakening of the buying power of that $250 represents a far greater disadvantage than any gain the average wage earner obtains by paying off small household bills in cheapening dollars.)

Inflation robs us all; and there is nothing in our future —individual, family, city, state, Federal and worldwide— to justify any hope that the deficit way of life, which is accepted at all levels and which breeds inflation, is to be altered.

If this is so, what can the investor to about it? What *must* the investor do about it?

He must place his surplus funds, extra dollars above and beyond those required to maintain life insurance protection and emergency savings accounts, into things—things which can be expected to rise in value as the dollar loses ground. He must become an owner of these things. He must assume an "equity" position, with his investment labeled: "an apartment house," or "a first edition of Whitman's *Leaves of Grass*," or a "Degas painting," or a "fine Louis XIV desk," or "200 acres of rich farmland," or 100 shares of stock which represents "1/10,000th of a company manufacturing shoes or nuts and bolts," and not in terms of dollars—$1,000, $5,000, or $10,000.

All these equities, over the years, have proved successful as either temporary or long-term storage places for protecting dollars from the inroads of inflation. For as the dollar dropped in value, the market price of these items has risen.

But most of these media for protecting dollars from the

inroads of inflation have one or several drawbacks:

The purchase of antiques, rare books, rare paintings and real estate requires a special knowledge of the field. A man who spends forty hours a week in an office or factory rarely qualifies as an expert in diamonds or rare furniture, especially to the degree required to find bargains in a specialized field dominated by full-time experts.

Furthermore, real estate must be managed—a profession in itself—and rare works of art must be stored safely to protect them from thieves and damage from the elements.

And, finally, a rare gem or book can provide no current income all the years the investor is holding it for a rise in market value. While the rewards, ultimately, may be great, not everyone can afford to keep $5,000 or $10,000 unproductive for ten or twenty years.

A notable exception to these handicaps is the equity sesecurity—corporate common shares or senior securities convertible into common shares.

For the common share is one of the few investments easily available to the layman which includes the price of management in the cost of the investment, which provides current income over the years, and which may be safely kept at no cost at all in the broker's vault.

How can common share ownership help you protect your surplus dollars from inflation?

Almost every adult who glances through the daily newspapers has read at one time or another of common stock price gyrations. There have been sensational rises—and sensational falls. No investment is guaranteed against loss. Fortunes have been made in common shares—and lost.

But in the field of common shares we do have a long-term average which has recorded investment progress over the years, and which gives us important clues to the role of equities in inflation protection.

The most popular, most widely used index to the stock market is the Dow Jones industrial average. It is based on the price movements of thirty leading U.S. corporations—better known, perhaps, than any other similar group of companies in the world, although not necessarily the most financially successful: Allied Chemical, Alcoa, American Can, A.T.&T., American Brands, Anaconda, Bethlehem Steel, Chrysler, du Pont, Eastman Kodak, General Electric, General Foods, General Motors, Goodyear, International Harvester, International Nickel, International Paper, Johns-Manville, Owens-Illinois Glass, Procter & Gamble, Sears Roebuck, Standard Oil of California, Standard Oil of N.J., Swift, Texaco, Union Carbide, United Aircraft, U.S. Steel, Westinghouse Electric, F. W. Woolworth.

The following table shows how an investment based on the Dow Jones averages would have protected your dollar during the most virulent inflation period in modern U.S. history:

The first column represents the U.S. Department of Labor's average annual consumer price index (cost of living) for each year since the depths of the Great Depression—adjusted to the base of 100 for 1967 living costs; the second, the closing price for the thirty stocks in the Dow industrial averages; and the last column the index to dividends paid by stocks included in that average. Notice how, despite often marked fluctuations, the long-term course of the stock prices and their dividend payments have more than offset the rising cost of living.

No one, of course, pays grocery, rent, clothing and medical bills exactly computed on the basis of the Bureau of Labor Statistics index. And not many investors' portfolios consist of exactly the same stocks listed in the D-J industrial average.

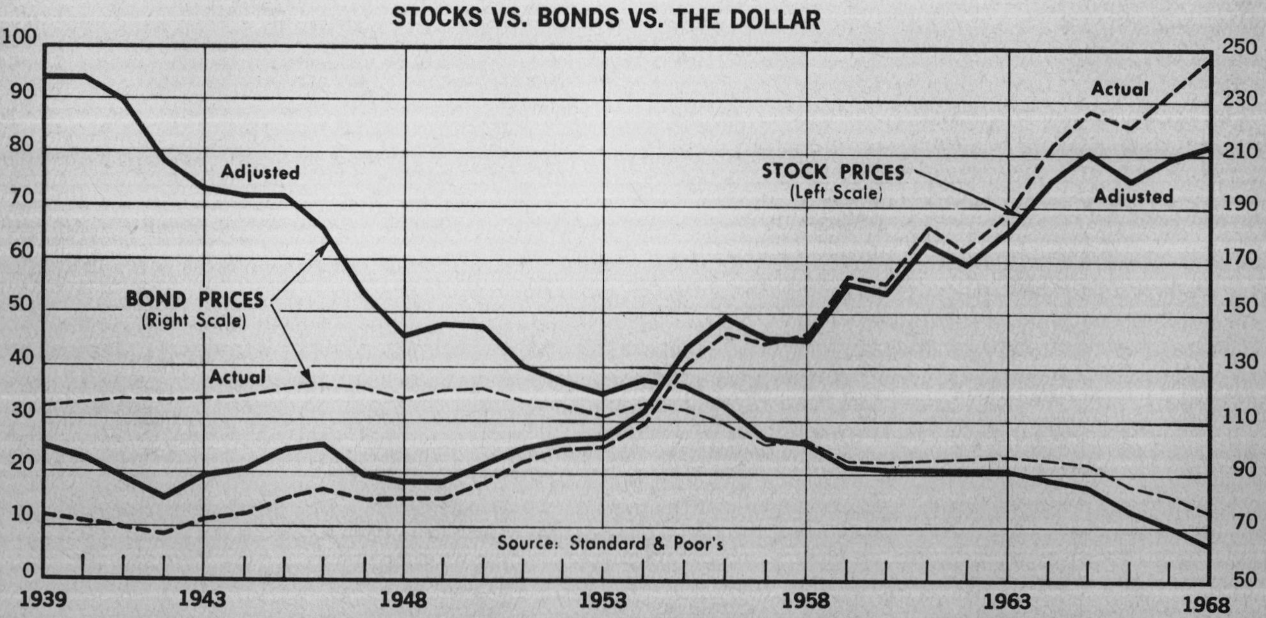

	Cost of living index (1967 = 100)	*Dow Jones industrial average*	*Dividend income from D-J issues*
1933	38.8	99.90	$ 3.40
1934	40.1	104.40	3.66
1935	41.1	144.13	4.55
1936	41.5	179.90	7.05
1937	43.0	120.85	8.78
1938	42.2	154.76	4.98
1939	41.6	150.24	6.11
1940	42.0	131.13	7.06
1941	44.1	110.96	7.59
1942	48.8	119.40	6.40
1943	51.8	135.89	6.30
1944	52.7	152.32	6.57
1945	53.9	192.91	6.69
1946	58.5	177.20	7.50
1947	66.9	181.16	9.21
1948	72.1	177.30	11.50
1949	71.4	200.13	12.79
1950	72.1	235.41	16.13
1951	77.8	269.23	16.34
1952	79.5	261.90	15.34
1953	80.1	280.90	16.11
1954	80.5	404.39	17.47
1955	80.2	488.40	21.58
1956	81.4	499.47	22.99
1957	84.3	435.69	21.61
1958	86.6	583.65	20.00
1959	87.3	679.36	20.74
1960	88.7	615.89	21.36
1961	89.6	731.13	22.71
1962	90.6	652.10	23.30
1963	91.7	762.95	23.41
1964	92.9	874.13	31.24
1965	94.5	969.26	28.61
1966	97.2	785.69	31.89
1967	100.0	905.11	30.19
1968	104.2	943.75	31.34
1969	109.8	800.36	33.90
1970	116.3	838.92	31.53
1971	121.3	890.20	30.86

It is fair to assume that many investors have achieved much less than the averages—both in market price appreciation and in dividend income. Others have done much better.

But taking the averages and their dividend payout as a base for discussion, we find that while the consumer price has gone up, since Depression days, from 38.8 to 121.3, an increase of about 200 per cent, the industrial stock index has risen nearly tenfold and the dividend index increased nearly that same amount.

To use food as an example of what this means to the investor relying on stock market prices and dividend income to meet living costs:

In 1933, a popular index to 31 most commonly used foods stood at around $1.50. So the $3.40 "dividend" paid by the D-J industrials would have been sufficient for slightly more than two "baskets" of food. By the end of 1971, cost of this food basket had soared to about $7.25. *But*—the dividend income from the same portfolio of stocks was sufficient to buy *four* such baskets.

There is no implication here that every investor, buying just any stocks, will thus be arming himself against inflation. But the table does indicate how a group of shares in the nation's leading industries has more than offset inflation.

SOME QUESTIONS AND ANSWERS

Q. *I plan to retire in two years, at age 55, with $150,000 now in savings, earning 5%. Could you send me a list of blue chip bonds that would pay a higher return?*

A. You can get current yields of 7 and even 7½% from bonds issued by leading corporations, so that part of your question presents no problem.

What deserves far more consideration, however, is the problem you pose by retiring at 55. (That's a problem? Yes, that's a problem.)

While you can, in today's market, get a generous yield from bonds, age 55 is far too young to fix your income in present-day dollars—whether it's $7,500 a year or $10,500—for the rest of your lifetime.

There may come a day in the next 20 or 30 years when $7,500 will cover only the rental of a comfortable apartment.

So your problem is not one of getting a fraction or a full percentage point above 5% on your $150,000, but of so investing the money that you will have the equivalent of today's $7,500 buying power in 1976, 1986 and for as much longer as you will need income.

Such an investment must involve equities—common shares or senior issues (convertible bonds or convertible preferreds) which may be exchanged for common shares.

That means far more market risk than merely investing in triple-A quality bonds.

Although the common stock market of the last few years has done very little indeed to keep up with inflation, the fact remains that over the long run (over the years of retirement ahead of you, for example) the prices of good common shares—and their dividend payments—will tend to rise and help offset the climbing cost of living.

I repeat, this hasn't been true in recent years. But if you go back over decades, you will see that the stock market has risen far more than the cost of ships and shoes and sealing wax.

So there's your twofold problem: generous income now and the promise of income keeping step with inflation in the years ahead. Better discuss a quality list of stocks, and some bonds, with your broker.

Q. *I inherited $7,500 which I have in savings at 5 per cent. I have no need for income now, but will when I retire in 9 years. I bought education policies for my boys but years later they fell far short of covering tuition.*

A. If there's anything you should have learned in this effort, it's that dollars "squirreled away" for years are not likely to come out buying as much as they did when they went in. And that applies to meeting college bills as well as retirement income needs.

So if you want this $7,500 to keep step with inflation over the next 9 years to retirement, and thereafter, you'd better see that at least some of it goes into equities. That's as clearly as I can say it.

Q. *I am a single woman of 51, with about $50,000 in assets—in banks and in savings and loans. Yesterday I bought a $10,000 Series E bond with a savings certificate*

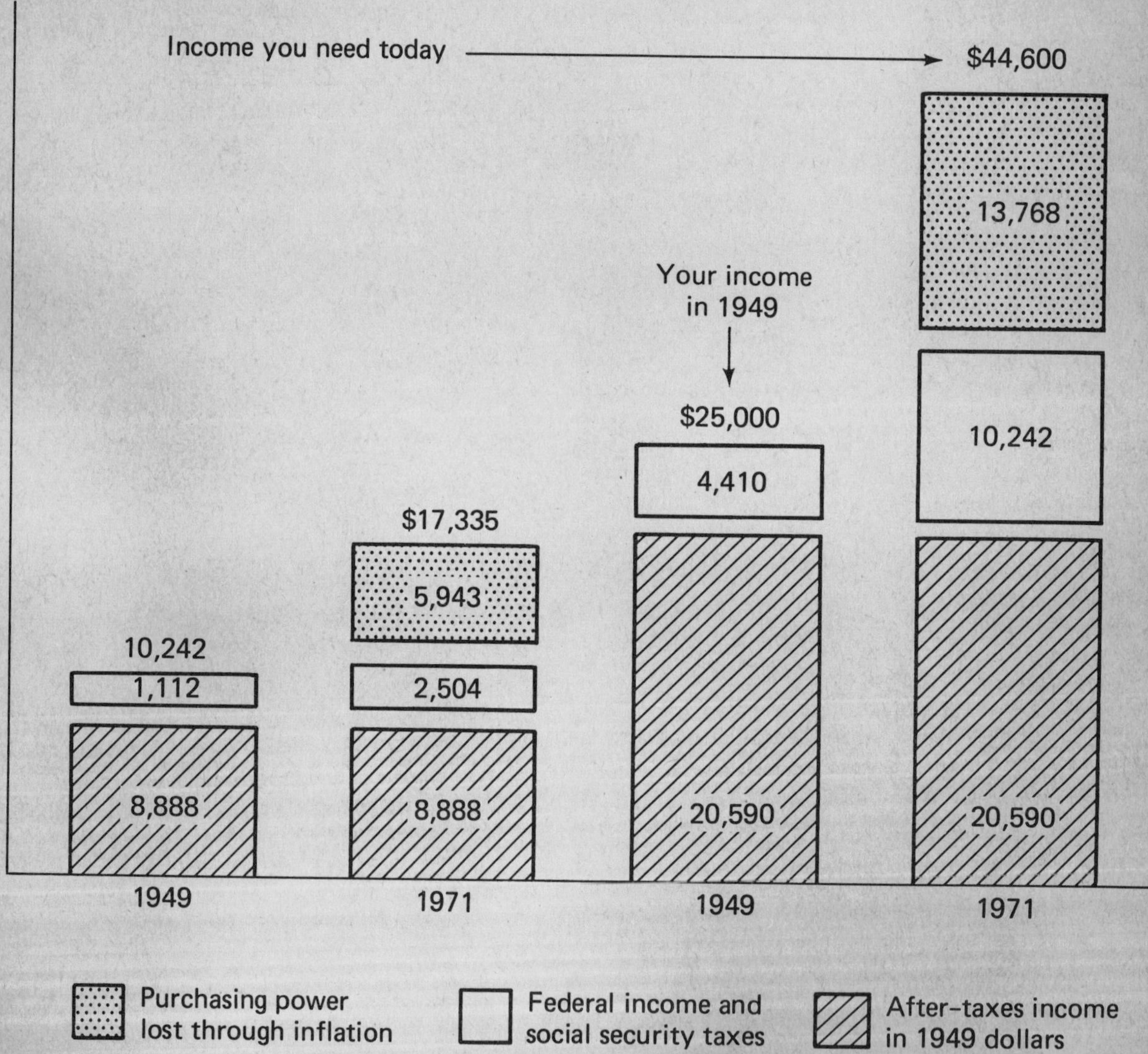

The Federal Income and Social Security taxes shown are for a married couple with two children. The average deductions for each bracket were based on data reported by taxpayers to the Internal Revenue Service, and the taxes were computed at the 1971 level. No allowance has been made for other taxes—Federal, state, or local. The amount of purchasing power lost through inflation is based on the change in the Consumer Price index of the Bureau of Labor Statistics. Sources: Treasury Department; Bureau of Labor Statistics, U.S. Department of Labor; The Conference Board. Copyright 1971 by The Conference Board.—from Brevits *which matured and next week intend to purchase more. My goal is to avoid the income tax bite on this money since I am now in my highest earnings and tax bracket. When I retire in 11 years I plan to switch to H bonds. I know nothing about stocks and bonds, and feel I am wise to stay away from them.*

A. I'm not going to argue you into stock ownership because any investment is wrong if it brings fears and uncertainty and worry with it. I can only point out to you that 11 years ago the consumer price index (the cost of living) stood at 90. Today it is around 122. So, what cost $9 then, will cost you $12.20 today. And that's only an average index. Medical and service expenditures have soared much more.

Eleven years ago, the Dow Jones industrial average stood at about 700; today it reads around 925. Eleven years ago, the dividends paid out by the Dow Jones average stocks were indexed at $22.71; for 1971, they stood at $30.86.

What the next 11 years will bring I don't know. But I'd hate to bet that prices will go down, that the dollar will gain in purchasing strength.

So—you fear stocks. But can you afford to hold ONLY dollars?

Come to think of it, I'm sorry you wrote. All I've done is jar you out of your feeling of well-being and substituted nothing but the harsh truth that there's nothing certain in investing for one's future.

Q. *I have about $85,000 invested in a savings and loan at 5¼%, adding the interest to the investment. I have confidence in the savings and loan company and feel I could, if I desired, get at the money. The $85,000 resulted from complete liquidation of securities three years ago. Now I am attempting to weigh the pros and cons of the current stock market. I follow the national and international developments and don't like what I see. Should I leave the $85,000 as is, or redistribute it?*

A. I can't see any defense for keeping $85,000 in one savings institution—no matter how much confidence you have in it—when Federal agency insurance goes up to only $20,000. There are plenty of places you can distribute that money and keep it all protected. If you think the economy is in for trouble, why tempt fate? That's point 1.

Secondly: Troubled times do not always indicate investment in dollars.

It seems to me we've had nothing but trouble since the start of World War I. (I realize we had almost a decade of euphoria in the Twenties—but that doesn't mean "times were good." It merely indicates we were blithely unaware of the economic stresses building up both at home and especially in Europe.)

In the last quarter-century we've had three shooting wars and any number of cold war incidents.

But that doesn't mean the best place for your money was in dollars. The dollar has lost more than 50% of its purchasing power since we entered World War II.

You evidently were frightened out of the market in 1963 at below current levels. So you missed the steady rise to the 1000 (D.J.) top—and subsequent sharp decline and fluctuations. But that's water over the dam.

What do you do now? I don't think you can continue to put 100% of your trust in dollars any more than you should put 100% into securities. A diversified list of holdings—common shares, Treasuries, cash—deserves consideration, with the common holdings aimed at inflation protection plus income or growth.

Inflation and Common Stocks

Probabilities of Gain in Value of Common Stocks Since 1870

Length of Investment Period	*Number of Periods Since 1870*	*Periods of Gain in Value*	*Periods of Loss in Value*	*Periods of No Change in Value*	*Chance of Gain in Value*
30 Years	71	71	0	0	**100%**
20 Years	81	77	4	0	**95%**
10 Years	91	78	13	0	**86%**
5 Years	96	68	28	0	**71%**
1 Year	100	58	41	1	**58%**

Probabilities of Decline in Value of the Dollar Since 1870

Length of Investment Period	*Number of Periods Since 1870*	*Periods of Gain in Value*	*Periods of Decline in Value*	*Periods of No Change in Value*	*Chance of Decline in Value*
30 Years	71	3	66	2	**93%**
20 Years	81	17	63	1	**78%**
10 Years	91	33	58	0	**64%**
5 Years	96	26	66	4	**69%**
1 Year	100	25	60	15	**60%**

Sources: Standard & Poor's Index of Industrial Stock Prices; U. S. Bureau of Labor Statistics

The table shows the performance of the Standard & Poor's Index of Industrial Stock Prices over varying time periods from 1870 through 1970. The statistics start with the Administration of President U.S. Grant and include the terms of the eighteen Chief Executives who have succeeded him.

Note that the longer the period the greater the chances of stock prices ending higher than they began. They showed a gain in every thirty-year period. Even in one-year periods they had a better than even chance of rising.

The lower table, based on data from the U.S. Bureau of Labor Statistics, shows the probabilities of a decline in the value of the dollar over the same time periods.

What it does not show is how inflation has been increasing in recent years. For example, 1954 was the only one-year period in the past twenty in which the value of the dollar did not decrease.

Together, the tables indicate why common stocks are considered an effective long-term hedge against inflation.—*from Brevits, December 1971, issued by Vance, Sanders & Co.*

3 Different Plans for Different Planners

Investing, ideally, is a lifetime pursuit.

Theoretically, your first investment should be made with part of your first week's salary.

And you should continue to invest to build capital for as long as you are employed, for as long as you are interested in and capable of building capital.

However, that's theory.

In practice, we all have individual problems which impose particular restrictions not only on our money management, but on our other pursuits as well.

Many of us can't save anything out of our first pay envelope. Many can't spare enough after meeting the primary requirements for life insurance and emergency savings account to invest in securities even after years of employment. We may all be created equal under the law, but our ability to earn and the responsibilities we must meet can vary so widely as to make any one formula for investing meaningless in many cases.

Nevertheless, the acquisition of capital—never a pleasant or easy task—can be facilitated if you do it according to some plan which suits your particular circumstances rather than by following some haphazard "dollar-when-you-catch-me" philosophy. In fact, habit is a far more basic component of both saving and investing than is generally understood.

You wouldn't attempt to build a house without first drawing up plans you could reasonably hope to follow.

You shouldn't attempt to build your financial future without first doing some planning—a survey of where you stand, a plan detailing your goal.

As a prudent investor, you, as a man or woman thinking of the future, should first be willing to sit down and take stock of what you have:

—in capital already accumulated,
—in earning power,
—in responsibilities and the money required to meet them,
—in saving power,
—in pensions abuilding (private and/or under Social Security),
—in years left to work.

Actually, this amounts to a formula with half a dozen variables, many of which can be altered even after you have begun to build on it. Conditions affecting the plan may change drastically over the years. Jobs and earning power may change drastically; responsibilities may be increased suddenly; and inheritance—fortunately—may cut your task in half or eliminate it entirely.

Nevertheless, the plan—some plan—must come first and be adhered to for so long as it is practical. If you have a plan, you can at least modify it to meet changing conditions. To invest without a plan renders one liable to all the cross currents which affect not only one's own affairs but which affect the investment world.

An investor who attempts to build capital without some program often winds up being driven by the financial winds rather than sailing by them. He becomes the emotional market plunger when the prices are high, when everybody is talking stock market; who is burnt by the market and sells out at the lows, disgusted and determined never to go there again.

Theoretically, the ideal investment program would be a plan as unique to us as our fingerprints. And within a limited sense, every man's investment plan does reflect his own personality.

But there are categories which fit most of us, which can serve as basic blueprints, subject to personal variations.

Phil Morse is only twenty-eight, but already he's begun to think of building capital via investing. He now earns $12,500 at a large engineering company. That means he also is building up a Social Security fund for his retirement years. But he will need capital long before that to educate his children.

With a wife and two children, life insurance and a mortgage, he has little left out of his income with which to acquire securities or other investments. Even so, what little there is—$400 to $500 a year—Phil is investing with the thought that, by putting his money to work for him he can meet his children's college tuition bills more easily, and some day later, provide the difference between mere existence on Social Security benefits and a comfortable retirement.

His supervisor, George Quinn, is 60, now earning $18,500 and with the youngest of his four children in his last year at college. Over the years, Quinn has had little opportunity to put money aside. His biggest family expenses came during the depression thirties when his salary was low. Raising four children and buying a home took most of his income. In the last ten years his earnings have risen steadily—in fact, about doubled. But with increased income came a substantially higher standard of living—a larger home, a vacation cottage, college educations. Now, with three children on their own, Quinn has begun to think of retirement. He figures he can put at least $3,000 a year into the plan.

Morse, only twenty-eight, now earns the smallest salary and has his heaviest expenses ahead of him. Yet, paradoxically, he can step out the most boldly on his investment program. Reason: He has more than thirty-five years ahead of him in which to build his stake. If he makes any mistakes in investing, he'll have time to reverse his course and correct them. With perhaps anywhere from a quarter to three-quarters of a million dollars of earnings still ahead of him, he can afford to take chances on growth stocks, new inventions, etc.

NO ROOM FOR "DUDS"

Quinn now has much more money to invest than Morse. In the next few years he will be able to put aside $6 for every $1 invested by his young colleague. But Quinn must "play it closer to the vest" if he wants to start taking it easy in five years, or sooner. Every dollar he invests until then must be solidly planted and bear fruit soon. There will be little time to replace any failures. Nor can he invest in companies which may be world-beaters in 1995.

Alan Lefferts, at age 64, is in his first year of retirement. He is no longer interested in capital building as No. 1 goal. He's worked for more than 40 years and he figures it is now time he enjoyed the fruits of that labor, even though he wants to leave the bulk of his assets to his three children.

Obviously, then, Lefferts wants results *now*—if, by results, we understand income from his invested assets. Therefore, he may well disregard taking any of the extreme risks assumed by Phil Morse or even practice the guarded growth optimism which rules Quinn's investing.

Leffers wants *income*—first and foremost. And, if possible, he wants income which will help him live comfortably now, and hopefully, increase sufficiently to keep him abreast of rising living costs.

Clearly, there can be no Plan A to suit all Morses, no Plan B to suit all Quinns or Plan C to fit all Leffertses. Each plan must be custom-made, even though general guidelines will be found in subsequent chapters

A PLAN YOU WANT TO LIVE WITH—FOR YEARS

An investment program is not a "sometime" thing, a weekend venture.

It is a long-time project which should be the core of your economic thinking for years, extending decades ahead. And so, while age, income, sum of present and future responsibilities all determine whether you will direct your course closer to Lefferts' or Quinn's than to Morse's, it will never do to overlook the fact that your program is inextricably bound up with you as a person. It is something you're going to have to live with for a long time.

This all adds up to this total:

You must have a program.

You should start it as soon as possible.

You must plot your course from today until the day you must turn to your capital for help and even thereafter, tending toward the financial program which fits in best with your temperament, earnings potential, retirement needs.

But you must not overlook the fact that you, as pilot of the ship, remain an individual with characteristics fixed by heredity and years of experience. That means the "course" —your program—must be corrected for what seamen call "compass error" but what we can better term "personality traits." There are enough variations possible to suit every need.

SOME QUESTIONS AND ANSWERS

Q. *I've enjoyed your columns but feel you err in arguing that a retired person should have all his holdings in bonds. Inflation is still rampant. To supplement our annuities and Social Security we have managed to build a portfolio of stocks—the residue of many years of in-and-out trading which was mainly an exercise in futility.*

A. Actually, we're not that far apart—and by withholding your age, your retirement income and retirement needs you're depriving me of material for discussion.

Firstly, I don't think every retired person should have 100 per cent of his investments in bonds, or even in fixed-dividend preferreds. I've never argued for 100 per cent of anything for anyone.

Secondly, age has a lot to do with facing up to inflation. If you retire at 60, you are sure to see plenty of inflation—whether it's "rampant" right now or not. In that case, I'd rely more on common shares from which you can hope to get increased dividends as the dollar loses purchasing value. If you are 80, the period of inflationary danger is obviously shorter. And I think that an elderly person getting 7¼ to 7½ per cent from bonds (say, 50 per cent more than he would get from stocks) has the ammunition with which to comfortably combat inflation for at least 10 years ahead.

I notice that of your $110,000 portfolio, only $10,000 is in bonds and a similar amount in convertible preferreds. These two items—adding up to under 20 per cent of your portfolio—provide close to 30 per cent of your investment income.

However, I'm not criticizing the list. If your years of trading were futile, you at least had the good sense to wind up with an excellent list of quality stocks—Smith Kline & French, General Telephone, Westinghouse, Continental Oil, S.O. of Jersey, Texaco, Santa Fe Industries, ITT, Tenneco, and a few solid electric utilities.

Your figures show you are deriving just under 5 per cent income from the full amount. If you don't need the 30 to 40 per cent increase you could get from a higher bond concentration, that's fine with me. But you must admit that a lot of retired people can't afford the luxury of retaining low-yield blue chip growth stocks for the sake of building a larger estate for their heirs.

But I never quarrel with success. It's a far better argument than any theory of mine.

Q. *I don't know why all people in ordinary circumstances don't buy quality bonds which pay good interest. My broker tells me to forget about bonds and buy stocks.*

A. I don't know what "ordinary circumstances" defines. Bonds are a good investment for elderly people requiring relatively safe and generous income. But bonds can't do much for a young man in a high tax bracket who wants to build capital for the future. For that he must take chances with stock.

Q. *I am holding some stock in my name for the benefit of my parents, who need income.*

A. You give me no reason for this arrangement, but I must point out to you that if these stocks are in your name, you are assuming an unwarranted tax burden, especially in the case of high-income stocks. (I assume your tax bracket is far above that of your retired, elderly parents.) I suggest you talk over with your attorney some other arrangement.

Q. *I'm a widow in need of income, with a large amount of Gulf Oil shares and about $35,000 in vacant land yielding nothing but tax bills. How much tax would I have to pay if I sold the Gulf Oil?*

A. I don't know because I don't know your tax bracket or what the stock cost you. But what I can't understand is your rush to sell a good stock yielding about 5.4 per cent (at recent market price) while holding land that yields zero.

Q. *I am in my mid-60s, interested in income, but also desirous of providing for my daughter. Thus, I feel, I should invest on a long-term (say, 25- to 30-year) program.*

A. A long-term program for one person is not the same as a long-term program for another. You need generous income and safety *now*. . .period. And that's for as long as you live. That should be your goal now–which, to my way of thinking, means the purchase of high-grade bonds yielding around 7¼ per cent.

Your daughter will require a long-term program which is much more inclined toward hedging against inflation. Time enough to think about that when the money passes on to her.

For the time being, your purchase of high-grade bonds will be helping you with generous income and protecting her by preserving principal.

Q. *We are an elderly, retired couple with investments in bank certificates, savings and loans and in U.S. Tresaury bonds. Comments, please.*

A. No need for change, but just make sure your banks are insured by FDIC and your savings and loans by FSLIC, and that your holdings in each bank are below the $20,000 insurance ceiling.

Q. *We are in our late 40s, with savings, investment in real estate mortgages and some stocks: CPC, Consolidated Natural Gas, Fedders . . . General Motors, Marathon Oil, Pacific Gas & Electric preferred, Pacific Lighting . . . Standard Oil of N.J., Tri-Continental, Union Electric, Washington Gas Light. We need more income for retirement.*

A. You *will* need more income for retirement–which means that people in their late 40s should not select stocks today for retirement income 15 or 20 years hence.

By and large, your list is a good one, although a bit heavy in some utilities which are not necessarily the most aggressive growth stocks you could own for the next decade at least (assuming you plan to retire in your early 60s).

4 Women as Investors

The professional world of finance is still, to a large extent, a man's world.

The old cliché that a woman can't be trusted to do a simple sum still persists in certain circles, although the truth is that when it comes to the everyday financing with which most of us are concerned it is very much a woman's world.

Man may earn the money, but woman disposes of it.

Our Federal government now spends a record-breaking (and to many a shocking) amount of about 240 billion dollars a year.

The American woman is the central figure in the disposition of about *800 billion* dollars of personal income every year!

And it is accepted that in so doing she won't be fooled by shoddy, bargain-priced merchandise, or that she won't be taken in by giant economy sizes which are neither giant nor economical.

And yet in this modern world–nearly half a century since women got the vote–there are men (husbands included) who insist that women don't know anything about money, are incapable of learning, and shouldn't be trusted with it under any circumstances.

The facts of the case are directly to the contrary.

As a wife, a woman controls perhaps 80 per cent of the family spending. (It's a fair assumption that if she doesn't handle this spending wisely, the family is going to be in financial trouble no matter how much her husband earns.)

As a working wife she contributes to the family income as well.

As a widow (and there is no sense disputing the surplus of widows over widowers) she winds up in possession of of whatever assets the two of them have managed to accumulate: savings, life insurance, real estate, securities. And yet men who spend a lifetime accumulating an estate will resist any effort of their wives to learn how best to use it.

For the career woman who doesn't marry, the importance of planning and carrying out a lifetime financial program is even greater. She must not only earn the money, but also manage it, alone.

So–single, married, widowed–the modern American woman is involved with finance all her adult life.

Fortunately, women in all categories are not awaiting men's permission to learn about finance. Investment courses and lectures on money management attract as many women as they do men, and the number of letters from women to financial counselors asking advice is easily as large as the number received from men.

How much should a woman know about handling money and investments?

Everything she can know.

It is ridiculous to assume that she will not be misled at the supermarket, but that she shouldn't be expected to realize that a $35 stock paying $1.75 in dividends provides more income than a $25 stock paying $1, even though the latter issue sells for less money and looks more like a "bargain." And if she does not know it, it's never too soon for her to learn. Money management, to be successful, should be a lifetime effort.

A young woman, even before she makes the commitment to either a career or marriage (or both), should know what she wants her money to do for her and how to implement such a program.

Young Jane Brown, just out of college or secretarial school, may plan on working a few years before considering marriage. The business world has just opened to her. She does not know how she will like it and, as of the moment, there is no young man around she is thinking about seriously anyway.

Yet whether she lives at home or is out "on her own," she realizes she must start some sort of investment program. And, as always, first things come first.

The very first thing is a savings account, if only for the sake of the independence it will grant her from either her parents' support or from reliance on high-cost personal loans. If she can manage to accumulate three to six months' earnings in savings she can rest assured that she's protected against most health emergencies and that she can gratify any sensible clothing and vacation requirements.

Life insurance plays some role–even in the life of a single young lady–although not necessarily as heavy a part as it would in the life of a young man who is planning on matrimony and family. Some consideration should be given to life and health insurance because (1) she does not want to be a burden on anyone, (2) life insurance taken out in her twenties is much cheaper than it will be later, and (3) if she marries, her insurance needs as a wife and mother will be even more significant. Still there is no need for Jane to commit herself to a back-breaking insurance premium program. A couple of thousand dollars' worth of protection, perhaps with the privilege of enlarging it later, and at the lowest lifetime rate, would seem in order.

From that point on her chief concern should be with building capital. That means investing for growth.

Many women, in this respect, have a built-in obstacle to investing for capital gain.

Being value conscious, they try to get the most for their money. And too often this "most" is expressed in current income. Thus, Jane would be only a normal young woman if she were attracted to a stock paying 5 per cent in dividends and discouraged from buying one which yields only 1 per cent. And she could be wrong.

Long-term capital is best built by investing in growth-type securities, mainly the common stocks of corporations which by virtue of their area of business or of their aggressive management have proved their ability to increase earnings per share 5 to 10 per cent a year, or even more; corporations which regularly plow back a substantial portion of their earnings into research and development of new products, or into extending the use of present products.

Such a company, of course, is not likely to pay large dividends–for the simple reason that it is using its profits for more important reasons: for building up the business.

Even a generous dividend will, by itself, not support a vigorous capital-building program. For every $1,000 invested in a 4½ per cent yielding stock, Jane will receive $45 a year. Of this she will pay–even if she is in a modest income tax bracket–$10 to $15 a year to the U.S. Treasury plus smaller amounts to her state and city, if these also impose income taxes. The balance, placed in a savings account and kept in dollars, remains vulnerable to inflation. But–receiving little current dividend income from a growth stock, Jane pays little or no tax on the money earned by her stock. Instead, the profits are put back into building up the asset value of her shares. During all the years this building up process is taking place, there is no income tax on the growing, reinvested earnings.

And if at some future date she should want to liquidate her investment and take her money out, the tax would be on a long-term capital gain basis which is reckoned at most likely only one-half her regular income tax bracket. Further characteristics of the capital gain investment will be discussed in Chapter 7.

Since it can be assumed that Jane's investable capital is limited, a logical method for acquiring these shares would be on a periodic investment basis, such as is offered by the New York Stock Exchange–the monthly investment plan. This program (discussed in detail in Chapter 5 "How and When to Buy Stocks") is ideally adapted to a young career girl's investment plan, since it allows payments of as little as $40 a month or $40 every quarter.

In effect, the $40 quarterly plan calls for investment of as little as $3 on a weekly basis, so that it should suit the young career girl earning even a modest salary. At the same time it helps establish the saving and investment habit which is the foundation stone of every successful lifetime program. She makes no commitment to continue investing any specific amount or for any length of time. This is significant in the case of a young girl whose "single" status may evaporate in a whirlwind courtship.

Mutual funds, of course, also provide an excellent investment vehicle for the young working woman. As in the case of the "monthly investment plan" they call for regular monthly or quarterly payments varying in size from $10 up to $100 and more. Here again, the habit is an important factor. Mutual funds (discussed in detail in Chapter 10) come in all sorts and sizes, directed at fulfilling almost any investment goal.

However, if Jane is attracted to the idea of merely sending in her monthly check to a mutual fund and letting professional investors do the work she should be conscious of one problem which applies to her investor class specifically.

Mutual funds are sold either on a voluntary or contractual basis. Under the voluntary plan she makes no commitment to continue for any length of time. Nor are selling commissions (if any) charged except for the current purchase.

The contractual mutual fund plan may run the same length of time as the voluntary–10 or 12½ years–but the investor's freedom to quit at any time is seriously hampered in this program by the fact that up to one-half the first year's monthly payments are deducted to prepay sales commissions for the balance of the 10- or 12½-year program. Thus, if Jane enters into a contractual program she must feel reasonably certain that she can maintain the $10, $20, or $50 monthly payments for the full life of the program even if the next 10 or 12 years should bring marriage, home-buying, babies and all the other expenses of setting up family living.

If she is unable to do this she stands in danger of losing all those prepaid commissions–fees prepaid for the acquisition of stock she is not going to acquire.

As will be developed in the chapter devoted to mutual funds, there are hundred of thousands of investors who prefer the contractual mutual fund program. Their most common reason is that since they know they will have to take a loss if they quit, the contractual plan proves a spur to their investing. This may make sense to investors who are "already set" in life and feel they need that additional pressure. But it seems an unreasonable burden to put on a young woman who most logically might want to change her status within a few years.

Young Jane Brown, just starting out in her career as a woman and as an investor, should rightly reserve to herself all the freedom she can, certainly the freedom to switch her investment from stock buying to home buying and family building.

THE WIFE AS AN INVESTOR

The old rhyme about "needles and pins" declares that when a man marries his troubles begin. No small portion of these troubles may be lifted from his shoulders if he marries a woman who has some appreciation of the use of money.

The saying goes that "behind every successful man stands a woman." Even more true is the claim that beside every financially sound man stands a woman who has some basic knowledge of money and the will power to use restraint and common sense.

Even a money-wise wife, it's true, can't make a palatial home if her husband earns only a tiny cottage salary. But it's also true that even a husband's country estate income will not bring contentment if his wife is incapable of practicing financial restraint or sensible budgeting and planning.

What are the things a wife should know about money?

She should know that a penny saved and transferred to a ready, available savings account is more than a penny earned. For it spells the difference between having emergency funds available if the old car suddenly goes, and having to borrow funds in a rush at 10 to 15 per cent interest, plus all sorts of fancy insurance costs and other usurious gimmicks.

She should know that rushing into the purchase of a too-expensive home can give her and her husband a thirty-year headache—not at all similar to the momentary embarrassment which might follow the purchase of a fancy $15 hat in place of her usual $10 number.

She should know that mortgage insurance can be obtained for a few extra cents per hundred dollars and can spell the difference between comfort and misery if tragedy should strike before the house has been fully paid for.

She should know that as budget manager it's up to her to see that money is saved and even invested if her husband hasn't set up this discipline.

She should understand the basic differences between investing surplus funds (surplus in the sense that they follow funds in savings and life insurance) in dollars and in equities.

Many women fear the stock market. That in itself is by no means the worst of diseases. A healthy fear of the stock market—for it can "bite"—does no one any harm. But if it leads to constant carping against the investment of any funds in any securities she is doing herself and her family an injustice. For though there is risk in owning securities, she must also realize that there is risk in owning dollars.

It is not at all unusual for a wife to declare: "I don't understand the stock market, I don't trust it. I want that money in the bank where I know it is safe and where I can get it any day."

She should make it her business to understand something about the stock market—at least the basic idea behind having some money invested in a share of American business.

She should realize that while money in a savings bank is a "must" for everyone—and especially for a young, growing family—it is not the only proper investment in a well-balanced lifetime financial program.

For cash savings, important as they are, are not 100 per cent "safe" in every sense either. The interest earned is subject to depletion by income taxes, and the principal itself is vulnerable to inflation. And inflation, in the last several decades, has run anywhere from 1½ per cent to more than 7 per cent a year.

She should understand that there is no riskless method of keeping investable funds; that there is a risk in securities and a risk in dollars. Her task, then, is to acknowledge this risk and stand by her husband in any sober, conservative attempt to acquire and hold quality securities for long-term appreciation.

Conversely, she should be realistic and sound enough to withstand the effects of careless gossip at her kaffee klatsch—the gossip centered around the "Did you hear that Millie made $150 last week trading Syntex and Annabelle bought Fairchild Camera Monday, sold it out Tuesday, and made enough profit to buy a new fur jacket?"

When she suddenly finds herself with children away at college and housework cut to the amount required by a three-room apartment, she ought to know enough about investments to realize that the public board room at the broker's is not merely another device for escaping boredom on a midweek afternoon. The ticker tape may look far more exciting than bridge—but it is far deadlier.

She should realize that her desire to make "just enough for a new dress" for her niece's wedding has no bearing whatsoever on the Dow Jones averages, or on the price of any stock to which she may be attracted. Wall Street is not that accommodating nor will it grant its rewards for the asking to those who approach it in the same fashion they attend a charity bazaar. A wife's role in investing is, at best, a partnership role. A partnership with her husband so that each may profit from the other's point of view and so that both may know what is being done with the family's investable funds—and why.

A share or stock selected or held by a woman does not perform any differently from the same issue held by a man. There are no "stocks for men" or "stocks for women."

But that does not indicate that a family's investing program should be carried out by husband or wife alone. In the first place, a woman being continually involved with corporate products may well have some valid opinions to contribute to an investment discussion. In the second place, a program carried out by only one-half of the husband and wife team (especially when the nonparticipating mate is opposed to any security buying at all) is likely to be far more speculative—in order to prove a point—than it would otherwise be or should be. Finally, if either husband or wife is steadfastly opposed to any securities investment, it may result in the family remaining with dollars all during the period it should properly be protecting itself against inflation and be building capital.

An informed and interested wife can prove a significant asset in a man's lifetime investment program.

THE WIDOW AS AN INVESTOR

Finally we come to the woman as widow—an unpleasant subject but a problem which is so well documented that it cannot be avoided.

A husband may feel "in the pink" and go through life

without a single ache or pain. But the statistics say his wife is far more likely to become a widow than he is to become a widower. Look at the insurance tables of any life insurance company–tables based on the mortality experiences of millions–and you will find that for $1,000 put into an annuity a man of sixty-five will receive about $7.20 a month for life, while a woman will be paid only about $6.30. The difference of about 90 cents a month does not reflect the insurance company's misogyny. It is based on pure statistics: the woman will live longer, so the insurance companies figure on paying her less per month than they pay the man.

Yet, statistics to the contrary, husbands–good husbands–insist on managing their financial affairs almost secretly, as though they will "be around" as long as their wives are. The result is that hundreds of thousands of successful men who have labored most of their lives to provide a competence for their wives and children leave behind them a sizable fortune in the hands of women who know as little about managing it as they do about repairing the basement oil burner. Why this condition should be so common is something for the psychologists to explain. Perhaps men enhance their self-respect by retaining full investment money management in their own hands, although many, in the course of their married life, will turn over far more dollars to their wives for food, furniture, etc., etc., with an "I leave it to you, dear."

Perhaps men, being mortal, don't like to think about death. (Although many do leave fortunes in life insurance taken out just for that eventuality.)

But whatever the reason, the facts are clear:

Hundreds of thousands of women are widowed every year and only a small percentage are prepared to cope with the money suddenly left in their hands–to provide for their own livelihood and to care for any small children.

The moral, of course, is obvious.

A woman should learn all she can about the family's financial program, should prepare for widowhood long before she becomes a widow.

She should know at least what investment programs are under way in savings, life insurance, securities, and real estate. And she should know who is handling them, where the securities and policies and mortgages are located. She should understand the reasoning behind each investment, the better to know whether it suits her book once she has become a widow.

Obviously, the sooner she becomes a partner in the family's investment planning, the better. Sometimes there are special considerations for having undertaken one investment instead of another–considerations which are not apparent on the surface. If these factors still hold, perhaps the investment makes sense even in widowhood.

There are two kinds of widows, financially speaking.

Those who have worked with their husbands in building the family estate and those who have this estate suddenly thrust upon them in the midst of tragedy and at a time when they are least equipped to handle it.

Both have things to learn about financial widowhood.

First, the widow who has kept in touch with the family's financial planning:

Perhaps the most important rule of all is "Do nothing for a while."

This is a difficult role to observe, and for good reason. The widow suddenly finds herself without her companion of many years. She realizes suddenly that in the split second of a heartbeat income has stopped; that a home which for years has seemed just right is suddenly far too large and, in fact, even superfluous.

Frightened, she decides she must do something and do it *now* in order to protect her inheritance, her income, her financial well-being. What is more, she has plenty of help in developing this frantic approach. It is rare that a new widow is not surrounded almost immediately by well-meaning friends who at once begin to offer her free advice and urge her to take steps at once to put her new financial house in order: "sell the house, buy a cooperative apartment, sell the car, sell the stocks, cash the savings bonds, buy an annuity, etc., etc., etc."

Whether the advice ultimately proves good or bad, more widows have imperiled their financial security and well-being by rushing into action than by any other investment move.

If there is any axiom which can be established for "financing widowhood" it could be: "The hurried action is likely to be the wrong one." (And in the case of a financially unsophisticated widow–the prey of sharks who scan the obituary columns–the results often are disastrous. Of them, more later.)

In ninety-nine cases out of a hundred, immediate action is rarely necessary. If any sizable estate is involved, some liquid funds are included or sufficient credit is available–certainly sufficient to keep the house going for several weeks or months.

Entering a new and totally different phase of her life, the widow should do absolutely nothing financially until she has had time to learn about her life as a widow, what it will entail in money needs and just how far her Social Security, pensions and other income go toward covering these needs.

The same holds true of any stocks and bonds which have appreciated since purchase. Time enough to liquidate these–*if* they should be liquidated–in the following year when her tax bracket as a widow will be far below what it was when her husband was alive.

The same warning against precipitate action pertains to home ownership. Some widows, it's true, may not want to stay on; others may derive some comfort from familiar surroundings. Financially, there may be an argument for selling a home, and then again there may not.

The widow who jumps to the conclusion that she no longer needs this "$48,000 house" and sells it may find that comparable rented quarters will cost her a good deal more than did the support of the house. In any event, a house suddenly thrown on the market after a death rarely brings as much as one which is sold in more leisurely fashion.

As a matter of fact, it is a rare investment indeed that

must be sold immediately under any circumstances.

Having overcome the shock of her husband's death, a financially sophisticated widow will begin to draw up two tables:

1. What she has.
2. What she needs.

The first should include all property—real estate, vacant land, savings accounts, life insurance, pensions, Social Security, mortgages, stocks and bonds, money owed her in the form of loans to friends or family.

The second should include what she feels she should have in the form of emergency savings accounts and in current income.

Now either one of two conditions prevail:

The widow is in "comfortable circumstances"—pensions, Social Security, annuities, mortgage payments and other income are more than sufficient to meet her living expenses; or

She is going to have trouble making ends meet.

If she is fortunate enough to fall into the first category, she should allow months or even a year or two to pass before disturbing her assets.

If she must generate more income to cover living expenses she should undertake a *slow, gradual* shifting of assets so as to arrive at maximum income, but without giving up any more safety and security of principal than she can bear.

What might these shifts involve?

• Putting up for sale any vacant land which currently represents a drain in the form of real estate taxes payable, and which brings in no revenues.

• Shifting life insurance funds from the company—where interest payments are generally below those paid by banks and government bonds—into an annuity or into savings banks and savings and loan associations insured by either Federal agency. (This means insurance by the Federal Deposit Insurance Corp. and the Federal Savings and Loan Insurance Corp.)

• Liquidating E bonds which grow at the rate of 5½ per cent a year but yield no current income. These bonds may be liquidated piecemeal, or converted in a lump sum into interest-paying H bonds, or redeemed and the proceeds put into other securities. (The advantages and disadvantages of the different programs are treated in the chapter on U.S. savings bonds.)

Selling her home—if she feels this would be psychologically as well as financially advantageous and if she feels she would be comfortable in rented quarters, and if she can rent, annually, for less than 10 per cent of the selling price of her home. In other words, a widow left with a $35,000 home could reasonably expect to be "money ahead" if she can rent suitable quarters for about $250 or less a month. This rule of thumb is based on the experience that a $35,000 home—even one owned free and clear—"down to the ground"—will cost about 10 per cent of that amount to maintain every year. This cost includes the income value of $35,000 at, say, 7 per cent, or roughly $2,450, (which this money could earn if it were invested in top quality corporate bonds) plus real estate taxes, heat, water, insurance and repairs. If there is still a mortgage against the home, her annual outlay would be even higher since it would include monthly amortization which, though a "savings," could prove burdensome on a widow's budget.

• Reshuffling of her securities portfolio so as to increase current income or by giving up some growth potential, but preserving as much of the safety factor via high quality securities as she can.

If, as a wife, she understood why her husband had long owned IBM for its growth potential, even though it yielded only about 1 per cent in income, then as a widow she will understand why she must consider liquidating IBM in order to switch the proceeds to a higher dividend- or interest-paying security. In the first place, she is no longer as much capital-gain oriented as she and her husband were thirty years ago, and in the second place she does need the income. To remain an investor in IBM because "it has been good to us" or because "it would seem disrespectful to my husband's judgment to sell it" is good sentiment, but very poor finance indeed.

A widow's investment needs are as different from a young wife's as in her food shopping list. And one great advantage of securities is that they may be easily adjusted to meet the changing needs of their owners.

These changes, it should be reiterated time and again, should be undertaken slowly and gradually and never without complete understanding of what is taking place, and why.

Even a financially sophisticated widow will find herself suddenly surrounded by securities salesmen, all urging some form of change—a switch from one stock to another, or a switch out of a long portfolio of stocks into a mutual fund (a popular gambit). It would be unfair to say flatly that all these salesmen are commission grubbers and bent on doing the widow harm. Far from it. But it is always likely that at least a few unnecessary changes will be urged.

An example: Mrs. Hayes inherited from her husband a long list of stocks and bonds accumulated over the last forty years. Joe Hayes learned about finance through experience and it's likely that some of his issues were good for him, some bad; also, that some are suited to his widow's needs and some are not.

A typical reaction of many securities salesmen would be: "Sell them all, Mrs. Hayes, and put the money into the XYZ mutual fund which my firm sells and from which you can withdraw $100 a month."

Now, it may well be that XYZ is a fine fund, and that a $100 monthly income from $20,000 so invested lies well within the boundaries of good finance. But it could also be true that some of the securities Mrs. Hayes inherited are well-suited to widowhood and are already paying 5 or 6 per cent in dividends. What is the point, then, of paying brokerage commissions to sell these issues and then to pay another commission, ranging up to 8½ or 9 per cent to acquire shares of the mutual fund which can do no more than the shares originally held?

Another favorite gambit is to switch a widow out of one or two mutual funds into a third.

Perhaps the third, as proved by its record, would better suit the widow's needs. But the switch will cost money in additional purchasing commissions, and time should be taken first to see whether the reduction of assets by the payment of an 8½ per cent commission is likely to result in increased income, net.

Real estate is frequently advanced as a "cozy" investment for widowhood.

Real estate, properly bought and managed, has provided the basis for more fortunes in this country than any other financial asset.

Further, income from real estate—again, properly bought and properly managed—often exceeds by as much as 50 per cent the income which can be obtained from high quality corporate stocks and bonds. *But*—

Real estate selection and management is a highly specialized occupation. The fact that you've lived in a house all your life does not make you a real estate expert, any more than the fact you have worn shoes for years makes you an expert bootmaker.

A widow who buys a single home on the premise that "at least I will always have a roof over my head" may be asking for nothing more than inflexible and burdensome rental costs for the rest of her life. And the argument that a multiple-dwelling piece of property will always give her "free rent and a comfortable income" could prove to be a cruel sales pitch.

Real estate management is for real estate experts. A widow shouldn't assume she can become one merely because she needs the income any more than she should assume that she can refit her car's main bearing merely because she can't afford the garage bill.

So far we have been discussing only the actions of a widow who has some familiarity with investments in general and her family's investments specifically. The pitfalls are many and the danger of losing part or all of the inheritance is great. She should move slowly, following always the motto: "If I'm not completely sure of what is proposed, I'll do nothing," at least until she can sit down with an investment manager she knows and trusts and discuss the matter thoroughly.

Snap, abrupt financial decisions by widows are 99.44 per cent wrong.

What, then, can be said of the widow who throughout her married life was kept in ignorance of the family's investments; who has no knowledge at all of stocks or bonds, or real estate mortgages; who looked to her husband for living expenses, but never entered into any discussion of where the money came from?

It is a sad and dangerous situation—one which she should approach with the same caution as she approaches the fuse box in the basement with which, heretofore, she has never had to come to grips.

A cardinal rule should be, again, to *do nothing* and to continue to do nothing until she has had the time to sit down with knowledgeable, expert financial advisers she can trust. That in itself is a large order.

All brokers and securities salesmen, of course, know more than she does about securities—but all of them may not be looking out for her financial welfare. Even her lifetime banker—while considerably more trustworthy—may urge her to put all the money into his bank, where it will no doubt be safe, but where it may not earn as much as it would employed elsewhere and where it definitely cannot protect a young widow against the inroads of inflation.

Nor does a male relative who has been dabbling in the market become, *ipso facto*, a knowledgeable adviser on income securities.

Her late husband's securities broker may prove an excellent source of advice, or again he may not—depending upon whether the family's portfolio represents a lifetime of successful investing or a list of securities misfits left over after years of "buying high and selling low."

There is no specific one-phrase answer.

The widow who finds herself with a sum of money—all she will have with which to support herself—and with no knowledge of how to handle it is in a bad spot.

She should move slowly.

She should keep her common sense about her, showing as much judgment as she does when she seeks medical or legal advice.

And, above all—she should NOT rush to do anything.

When she finally does decide to do something about rearranging her assets she should move *only* with the help of an adviser she trusts completely and who has taken the time to explain to her *fully* the changes she is making and why she is making them.

SOME QUESTIONS AND ANSWERS

Q. *I'd suggest you add this advice for your single women readers: Never let anyone know that you have any interest in or understanding of the stock market. I don't go around talking stocks, but when the subject has come up I've felt I could join in. Whenever this has happened, with men present, I find it's the last time I see them.*

Women, too, often think I'm peculiar if I express any interest in the market, or admit to any investments. Maybe it's just a reflection of the times—saving is square and solvency is "outsville"—but apparently it's better for a woman to look and act as fluffyheaded as possible while quietly piling up profits.

A. Maybe it's just as well that you don't see these men again. Any man whose ego is threatened by a woman's knowing something about stocks and bonds is probably holding tight to his medieval concept of womanhood because he isn't quite sure of himself as a modern man.

Nor, for that matter, has he learned that not only do women often control about 80 per cent of the family budget but generally wind up with 100 per cent of a couple's capital. (If men are so smart, how come women live longer?)

And women who think you peculiar because of your knowledge of finance are either envious or simply unaware of what's going on. About half the letters I receive that are concerned with individual or family finances and investments are written by women. I don't think that's too surprising.

A single woman must manage her own finances and plan for her financial security. A wife is often the most important member of the household's financial team because she is closest to the "checkout counter." She knows best where the family's money is going, and how much. And the widow who doesn't understand anything about the estate left her is in a bad way, indeed—often the victim of all sorts of sharp operators, at worst, or merely badly informed friends, at best.

I don't know about being "fluffyheaded," but if these poor benighted males think that acquaintance with finance robs a woman of her femininity they haven't been girl-watching in any of the country's financial centers. Any man who frowns upon a woman's knowing something about finance is a square.

Q. *I am single, a business woman in my 50s, earning $6,500, with total assets of about $47,000—mostly inherited. I hold small lots of Grolier, John Sexton, Weyerhaeuser, Bank of America, Standard Oil of N.J. and $3,000 in Series E bonds and $40,000 in savings. Is this properly distributed?*

A. $43,000 in dollars and only $4,000 in common shares is not what I would label an ideally balanced portfolio for a person in your position.

Assuming you intend to work another 5 to 10 years before retirement, more of your assets should be at work in stocks hedging against inflation.

The E bonds make sense because they provide an emergency fund, growing at the rate of 5½% with tax on that growth deferrable until your retirement years.

Q. *My mother holds a World War I Liberty bond for $1,000. She has tried to cash it but was unable to do so. It seems to me it ought to be worth something.*

A. It certainly is—$1,000! At least.

Your mother has been careless in holding this bond long after it has stopped paying interest. But there's no question about the face value.

Your best bet is to write a letter to Division of Loans and Currency, Treasury Department, Washington, D.C., and tell them exactly what you have. If you send the bond itself be sure to use registered mail.

Q. *I am a widow living on income from securities which include such issues as Coca Cola, Am. Natural Gas, Bethlehem Steel, General Tire, Parke Davis, Continental Can, American Home Products and U.S. Steel. Some show losses. Would it be advisable to sell them and deduct $1,000 from my taxable income? Could I increase income and, at the same time invest for an increase in capital?*

A. Tax deductions are one thing and common stock income is another. You fail to give your age—which is another way of saying you fail to indicate how important the anti-inflation factor is in your investing. A young widow should have more in common shares than in bonds—which offer a generous return, but no hedge against inflation. An older woman would be justified in arguing that the 7 per cent to 7½ per cent she can receive from bonds is sufficiently more than, say, the 5 per cent she gets from stocks to keep her ahead of any inflation for a decade.

In any event, while a $1,000 taxable deduction is desirable, it is best obtained by getting out of an unsuitable stock which no longer offers a generous return—computed on present market price. Don't rush to sell out quality stocks which for cyclical reasons may be down in price, but still yield a good return on present market price.

Some of your issues are, by nature, growth types which cannot be expected to yield a generous amount—American Home Products, for example. If you are meeting your living costs by a comfortable margin, there is no reason why you can't continue to hold it. If you need more income, it will have to be replaced by a higher-yielding stock even though the latter might not promise as much growth.

As far as reinvesting for more income and more growth potential is concerned: That's what we all want. But you can't have 100% of both.

I guess it's very much like your asking for a high-heeled, good-looking dance slipper which you could also use for comfortable hiking. You have to compromise somewhere between the two, or else buy one or the other.

Q. *I am a widow, 60, intend to semi-retire in a couple of years. I have a savings account of $2,100 and would like to invest half for a fast turnover. No long-term thing like a mutual fund—that's where I lost money. At the end of 10 years I withdrew my money, losing a few hundred dollars. I don't trust the mutual-fund company because the agent told me my investment would double in 10 years. Now I have been advised to invest in a race track, but I don't know where to go. I've followed your columns, but I've never found one that would help me.*

A. I'm afraid I'm going to continue striking out, if you're asking me for "fast turnover" investments. A woman of 60 with $2,100 in savings has no money for fast or slow turnovers, or anything but a bank account. Certainly, taking half of that money and trying to pyramid it into any sum which would make any difference to your retirement budget would be foolhardy.

I can't find that race-track stock. If you must gamble, why not take $25 and go directly to the track?

Q. *A few weeks ago I received 68 shares of Wisconsin Power & Light common stock. I know nothing of stocks and bonds. I am a 39-year-old housewife. Will we get anything from this stock? Must it be declared on our income-tax report? Can you recommend a book for beginners, so I won't be so dumb on the subject?*

A. Wisconsin Power & Light serves primarily southern and central Wisconsin. Its ownership is represented by 450,000 shares of preferred stock and 6,300,000 of the common. You now own 68 of those 6,300,000 shares, so you are part owner of the utility.

The shares, which carry a high rating of "A minus," pay quarterly dividends of 35 cents a share, or $1.40 a year, so you can expect annual income of 68 times $1.40. This is taxable income. Currently the shares are selling at around $21½, so your investment is yielding income at the rate of about 6½ per cent.

The libraries offer a wide variety of elementary books explaining stocks, bonds and other forms of investment. You can get a good beginner booklet, "Understanding the New York Stock Exchange" as well as other booklets, such as "Investment Facts," by sending $1.50 to the New York Stock Exchange, Dept. SU, Box 252, New York, N.Y. 10005.

Q. *I am a woman of 69, living on income from stocks, two annuities, and $20,000 in one bank and $95,000 in another. Would you advise more stocks?*

A. Not necessarily. You have an excellent list of securities now and, evidently, sufficient income.

The only point which raises an eyebrow: Why $95,000 in one bank when only $20,000 of it is insured? Your bank may be perfectly sound, but why not have all your money insured by spreading it around among other banks in $20,000 amounts?

Q. *When my husband passed away 9 years ago a friend helped me set up a portfolio consisting of Columbia Gas, International Minerals, Ohio Edison, Public Service of Indiana, Mobil, American Home Products and bonds of Potomac Electric and Tenneco. Now I must pay up a $3,000 note and a $6,500 mortgage, and must sell something. Should the bonds—which have gone down in price—be sold and the money put into the bank?*

A. Since your portfolio obviously is being called on to provide income, I would hesitate to sell these good-quality bonds which provide a generous yield while retaining high-quality growth stocks which yield around 2 per cent.

It's true the bonds have sold off since you bought them in 1957. Most bonds have. But if you sold them now you would be giving up good current yields of around 7 per cent not to mention the built-in appreciation over the years of maturity.

It seems to me that the money you need to pay off debts should come from the low-yield growth stocks. The fact that a good quality bond goes down a few points in price does not mean it's a sale, in your case, but merely that its yield is now higher.

Q. *My husband died a year ago and I asked the bank's trust department to manage the estate. It sold out my mutual funds and reinvested in its own trust funds. But $16,000 in cash has not been reinvested. It brought in nothing last year. I also have $4,000 in a checking account. I don't use these funds, either. What stocks should I buy?*

A. I have no way of judging the wisdom of the move from mutual fund to the bank's own trust funds. But in this day of 5½ per cent Treasury issues there is absolutely no reason for $16,000 to lie idle for a year. Wasn't it at least put into an interest-bearing savings account? Unless you're writing a lot of checks, I see no reason for keeping $4,000 in a checking account, either. That could earn at least $200 a year.

Since you have a bank managing your funds, I'm reluctant to suggest specific stocks. After all, they have a far better view of your overall picture than I have. But that's no excuse for letting all this money lie idle.

Q. *I'm a working widow, in my 50s, with 2 children and have 100-share holdings in Goodrich, Parke Davis, International Paper, Lorillard, Santa Fe, Abbott Lab., Illinois Power, Tenneco, El Paso Natural Gas, Borg-Warner, Marcor, Standard Oil of N.J. and California, National Aviation, U.S. Gypsum. My broker feels capital gains should be taken when a stock shows $1,000 profit.*

A. This "$1,000-profit limit" rule is a new one to me. Why $1,000? Why not $5,000 or $10,000? Anyway, I think it's all wrong.

You have a fine list of stocks—some growth situations, others excellent income providers for a widow with 2 children to educate. So far so good. But if you sell out whenever an issue shows $1,000 profit you're going to sell yourself out of market "winners" and leave yourself with "losers." And that is just what you have done.

I don't think there is any reason to panic because Santa Fe or Borg-Warner or Marcor or U.S. Gypsum, for example, are below your cost price. But what sense was there in taking profits on equally fine stocks and not offsetting these gains with losses? So much for poor tax tactics.

I think a widow who is working and rearing 2 children would do well enough buying top-quality issues and holding them for whatever growth she can afford and for whatever income she requires. If you're going to sell any, sell those that aren't doing a job—not those that are moving ahead.

In today's "bargain" market for bonds and preferreds, I think you could own some, as a balance to your heavy common-stock investment.

Q. *I am a 40-year-old woman, alone and self-employed, who must look ahead to retirement 20 years from now. I have been considering an insurance plan which would give me $10,000 at retirement and which would cost me $70 a month until then. Or should I consider bonds or savings? I don't particularly like the idea of stock, because I don't want to gamble. I can invest about $100 a month.*

A. Most of us don't want to gamble, and shouldn't. But what are the alternatives?

I'm not sure I understand the insurance proposal. Certainly, payment of $70 a month, $840 a year, $16,800 total, over the next 20 years should wind up more than a $10,000 fund. But even if you've made an error in the total figure, I can't get excited about it, because we have no way of predicting the course of the dollar over the next 20 years, so we have no way of knowing what $10,000 (or $20,000) will do for you in 1992. Similarly, you could apply $100 a month to savings accounts and/or savings bonds and be able to predict pretty closely what it will amount to in 20 years—but again, you would have no idea of what those dollars will do for you.

In other words, whether you want to gamble or not, insurance, savings or bonds are all "gambles" on the course of the dollar's purchasing power, just as stock purchases are "gambles" on corporate success and the stock market.

All I've done so far is add to your concern, because I

don't know any easy, pleasant, sure routine.

Every investor planning his future must choose between accumulating a fixed number of dollars (but without knowing what those dollars will buy) and putting his present dollars into equity securities which may rise or fall in dollar value (but with the hope that the purchasing power of his investment will retain some link with the cost of living). There is no foolproof choice. You should have some savings and savings bonds. You should have some money in common shares (or senior issues convertible into common shares). Compromises often smack of indecision. But I still feel a "balanced diet" is a fair compromise.

(Incidentally, if you are self-employed, be sure to investigate the tax savings open to you under the Keogh Bill. Your bank, mutual-fund agent or local Internal Revenue office can give you some pointers.)

Q. *I'm a widow who would like about $400 a month from $50,000 invested in something without risk, and without cutting into capital.*

A. That's a tall order–in fact, too tall for me. First–there is no "riskless" investment. Second–$4,800 a year from $50,000 means a yield of 9.6% and I can't find many like that in any investment except some so risky that I would not suggest them.

Q. *I'm a working widow, in my mid-50s. My earnings are modest (I had never worked before) so I must have additional income from investments. But I've been losing money steadily. It seems I always buy at the high price and get caught in market slumps. Any comments?*

A. One thing is certain: You're going to feel ever so much better once you stop banging your head against that brick wall.

I can't imagine where you got the idea that at 54–with no business experience and with no previous knowledge of the stock market–you can suddenly begin getting a steady income by trading stocks with $25,000 of insurance money.

I'm not going to print the long list of speculative stocks you've been buying at their tops because I don't care to give them prominence. But take my word for it, they represented foolish shopping, all bought at the wrong time and for the wrong reasons.

The $20,000 or so you have left, it seems to me, ought to be put to work bringing in solid income, with some measure of inflation protection. Buy a few quality issues, hold them–and start getting some substantial dividends, instead of fattening up your broker's commissions account.

Q. *I'm a widow with a $45,000 two-family house, free and clear. The rent I receive pays all expenses, so that I get my own apartment rent-free (except for electricity and telephone). But I do need more income. Should I sell?*

A. If you could get $45,000 out of the house and invested it at 7½ per cent your income would be $3,300 a year or $275 a month. If you could rent for less than that you would be money ahead by selling.

Q. *I'm a widow who knows nothing about the market. I purchased a few good utility stocks but last year was advised to buy some real estate trust stock on the promise that it would pay 8 per cent. Now the broker tells me a market drop is coming and that I should get out.*

A. It just so happens that the date of your letter coincided with the start of the late 1971 rally in the market. So much for predictions.

I can't find the real estate trust you bought. I assume it is a small local outfit. It could pay 8 per cent, or more, or less. Promises on dividends often aren't worth the breath used in making them.

You neglect to give your age, and other data, but if you are elderly and in need of income, I think you should go into bonds and stay there. If you are in the early 60s, I can see some argument for sound utility, rail and manufacturing common shares. But buy and hold, and don't try to catch market swings.

Q. *I'm a 42-year-old widow who will inherit a large sum of money soon. I've never invested before. What do you suggest besides bank accounts? I will be in a high tax bracket.*

A. Speaking broadly, you should have low-yield growth stocks to protect you against long-term inflation and tax-exempt bonds to ease your income tax burden.

Q. *I have been willed some blue chip stocks. I know nothing about their value, what they yield, and don't know whether to keep them or sell them.*

A. You're not giving me much to go on–neither the names of the stocks nor your individual investment needs: income, growth?

If you don't need the income, and the stocks are quality growth issues, you should keep them. If you are retired and in need of income, perhaps you could get more by reinvesting elsewhere.

If they are well-established stocks, you can find their value by looking in the stock tables. Their yield is arrived at by simply dividing the annual dividend by the market price, thus: A $1.50 annual dividend paid by a stock selling at $33 represents a yield of 4½ per cent.

No one can tell you whether to sell or retain the stocks without knowing the names of the stocks and without some idea of what your investments must do for you as an individual.

Q. *A bank is keeping the account of my mother (75) in A.T.&T., Ford, McDonalds, Texaco, Woolworth. It seems to me half the dividend income is consumed by management fees.*

A. As commendable as such a portfolio might be for a business man I can't see yields of as low as 2¾ and 3½ for a woman of 75–not when high-grade bonds yield 7¼ per cent and require a minimum of management.

5 How and When to Buy Stocks

There are as many theories about when and how to buy stocks as there are people who are willing to be quoted.

Many an expert—with a fortune in stocks to prove it—will declare that he buys securities only once in every seven or eight or nine years. The theory is that the average adult will live through—even though he may not recognize it until later—several eight- or nine-year cycles in his lifetime when he should have mortgaged his grandmother and plunged into the market.

A review of the stock market's history does indicate that there is, in fact, a cyclical character to prices. The trouble, however, is that these peaks and valleys stand out clearly *only in retrospect,* on charts already drawn, charts showing "where we've been."

When you study the current chart, when you move your finger along the line to the last point—the position of the market today, right now—it is a good deal more difficult to visualize the future than it is to rationalize the peaks and valleys of the past.

And there have been many peaks and valleys.

There will always be peaks and valleys—because one of the basic laws of the world of securities, of all investments, is change. Inertia is a basic law of physics. It does not apply to investments.

Spread out a chart of the stock market covering only the last quarter century and you will see a dramatic story of securities prices, of men's (and nations') hopes and fears, victories and defeats, all reflected in their evaluation of the future.

Such a story would begin in the despair of the darkest days of World War II and tell:

The story of the long fight against dictatorship;
the postwar years of rebuilding destroyed nations;
the rising prominence of the United States as a world power and the increasing burdens which are the price of that position of leadership;
the growing tension between capitalism and communism;
the years of labor-management discord;
the conflict of government and business;
the development of the new wonder ages in electronics, outer space, drugs;
the growth of leisure time and the new economics it brought about;
the horrifying assassination of a President;
the rise of new independent nations in what had been for centuries colonial outposts;
the long battle in Vietnam;
the rise of Communist China to a position of world power, to the point, in fact, where it challenges Russia for the distinction of being Number 1 advocate of world communism;
the weakening of U.S. industry's position in world commerce;
the first U.S. international trade deficit in decades;
the first devaluation of the U.S. dollar since the Great Depression;
the rise to world industrial leadership by countries which were all but wrecked during World War II;
the spreading worldwide concern about the wasting and pollution of natural resources.

All these developments, and many more, have made history in the last quarter-century, and have affected the world of investments as well, for investing is little more than evaluating what is occurring now and attempting to estimate how it will affect the future.

As is the case with all history, we can learn little from investment history. An event which may bring lower prices to the stock market one year may spark an advance in prices the next. Oftentimes, the internal, technical condition of the stock market may be more important than the outside stimulus bearing on prices.

But two related truths do emerge from any study of the investment history—whether it covers a period of twenty-five years, or fifty years, or one hundred years:

The general, long-term trend of the dollar (as well as other world currencies) is toward lower values, lower purchasing power. In a word—inflation.

The general, long-term trend of securities prices (despite any and all violent interim fluctuations) is toward higher levels.

To the investor trying to find his way through what is at best a murky fog, these truths represent both a warning and a comfort.

He cannot entirely rely on accumulating dollars.

He can be comforted by the hope that though the stock he bought last month is lower in price today, the heavy odds are that the price of any standard investment issue will be higher ten years from now and even higher still twenty years from now.

As this is written, the stock market, which dropped after approaching the peak of 1,000 in the Dow Jones industrial stock averages, is now once more approaching that level. For years, that figure stood as a Mount Everest sort of peak—one more important as a point of reference than as one which we could expect the stock market to scale. It would be foolhardy to predict that the peak will be reached by next May 1 or October 15.

But it takes little bravery to predict that within the next ten years we will be looking back at the 1,000 level as complacently as we now look back at the Boom Twenties high of 381.17 in that same index. That peak, reached in 1929, was not touched again until a full quarter century had passed. And when it was reached there were not a few who said, in effect: "That's high enough. If we have gotten back to 1929 peak prices, we are once more in dangerous territory."

But in the next ten years, that high of 381.17 was more than doubled. And since the end of that decade, stock prices have risen even further. (As have the prices of ships and shoes and sealing wax.)

HOW HIGH IS UP?

It does no good to say "stocks are high, they'll have to come down," or that "stocks are a bargain." Because no one knows that exact arithmetical definition of "high" and "bargain"—and if by some occult power someone did, he'd be a fool to waste his time telling other people.

Curiously enough, it is only the securities-buying phase of a prudent man's investment program which is always being twisted and tortured by the question: "Is this a good time to buy?" He doesn't ask that question in other related matters.

He makes regular deposits in the savings bank—summer, winter, high prices or low. The same for his E bond payroll deduction payments. The same for his life insurance. The same for his home mortgage amortization.

He never asks: "Is this a good time to buy E bonds, or put money in the bank, or pay my life insurance premium, or make a payment on the mortgage?" He may even be conscious of the fact that most likely the dollars he will get back will not be as strong as the dollars he is putting in.

But he keeps on making his payments nonetheless. He's saving for the future, he's saving as he earns. That's the only way he can save, and there's no point in arguing with him about it.

And he's right.

But when it comes to securities, he suddenly gets cagey. You didn't catch him buying stocks late in 1954, at 381 in the Dow Jones industrial price average. Any fool knew that was the level on the fatal day in 1929 when the dizzy '20s, came to an end, and with them world prosperity.

By the time this is read, the averages may, in truth, have reacted to 600, or gone up to 1,000 or beyond.

An investment program in securities is no more foolproof than any other method for accumulating capital. There is a best time to buy stocks. But most of us have to learn this from history. Meanwhile, the business of earning, spending and putting aside for the future must go on every day.

One of the most widely circulated stock market charts shows the vagaries of the market since 1900. Superimposed on its long-range upward trend are boundary lines which attempt to show that during this period the market has held roughly between constantly rising upper and lower limits. In addition, there are intermediate lines which attempt to indicate when the market is on the "high" side and therefore not a "buy" and conversely when it is on the "low" side. Judging from this chart, the last time any sober chart follower should have bought stock was back in 1950! Since the highest point of that year, stocks have risen more than 300 percent.

There has *never* been a moment in Wall Street when a consensus of market analysts showed 100—or even 75—per cent unanimity on the future of the market. In fact, any substantial or unusually large agreement on any prediction is accepted as proof positive that it won't happen.

Since we lack the power to peer into the future, why not give up any thought of "beating the market"? Why not set up for ourselves a comfortable, worry-free program of *paying today's securities prices with today's earnings?*

Why not leave the fingernail biting to those who are constantly looking for bargains, and instead, concentrate on getting *going* values with our *current* dollars?

KEEP STEP WITH COSTS

There is one comforting thought when we contemplate the purchase of corporate shares. These securities will tend—in market value as well as yield—to keep step with current living costs. Since the long-term trend of prices in this country has been upward—inflationary—it follows that a safe rule of thumb would be to buy quality securities on a regular basis, steadily, and to trust that the long term uptrend will continue in the next twenty to forty years just as it has over the last hundred and fifty. Let the day-to-day, month-to-month, and perhaps even the year-to-year price swings average themselves out.

Consider our young man, Morse, now 28, with thirty-five years of investing ahead of him. He has, it is true, more leeway than most investors. He could, theoretically, hold his cash intact and buy "once in eight years," or whenever he thought the stock market was "in a buying range." It might as well be made clear right here, though, that no bell rings when the market is "a buy" and all theoretical attempts to pinpoint such a moment have failed. (Nor for that matter does the stock market move up and down as a unit. With the stock market averages around 935 early in 1971, there were still many issues which were selling well below their individual highs reached years earlier.)

Young Morse, who should devote himself to growth industries, should be little guided by the course of the general market, anyway. The fact that the averages are high is of little value in making a decision on investing in a new chemical, or plastic, or electronic company. If he is able to learn enough about the particular company to consider it a worthy investment, he cannot afford to be swayed by the current standing of the Dow Jones industrial averages which are made up entirely of old-line, large, successful companies. Should he decide to wait until the averages come down to what, chartwise, is considered to be a "fair" price, he may find that his little company, in the meantime, has had a couple of successful years during which time its stock has trebled in price.

It may sound tiresome to repeat the old cliché, "it's not a stock market, but a market of stocks." Nevertheless, when you are dealing with young, growth companies, nothing could be closer to the truth.

WHICH COMPANIES HAVE A BRIGHT FUTURE?

For the maximum gain over the years, Morse must devote his investment study time to seeking out companies which, to mangle a phrase, "have their future ahead of them." He is fortunate in that he can wait even ten years for the company to prove its worth (although in today's rapid development of business, less than half that time is generally sufficient). But to get the lowest price, to get in on the ground floor–and especially since he can afford to take the risk–he must "get 'em while they're young," regardless of what the price for du Pont, U.S. Steel, or General Electric may be at the moment. Morse can't afford to try to mastermind the whole stock market. He'll be doing himself the most good if he can learn all there is to know about one young and growing company at a time. But if he can't decide on a young company, he will do well to ride along with an established leader in a growth field.

For that matter, no person who is making a living in a factory, office or classroom can expect to develop the sixth sense which will tell him when stocks ought to be bought and when cash should be hoarded in the bank against the day when shares once more become a bargain.

He should, instead, set his sights on accumulating investments which fit his needs as he goes along, hoping that he will benefit by the long-range growth of the country and ignoring the peaks and valleys in stock prices which rightfully claim 100 per cent of the attention of the professional stock market trader.

Such a regular purchase policy would work equally well for older Lefferts and Quinn even though their investment plans are different from Morse's and are concentrated in the established leaders.

The stock-buying system proven best by both actual experience and theoretical computation is that of "dollar averaging." That means the purchase at stated intervals of equal dollar amounts of whatever securities satisfy the investor's particular program. The investor is thus assured of acquiring more shares for his money when prices are low, and fewer shares when prices are high. Also, he is never in the position of trying to guess whether the market is going up or down, but instead is constantly taking advantage of price fluctuations to get his stock at a price which will be below the straight mathematical average for the period of time covered.

There are many ways our retirement planners can take advantage of the "dollar averaging" technique.

AS LITTLE AS $40 A QUARTER

Morse, with only a few hundred dollars a year to invest, could come under a New York Stock Exchange's "invest as you go" program, whereby his broker will accept payments as small as $40 a month, or even $40 every three months. If he felt he could withstand the temptation to spend his money for luxuries, he could save on commissions by keeping his money in the bank until he has acquired $400 or $500 for a single purchase.

Obviously, if he were buying shares in young companies not traded on the New York Stock Exchange, he would have to follow the latter procedure anyway.

However, since he would be concentrating on growth stocks, which yield few, if any, dividends, the interest his funds pick up while waiting in the savings bank would probably more than offset his loss of dividends.

HOW DOLLAR COST AVERAGING WORKS

An investment of $1,000 at ten regular time intervals, assuming fluctuations in market price of shares being acquired:

Assumed Regular Investment	Assumed Share Prices	No. of Shares Acquired
$1,000	$ 8.00	125
1,000	11.50	87
1,000	12.50	80
1,000	11.50	87
1,000	14.25	70
1,000	12.50	80
1,000	14.50	69
1,000	16.40	61
1,000	17.50	57
1,000	15.00	67
$10,000	$13.36 (average cost)	783

–Table from Brevits, by Vance, Sanders & Co.

It can be seen at a glance that the regular $1,000 investment acquired more shares when prices were low and fewer shares when prices were high. (This is the reverse of what happens when an uninformed, emotional investor is left to his own devices. He generally buys more shares when prices are high and often, disillusioned, won't go near the stock market when prices are low and stocks are a "buy.") The result of the dollar averaging is that the investor acquired 783 shares for $10,000 at an average cost of $12.77 a share even though the price average over the period of investment was $13.37 a share.

One thing seems certain, however. Investors using the Stock Exchange's monthly investment plan are far more quality-minded as a group than the general run of non-professional small investors. To this extent, we can agree that the monthly investment plan represents a solid plus for the average investor.

Here are stocks which have been most popular with monthly investment plan investors.

American Telephone & Telegraph, General Motors, Radio Corp. of America, General Telephone, International Business Machines, Sears, Roebuck, General Electric, Eastman Kodak, Tri-Continental, Standard Oil of N.J., Standard Oil of California, Xerox, Pacific Gas & Electric, Merck, Scott Paper, Safeway, Dow Chemical, Litton, Texaco;

Gulf Oil, Union Carbide, du Pont, Pfizer, Phillips Petroleum, Corn Products, Communications Satellite, Lehman, Monsanto, Chrysler, Sperry Rand, International Telephone and Telegraph, Consolidated Edison, American Cyanamid, Honeywell, Pan American;

Caterpillar Tractor, FMC, Polaroid, Long Island Lighting, Westinghouse, American Hospital Supply, U.S. Steel, Baxter Laboratories, Madison Fund, General Foods, Lone Star Gas, Tenneco, Chesebrough-Pond's.

It so happens that this list includes some of the most spectacular price gainers of the last several years, as well as several which have shown little gain.

But one thing is obvious: Monthly investment plan stock buyers will never be left holding the bag after some fast-talking telephone salesman pulls up his stakes and fades into the night.

PERFECT VEHICLE FOR DOLLAR AVERAGING

The perfect vehicle for dollar averaging is, of course, the open-end mutual fund. Open-end funds will accept monthly payments of as low as $10 and credit that to as many shares—worked out to two or three decimal places—as the money will buy after payment of commissions. These commission charges often are high—running to 8½ to 9 per cent—even when one takes into consideration the fact that the fee on buying covers the expense of selling as well. However, the mutual fund does provide diversification of investment and professional management far beyond those the small investor can command by himself. (Furthermore, as we shall discuss in the chapter on Mutual Funds [Chapter 10], there are some funds which charge no commissions.)

It might be that Quinn, our oldest investor, who is going for safety first and has large sums to invest, would be tempted to buy the generally accepted safe stocks on his own and avoid the mutual fund fee which is the equivalent of two years' dividend income. If he sticks to quality, he doesn't need the diversification or fund management which the mutuals provide. The leading auto and food companies, the conservative banks and finance companies, the big electric utilities, could all be selected pretty much from the standard quality lists available at any brokerage house, and go into his portfolio for keeps. But even in buying these, a steady dollar averaging program of acquisition will prove advantageous in the long run.

In recent years, investment clubs have enjoyed growing popularity—aided no little by the long upward sweep of stock market prices. The investment club is a simple organization of a dozen or so friends who regularly (mostly monthly) meet and deposit a fixed amount of money in the club treasury. At the same meeting, several members and/or a professional analyst invited for the purpose report on some securities and the members decide on a purchase.

The aims of the clubs and the intelligent way most memberships go about making an investment are, of course, commendable. But membership in such a club is definitely only a small part of a well-thought-out personal program.

Investment planning is nothing if not individualistic by its very nature. A dozen people may be close friends by virtue of their common interest in golf, fishing, poker or church activities. But it is not likely that all of them, or even most of them can afford to take the same amount of risk, or have the same investment goals.

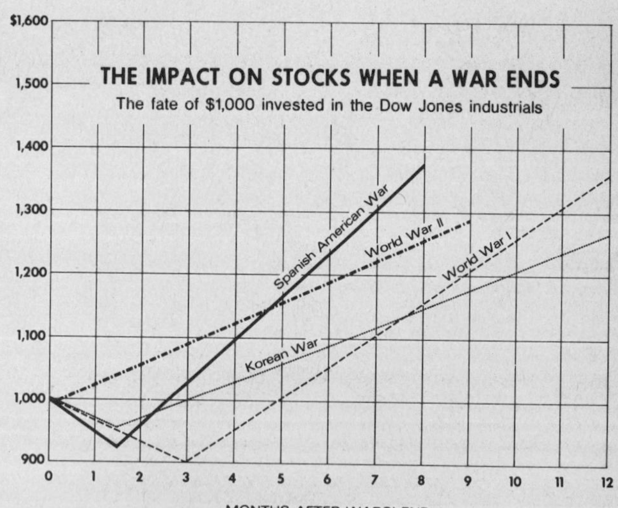

PEACE IS "BULLISH"

The market's reaction to "peace breaking out" is graphically shown in this chart compiled by Ralph A. Rotnem, veteran stock market analyst with Harris, Upham & Co. The termination of fighting brought a sharp rise in the Dow-Jones industrial averages following every war in the last 75 years. Almost immediately after V-J Day, marking the end of World War II, a rally started. Following the 1918 armistice, the market declined for 3 months before starting its sharp rise.

SOME QUESTIONS AND ANSWERS

Q. *Do brokers require payment for purchases after 5 business days? And, if so, what happens when one gets a confirmation 2 weeks late, with the excuse that the "office was busy"? In the meantime the stock may have dropped in price.*

A. Generally, securities must be paid for in 5 days after purchase. Confirmation of a purchase should usually arrive a day or two after the day the order was executed. From here on, you're pretty much on your own. If the broker is reputable, well known and respected in the community, you'll have to give him the benefit of the doubt and assume there was some carelessness in the office (in which case he will take some steps to satisfy you that the stock was actually bought at the price and on the day he said it was).

Q. *How can a stockbroker ethically buy and sell stock in the same company? When he represents a buyer he theoretically tries to buy the stock at the lowest price possible; when he represents a seller, he tries to get the highest price. An attorney isn't allowed to represent both sides of the transaction.*

A. I think you're overlooking one significant point. A stockbroker executes his clients' orders on the floor of the Stock Exchange, where prices are set by public, 2-way auction. He doesn't control the price at which the trades are made. Further, prices fluctuate from minute to minute, so that your order to buy, say, 100 A.T.&T. at 11 A.M. and your neighbor's order to sell 100 at 1:30 P.M. are executed in 2 different market climates.

But let's say you both call in your orders–one to buy, one to sell–at the same moment. What happens then?

Stock Exchange rule 76 requires that both orders must be taken to the American Telephone trading post on the floor of the exchange. Your firm's broker walks up to the post and learns that "T" is 45 bid, 45¼ asked. He thereupon would call out in a loud voice: "⅛ for 100"–"100 at ¼"–"Sold at ⅛." Translation: "I'm bidding 45⅛ for 100 shares, offering 100 for sale at 45¼, and executing both deals at 45⅛." The $45 price level was set by the open market.

Even so, he isn't free from all competition. Any other broker standing in the crowd could call out "Sold" and force your broker to buy *his* 100 shares at 45⅛, and another broker could yell "Take it" after the call of "100 at ¼" and claim the 100 shares being offered. But this doesn't occur too often since your broker, who is the only one who knows he has 100 to buy and 100 to sell, can rattle off his calls in rapid sequence.

In any event, you have to admit that the deal is not carried out in secret and that both customers are getting the benefit of public competition and public price-setting.

Q. *A recent article discussing investments said that no longer can a person buy good securities and forget about them–as I have done since the late '20s. Considering that I am 75 and my husband a semi-invalid, it would be quite a chore for me to be in and out of the market. Our portfolio includes odd lots of Ford of Canada, IBM, National Steel, Standard Oil of California, and 100- to 250-share blocks of Anaconda, Chrysler, Dow, Detroit Edison, Ford, General Telephone, General Motors, Monsanto, Phelps Dodge and Excello. Should we turn over our securities to a fund for management?*

A. You've touched on one of the oldest arguments in investing: the need for constant supervision and portfolio adjustment. Obviously, it would be silly to say that one should buy securities, put them away and forget about them–today, 40 years ago, or 40 years hence. As between supervision and no supervision–whether of securities, or gardens, or children–one must always take a blanket stand *for* supervision.

But then you get to the question: What quality supervision?

If you're talking about gardening, you could get a close observer to testify that my garden does better when I don't "supervise" it. And we've seen children who have gotten the kind of parental supervision they could have done better without.

And–getting back to your specific question–any financial observer can testify that investment counselors and mutual fund managements have bought stock before a fall and sold them before a rise. The good managements and counselors are merely right more times than they're wrong.

In your own specific case, I'm sure that there have been times in the last 40 years when you should have sold Anaconda or IBM or Chrysler or practically any of the others and then bought them back at much lower prices. I'm sure a professional manager would have tried to do that–and succeeded according to his ability. Whether he would wind up today with a portfolio worth more than yours there is no way of telling. Selling and rebuying costs money. Capital-gains taxes have to be paid. And there is never any guaranty that a sale or repurchase is well timed.

I realize I'm begging the question, but I have no definite answer.

Should securities be watched? Yes. Would portfolio adjustments over the last 40 years have increased your fortune substantially? I don't know. Should constant portfolio adjustment be your course for the future? I don't know.

If you want more current cash income, the obvious course would be to sell IBM, General Telephone and other low yielders and, at your age, put proceeds into 7¼ per cent good-grade, long-term utility bonds. Then do nothing.

Actually, what you did about 40 years ago was to turn your money over to about a dozen leading corporations and say, in effect: "Here's my money. Use it and repay me in dividends and/or capital appreciation. I don't know how to make automobiles, or refine copper, or develop computers. But I leave it to you and will go along with your judgment."

I think that on the whole your trust has been well placed. To argue that you should have sold out of any specific company at any specific time is to argue that you would be capable of:

Foreseeing a drop in that company's business which its own management either could not foresee or could not avoid; or

Foreseeing a downtrend in public acceptance of the shares of the particular industry; or

Foreseeing a drop in the economy in general and, consequently, a decline in overall market prices.

I'm not saying you could do any or all these things. But you must admit you'd most likely have to make it a full-time job.

Q. *Although our income is about $90,000 a year, I find we are in debt for $48,000 in order to take advantage of a stock option. Isn't that dangerous?*

A. It could be or couldn't be—depending upon the terms of the option, the amount of stock involved, the quality of the stock involved and a lot of other matters.

Generally, I don't favor buying stock with borrowed money, but the option situation and the amounts of money involved here place this investment outside the norm.

Q. *I know nothing about buying stock in a corporation. What might I expect if I invest my money in this way?*

A. Corporations and partnerships differ in many respects. But just the same, when you buy stock in a company, you acquire part of that company and you become a sort of limited-risk partner (your risk is limited to the amount you put into the company. You can lose all of that, but no more). As a partner you can expect to see the value of your shares and the amount of your dividends go up when the company's business is good, and see them go down when business is bad. You can expect to have a vote for each share you hold. But having a vote and exercising any significant control on the management are two different things. Don't buy common shares just because you think this is going to give you a voice in running a giant automobile company or electric utility or railroad. It won't.

But, as simply as I can put it, a purchase of shares in a company means you become part owner of the enterprise. From then on—and as long as you remain a shareholder—the fortunes of your investment are tied to that company, to the industry it's in, to the state of the national economy, to the international situation, and to the state of mind of millions of investors and speculators whose emotions converge on a trading floor about two-thirds the size of a football field, located at the corner of Broad and Wall Streets in downtown New York City.

"Investment Facts," a booklet published by the New York Stock Exchange, explains some of the basic terms involved in investing.

Q. *How does one go about getting information on the different companies which have stock for sale, other than going to a broker? Is there a booklet giving ticker-code letters? Please send me a list of investments. I'd like to speculate with $400.*

A. I guess you'd be the first to admit you are a novice in securities investment. Certainly you are going about it the wrong way when you ask first for a list of ticker symbols. Of all the trappings of securities investments, I think that the ticker symbol is just about the least important piece of information a novice could have. You could profitably own a list of stocks as long as your arm without ever knowing that "J" stands for Standard Oil of N.J., "T" for American Telephone and "GRL" for General Instrument.

There are thousands of corporations with shares already in the hands of the public. Their stock is not "for sale" in the same sense that television sets are for sale in stores. RCA, for example, is not in the business of selling shares of stock. Its capitalization consists of debt, preferred shares and 74,437,000 shares of common stock. If you want to own 100 or 5,000 of those shares you ask a broker to send his representative to the RCA trading post on the floor of the New York Stock Exchange and buy the shares for you from some investor who already owns them and is willing to sell.

If you want information on RCA (or General Motors, or U.S. Steel, or N.Y. Central, etc.) you can either go to a broker and discuss it with him, or look it up in Standard & Poor's or Moody's at a brokerage office or at the public library.

It might also help you get some basic facts straight if you sent $1.50 to the New York Stock Exchange, Dept. SU, Box 252, New York, N.Y. 10005 for an "investment kit."

You can put your $400 into investment-grade companies. If you want to gamble, you should turn to a better source of advice than yours truly. Over the years I've been a consistent (although, thankfully, a small and infrequent) loser at matching pennies, penny-ante poker and all forms of parchesi.

Q. *I sold some stock just 4 days before a 2-for-1 split. The broker has asked me to return the additional stock. Is he right?*

A. This stock-split bit causes more suspicion than almost any other item involving customer and broker.

Strangely, while the technical data involved in a split are complicated, the matter itself is extremely simple.

When you say "4 days before a split" you are speaking too vaguely. A stock split is declared by directors on one day, approved by shareholders on another. The stock goes "ex split" on still another day—generally 4 business days before the day of record. And the additional shares, finally, are mailed out on still another, later date.

After this lengthy and, admittedly, complicated dissertation, I should add that all this explanation is unnecessary. For—

If you got the "pre-split" price for your stock, you evidently sold the stock before the split; therefore you are not entitled to the additional shares.

Let's assume a stock sells for $90 a share. A 2-for-1 split is announced and approved by shareholders. If you sell 100 shares and get $9,000 proceeds, you obviously sold the old stock—the pre-split stock—and the investor who bought it will be entitled to the 2-for-1 split. If you sell 100 shares and receive only $4,500, you obviously sold the new, split stock and the 100 shares additional are due you.

Actually, there is little difference. You either sold 100 shares for $9,000 or sold 100 for $4,500 and have another 100 shares due you at 45. Either way you slice it, your investment stands at $9,000.

Q. *Which type of trader is most successful: tape reader, short-term chartist, 1-to-3 year investor, long-term investor (15 to 20 years)? Do brokerage houses buy and sell stock for their own accounts? If so, is this fair to the public? Are short sales profitable if protected by stops? If so, why are they shunned by brokers? For the last 15 years I have owned stocks, usually selling too soon, or buying at bad times. I own and operate real estate, which has been far more profitable.*

A. Your first question is a futile attempt to get a pat answer to a complicated question.

Obviously some professional tape readers make money, others don't. I doubt that a man making a living by working in an office or factory can make money as a tape reader. The same is true of short-term traders. I think most money made by nonprofessional investors is made long-term, whether it's 3 years or 30 years.

Brokerage houses often do take a position in a stock. I don't see that that is unfair to the public, even if you consider the firm's customers part of the public. Often the firm's position is in a special situation far from the path along which the public moves.

This is all part of the vague but widely held belief that brokerage firms make their money at the expense of their customers. Naturally, they do make their commissions from purchases and sales by customers. But it would be unfair to carry that further and intimate that a broker can't make any money unless his customer loses. When you buy stock it is most often from some investor represented by another broker; when you sell, it is most often to some investor represented by another broker. In other words, it isn't you against your broker, but you against another investor who is also acting on his own initiative.

A stop-loss order on a short sale sets a price at which, when reached, your broker goes into action. A stop order will limit your loss, but certainly there is no reason for believing it automatically guarantees a profit.

If you sell a stock short at 50 and place a stop order to buy it back at 47½, your broker will go onto the floor to buy the stock if and when the price drops to 47½. If he can get the stock at that level, you've made a profit of 2½ points, minus commissions.

If you place a stop-loss order to buy it back at 52½—assuming the stock rises against you—he will go into action when the stock reaches 52½ and buy at the best market price he can get. You thus attempt to limit your loss on the short sale at around 2½ points, plus commissions.

In either event, a stop order sends your broker into action automatically, but doesn't assure you of a profit.

I don't know what rules you follow in your real-estate operation. But if the business is profitable, it must be because you know what you're doing and making a career of doing it. I get the impression you're willing to work hard at your real estate but would like to make some easy money in the market. Doesn't it follow, then, that you consider real estate a business deserving your full attention, but Wall Street is something you feel you can beat with one hand behind your back? It ain't necessarily so.

Q. *A group of young friends are considering starting an investment club. There will be 8 to 12 of us paying about $10 a month dues. We have already asked the National Association of Investment Clubs for material. I would appreciate your do's and don't's and a list of stocks we might study for our first investment.*

A. I think you will get all the necessary background material from the association.

The problems most often referred to me by investment clubs deal with program and settling differences which arise—most often in troublesome markets.

It seems to me a group of young people forming a club should aim for growth—first, foremost and to the exclusion of anything else, including dividends. There is absolutely no point to giving any weight to one stock because it pays 4½%, rather than to another which pays 2½%, or no per cent at all.

Your most difficult question will be whether to work toward this goal by taking wild chances on unseasoned and generally low-priced issues or by investing in the IBMs, Kodaks, General Electrics, etc., etc. Only you can decide.

I assume this $10 a month is not your "last dollar," that you can take chances with it. If any member has any special "inside" knowledge of any specific glamor fields or specific new companies in this field, I'd say go to it. You have nothing to lose but the $10 and you're all young enough to escape being scarred for life if you do.

If you feel you don't want to take the wilder chances, stick with the tried and true.

This second course will present another problem. With only $120 a month to invest you're going to be hard pressed to find much to talk about if you are in the process of accumulating, for example, IBM. That much money will, currently, get you about one-third of a share, which is hardly a subject for an evening of exciting discussion as worthwhile as the program may prove in the long run. So if you decide to go for the blue chips you might appoint a program chairman to present something interesting once the $120 has been collected.

Whichever you do, make the hard and fast decision first, because a change in midstream will cost you membership, and you haven't any to lose.

It helps to set up termination policy (or a system for handling dropouts) before you get started, thus avoiding any bad feelings. Also decide at the very start that you are going to invest *every* month, even if it's only $120. Once you start guessing the market "let's not buy this month; prices may be lower next month" you're in for trouble.

Q. *I am in the service—out in the "boondocks." How can I invest?*

A. Letters from members of the armed forces raise the pertinent question of investment techniques best suited to their term of service.

In many cases, the problem seems (to them) complicated by the fact that duty assignments will be overseas—in Europe, the Far East, etc.

I suppose, to a first-time investor, the problems of investing in U.S. industry from Vietnam, Japan or West Germany seem almost insurmountable. As one officer based in a tiny country put it: "We don't get daily quotations here." (To which I am inclined to murmur: thank heaven!)

Actually, a conservative, sober and sensible long-term investment program can be carried on just as easily from any military post thousands of miles away as it can from any point within sight of Wall Street's towers. And more safely—that is, more immune from transitory rumors, fevers, and other influences which so often wreck a solid lifetime plan.

If you are about to go into military service, all you need do is talk over your aims with a broker in or near your home town.

If you are already stationed in some far-off land, a letter to a U.S. brokerage firm which may have an office in that country or in your home town will bring you all the help you need, insofar as investing in corporate shares and most mutual funds is concerned.

While some brokers will discuss no-load (noncommission) funds, you can't expect them to put too much emphasis on an investment plan which yields them no commissions. For a list of all funds which are members of the Investment Company Institute, the mutual fund organization, you need only write to the institute at 1775 K Street N.W., Washington, D.C. 20006.

But whether you decide to buy mutual funds or corporate shares directly, your distance from Wall Street is of little importance.

The funds provide a monthly program. You send in your check and they do the rest—even to re-investing income and capital gains and having a custodian bank hold the shares. The confirmation slip—which is the receipt for money sent in and which indicates the shares acquired—can be sent to your home for safekeeping.

The same sort of service is provided by N.Y. Stock Exchange member firms (under the Monthly Investment Plan—MIP) if you should decide to buy listed stocks directly. All you need do is send in your monthly or quarterly check for as little as $40 and the firm will do the rest, reinvesting your dividends in additional shares of whatever stock you are then accumulating, and holding the stock certificates in its vault.

I think either of these programs is ideal for servicemen. Merely select the fund or common stock you want to own, and send in your monthly check to the bank acting as custodian for the fund, or to the brokerage firm.

If you can get mail out of your military post, you can invest.

Q. *I have a "monthly investment plan" account, with 48 shares of Standard Oil of N.J. But I never received the last (June) dividend payment.*

A. Generally, MIP accounts apply the dividend to purchase of additional shares of the stock then under acquisition. Check your statements and see whether that wasn't done.

Q. *My broker would recommend one stock and discourage purchase of something I wanted to buy. So I'd buy what he suggested and watch the other stock skyrocket. Finally, I became so frantic I began spreading my money out as thin as I could—buying 10 shares of this and 15 of another. It's been a failure.*

A. Anyone who attempts to make quick profits trading 10- and 15-share blocks of stock goes to bat with 2½ strikes against him.

Minimum commissions, plus the odd-lot differential given up on both purchase and sale, make this form of penny-ante poker almost impossible to beat.

You will find that these total charges are so heavy, proportionately, that if you suffer a 2-point decline in the stock, your loss in dollars will be twice as much as what you could expect to gain from a 2-point rise. I don't think you'd care for those "odds" in the long run.

Q. *I am a 25-year-old salesman, owning 600 shares of California Financial bought at 7¾; 100 shares of Pan Am at 29⅝; 10 shares of General Motors at 74⅝. I sold Chrysler at 43 to buy the Pan Am and sold 50 shares of Burroughs at 64 for an 8-point profit. To be honest with you, I don't like my investment methods. I've tried working with a broker, but the older ones treat me like a kid; the middle-aged ones do not like my ideas; and the young ones can't answer my questions.*

A. I think the trouble with your investment method is that it isn't an investment method at all, but an attempt to scalp quick profits by in-and-out trading.

Let me hasten to add that I have no objection to trading. But if you go in for it, you must realize that you have to pretty much "go it alone." A broker can advise you and you can do everything from ignoring his advice completely to taking it 100%. The choice is yours. Furthermore any position up or down the scale from completely ignoring his advice to accepting it 100% is perfectly proper and could prove profitable or costly.

As of the moment, you are displaying the popular (and dangerous) tendency of the amateur trader to take quick (and generally, small) profits but to dig in with your losses (and stubbornly watch them grow).

I think you will find that most "pro" traders, as a general rule, will let their profits run and cut their losses at 5%, 10% or some predetermined level.

Some of your issues are more speculative than others, but at 25 they're all "in the ball park." All *could* show you profits in the next 5 years.

I'd say you'd do far better by latching on to something which is growing—and staying with it—than by this "in and out" stuff.

Finally, I notice you're doing well in real estate. Fortunes have been made in real estate. How come you're not putting your money where your knowledge and experience are?

Q. *I am a student, 19, with $700 with which I would like to speculate in fast trading. I'm not interested in long term investment.*

A. This is a perfectly proper program—for you. At 19, and with a modest sum for experimentation, there's no reason why you should not try your hand at speculating.

If you're successful, you may have a profitable career as a trader before you.

If you lose the money, there's no great harm done. You're young enough to make a fresh start and, in fact, the $700 loss is a cheap price to pay for a course in speculation.

However, I can't be of much help since I'm not a successful speculator myself. I, too, learned my lesson many years ago. I wouldn't deny you a chance to learn yours.

Talk over your plans with a broker who is willing to take you on and whose firm issues trading suggestions from time to time.

Also, get someone over 21 to act as custodian for your account. At 19, you generally cannot make a legally binding commitment to buy or sell securities.

Keep in mind, also, that you go to bat with two strikes against you: (1) you're new at the game; (2) you have limited capital—which means either that you will buy "penny" stocks in order to acquire 100-share lots or that if you trade in odd lots of higher priced issues, you will have to give up an eighth or a quarter of a point buying and selling.

But, in any event, go to it and good luck!

Q. *Some investment experts say one should always average up, never down. They also say: buy when others are selling, not when others are buying. Don't these two principles conflict? If you buy when the price is rising, that price is going up because others are buying, too.*

A. Sure there is a conflict. For that matter, how about those old proverbs: "Look before you leap" vs. "He who hesitates is lost." I've never been able to reconcile them.

Or how about the praise for the man "who can keep his head while all about him are losing theirs"? (Translated into stock market terms: the man who keeps buying while everybody is panicking and dumping stock.) The only trouble with that praise for the man who can remain unruffled is that some wise guy added: "Maybe this calm guy doesn't really know what's going on."

Seriously, I think we must first clarify those words "buying" and "selling." Every time a share of stock is bought you can be sure someone else is selling it. So when you say "buy when others are selling" you really mean "buy when those who don't know as much as you think you know are selling."

Sometimes the buyers are right; sometimes the sellers. In any given transaction, someone is making a mistake.

I've seen averaging up (buying steadily as the price rises) which has resulted in whopping profits, and vice versa. I've seen averaging down which has ultimately resulted in big profits when the stock finally turned around, as the buyer was betting all along. And I've seen records of "averaging down" on a declining stock which continued until the stock disappeared as worthless.

Each market situation must be evaluated on its own merits. In other words, before you average up you must satisfy yourself that the company's progress is likely to continue for a long time and that the current market price does not represent an over-evaluation of its prospects. And when you average down in a falling stock you must feel assured that its troubles are only temporary, that the company will once again reassert itself. And always, of course, you must take the general market picture into consideration.

You need more than a slogan to make money in Wall Street.

Q. *I have income which leaves me, after expenses, about $300 a month to save or play with. I've been reading market books, but I'm still too scared to move. Inflation is cutting into my dollars. Penny stocks are sold by crooks. Blue chips pay a small dividend. Bonds provide no inflation protection. Mutual funds and their brokers charge a lot for their service. Warrants I don't understand.*

A. It's never been an easy world to live in, and certainly the world of investments is no exception. However, it's a case of "durned if you do, durned if you don't"—as you yourself seem to realize. There is no safe "hiding place down here." That being so, you look for the best odds you can get.

First, however, I'd like to clear up one point: It's difficult to imagine money that can be saved OR "played with."

If you need more savings in order to protect yourself against emergencies, you have NO money to "play with." In that case, the $300 a month should continue going into savings until you have reached an adequate protection level.

If you already have substantial emergency savings and, of course, adequate life insurance, then you DO have a choice:

1. You can "play" the market with the extra money; or
2. You can invest it for long-term growth.

I'm not going to dictate which course you should follow, because only you know your abilities, financial needs, resources, responsibilities.

As to your other complaints:

If you're afraid of penny stocks—stay away from them. You can buy the highest-priced quality issues on the market at the rate of $300 a month (and even less.)

Warrants are basically a speculative device. If you don't understand them, stay away.

Mutual fund sales commissions run from more than 9% down to zero. So that field is wide open.

Growth-type blue chips do, generally, pay a small dividend—or no dividend at all. So what? You just said you had $300 a month left over, so you can't be in need of income. If you're investing for long-term capital gain, don't become too involved with getting 5% return on your money now. Most growth companies can build capital faster in the long run than most high-yielding common stocks.

All I'm saying is that if you are uncertain, buy quality, buy for growth, and continue to hold the stock so long as it satisfies both criteria.

Q. *I recently bought 100 shares of A.T. & T. but was told by the broker that I did not have enough stock to qualify for the dividend reinvestment program you mentioned in a recent column. How many shares do I need?*

A. You have enough now. I think the problem must be that the shares are being kept at the brokerage firm—in "street" name—instead of being registered in your own name.

If the shares had been transferred to your name you would have received a welcoming letter from A.T. & T. as a new shareowner plus an explanation of how the reinvestment plan works.

Any shareholder may enroll, although the company has taken pains to point out to small shareowners (1 to 15 shares) that the program might not be attractive for them since the costs—75 cents a quarter plus the proportionate share of the bulk commission—might represent too large a part of their quarterly dividend income.

But certainly a 100-share owner could use the plan advantageously. Have the shares transferred to your name.

Q. *Why is a dividend distribution of one share for every share already held called a "2-for-1" split? Is it also called a 100 per cent stock dividend?*

A. Because if you held 10 shares before the distribution, you will have 20 shares to your credit thereafter. It is also labeled a 100 per cent stock dividend because it increases your holdings by 100 per cent.

Q. *Does the plowing back of dividends into more corporate shares make sense taxwise?*

A. There is no tax gain or loss in this procedure. The dividends you plow back into new shares are taxed as income—in the same way they would be taxed if you took them in cash and bought a new hat.

If you don't need the dividend income, it can be a convenient, dollar-averaging method of acquiring more shares.

Q. *I bought some Japanese motor stock at 77 cents a share. Why would this large company's shares sell at so low a price when ours sell so much higher?*

A. Japan went through a postwar securities boom which attracted wide public support. In fact, securities were being sold in department stores.

In order to attract more working-class customers, many corporations there split their capital into many millions of shares, thus bringing the price down to below the equivalent of the U.S. dollar.

Q. *Where can I get advice on investing $40 a month in stocks?*

A. By asking the New York Stock Exchange, Dept. SU, Box 252, New York, N.Y. 10005 or a broker for a copy of "How to Invest on a Budget."

Q. *We have a home, free and clear, some life insurance and $5,500 in savings. Our children are married. Now I realize I've done nothing about planning for retirement. Is it too late for me to start an investment program at age 51?*

A. It is never too early or never too late to consider investments. Investment needs as is the case with food and dress, change with one's age, but they must be considered at every age.

Assuming you want to quit work in the 60–65 area, you have 10 to 15 years to build a portfolio that will supplement your pensions, social security and other retirement benefits. Since you are still *so young*, your investments now should be directed primarily at capital gain, ignoring current income.

You can start right now to accumulate growth stocks or growth-type mutual funds, whichever suits your fancy, and makes you feel more comfortable.

Time enough when you retire to switch your portfolio to income-producers.

Q. *I bought 400 shares of a plastics stock at $3 a share. It subsequently fell to 25 cents a share before recovering. I told the broker I wanted to get my money out if I could. He called me one day and said he thought he could get $3 a share, so I sold. My confirmation showed I had received $1,200—net, no commission. Why should he have acted as a principal, rather than as agent—as he had done before? Was he able to sell the stock for more?*

A. An over-the-counter trader may act either as broker or principal. Only he and the broker to whom he sold the stock know what he got for the stock when he sold it. Obviously he got more than $3, otherwise he would have nothing to show for his effort. Whether it was $3.10 or $3.25 or $5 a share I haven't the slightest idea and only an examination of the over-the-counter "pink sheets" as of the day of the sale can give you an idea. And that would by no means be conclusive.

Q. *Several years ago I bought 300 warrants of an over-the-counter food company. I paid 3¹/₈ and they haven't sold at that level since. I understand these warrants expire later this year and may then become worthless. Do I take my loss now, or wait?*

A. I'm not going to give you any answer because I don't know.

What I can tell you:

The warrants entitle you to claim one share of stock, now selling around $6, by turning in one warrant and $3.50 in cash. So on a straight arithmetical basis, the warrant is worth $2.50. But it also represents a 7-month speculative claim on the stock and that's worth something, too—although that factor may decrease in value steadily as expiration date approaches. This leaves you with the problem: will the common stock sell above 6⁵/₈ before the warrant expires to make the warrant worth more than 3¹/₈.

One more thing you should understand perfectly: There's no MAYBE about the warrant becoming worthless. The day after the last day it can be used to acquire common, the warrant is WORTHLESS—and don't you lose sight of that! You've got to either fish (turn it in) or cut bait (sell) before that last day.

Q. *Recently you wrote that you take a dim view of giving someone power to act on one's behalf in trading securities. This disturbed me because as a professional I find myself with longer-than-ordinary long office hours and without the time to keep myself well-informed in the field of finance. Also, as a professional, I recognize the competency of other professionals in different areas.*

A. I by no means intended to run down the competency of professional investors. In fact, I have always stressed that if you don't know and haven't the time to find out, go to someone who does know and who devotes his working days to finance.

The column you refer to discussed the query of a reader who asked about giving his broker full discretion to trade his account. I think such powers should be delegated with extreme caution and only if you have known the broker long enough to feel assured that he is a competent trader and takes risks which you can assume. Incidentally, many leading brokerage firms are even more cautious about this than I am. They either prohibit such arrangement—period—or else require that the account be supervised by a senior officer or partner of the firm.

However, turning a trading account over to a broker is only one way to get professional help—and, perhaps, the least common.

An investment company—either mutual fund or closed-end—is one of the most popular methods of getting professional management for your investment funds. Mutuals, alone, are managing more than 9 million individual investment accounts, with upward of $50 billions involved. Many banks, statistical organizations, and investment counseling firms offer professional management at a fee. If, as you say, you don't feel you can devote the time to investing, there's no reason you shouldn't consider any or all of these services.

Q. *How may one transmit a common share certificate to a relative without going through a broker?*

A. By writing to the transfer bank, the name of which appears on the front of the stock certificate.

Q. *When one opens a brokerage account he is asked to sign all sorts of agreements, one of which gives the broker the right to pledge any stock. Must one sign such an agreement?*

A. No. If you intend to pay 100% for any securities you buy, you need not sign any such agreement even if you leave the securities in the broker's safekeeping. Of course, if you intend to use margin, you must give him the right to pledge the stock.

Q. *My broker says he could give me better service if my stocks were in "street name." What would this mean?*

A. It would mean that you'd endorse your stock over to the broker and that he would hold it in his name. Many investors follow this plan since it relieves them of the safekeeping chores. Dividends would then be paid to the broker, who would send you his check in payment, if you requested it, or else credited to your account.

Also, if you wanted to sell the stock, a phone call would suffice.

All stock owned on margin is held in "street name." Stock fully paid for may be held in "street name." The risk you assume by turning the stock over to your broker depends, of course, entirely on the reputability of the broker.

I don't follow his promise of "better service." He can watch your account just as closely if the shares are in your own vault. Investors who trade in and out a lot prefer to leave their stock in street name and thus avoid having to receive and send out certificates through the mail.

Q. *I am a schoolteacher. Several months ago my wife and I took our $1,000 savings and decided to give the stock market a try. I have had difficulty getting good advice. My broker suggested a construction stock which was so expensive I could buy only 36 shares. He discouraged my interest in $5 to $10 stocks. Yet I had plotted 50 stocks in this range, the majority of which have risen while my investment eased a trifle. So I sold it at a slight loss. I then bought an oil stock at 7³/₄ and placed an order to sell it at 9¹/₂. In three days I netted $150. I then bought another stock at 9³/₄ and sold at 11. I now have another, bought at 6³/₄, with an order to sell at 8¹/₄. I realize this approach would have to be modified as the overall market picture changes. Comments, please.*

A. I can't fault anyone who wants to speculate, although I hope you meant to write "$1,000 of our savings" and not "our $1,000 savings." Leaving the bank book empty is hardly a wise move.

You're young enough to take the risks involved. Presumably the loss of the $1,000 won't cripple you financially for life. You are trying a "scientific" approach. Charting, backed up by some knowledge of the fundamentals, is a reasonable approach.

You also realize that part of your success derives from the popular enthusiasm for low-priced issues, which, a study of stock market history will show you, can disappear almost as fast as it arises.

Evidently you don't have much faith in these issues yourself since you immediately place a sell order that gives you a net profit of $100 or $150. Here again, it's O.K. with me (and certainly must please your broker). But if you actually sold that 6³/₄ stock at 8¹/₄ you missed out on a further rise of nearly five points.

You say, "I'm not greedy,"—which is a valuable attribute in a market where "bulls make money and bears make money, but pigs never do." I must point out to you that if you had had to sell that second stock—bought at 9³/₄—for its current price of 9¹/₂, you would have incurred a total loss of about $60 on a decline of only ¹/₄ point whereas your net profit on a 1¹/₄-point rise was only about $90.

So it will not do to think you can come out with a whole skin by keeping both gains and losses small. If whatever portents you follow remain favorable, try to let your profits run. Setting a selling price 1¹/₂ points higher on the day you buy would, logically, have to be matched with a stop loss selling order only ¹/₄ to ³/₈ points below your buying price, and that is by no means feasible.

Good luck. Have fun. And be wise enough to admit it if this sort of trading should become costly.

WHAT IT COSTS TO BUY AND SELL STOCKS

Brokerage commissions established by the N.Y. Stock Exchange generally set the scale for the entire securities industry. In March 1972 the Stock Exchange revised buying and selling fees for the first time since 1958. Following is the new schedule, as it applies to the buying and selling of "round lots" (100-share blocks) of stock and "odd lots" (less than 100-share amounts).

The schedule eliminates the surcharge which had been in effect since April 1970:

ROUND LOTS

Shares Per Order	*Price of Stock* *$5*	*$10*	*$20*	*$30*	*$40*	*$50*	*$75*	*$100*	*$200*	*$400*
100	$16.40	$25.00	$ 38.00	$ 49.00	$ 58.00	$ 65.00	$ 65.00	$ 65.00	$ 65.00	$65.00
200	32.80	50.00	70.00	88.00	106.00	124.00	130.00	130.00	130.00	130.00
300	49.20	67.00	94.00	121.00	148.00	175.00	195.00	195.00	195.00	195.00
400	62.00	82.00	118.00	154.00	190.00	226.00	260.00	260.00	260.00	260.00
500	74.50	97.00	142.00	187.00	232.00	262.00	322.00	325.00	325.00	325.00
600	85.00	112.00	166.00	220.00	262.00	298.00	358.00	390.00	390.00	390.00
700	95.50	127.00	190.00	250.00	292.00	324.00	394.00	455.00	455.00	455.00
800	106.00	142.00	214.00	274.00	318.00	350.00	430.00	510.00	520.00	520.00
900	116.50	157.00	238.00	298.00	340.00	376.00	466.00	556.00	585.00	585.00
1,000	127.00	172.00	262.00	322.00	362.00	402.00	502.00	602.00	650.00	650.00
2,000	212.00	302.00	402.00	482.00	562.00	642.00	842.00	1,042.00	1,300.00	*
2,500	254.50	352.00	462.00	562.00	662.00	762.00	1,012.00	1,262.00	1,625.00	*
5,000	452.00	562.00	762.00	962.00	1,162.00	1,372.00	1,862.00	2,362.00	*	*
10,000	762.00	962.00	1,362.00	1,762.00	2,162.00	2,562.00	*	*	*	*

ODD LOTS

Shares Per Order	*Price of Stock* *$5*	*$10*	*$20*	*$30*	*$40*	*$50*	*$75*	*$100*	*$200*	*$400*
10	*	$ 6.40	$ 8.40	$10.40	$12.40	$14.40	$19.75	$23.00	$36.00	$56.00
20	$ 6.40	8.40	12.40	16.40	20.40	23.00	29.50	36.00	56.00	65.00
30	7.40	10.40	16.40	21.70	25.60	29.50	39.25	47.00	65.00	65.00
40	8.40	12.40	20.40	25.60	30.80	36.00	47.00	56.00	65.00	65.00
50	9.40	14.40	23.00	29.50	36.00	42.50	53.75	65.00	65.00	65.00
60	10.40	16.40	25.60	33.40	41.20	47.00	60.50	65.00	65.00	65.00
70	11.40	18.40	28.20	37.30	45.20	51.50	65.00	65.00	65.00	65.00
80	12.40	20.40	30.80	41.20	48.80	56.00	65.00	65.00	65.00	65.00
90	13.40	21.70	33.40	44.30	52.40	60.50	65.00	65.00	65.00	65.00
99	14.30	22.87	35.74	46.73	55.64	64.55	65.00	65.00	65.00	65.00

*Not computed; negotiated rates.

6 Yes—But What Stocks?

There are about 1,350 companies with nearly 1,850 securities issues listed on the New York Stock Exchange, a smaller number on the American Stock Exchange, still smaller amounts on the dozen and a half regional exchanges scattered around the United States. And finally, there are over 50,000 companies with publicly held securities which are traded on no exchange, but are bought and sold over the counter, meaning directly between brokers who may be acting as agents for others or as principals.

Deciding where to put your money is not easy. How does one select the stock or stocks on which to pin his hopes for the future?

The Number 1 consideration, perhaps, is corporate management. It is a paradox that with all the balance sheets and slide rule computations which are the invariable ingredients of financial analysis, the one factor which more than anything else will determine how X shares will serve you twenty years hence cannot be measured in tons of output, dollars of sales, or debt/equity ratios.

A company's capitalization, its ratios of current assets to current liabilities, its net per dollar of sales can all be figured out to two or more decimal places from the earnings statement and balance sheet. But these are not enough. A few lucky years may provide earnings and cash position which will cover up a multitude of previous fiscal sins and offer no worthwhile indication of what may be expected in the future.

The answer to what any particular company may be reasonably expected to do in the future must be found in the quality of its management.

GOOD MANAGEMENT LOOKS AHEAD

No company, it is true, lives in a vacuum. All are influenced by the times. But that does not mean all suffer as much in depression, or make as much progress when times are good. Good management is that factor in a business which constantly carries on a two-front campaign–which not only manages successfully today, but prepares for the future. Its fiscal health, production efficiency and sales vigor *now* are matched almost equally by its research and development of products as well as manpower for the future. A well-managed company lives simultaneously in two time zones–today and tomorrow. It will never be caught still making only thingamabobs when the public already has switched 100 per cent to widgets.

Technically, management analysis is a fine art and far beyond the ken of the average man who can devote only a fraction of his time to investments. But there can be a layman's approach which, while it may not uncover some little known company destined to become the General Motors of Interplanetary Travel of 2100, will certainly go a long way toward preventing your investment from melting away to zero by 1980. And that approach is to measure a corporation's management by its standing *in the everyday marketplace.*

Does its product have acceptance?
Has its management shown an ability to meet, or even anticipate, public demand?
Does its label stand for reassuring quality in the same way that the stamp of "sterling" does?

In other words, how do the company and its products rate with you and with people in general?

If the rating is high, and has remained high over the years, you can trust your own judgment as to its quality as an investment. For, after all, what makes a company successful if it isn't the ready acceptance you, and millions like you, have given it?

You might ask: "What are the stocks most popular with the professionals who invest millions of dollars for investment companies?"

If most of the names on the list that follows sound familiar to you it is only because their managements have been successful in attracting your patronage over the years, in operating the properties efficiently, in planning for the future.

Here is a list of investment-grade companies which have paid dividends without interruption for many years. It is by no means all-inclusive. Every issue listed is not suited to every investor. Nor does the fact that an issue is omitted imply any criticism of its investment standing. This is merely a sampling of the type of securities you should consider if safety is important to you. Only a reputable broker can help you decide.

Income varies, but in some cases current yields of 5 per cent and more are obtainable:

Industrials: Allied Chemical, Allied Stores, American

Brands, American Can, American Cyanamid, American Standard, Ancorp National Services, Anaconda, Armco, Bethlehem Steel, Borden, Borg-Warner, Briggs & Stratton, Campbell Soup, Cannon Mills, Chesebrough-Pond's, CIT Financial, Coca-Cola, Continental Can, Continental Oil, CPC International, Dow Chemical, E. I. duPont, Eastman Kodak, Ford.

General Electric, General Foods, General Mills, General Motors, Gimbel Brothers, W. R. Grace, W. T. Grant, Goodyear Tire, Great Atlantic & Pacific, Gulf Oil, H. J. Heinz, Hercules, Ingersoll-Rand, Inland Steel, International Harvester, Kennecott, Kimberly-Clark, Kraftco, Libby-Owens-Ford, Liggett & Myers, R. H. Macy, National Biscuit, National Distillers, National Gypsum, Phelps Dodge, Pfizer, Inc., Philip Morris, Phillips Petroleum, PPG Industries, Procter & Gamble, Quaker Oats.

RCA Corp., Reynolds Industries, Safeway Stores, Scott Paper, Sears, Roebuck, Sherwin-Williams, Mobil Oil, Standard Oil of California, Standard Oil of N.J., Sterling Drug, Stone & Webster, Texaco, Union Carbide, U.S. Tobacco, F. W. Woolworth, Wm. Wrigley.

Railroads: Burlington Northern, Chesapeake & Ohio, Kansas City Southern, Louisville & Nashville, Norfolk & Western, Pullman, Santa Fe Industries, Southern Pacific, Southern Ry., Union Pacific.

Utilities: Allegheny Power, American Electric Power, American Natural Gas, American Telephone & Telegraph, Baltimore Gas & Electric, Boston Edison, Brooklyn Union Gas, Cincinnati Gas & Electric, Columbia Gas, Cleveland Electric Illuminating, Commonwealth Edison, Consolidated Edison, Consolidated Natural Gas, Dayton P. & L., Detroit Edison, Duquesne Light, El Paso Natural Gas, Equitable Gas, General Public Utilities, National Fuel Gas, New England Telephone and Telegraph, New York State Electric & Gas, Niagara Mohawk, Pacific Gas & Electric, Pacific Lighting, Peoples Gas, Philadelphia Electric, Potomac Electric, Providence Gas, Public Service Electric & Gas, Puget Sound Power & Light, Southern Natural Gas, Tenneco, Toledo Edison, Union Electric, United Gas Corp., United Gas Improvement, Washington Gas Light, Washington Water Power, Wisconsin Electric Power.

Moody's Stock Survey, a weekly advisory letter published since 1909 by Moody's Investor Service in New York, devotes much of one letter each month to a "stock selector"–listings of stocks it suggests for various investing purposes. The March 1972 listing showed these groups.

Naturally, these listings are subject to revision, especially when discussing speculative issues. But, as always, it is interesting to note that many of the stocks favored are companies known to almost every housewife and her husband. In other words, wide public acceptance is, as always, one of the most important criteria in selecting a company's shares for investment.

Again, if only to emphasize the concentration in quality stocks, here are the 10 largest stock holdings in four large university endowment funds as of June 30, 1971 compared with the amount invested in the same stocks a year earlier. All figures are in the millions of dollars:

HARVARD

	1971	*1970*
1. Int'l. Business Machines	$60.6	$46.9
2. Texaco, Inc.	29.7	20.0
3. Gulf Oil Corp.	21.5	15.4
4. General Motors Corp.	21.0	18.0
5. General Reinsurance	19.9	10.5
6. Standard Oil (N.J.)	19.9	13.5
7. Eastman Kodak	19.0	15.3
8. Ford Motor Co.	18.3	12.9
9. Polaroid Corp.	16.6	7.5
10. Middle South Utilities	14.2	11.4

YALE

1. Cities Service	$26.9	$20.8
2. Polaroid Corp.	20.8	–
3. Matsushita ADRs	19.2	–
4. Sperry & Hutchinson	19.1	3.2
5. Atlantic Richfield	14.2	8.2
6. Grace (W.R.) & Co.	12.6	6.1
7. Bank America Corp.	11.9	–
8. FNMA	10.9	–
9. Fujitsu Ltd. ADRs	10.3	–
10. Simmons Co.	9.6	6.9

PRINCETON

1. Int'l. Business Machines	$22.0	$17.3
2. Xerox Corp.	20.9	16.1
3. Louisiana Land	14.3	7.6
4. Coastal States Gas	13.4	10.3
5. Amer. Home Products	12.8	9.5
6. Texaco, Inc.	12.7	9.0
7. Texas Oil & Gas	11.5	4.9
8. Standard Oil (N.J.)	9.3	6.5
9. Bristol-Myers	9.0	7.5
10. Gulf Oil Corp.	8.4	6.3

UNIVERSITY OF CALIFORNIA

	1971	*1970*
1. Caterpillar Tractor*	$16.0	$ 7.4
2. Int'l. Business Machines	15.1	11.8
3. Eastman Kodak	6.5	5.3
4. General Electric	5.5	3.0
5. General Motors	4.6	3.5
6. Sears Roebuck	4.4	2.8
7. American Telephone	3.6	3.2
8. Texaco, Inc.	3.5	2.8
9. Standard Oil (N.J.)	3.0	2.4
10. Pacific Gas & Electric	2.8	1.9

*Large bequest a factor in gain

I—GROWTH STOCKS

	Per-Share Earnings Est. 1972	1971	1970	1969	Indicated Dividend	1969-72 Price Range	Recent Price	Current Yield	Ratio of Price to Est. 1972 Earnings
Burroughs	$4.60	$4.03	$3.83	$3.32	$0.60	173 - 78 5/8	171	0.4%	37.2
[1]Cenco Instruments	2.65	E2.40	2.21	1.93	0.30	64 1/2 - 16 1/2	58	0.5	21.9
IBM	10.50	9.38	8.92	8.21	5.20	387 - 216 3/4	383	1.4	36.5
Merck	3.80	3.48	3.11	2.79	2.20	138 1/2 - 73 1/2	137	1.6	36.1
Tampax[oc]	9.00	7.97	6.58	5.34	4.70	392 - 146	380	1.2	42.2
Xerox	3.25	2.71	2.40	2.08	0.80	144 1/2 - 65 1/4	142	0.6	43.7

[1]Fiscal years end April 30 of following years. oc—Traded over the counter. E—Estimated.

II—STOCKS FOR LONGER TERM CAPITAL GAINS

	Est. 1972	1971	1970	1969	Indicated Dividend	1969-72 Price Range	Recent Price	Current Yield	Ratio of Price to Est. 1972 Earnings
American Metal Climax	$2.75	$2.20	$3.40	$2.92	$1.40	40 - 25 1/4	33	4.2%	12.0
Borg-Warner	3.00	2.45	2.28	2.73	1.25	36 1/8 - 18 1/8	32	3.9	10.7
CPC International	2.60	2.30	2.56	2.42	1.70	42 7/8 - 26 3/8	36	4.7	13.8
Champion Spark Plug	3.10	2.79	2.39	2.24	1.20	52 1/2 - 19 3/4	52	2.3	16.8
E. I. du Pont de Nemours	8.50	7.19	6.76	7.35	5.00	175 1/2 - 92 1/2	173	2.9	20.4
Ford Motor	6.75	6.18	4.73	5.00	2.40	74 5/8 - 37 1/8	72	3.3	10.7
General Motors	7.25	6.72	2.08	5.94	3.40	91 1/8 - 59 1/2	82	4.1	11.3
B. F. Goodrich	3.00	[1]2.06	0.85	2.74	1.00	66 - 19 3/4	27	3.7	9.0
[2]Heublein	1.95	E[3]1.65	1.46	1.30	0.85	56 - 28 1/2	53	1.6	27.2
Ingersoll-Rand	4.25	3.81	3.84	3.90	2.00	62 3/8 - 32	61	3.3	14.4
Jefferson-Pilot	[3]3.10	E[3]2.80	[3]2.52	[3]2.27	0.88	49 3/4 - 23 1/2	47	1.9	15.2
Johnson Service	2.55	2.29	2.12	1.87	0.80	39 3/4 - 21 7/8	39	2.1	15.3
Nabisco	3.70	3.31	3.00	2.27	2.20	60 1/8 - 37	58	3.8	15.7
[4]Sears, Roebuck	3.95	E3.45	3.01	2.87	1.55	116 1/4 - 51	112	1.4	28.4
Standard Oil of Indiana	5.25	4.95	4.55	4.54	2.39	70 3/4 - 35	68	3.5	13.0
Sun Oil	3.65	3.42	3.04	3.69	1.00	68 7/8 - 36 3/8	49	2.0	13.4

[1]Before nonrecurring charge of $1.94. [2]Fiscal years end June 30. [3]As adjusted by Moody's. [4]Fiscal years end January 31 of following years. E—Estimated.

III—STOCKS WITH SPECULATIVE APPEAL

	Per-Share Earnings Est. 1972	1971	1970	1969	Indicated Dividend	1969-72 Price Range	Recent Price	Current Yield	Ratio of Price to Est. 1972 Earnings
Budd	$1.50	$0.83	[1]d$1.50	$1.63	Nil	33 7/8 6	17	...	11.3
Carlisle	1.80	1.40	1.37	1.34	$0.60	33 1/2 - 9 1/2	23	2.6%	12.8
Certain-teed Products	3.45	3.04	0.72	1.57	0.80	50 3/4 - 13 1/4	47	1.7	13.6
[4]Drug Fair[A]	1.75	1.34	2.00	1.47	0.40	34 3/8 - 12	25	1.6	14.3
[2]Foremost-McKesson	2.15	E1.95	[3]1.62	2.00	0.80	36 1/4 - 16 1/4	27	3.0	12.6
Itek	1.75	1.22	1.20	2.01	Nil	93 3/4 - 21 5/8	54	...	30.9
Londontown Manufacturing	1.50	E1.20	0.72	0.89	Nil	40 1/2 - 6 1/4	18	...	12.0
PEPI[A]	1.90	1.44	1.94	1.65	Nil	46 1/4 - 21	29	...	15.3
Phelps Dodge	4.25	3.62	5.36	4.43	2.10	56 1/2 - 28	42	5.0	9.9
Sonesta Int'l Hotels	0.25	Ed1.00	d1.17	0.27	Nil	21 - 4 1/8	9	...	36.0

[1]Excluding special items. [2]Fiscal years end March 31 of following years. [3]Before 58c nonrecurring charge. [4]Fiscal years end June 30. A—Traded on the American Stock Exchange. E—Estimated. d—Deficit.

IV—STOCKS FOR LARGE CURRENT INCOME

	[1]Per-Share Earnings Est. 1972	1971	1970	1969	Indicated Dividend	1969-72 Price Range	Recent Price	Current Yield	Ratio of Price to Est. 1972 Earnings
Cleveland Elec. Illuminating	$3.10	$3.06	$3.01	$2.91	$2.28	43 - 28	36	6.3%	11.6
Interstate Power	1.65	1.57	1.53	1.50	[2]1.28	22 7/8 - 16	18	7.1	10.9
New England Electric	2.30	2.05	1.98	1.96	[2]1.56	25 1/4 - 13 7/8	24	6.5	10.4
New England Tel. & Tel.	2.80	2.53	2.65	2.45	2.36	43 - 30	34	6.9	12.1
Northern Illinois Gas	2.85	2.73	2.79	2.57	1.78	38 1/2 - 26 1/8	29	6.1	10.2

[1]On year-end shares. [2]Some part of the dividend is nontaxable as ordinary income. E—Estimated.

GIANT BANKS' INVESTMENTS

Early in 1971, the Chase Manhattan Corp., one of the world's largest banks, published its portfolio for the first time. The 20 largest investment positions were in:

International Business Machines, Standard Oil (New Jersey), General Electric, General Motors, International Telephone and Telegraph, Mobil Oil, Xerox, Eastman Kodak, American Telephone and Telegraph, Polaroid, Aetna Life and Casualty, Atlantic Richfield, E. I. du Pont, Standard Oil of California, Warner - Lambert, Sears, Union Carbide, Honeywell, Connecticut General Life and American Airlines.

Not suprisingly, for all its financial acumen and research facilities, the bank's major investments prove to be in the securities of corporations known to every average American.

The giant First National City Bank also—as would be assumed—leans heavily on quality stocks. Its investment management division listed, as of December 31, 1971, these stocks among its largest holdings: Nearly a billion dollars worth of IBM, 4,668,000 shares of Xerox with a value of upward of $700 million, 3,197,000 shares of Kodak, 2,858,000 shares of Avon Products, 2,208,000 shares of Coca-Cola. These few blue chips alone represent about 25 per cent of the value of the bank's total common share holdings.

They are all "good" investments, in the general sense of the term.

But if we are to get particular, some of them are better investments for Lefferts than they would be for young Morse. And some would fare better for Quinn than for Lefferts.

Kodak, for example, has an uninterrupted dividend record going back to 1902. But the current yield is modest, which represents little comfort to Lefferts, who is trying to get high income from his investment.

Standard Oil of N.J. common is a sound security of generous yield, but it might offer less in the way of long-term growth to Morse. Quinn, looking for high safety, might well consider a substantial investment in A.T.&T.

The beauty of investing in securities is that there are enough gradations in safety, yield and growth to satisfy almost any particular need.

Investment is not far different from food intake. Every school youngster learns that fats, proteins, carbohydrates are all essential parts of the diet, but every adult soon discovers that his particular needs require him to *concentrate* on some and take only little of the others. Investment portfolios should be made up the same way. If there were one perfect investment stock, it would soon be priced way out of reach and we should all be as unhappy as though there were only one item of food, one design of house and one make of car.

N. Y. STOCK EXCHANGE "BOX SCORE"

Top Percentage Gains	*Closing Market Price #*		
	1971	*1970*	*% Increase*
Winnebago Industries	$ 48½	$ 8⅝	462.3%
Bausch & Lomb	177	47¾	270.7
Maremont	32	10	220.0
Trans World Airlines	41	13¾	198.2
Gable Industries	24	9	166.7
Rite Aid	83½	33	153.0
Hoffman Electronics	17⅛	6⅞	149.1
Overnite Transportation	33⅛	13½	145.4
McDonald's	75¾	30⅞	145.3
Leaseway Transportation	64½	26½	143.4
Murray Ohio Manufacturing	37¼	15½	140.3
U. S. Leasing International	36½	15⅜	137.4
Belding Heminway	19¾	8⅝	129.0
Admiral	17⅞	8⅛	120.0
Tropicana Products	62	29	113.8
Gateway Industries	14⅝	6⅞	112.7
Royal Crown Cola	35¼	16⅝	112.0
Bath Industries	49	23⅛	111.9
Berkey Photo	16⅜	7¾	111.3
Milton Bradley	44⅞	21¼	111.2

Top Percentage Losses			*% Decrease*
Boise Cascade	$18¾	$ 45⅜	58.7%
Reading	2¾	5⅞	53.2
GAC	11⅛	23	51.6
American Standard	15⅜	30½	49.6
Technicon	20	39⅜	49.2
RTE Corp.	8⅜	16¼	48.5
American Export Industries	5¾	11⅛	48.3
Alberto-Culver	22¼	42	47.0
McIntyre Porcupine Mines	75½	142	46.8
International Industries	5⅝	10½	46.4
Chadbourn	3⅜	6⅛	44.9
Arlan's Dept. Stores	5	9	44.4
Northgate Exploration	5⅛	9⅛	43.8
General Steel Industries	7⅜	12⅞	42.7
International Mining	6⅞	12	42.7
Kaiser Aluminum & Chem.	20⅛	35	42.5
MacAndrews & Forbes	12⅜	21½	42.4
Molybdenum Corp.	14	24⅛	42.0
Memorex	33¼	57	41.7
Republic	5⅛	8¾	41.4

Adjusted for stock dividends, splits, etc., where applicable.

SOME QUESTIONS AND ANSWERS

Q. *I am planning my first venture in buying common shares—to me a mysterious field. What can you tell me about Benguet, Lionel, Atlas Corp. . . .?*

A. I can tell you right off that you are approaching this "mysterious field" strictly from the point of view of low price. In other words, you're running your finger down the right hand side of the "menu" and looking for what you think are "bargain prices." That could be dangerous.

I'm not going to discuss these or any other stocks selected merely because of low price, because I am opposed to evaluating securities solely on the basis of their price bracket ("under $10, $10 to $20, $20 to $30," etc., etc.). Further, many such low-priced issues are speculative in nature and that means careful matching of the risk involved to the amount of risk the particular investor should assume.

I realize that profits have been made on low-priced stocks. In fact, all the activity and excitement so generated most likely attracted you in the first place. But I have no way of telling whether this "sport" will continue and, if it does, for how long. It's quite likely that just about the time new stock buyers become excited about cheap stocks the boat has already sailed. It's happened before—many, many times.

A stock is not a bargain merely because it sells for $5. As in the case of the $50 jalopy or the $2 watch the answer may be: "That's all it is worth." In fact, the $5 stock may be overpriced because so many novices—such as yourself—are so eager to buy it merely because it is low priced.

A successful bargain hunter, it seems to me, must have a professional knowledge of the field in which he is doing his hunting. I'm confident a good auto mechanic can find a better used car than I can, just as an expert corporate analyst may find a new company which is going places, or an old, tired corporation which is turning over a new leaf and will soon start to roll up some profits. In either case, he may buy $5 shares which are headed for higher prices for basic, underlying reasons and *not* merely because they are now at $5.

But you are not an expert, and buying a stock merely because it sells for a few dollars a share and therefore "has more room to rise" can prove as futile as ordering a hamburger on a bun because it is modestly priced and hoping it will somehow turn into a filet mignon by the time it reaches your table.

I repeat, I'm not going to discuss your stocks because I think your approach is all wrong, even though some expert may come along some day and select any or all of them as good vehicles for a stock market "killing."

I would urge you to sit down with a reputable broker and discuss a long-term investment program suited to your individual needs. And remember, it isn't the number of shares you acquire, but the growth potential that counts. An $8 stock may remain at $8 for decades—or even go lower. You can often make more money, over the long term, with 10 shares of an $80 stock than with 100 shares of an $8 issue.

Q. *In spite of my study of financial sections and corporate reports I still do not understand the stock market—and the stock market certainly does not like me.*

The day I buy, the entire market decides to sell and the stocks fall from the moment of my purchase. I'm now retired, need solid income, own substantial amounts of AMF, A.T.&T., Con Edison, Columbia Gas, Libbey-Owens-Ford, General Motors, Reynolds Industries and International Paper. I feel I should hold more stocks (and less cash) because of inflation, but I don't think inflation can hurt as much as some stocks have. What do you think?

A. I think you're nagging yourself unnecessarily.

1. You have an excellent retirement portfolio—all are fair to good quality and most are generous income providers.

2. I don't see why a man with your resources should fret over market declines of 8 points in G.M., 6 in Reynolds Industries and a point or so in L-O-F. Both from the point of view of percentage decline and investment quality such market changes have no significance whatsoever for a long-term investor seeking income. (And how come you don't credit your account with gains in AMF, A.T.&T., and Columbia Gas?)

3. I think you have good inflation protection now and a fair balance between securities and cash—although some people, I admit, would make a case for reduction of the savings accounts.

4. If you want more income—and at the same time want to reduce your commitment in common shares—there is no reason you can't sell some of your lower-yielding stocks and put the proceeds into high-grade bonds.

In other words, my friend, I'd think you'd spend your time enjoying your retirement—"live and laugh" is the motto—and let expert management worry about the future of the automobile, tobacco and glass business.

If you don't do any worse for the next 50 years, you ought to have a happy old age.

Q. *My broker has not been able to give me any new issues, so I've missed out on a lot of fast profits. What can I do about it?*

A. Perhaps he hasn't been giving you any "hot" issues because he hasn't been involved in their underwriting or selling and doesn't want to be. And I wouldn't shoot him for that. The insanity that has gripped the new issues market from time to time forms one of the biggest clouds over the stock market and is one of the prime reasons for concern felt by professional, veteran market observers in Wall Street.

The rush to buy new issues—any new issues—whether they have any intrinsic merit or not is of a piece with the madness that has gripped speculators all through history. In those previous eras of wild speculation, the rush was to tulip bulbs or land or what have you, all based on the conviction that no matter what price you paid today, a bigger fool would pay you a higher price tomorrow. As has always happened, there came a day when we ran out of bigger fools, and the bottom dropped out of the market.

We've had these "hot" new issues markets before—even though you may think you've just discovered a new way to coin money. And following every such era of insanity there was a collapse. As Merrill Lynch, Pierce, Fenner & Smith once pointed out in an advertisement, the SEC found after the 1962 market break that fewer than 40% of the companies which had "gone public" in the previous ten years were still in good health, either as the same corporation or as part of another firm. More than 60% were in trouble—still showing losses, dissolved, inactive, bankrupt, or just plain disappeared.

I grant you that those quick profits are attractive, but that presupposes you are agile enough to get in and get out while the fever is still high. In the long run, more money has been lost than made on these hot new issues.

Q. *Several months ago I bought some shares of uranium stock. The stock began to rise but the SEC stepped in and suspended trading. If it weren't for the commission's interference, a lot of us would have been able to sell at a good profit. What is the purpose of this sort of action?*

A. To protect the people who would have bought the stock from you.

I don't know the company; never heard the name. But the fact the price was going up and up was no proof at all that the company itself or the dealers in the stock were on the up and up.

Q. *Why do companies split their stock? I own some stock that is soon to be split. The company pays good dividends now. Will the split affect that? I need income.*

A. Companies split stock for a variety of reasons. They may be interested in the widest possible ownership of shares and their stock is now selling at a price so high as to discourage wide ownership. Their earnings per share may be high enough to attract governmental attention and a company in a regulated industry may not like that.

A young company may split its stock to attract more attention and make it seem more glamorous.

Generally, a dividend is readjusted downward to the point where the total income you will receive after the split on the increased shares is the same as you received before the split, although slight increases in total payments are not uncommon.

You can't make a decision on whether you should hold or sell a stock merely on the basis of its declaring a split.

Q. *We hold some over-the-counter shares selling around 11 to 11¾. My broker says he could sell it for 10¾, no commission. Is this true or should I be able to sell it for more?*

A. A counter broker may act as your agent—in which case he charges a commission for buying or selling; or he may act as a principal, buying your stock himself, or selling you shares from his own inventory. In the latter case he charges no commission, but makes his profit on the price markup.

There is *no* way for you to determine which is the better method without checking the market price with several brokers—*as of the moment* you want to trade.

The brokerage commission for the purchase or sale of 100 shares of a stock selling as $11 would be about $27. If you find a broker who will get you a bid of, say, 11½, it would obviously be better to sell through him, and pay the commission, than to take 10¾ net from the broker who wants to act as principal.

I want to emphasize, however, that whenever you buy or sell securities—exchange-listed or over-the-counter—it is best to get a "fresh" quote—that is, a quotation "hot off the griddle." For that you must talk to a broker.

A "SELECTED" STOCK LIST

Selecting common stocks for investment raises as many differences of opinion as picking the winner at the race track. But that doesn't mean you can't find common sense suggestions.

Late in March 1972 *Financial World* magazine—one of the leading publications in the field of finance—listed these issues "as a guide to intelligent investment decisions," as of that date. (The magazine makes additions or deletions as it feels circumstances warrant.)

CONSERVATIVE BLUE CHIPS

High quality issues such as these should form the backbone of the equity portion of a conservative portfolio.

	**Earnings*	*†Dividends*	*Recent Price*	*Yield*	*‡P/E Ratio*
American Cyanamid	$1.95	$1.25	40	3.1%	20.5
American Electric Power	2.43	1.75	30	5.8	12.3
American Home Products	2.86	1.77	98	1.8	33.9
American Telephone & Telegraph	4.02	2.60	44	5.9	10.9
Coca-Cola Co.	2.82	1.58	129	1.2	45.7
Eastman Kodak	2.52	1.32	111	1.2	44.4
General Electric	2.60	1.40	64	2.2	24.6
Kimberly-Clark	1.34	1.20	26	4.6	19.4
Kraftco Corp.	3.25	1.77	45	3.9	13.8
Procter & Gamble	3.12	1.50	87	1.7	27.8
Safeway Stores	3.14	1.35	39	3.5	12.4
Sears, Roebuck	3.31	1.55	112	1.4	33.8
Standard Oil (N.J.)	6.76	3.90	76	5.1	11.2

SOUND STOCKS FOR DIVERSIFIED PORTFOLIOS

These good quality equities offer appreciation potential plus moderate yields and prospect of increased dividends.

	**Earnings*	*†Dividends*	*Recent Price*	*Yield*	*‡P/E Ratio*
Allegheny Power System	$2.15	$1.40	22	6.4%	10.2
American Brands	4.30	2.29	44	5.2	10.2
American Can	2.66	2.20	35	6.3	13.1
C.I.T. Financial	3.70	2.00	46	4.3	12.4
Columbia Gas System	2.90	1.82	34	5.4	11.7
First National City Corp.	3.08	1.32	49	2.7	15.9
General Motors	6.72	3.40	80	4.3	11.9
Grace (W.R.)	1.92	1.50	28	5.4	14.6
Liggett & Myers	4.42	2.50	63	4.0	14.2
National Distillers & Chemical	1.10	0.90	17	5.3	15.4
Phillips Petroleum	1.66	1.30	30	4.3	18.1
Public Service Electric & Gas	3.00	1.64	25	6.6	8.3
Southern Pacific	3.81	2.00	48	4.2	12.6

Earnings were for the latest 12-month period to February 1972. Dividends are as indicated as of that day of publication.

Last night's closing price of an exchange-listed stock is proof only of where the trade took place yesterday. Similarly, a counter quotation of 11 bid, 11¾ asked signifies only that whenever that quote was turned in yesterday those were the highest bid and the lowest offering prices. Anything could have happened in the interim to change the prices markedly.

Q. *Why does the government allow trading in a bankrupt company's stock?*

A. Because it's a free market. If you think the company will be reorganized in a fashion that will ultimately give some value to the stock it's your privilege to take that chance.

Q. *In January, 1961, I bought 50 shares of a stock. There was a 2-for-1 split in March 1966, a 3-for-1 and later a 4-for-3 in 1970, a 2-for-1 early in 1971 and another 2-for-1 in July, 1971. How many shares should I have?*

A. The March 1966 2-for-1 split gave you a total of 100 shares. The 3-for-1 made this 300 shares. The 4-for-3 lifted the total to 400 shares. The early 1971 2-for-1 boosted the total to 800, and the July 1971 2-for-1 made the total 1,600.

Q. *I bought a speculative oil stock at 46 just before it tumbled. I bought 500 more at 12½, in order to get even. My average cost is now about 19. Did I do the right thing?*

A. Evidently not. The stock is now around 13.

Your question is the perfect example of a type I've never tried to answer, because my guesses on speculative stocks are valueless.

7 Growth Stocks for Capital Gain

Theoretically, a growth stock is the equity of a company which is expanding its business at more than the average 3 per cent annual rate of gain for all U.S. industry.

Actually, the term "growth stock" has been bandied around in recent years in an extremely offhand fashion. It has been applied—almost automatically—to companies which are at work in the exciting new fields of petrochemicals, air conditioning, atomic energy, light metals, automation, electronics, synthetic fibers, aviation. And this seems proper.

But it also has been applied by the more daring—and perhaps the more thorough—securities analysts to the glass, paper, shoe, and even the coal industry, none of which is exactly new and the last of which had for years been considered to be on the downgrade.

DOESN'T HAVE TO BE YOUNG TO GROW

The answer to this paradox, it would seem, is that the term "growth" is really just another label for wide-awake, aggressive and forward-looking management which can be expected to make the most of new opportunities whether they present themselves in titanium or in coal—in some of the newest or some of the oldest known materials.

What qualities should a growth company have?

It should have:

- Strong and increasing consumer demand for its product or services;
- Financial strength which can finance expansion and carry it over periods of business slumps;
- Aggressive management—not only currently, but "in depth" so as to assure good leadership in the years ahead;
- A strong research program, supported by management's willingness to plow back earnings.

The term "growth" should not be applied indiscriminately to any new company or denied any old corporation merely because it has been operating for a hundred and fifty years. The new firm, even though it has announced its plans of building a platform in outer space, may turn out to be only a flash in the pan, whereas the old, established Eastman Kodak is a safe bet to continue coming up with profitable ideas for many years to come. A corporation's chronological age has nothing to do with its growth potential.

A "SELECTED" GROWTH LIST

Financial World magazine late in February 1972 listed these stocks in its growth categories. The first "established" stocks offer less risk than the stocks suggested for "aggressive investors" who can assume higher risk. (The magazine makes additions to and deletions from its lists as it feels circumstances warrant.)

ESTABLISHED GROWTH STOCKS

Appeal of these issues is based on prospect for above-average long term growth, with income unimportant.

	**Earnings*	*†Dividends*	*Recent Price*	*Yield*	*‡P/E Ratio*
Baxter Laboratories	$0.68	$0.11	37	0.3%	54.4
Chesebrough-Pond's	1.89	1.04	63	1.7	33.3
International Business Machines	9.38	5.40	370	1.5	39.4
International Tel. & Tel.	3.32	1.19	62	1.9	18.7
Johnson & Johnson	1.78	0.47	105	0.4	59.0
Kresge (S.S.)	2.28	0.50	99	0.5	43.4
PepsiCo, Inc.	2.65	1.00	72	1.4	27.2
Philip Morris	4.02	1.24	73	1.7	18.1
Squibb Corp.	2.78	1.50	88	1.7	31.6
Standard Brands	2.96	1.60	46	3.5	15.5

STOCKS FOR AGGRESSIVE INVESTORS

These issues appear to offer outstanding capital gains potential but may carry commensurately higher risks.

	**Earnings*	*†Dividends*	*Recent Price*	*Yield*	*‡P/E Ratio*
American Metal Climax	$2.20	$1.40	29	4.8%	13.2
Burroughs	4.03	0.60	165	0.4	40.9
Coastal States Gas	2.01	.....	53	....	26.3
Combustion Engineering	3.36	1.40	62	2.3	18.4
Dart Industries	1.96	s0.30	52	0.6	26.5
Flintkote Co.	1.94	1.00	29	3.5	14.9
Lowenstein (M.) & Sons	2.65	0.90	32	2.8	12.1
Pittston Co.	2.17	s0.60	47	1.3	21.6

Earnings are for latest 12-month period to February 1972. Dividends are as indicated as of date of publication. "S" indicates "plus stock."

Young Phil Morse, who has his working lifetime ahead of him, is the perfect example of a growth stock buyer—in either a young or an old company. He can afford to pass up safety of principal because he has years in which to rectify any mistakes. There is no point to his stressing income since his annual investment is too small to yield any appreciable return no matter how much safety he is prepared to give up in return for a high dividend rate. And besides, any dividends he receives for the next four decades will be taxed at his top income bracket.

But if he can latch on to even a couple of thousand dollars' worth of stock in the company which will become the "General Motors" of the automation business in 1980 he and his heirs will live on Easy Street for generations, even though the company for the next ten years plows most of its earnings back into research and development and pays little or no dividends.

Such a prize is not easily come by.

Go back about 60 or 70 years when—as we now know—the automobile industry deserved the title of "growth industry." Phil Morse's father may have been one of the youngsters who yelled "get a horse," but certainly Phil's grandfather must have realized, deep down, that this noisy, self-propelled contrivance (or some form of it) was here to stay. He and many of his fellow citizens may well have sunk some of their money in the intervening years into one or more of the two thousand-plus companies organized to supply the horseless carriage market.

The rest is history and the lesson obvious. Merely putting your money into an auto company—any auto company—was no guaranty at all that you would wind up a millionaire—although a few thousand dollars invested with the elder Henry Ford would have, today, made academic all Phil Morse's worries about retirement. Or even about working for a living, for that matter.

Today, only four major U.S. automobile makers remain—about one quarter of 1 per cent of the hundreds that started. Any of our grandfathers who plunked their money down indiscriminately on just any auto company because the securities analysts of 1905 labeled it a "growth" company must have long ago learned their lesson.

And just so today, after Phil Morse agrees that atomic power and electronics will play an increasingly important role in the latter half of the twentieth century, he's got to get down to cases and decide *which* company in these dramatic industries is going to carry his few hundred dollars a year into battle for new business.

And even after he has decided, he must then satisfy himself that investors thinking similarly haven't already pushed the price of its stock up to a level which the company will not be able to justify for years to come. There are electronic and space companies today with stocks selling at 30 to 50 times earnings. These companies may be the successes of the future, but it's only a guess at what price they will stabilize and when they will begin paying their investors for the use of their money—and how much. In other words, before young Phil can buy ABC stock, he must decide how much of its price represents future prospects and how much of it is due to current popular enthusiasm.

In the stock market's historic climb to levels well above the boom Twenties peak, these wonderful "growth" stocks enjoyed a field day. Light metal securities rose tenfold and more, atomic power stocks originally sold for a few dollars a share are now twenty times that sum. Ditto for some of the chemicals, aviations, automation machinery manufacturers, as well as electronic data and "space" stocks.

Young Morse is faced with two problems. He will have to reconcile himself to much more study than Quinn, who can choose his safety stocks from their records, or Lefferts, who can select high-income securities on the basis of past performances and the companies' established position in a basic industry. Secondly, Morse will have to have faith that all the giant steps already taken in these new fields are only the beginning.

Here is a *small sample* of the companies he will have to study before he makes an investment:

Abbott Laboratories
Aluminum Co.
Amerada Hess
American Cyanamid
American Electric Power
American Home Products
American Hospital Supply
American Metal Climax
American Tel. & Tel.
AMP, Inc.
Anchor Hocking
Ashland Oil
Atlantic Richfield
Avon Products

Baxter Laboratories
Beckman
Bell & Howell
Black & Decker
Boise Cascade
Borden
Borg-Warner
Bristol-Myers
Burroughs

Cenco Instruments
Champion Spark Plug
Chesebrough-Pond's
Cleveland Electric
Corning Glass
CPC International

Detroit Edison
Duke Power
Du Pont

Eastman Kodak
Emerson Electric

FMC Corp.
Florida Gas

Florida Power
Ford Motor

General Electric
General Foods
General Mills
General Telephone
B. F. Goodrich
Goodyear Tire & Rubber
W. R. Grace
Gulf Oil

Hanna Mining
Heublein
Honeywell
Houston Lighting & Power

Ingersoll-Rand
International Business Mach.
International Flavors
International Paper
International Tel. & Tel.

Johnson & Johnson

Kraftco
Kresge

Lilly (Eli) and Co.
Long Island Lighting

Magnavox
Merck & Co.
Middle South Utilities
Miles Laboratories
Minnesota Mining & Mfg.
Mobil Oil

Nalco Chemical
National Biscuit
National Cash Register
Nevada Power

Owens-Corning

Pacific Gas & Electric
Pfizer
Philip Morris
Phillips Petroeum
Polároid
Procter & Gamble

Quaker Oats

RCA Corp.
Raytheon
Reynolds Industries
Robertshaw Controls

San Diego Gas
Schering–Plough
SCM Corp.
Scott Paper
Sears Roebuck
Shell Oil
Smith, Kline & French
Sonderling
Southern California Ed.
Squibb
Standard Oil of California
Standard Oil of Indiana
Standard Oil of Ohio
Sterling Drug
Sun Oil
Sybron

Tampa Electric
Texaco
Texas Instruments
Texas Utilities
Transamerica
Tucson Gas & Electric

Union Carbide
Union Oil
Union Pacific
U.S. Freight

Virginia Elect. & Pwr.

Warner-Lambert
Western Union
Westinghouse
Westvaco
Whirlpool
Wisconsin Electric Power

Xerox

Zenith Radio

Even the newest of fields has a liberal sprinkling of old, established, successful corporate names. Thus, for example, a company which has been a successful boiler maker for years, keeping step with the many advances in the production of power, might well be successful in competition for atomic energy business. In addition, it has the decided advantages of being well known in its field; of having access to capital, when needed, at more favorable rates than a new company; of having an experienced management which evidently has already displayed its ability to make the most of new opportunities.

In other words, Morse may feel that the better part of valor would be to apportion some of his future investment funds among the General Electrics, and the Union Carbides as well as among the smaller, seemingly more exciting companies just now getting started in the field of atomic energy.

What about air conditioning?

The nation's manufacturers of air conditioning equipment have had their ups and downs in recent years, to a great extent due to fickle weather conditions as well as to merchandising problems. However, there can be little doubt but that the future trend of air conditioning, as an industry, must be upward. Here are some corporations that play roles in the industry:

Borg-Warner, Buffalo Forge, Carrier Corp., Fedders, Tecumseh Products, Trane.

As noted earlier in this chapter, an industry need not be involved exclusively with landing on the moon to be considered a growth industry. Oftentimes, new aggressive management and a new marketing approach can do wonders for an old industry.

There is nothing particularly new about furniture, yet some of the biggest market gains in recent years have turned this fundamental need into a glamour industry: American Furniture, Barwick Industries, Bassett Furniture, Baumritter Corp., Hamilton Cosco, Henredon Furniture, Hickory Furniture, Kroehler Mfg., Lane Co., Levitz Furniture, Rowe Furniture, Wickes Corp.

Paper is another industry as old as history. But tremendous new fields have recently been opened for its use. For Morse, a list to consider would include:

Boise Cascade, Crown Zellerbach, Hammermill, Hudson Pulp & Paper, International Paper, Kimberly-Clark, Mead Corp., St. Regis Paper, Scott Paper, Union Camp, Westvaco, Weyerhaeuser.

Similarly, growing enthusiasm is being shown for the rapidly expanding field of labor-saving materials-handling equipment. Among the well-known firms in this field are Allis-Chalmers, American Hoist & Derrick, Bucyrus-Erie, Clark Equipment, Deere & Co., Eaton Corp., Harnischfeger, International Harvester, Jaeger Machine, Studebaker-Worthington, Tenneco, Whiting Corp.

In the chemicals, among the leaders are Allied Chemical, American Cyanamid, Dow, du Pont, Eastman Kodak, W. R. Grace, Hercules, International Minerals, Monsanto Chemical, Olin Corp., Rohm & Haas, Union Carbide. These make a paradoxical group of investment quality securities. Investor Quinn could buy them for complete safety. Young Morse could buy them for future growth—and both for the same reason: These companies over the years have shown themselves to be leaders in their field.

One of them may have the inside track on a new synthetic thread, another may be the leader in producing a specific plastic. But no matter where the new age of wonder chemistry may lead industry, it's a safe bet that these companies will always be in step with future trends. Their excellent managements, their heavy concentration in research assures that. Yields are low. Alan Lefferts may well feel that he can get a better income from high grade steels and rails and leave the chemicals to those who want gilt-edged safety and future potential. But for the latter, chemicals are a must.

Similarly, good advances have been scored in recent years by the producers of ethical drugs, thanks to a steady rise in population, increase in the older age groups, more health insurance plans and—as ever—basic American research. Yields by these companies are low—mostly 2 and 3 per cent. Specializing as they do, they would not seem to have the solid-rock foundation of the industrial chemicals. But for future growth they are standout choices. The fight against disease is unremitting. As a believer in a better and healthier nation, Morse should consider investments in American Home Products, Smith, Kline & French, G. D. Searle, Schering Corp., Pfizer, Abbott Laboratories, Merck & Co., Warner-Lambert, Richardson-Merrell, Eli Lilly, Upjohn, Miles Laboratories, Sterling Drug, Plough, Inc., Becton, Dickinson & Co., Baxter, Bristol-Myers, Johnson & Johnson.

Presumably there is nothing exciting about running a store. But, evidently, exciting things have been happening in the age-old field of merchandising, as witness strong advances in retailing stocks and the marked decline in yields which forward-looking investors are ready to accept in return for potential growth. Look at Allied Stores, Associated Dry Goods, Federated, Gimbels, S. S. Kresge, Marshall Field, R. H. Macy, Marcor (formerly Mont-

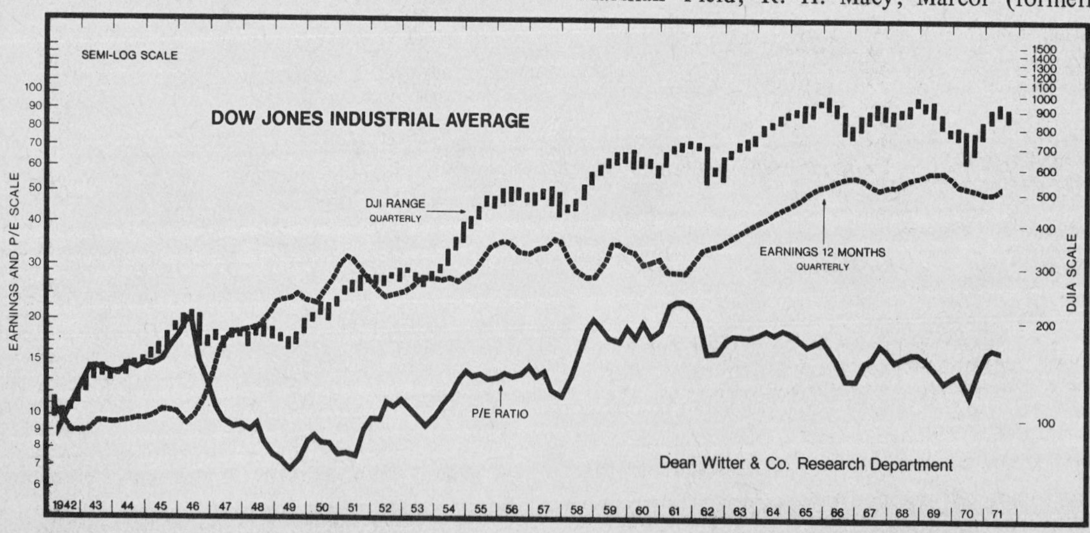

The price/earnings ratio is the relationship between the market price of a share of stock and the earnings per share. A stock selling at $50 when the company is earning $2 a share is said to be selling at a p/e ratio of 25. If the company were earning $2.50 a share, the p/e ratio would be 20 ($50 divided by $2.50). The p/e ratio is a significant statistic in investing, but—as can be seen by the chart—is by no means the sole answer to stock prices. Back in postwar 1946, when optimism was high, stocks in the Dow Jones industrial average sold at 20 times per share earnings. Even though earnings per share and stock prices themselves rose in the ensuing years, investor enthusiasm cooled to the point where these same stocks at one time were being priced at only 7 and 8 times annual per share earnings. Investor enthusiasm, or lack of it, can be a more important market factor than earnings, themselves—as basic as earnings may be in the long-run evaluation of a corporation.

gomery Ward) and Sears as examples of how old names in an old industry can become the favorites of a new generation of investors.

Although utility stocks are generally discussed as widows' and orphans' stocks—because of their safety and stable earning power—recent shifts in both population and industry in this country, as well as in techniques of power production have singled out some utility companies as distinct growth situations.

Keeping ever in mind that the term "growth" should be considered a relative term, here are some electric power companies which have earned the investment community's label of "growth companies":

American Electric Power, Central & South West, Duke Power, Florida Power Corp., Florida Power & Light, Gulf States Utilities, Houston Lighting & Power, Southern Co., Tampa Electric, Texas Utilities, Utah Power & Light, Virginia Electric & Power.

In the last few years, these issues not only have advanced in price but have consistently increased dividend distributions.

Of course, Morse may ask the same question that has perplexed many a young man trying to invest in the future: "Sure, I believe in the future of 'atomic' stocks, in the aviations, in the chemicals. But how can I make a choice between Dow and du Pont, between Pfizer and Merck?"

If he wants to leave that admittedly technical decision to experts, he can always turn his problem over to the specialized funds, i.e., investment companies which concentrate on one particular field. It is a fair assumption that a group composed of both investment bankers and, say, chemical engineers can do a better job of picking the chemical leaders of 1985 than can Morse who is expected to put in eight hours a day on his engineering work. Not that these mutual funds have any magic crystal balls. They pick lemons, too. But thanks to their ability to spread their risk, they represent a measure of safety which a lone investor cannot hope to attain.

As in the case of any service, however, you are expected to pay. But it may be worth it if you don't have the time to study the entire field.

Examples of such specialized funds are legion. Group Securities, Inc., for example, have the following funds: Automobile, aviation, building, chemical, electronics, food, industrial machinery, merchandising, mining, petroleum, railroad equipment, railroad stock, steel, tobacco, utilities. Then there are independent funds specializing in certain fields, such as Chemical Fund, Inc., Axe Science, Technology.

If young Morse should decide to turn his investing in chemicals over to Chemical Fund, Inc., his very first purchase would give him a stake in more than a score of chemical and allied corporations; in nearly ten drug firms; in three glass companies; in several oil companies, plus about a dozen related miscellaneous companies. That's the sort of risk spreading that ordinarily takes a lot of money—in this case about $515 million.

Mutual funds will be discussed at greater length in a later chapter. The point made here is that merely because they are devices for attaining diversification does not mean that they cannot be vehicles for investment in the future, also.

SOME QUESTIONS AND ANSWERS

Q. *I'm 30, married, 3 children, have an income of $12,000. I've been investing in securities since 1962 and have built an investment of $9,000 up to about $17,500. I presently owe a debit balance on substantial amounts of Brunswick, Addressograph, Lukens Steel, Sperry Rand, Sperry warrants and General Steel Industries. I am considering changing my course to investing for long-term growth in companies with less volatile reaction to economic conditions. At about what age should a man switch to a stable portfolio from trading?*

A. I don't know. At what age should a man forget about women? Evidently you've been successful in your trading. Now, for some reason (could it be the recent price drop?) you want to switch to long-term investing.

I don't think there's anything wrong with trading—*provided* you don't lose money at it. I certainly don't think there is anything wrong with long-term investing, either.

A man who is a successful trader could, presumably, trade right up to retirement—when he'd want to put his money to work bringing in stable income—and possibly even longer. I've had letters from successful traders who are retired. As long as they have the resources—financial and mental—for trading, and as long as they have a cushion to fall back on, I can see no objection.

I don't think age has anything to do with your question. If I may be permitted a bit of amateur psychology, I think you're tired of "the whole frantic bit," despite your past successes, and now want to buy a portfolio of long-term growth stocks and sit back and relax. If that's so, go to it, whether you're 30 or 40, or 70. You've worked for that money. It should not be a cause of worry to you.

Q. *I am 36, not married, holding odd lots of 3 stock issues, $8,000 in corporate bonds, $9,000 in Treasury bonds, $6,000 in H bonds, $20,000 in savings. Any suggestions?*

A. It would seem to me that a man of 36 ought to look more to future capital gains—even with the implied risk—and less to security for a fixed number of dollars. If you've accumulated all this money at your age you must be able to earn money. And if you are a successful wage earner, all that these high-yield bonds and savings accounts are doing is adding to your income tax burden.

E bonds would make sense for you as an emergency fund without any current tax liability on the 5.5 per cent annual gain. But why H bonds, which bring you 2 taxable checks a year?

Q. *I bought 300 shares of utility stock at 36. The price is now around 56. But the yield is only 3½ per cent. Should I sell and put the money in 5 per cent savings? There seems to be so much talk about a drop in the market. Or should I switch to another utility? This would leave me subject to a capital-gains tax. Does one figure yield on a stock's cost or on present price?*

A. You leave me in the dark by withholding the name of the utility. However, in general, utilities today are depressed, so I doubt that as a group they would be as vulnerable in any serious market drop as would be, for example, the electronics and other recent high fliers.

If you need maximum income from your money, your course is clear–5 is more than 3½.

I see no point to switching to another utility, unless you switch to a preferred or bond for higher income.

You figure your yield on the stock's present market price.

Q. *We plan to retire in 6 years; will not need more income until then. We already have $25,000 in E bonds and $10,000 in bank-deposit certificates. We can put aside $15 to $20 more monthly. Is it too late for us to buy growth stocks?*

A. There's no way to determine the rate of growth in "growth" stocks. You might select some stocks which will show you excellent growth in the next 18 months; others may be much slower.

But since you already have $35,000 working on the side of dollars, I can't see why you should hesitate to put some money into equities, even if only at the rate of $300 to $350 a year.

Q. *What do you think of this financial set-up for a man of 51, married, with ample insurance: $15,000 in savings, $8,000 in E bonds, 100 each of A.T.&T., Pacific Gas & Electric, Southern California Edison; 50 Florida Power, General Telephone & Electronics and 10 Ford? Bear in mind that I am a conservative sort of person.*

A. I'd say you've well followed Shakespeare's advice: "To thine own self be true." Some might point out that you're a bit heavy in dollars and utility shares. But these are minor matters. If you're comfortable, don't change.

Q. *We have held some issues for 6 years with little price appreciation. We've been thinking of selling and switching to stocks that are heavily traded, with growth potential.*

A. If you are in your capital-accumulating years, you should, of course, aim for growth. But whatever you do, don't be lured into a stock merely because it is heavily traded. That heavy trading could represent liquidation by well-informed persons just as much as it could indicate informed buying. Some extremely heavy trading in recent months has been in low-priced stocks of little merit.

Q. *Stock-market analysts continually label certain stocks as "glamour" stocks until it almost sounds like a dirty word. I hold Zenith, RCA and Raytheon. I consider Zenith and RCA as much blue chips as A.T.&T. and General Motors, and I think Raytheon is a growth stock. Should I be influenced by the sneers of "glamour" stock?*

A. A "glamour" stock, it seems to me, is any stock which is currently in the public eye. Now, it could be in the public eye because it is making giant strides or merely because it is turning out hula hoops just when everybody is crazy about hula hoops. There's a difference. (Bowling and boating stocks, for example, were bid up to outrageous prices a few years ago because so many people decided we were all going to spend half our days in bowling alleys and the other half aboard yachts.)

Electronic stocks of sound companies are certainly growth stocks and–whenever public attention is attracted to some exciting computer or outer space development–might also be called "glamour" stocks, with no sneer intended.

I wouldn't allow any appellation to discourage me from ownership of an aggressive, sound electronics company's shares. I must emphasize, however, that you should be selective. Literally thousands of young companies that started in garages, using "electronic" in their name, have gone bankrupt in the last decade. But that doesn't diminish one whit the importance of the electronics industry.

A thought-provoking publication from Kaiser Aluminum & Chemical explores changes in the world we live in.

HOW SOME INVESTMENTS GROW

Results of an assumed investment of $10,000 made August 1, 1944 in each of the 30 stocks now in the Dow-Jones Industrial Average:

Company	*Market Value of Investment December 31, 1971*
Kodak	$380,546
Sears Roebuck	264,152
International Paper	206,990
Goodyear	196,670
Procter & Gamble	168,590
Texaco	130,189
G.E.	100,535
Standard Oil (Cal.)	95,258
Standard Oil (N.J.)	85,777
G.M.	79,343
Westinghouse	71,961
General Foods	67,729
DuPont	65,778
Bethlehem Steel	55,791
International Nickel	54,219
Johns-Manville	50,937
Alcoa	50,216
United Aircraft	38,585
Woolworth	33,306
Union Carbide	32,089
U.S. Steel	31,159
Owens-Illinois	30,871
Swift & Co.	24,202
International Harvester	23,508
American Brands	23,103
Allied Chemical	18,007
Chrysler	17,011
American Tel. & Tel.	16,472
American Can	14,511
Anaconda Co.	12,039

A quote from this publication that should bolster your preference for sound electronic stocks:

> We will begin to live more and more in the shock wave that is created when an electron drops to an orbit closer to the nucleus. We will begin more and more to ride the waves of the oscilloscope; to swim in the blue-green phosphorus of our television screens. . . . We will exchange the wheel for the dance of the photons, as once we traded the horse for the wheel, and it will be another world, altogether, when we do that. . . . Swarms of electrons are nibbling away the mechanical world we all grew up in.

Q. *What would be the best $2,000 investment for a brand-new grandson, with the idea of providing for his college tuition?*

A. I'd vote for a growth stock, or a growth-type mutual fund.

Q. *I shall soon have about $50,000 to invest. Assuming I won't need income from this investment for the next 5 years, what should I buy for growth of capital? I would want stocks that do not demand constant supervision. In 5 years, when I am 57, I will want to think of income, although I could continue to hold growth stocks for another year or so if necessary. I am tired of buying, selling, switching, winning some, losing others, and piling up commissions. I want something I can hold on to for a while, with some hope of future gain. I have thought about Standard Oil of California, RCA, American Hospital Supply, International T. & T.–but these are just thoughts, not supported by research.*

A. 1. If you're tired of buying, selling, winning, losing –quit. That's easy. It's a free country.

2. The amount of supervision one should give his portfolio has never been settled to my satisfaction. Successful investment-company advisers, of course, watch their holdings very closely and continuously. And if they can't get enough information out of the various reports, proxy statements, annual meetings, they go out to the plant, look around and ask questions. That's their business. Whether you or any other layman can or should devote that much time and energy, and still make a living at your job is another matter.

I think an investor ought to learn as much about his company as he can. But frankly, I am not sure that such a policy will be more rewarding, in the long run, than the far simpler one of buying the stock of a long-time leader in any important field of industry and staying with it for as long as you are interested in building capital.

This is *not* the professional approach. Multi-million-dollar mutual-fund managers reveal quarterly that they have sold 10,000 shares of X and bought 10,000 of Y –both X and Y being popular, successful corporations of good reputation. I'm sure they have good reasons (although if there are any funds that can claim they never missed out on a good market rise, I don't know them). Mutual-fund managers do not ask my advice, so I don't know why they buy or sell.

But thousands of laymen investors have shown me their portfolios, and for every one who can boast of having gotten out of one good company and into another just before the first retreated and just before the second began to climb, I can show you 25 who have stored up mouth-watering profits by having bought–10, 20, or 25 years ago–Kodak, IBM, RCA, Standard Oil of California, General Motors, American Electric Power, International Telephone, Sears, Roebuck, etc., and never sold a share. These are only a few of the typical growth stocks.

Of course you will be told–and rightly–that there have been times when you should have sold Kodak, or IBM or I.T.&T. and bought them back later at lower prices. But that's 20/20 hindsight. No bells are rung when it's time for a sale or time for a repurchase.

So give your stocks as much or as little "constant supervision" as you like–but meanwhile buy and hold the leaders.

Q. *About a year ago I endorsed a stock certificate over to a broker for sale. The stock never reached my price, and when I asked for the return of the certificate, I received a new one. Also, for a time, the dividends went to the broker. Is this customary?*

A. Yes. When you endorsed the certificate for sale you turned it over to the broker. When you asked for its return, he had to get a new one, unendorsed, issued to you. For the period the stock was in the broker's name, he received the dividends and credited them to your account.

Q. *I would like your comments on timing purchases of growth stocks. Should one buy any time he has the cash, or should he accumulate funds and make purchases when the price recedes? Although the major trend of good growth securities is generally upward, there are usually periods during the year when the price recedes 10 or 15%.*

A. A basic law of the securities market is that prices fluctuate. That's one point for you.

If you look over the price charts of some cyclical companies–steels and coppers and oils–for example, you will note a cyclical picture, even though I doubt you will find any 10 to 15% annual fluctuations. And I am quite sure you will find it difficult to spot any such pattern in growth stocks.

There are problems, however, in applying your scheme. Even in a cyclical stock and industry, fluctuating price patterns are far easier to spot in retrospect–when they're already part of history–than they are to project into the future. History doesn't always repeat, and there are few trustworthy ouija boards in Wall Street.

So, when you say "when the price recedes" you should be more specific. Would you buy when a stock has fallen to 45 from 50? (What if there is something fundamentally wrong with it and the stock is headed for 25?)

Would you pass up buying a growth stock which doesn't recede at all even though the general market averages have come down 5 or 10? (Many an expert technician will argue that is the time to buy, especially BECAUSE the stock has not receded in an otherwise weak market.)

If you are a serious investor you should by all means consider charts, too. Many professionals do and some won't move into a stock unless they consider the chart pattern favorable.

But don't look for any sure thing patterns, because—by definition—a "sure thing" as readily available as a chart picture can't come true. Too many pros would be playing all the angles against it.

Unless you have something more concrete to go on, I'd buy growth stocks periodically as you develop the investable cash. Trust to dollar averaging to give you a "fair" price.

Q. *I don't understand why a giant such as General Electric can't pay out better dividends. At current prices, it yields less than 3%.*

A. GE is the largest and most diversified producer of electrical equipment—and (what's important) has been for years. That indicates GE doesn't work only at turning out today's radios and refrigerators, but at developing products for next year, and ten years from now. That requires research. And research is costly.

Over the last half century, GE has paid out on average just under 70% of net earnings in cash dividends. If it cut back research, it could, of course, pay out more. But what, then, would happen to the development of new products which over the years have kept GE the largest in the field?

A business, to be successful, must constantly modernize and meet competition with better and newer products. In recent years, GE research has developed new avenues of business with silicone chemicals, man-made industrial diamonds, new lubricants, new types of rechargeable batteries, etc., etc.

Finally, you don't buy GE for current income, but for growth. In 1950 the shares (adjusted for stock split) sold under $10 a share. In 1962 they sold around $30. Recently, above $60. It would seem to me the proof of the pudding. . . .

8 Life Insurance Stocks for the Long Pull

One of the few industries in the United States with a built-in growth potential is life insurance.

Over the years, shares of the stock life insurance companies have proven outstanding vehicles for capital appreciation. (Mutual companies–e.g., Metropolitan Life, Prudential, Equitable, etc., of course, do not have shares outstanding, but are owned by their policy holders.)

For many years, life insurance stocks were virtually a closed book as far as the general population of investors was concerned.

In the earlier years of the industry–now into its second century in this country–most life insurance company shares were closely held, rarely traded. It is only within the last few decades that increased capitalization and formation of new companies provided a number of shares sufficient for trading purposes. Even today, however, it is far from an active market, with most of the shares traded over-the-counter and with price spreads generally much wider than in industrial issues.

What is more, analysis of life insurance company shares for the purposes of investment is probably the most difficult of any industry. The usual total sales, operating earnings, and net profit per share statistics which serve as the backbone of industrial share analysis are here only a minor part of the story.

A life insurance company actually is involved in two lines of business at the same time. First, it insures lives. Secondly, it is an institutional investor of capital, surplus and other reserves in the securities of other industries and in real estate mortgages.

The second activity is no different from that pursued by mutual funds, closed-end funds, bank and college trustees and other institutional investors.

But the primary activity–the selling and servicing of contracts to cover lives–presents unique problems in securities analysis.

Before one can make a valid judgment on investing in life insurance stocks, one should be able to study and analyze the growth rate in capital funds, insurance in force, the types of insurance (participating and non-participating), the type of business written (whole life, term, endowment, group), the method of reserve accumulation, amount of new business written in relation to the business already in force, lapse rate, etc.

It can be seen at a glance that, in the main, this is a field which one should go into only with professional help.

There are many other warnings:

> Marketability of shares–generally less than that enjoyed by large industrial corporations with shares traded on the exchanges; low yield–often only 1 to 2 per cent on the current market price of the stock and quite often even much less, or none at all; price/earnings ratios–frequently higher than in most other industries.

Life insurance company shares are *not* speculative vehicles for amateurs. If it can be said of any group of securities, it can be said of life insurance stocks that in nine markets out of ten they are usually "fully priced," if not overpriced. The redeeming feature lies in the fact that though you may pay a full price, or too high a price today for a well-managed company, the natural, built-in growth in the industry will most likely show you a profit in ten years.

This does not mean that you may not have a serious loss next month. Periods of popular enthusiasm for these shares have come and gone–often in exaggerated fashion so that price swings are accentuated.

One such period of enthusiasm reached boiling temperature levels in the spring of 1964 when popularly written books on the subject of life insurance shares hit the investing public with all the force of the discovery of a new planet.

Small investors who had never heard of life stocks before poured into the market, buying the shares with all the fervor which, in earlier years, they had lavished on uranium, electronic, bowling, boating issues. Prices were feverishly bid up to new all-time highs.

Accompanying the bidding up of prices for the shares of established life insurance companies (and adding to the speculative hysteria) was a rash of formation of new companies, especially in the South and West. In 1964 alone, 150 new legal reserve life insurance companies were formed in thirty-nine of the fifty states–the most active year in new company formation since 1955. From 1950, when there were 611 life insurance companies in the United States, to July, 1964, 1,570 new companies were organized.

Despite the fact that, by the very nature of the business, new life companies cannot be expected to show any profits for at least five to ten years after formation, thousands upon thousands of novice investors were lured into these new shares, often with tie-ins of "charter" life insurance policies and frequently with the promise that within a year or two the profits and income from the stock investment would more than cover the cost of insurance premiums.

But by the fall of 1965, at least 30 per cent of the companies formed in the previous fifteen-year period were no longer in business and ultimate shrinkage is expected by insurance experts to come to as much as 60 per cent.

But the folding up of these companies attracted far less attention than the selling campaigns mounted for the sale of new company shares and far less than the flood of bullish publicity which swept over the entire insurance stock market—old, established companies, as well as new.

Established life company shares, which had sold at anywhere from 4 to 6 times adjusted per share earnings in the previous decade, were bid up wildly. By the time the April 1964 peak was reached, the average price/earnings ratio for the fifty leading life companies was 34 times 1963 earnings!

As we have constantly stressed in this book, excesses always carry the seeds of their own correction. The life insurance stock field was no exception.

Beginning with the spring of 1964, these shares went into a sustained price decline. Through 1965 and 1966 there were various flurries interpreted as rallies, but these failed to hold. It was not until 1968 that the more-than-three-year bear market seemed to attract some support.

It is not the purpose of this book to attempt to predict stock market prices.

But it may be of some comfort to disconcerted life insurance stock investors to know that the pattern of recent years is not new to the life stock field (or to *any* field of investment).

Using the Alfred M. Best index to life insurance stocks, we find that this phenomenon of surging prices followed by decline has been repeated several times in recent years. In the six years to 1955, this index rose phenomenally to a high of 180. In the next two years it backed down to about 130. Then followed a two-year climb to about the 200 mark, followed by a correction in little more than a year and a half to 170. In a little more than two years, the index then rose to close to 400. This was in the spring of 1962, but the 1962 bear market in all stocks brought it back down to about 265. The climb was then renewed, reaching the aforementioned peak in April 1964 of 459, from which point it declined 48% before turning firm.

But the insurance industry still has built-in growth factors working for it.

> Increasing population; steadily increasing insurance coverage per person and per family; a constantly improving mortality experience; more efficient operations made possible by the wide adoption of electronic data processing.

The life insurance industry remains a solid, basic business, woven inextricably into the financial, industrial and social fiber of the country. Quotations for its common shares are, of course, at the mercy of the public greed. That means, again, prices will fluctuate. It does not undermine the value of the industry's quality shares as an investment medium for those who strive for long-term capital growth.

Do not buy without the advice of experts, do not buy for the short term, do not buy into new, young companies unless you are prepared to assume the risks which take a high toll of such companies.

Over the years, the shares of the large, long-established companies have proved the most rewarding.

Among them are:

> Aetna, Travelers, Combined Insurance, Farmers New World, Fidelity Union, Connecticut General, Lincoln National Life, Jefferson Standard, Massachusetts Indemnity and Life, Business Men's Assurance, Commonwealth Life, Gulf Life, Liberty Life, Liberty National, Life Insurance Co. of Virginia, Massachusetts Protective, Monumental Life, Provident Life, Southwestern Life, U.S. Life, Philadelphia Life, Phoenix, Republic National Life.

If you are interested in what insurance stocks the experts buy, here is the 1971 year-end portfolio of Century Shares Trust, a 45-year-old mutual fund specializing in the shares of insurance and banking companies. Of $115,208,404 total assets reported, the fund has $103,105,305 invested in insurance company stocks. These included:

> Aetna Life & Casualty, American General Insurance common and convertible preferred, BMA Corp., Capital Holding, Chubb Corp., CNA Financial common and $1.10 convertible preferred "A," Colonial Life & Accident, Combined Insurance, Connecticut General Insurance, Continental common and $2.50 convertible preferred "A," ERC Corp.
>
> Fidelity Union Life, Globe Life & Accident, Government Employees Life, Home Security Life, INA Corp., Independent Life & Accident, Integon Corp., Interstate Corp., Jefferson-Pilot.
>
> Kansas City Life Insurance, Liberty National Life, Life Insurance Co. of Georgia, Lincoln National common and $3 convertible preferred, Monarch Capital, Monumental Corp., NLT Corp., Northwestern National Life, Ohio Casualty, Protective Life Insurance, Provident Life & Accident, Republic National Life, Richmond Corp., Safeco Corp., Southland Financial Corp., Travelers Corp., United States Fidelity & Guaranty.

Life insurance stock investment is a long-term proposition. Take your time investigating. Get the best help you can. And when you do buy, buy to hold.

In most cases, insurance stocks are traded over-the-counter. As of early 1972, here is a price list of representative issues as quoted by Salomon Brothers, large New York banking house which is one of the leaders in this market.

	Bid	*Asked*
Alexander & Alexander, Inc.	49	49¾
American Int'l Group	99½	100¼
American Int'l Group $2.00 Cvt. Pfd.	149	152
American National Ins.	9½	9⅞
American Re-Insurance	113	113¾
American Reserve Corp.	70¾	71½
Chubb Corp	65	65½
Colonial Penn.	84¼	84¾
Combined Insurance Co. Amer.	29¼	29¾
Connecticut General Ins.	68¾	69¼
Crum & Forster–N.Y.	34	34½
Farmers Group	40	40½
Farmers New World Life	42¼	42¾
Fidelity Union Life Ins.	35½	36
Frank B. Hall	62¼	63¼
Franklin Life Ins.	21⅜	21¾
Georgia Int'l Corp.	14⅞	15⅜
Government Employees Ins.	96	96½
Integon Corp.	12	12⅜
Interstate Corp.	27¼	27¾
Kemperco Inc.	45	45½
Liberty National Life Ins.	34	34½
Lomas & Nettleton Financial Corp.	22⅜	22¾
Monarch Capital Corp.	22¼	22¾
Nat'l Liberty Corp.	45¾	46½
NLT Corp.	34¼	34¾
NN Corporation	44½	45½
Northwestern National Life	19¾	20¼
Ohio Casualty Corp.	48¾	49¼
Pennsylvania Life Co.–Com.	35¼	35¾
Pennsylvania Life Co.–Wts.	19¼	20
Richmond Corp.	53½	54
St. Paul Cos., Inc.	66½	67
Safeco Corp.	42	42⅛
Safeco Corp. 4½ Cvt. Pfd.	28⅝	29½
Southwestern Life Ins.	49	49½
Union Fidelity Corp.	41	41½
Variable Annuity Life	15	15½

SOME QUESTIONS AND ANSWERS

Q. *I'd like to speculate and would appreciate a list of growth-type stocks. I have a chance to buy some life insurance with a cash value option on the stock of another company. I am told that insurance stocks have an average growth of 22 per cent (as against 9 per cent for mutuals) but that they are not readily available on the open market.*

A. I think you're being conned.

1. That phrase "I have a chance to buy" has always been connected, it generally develops, with some sort of "only-for-you" type of bargain. It reminds me of that tip-peddling scene in the Marx Brothers' "A Day at the Races."

2. As a rule, I don't like these combination insurance and new company stock deals—and, more important, neither do an increasing number of state insurance superintendents.

3. I don't know what you've been told about insurance stocks' "average" growth, but the fact is that in one recent period established insurance stocks fell about 40 per cent. In the last decade hundreds of new insurance companies have failed.

4. I don't know at what rate all mutual funds grow, and any blanket statement covering the entire industry, you can be sure, is being made for an ulterior motive.

5. Practically all life insurance stocks are traded over the counter—as are Treasury bonds, most bank stocks and thousands of corporate securities—and you can buy them any time you want to meet the asking price.

When a salesman says he is offering you any stock which is "not readily available," tell him you don't want any either.

Q. *I have been considering buying 100 shares of a life insurance company at $1 a share. What can I expect in the way of losses or gains? It's not money I can throw away, but I'd like to buy a good growth company.*

A. You're asking for a book. In fact, there is a 155-page study called "New Life Insurance Companies: Their Promotion and Regulation" in the *Marquette Law Review* for Fall 1965, which should make any investor in new life stocks pause—at least until he can find out what he is doing.

I don't know the company you are interested in and won't even guess as to its chances of success. All I can tell you is that of the 1,570 new insurance firms formed from 1950 to 1964, only about two thirds were still alive in mid-1964.

Q. *A few years ago I bought 50 shares of insurance stock at $70. The stock is now down to less than half that. Yet every year I get reports of the business increasing. How come?*

A. There are at least 4 reasons for the decline in price:

First: in the last few years, there have been stock dividends of 25 per cent, 20 per cent, 16⅔ per cent and 10 per cent. The total result of these 4 dividends has been to almost double the number of shares you hold. (Your 50 shares became 62½ with the first dividends, 75 with the second, 87½ with the third and 96¼ with the fourth.) That alone—all other things remaining the same—would have tended to cut the market price nearly in half. But all other things did not remain the same.

Second: while total business may have increased, net earnings have shown little improvement. Evidently the casualty end of the business has suffered from heavy underwriting losses, as has been the case with other casualty companies.

Third: the enthusiasm for insurance shares a few years ago brought market prices 30 to 35 and even more times annual per share earnings. Insurance stocks were hailed as the royal road to riches, and a lot of people who had never heard of them before were lured into buying them at outrageous prices. Recent disillusionment with insurance shares brought these price multiples down to 15 and and 20 times earnings.

This price/earnings factor, it seems to me, is too little understood. It's easy enough to figure out that a stock selling for $45 and earning $3 a share is selling at a price/

earnings multiple of 15, while another earning the same $3 and selling at $75 is selling at 25 times earnings. It is no help at all to point out that 15 is a cheaper price/earnings ratio than 25. Because if you buy the first stock as a "bargain" it may go still lower, while the second stock, which you may consider too high, may continue to climb to a point where it sells at 30 times earnings.

The answer to this seeming paradox is not to be found in arithmetic. It is based on the company's potential and, even more important, on what the bulk of investors *think* is its potential. Or, put it another way, it depends upon whether the stock (or the industry) is "in style." In the last decade we have had bowling, boating, rare metals, electronic, color TV, airline, as well as insurance-stock "styles." And a stock in style can command as high a price as public emotion will support, in exactly the same way that a popular dress may carry a price tag of $75 at the peak of its popularity but be marked down to $20 when that popularity has waned, even though there has been no change in the material and workmanship involved.

Insurance stocks today are definitely out of style—have been out of style for years. Are they on the bargain rack? Only time will tell.

Fourth, and finally, the entire market has come down in recent months. In a general market decline, very few industries escape—even those that hadn't shared in the previous boom.

So all you have going against you, as of the moment, is your company's failure to show substantial earnings gains, the disillusionment with insurance stocks, and the disillusionment with the entire market.

Q. *I have a small amount of a life insurance issue which I bought for growth. The stock has been as high as 22, but is now selling for less than 10. In view of the apparent health of the company, I can't account for the decline in the stock.*

A. I know nothing of your company, so can point out to you only that no single stock issue exists in a vacuum. This is especially so when it is an issue of a company in a field so specialized as life insurance. Life insurance stocks today are in the doghouse.

I suppose some day these prices on quality life companies will look as some of the 50- and 60-times-earnings prices that were paid not so long ago for glamour issues. Meanwhile, you either sit it out with your life stocks or sell out.

Q. *My investments are concentrated in life-insurance issues bought between 1940 and 1966. I am retired, and feel that, based upon my knowledge of the industry, I can set up my own level withdrawal plan, rather than sell all, pay huge taxes and reinvest net proceeds in income stock. My broker says I'm wrong and ought to listen to you, who have argued against such a plan.*

A. Anyone who has accumulated as much stock as you have here—blocks running from 500 to nearly 3,800 shares—actually doesn't have to listen to anyone. I can't imagine your running out of money, no matter which course you follow.

However, why not compromise?

If you bought insurance stocks as late as 1964-65-66, you could well have some losses on those purchases. I admit that some insurance stocks are depressed now and should not be sold in panic. But why not, for the sake of balance, take some of these losses and reinvest the proceeds in some industrial issues—tobaccos, utilities, motors, rails, metals—for the sake of a more generous income? Your earlier insurance purchases should be retained, I think, because your gains there must be astronomical.

Q. *I own some mutual funds invested in insurance shares. I intend to retire next year. Should I take my losses now and switch to income stocks?*

A. The insurance stock market has been one of the more disappointing investment areas of recent years. From time to time—as at present—there have been signs of recovery. I haven't the slightest idea whether this latest recovery will be sustained, or will fade out as have several previous ones. Nor can I guess whether these stocks will recover to previous highs, or exceed them.

However, it seems to me that since (1) you don't need income until next year, and (2) you can take the tax loss as an offset against your earnings any time until 3:30 P.M. on the last trading day of the year, there's not much need to jump now. Give the insurance stocks a bit more time.

Q. *Several years ago I bought stock in a new life insurance company for $4 a share, expecting to sell it when it went up a few dollars. But it has gone steadily lower and now I can't find a quotation. I asked the broker to sell it when it went up, but he said I'd have to watch it and tell him when. How can I watch it when the stock no longer appears in the listings?*

A. I guess you were caught in that rash of new insurance stock ventures a few years back. These were extreme gambles and the mortality rate was high. The last, out-of-date quote I can find on your stock is about $1¾.

Your letter is valuable as an object lesson for other uninformed speculators.

First, there is your intention to sell "when it went up a few dollars." When you take a gamble such as this one, you shouldn't try for a "few dollars," but for a "killing." Why else would you go into a new, unknown venture? If you wanted to make only a few dollars, you could have bought say, General Motors or U.S. Steel and hoped to catch a 2-point rise.

Second, there is your rather naive instruction to the broker to sell the stock "when it went up." A little thought should point out to you that no broker can operate efficiently under such vague instructions. No two people agree on what "up" means. If you told him you wanted to sell at 2½, I'm sure he would have taken the order.

The only way you can now keep tabs on the stock is to ask an over-the-counter dealer periodically. It isn't convenient, I know, but that's the price you pay for taking off-beat gambles.

9 How to Meet Your Current Needs with Income Stocks

For facility in labeling, investment shares are generally classified into stocks for growth, stocks for income, stocks for safety. It's a loose classification at best. Obviously there is some percentage of each quality in every stock. Just as clearly, no stock has 100 per cent of any quality.

Alan Lefferts seeks primarily high current income—as high as he can get without losing too much of the other qualities of safety and growth. For he cannot—in fact, would not want to—ignore the other factors completely, any more than his wife would want to exclude carrots and potatoes from a beef stew. When Lefferts shops for high income stocks he is merely emphasizing yield and placing safety and growth in secondary positions—not ignoring them.

As this is written, the stock market has fluctuated after having reached new high ground in the late months of 1968. Around the highs near the legendary 1,000 level in the Dow Jones industrial index, the average yield was down to about 3 per cent. The market drop, of course, resulted in slightly higher yields, but they are still far below the generous figure of 7.8 per cent recorded for the leading industrial common stocks in 1948 when the averages were around the 180 level.

And yet, even at current price levels, you and Lefferts may hope for a fair return. If you are willing to scout around, accept a few risks which go with cyclical businesses and give up a bit of glamour and popular appeal in return for time-proven dividend performance.

Common stocks listed on the New York Stock Exchange in 1971 paid a record dividend total of $20.3 billion to shareholders.

Of the 1,132 common stocks paying dividends, a total of 976 stocks—or 86 per cent—paid out the same or more in dividends than in the previous year. The $20.3 billion in total dividends represented a 1.8 per cent increase over the previous year's figures, which also had been a record.

Average dividends paid on stocks in the industrial, utilities, finance and real estate categories were as much as 6.2 per cent more than in 1970. Only the transportation category, consisting of 63 listed stocks, failed to better its 1970 average.

Early in 1972, *Financial World* magazine listed these corporations in its "aristocrat" list. To qualify, a company must have operated profitably since incorporation and must have paid dividends in each of the last 25 years:

25 TO 39 YEARS

	Year Incor-porated	*Dividends Paid Since*	*Dividends Total 1971*	*Recent Price*	**Yield*
Beco Industries	1924	1934	$1.00	26	3.8%
Columbia Gas System	1926	1943	1.76	32	5.5
Consolidated Natural Gas	1942	1944	1.88	30	6.5
Esquire, Inc.	1937	1937	0.30	11	2.7
Genesco Incorporated	1925	1934	1.70	34	5.0
Iowa-Illinois Gas & Electric	1940	1942	1.38	20	6.9
Madison Fund	1929	1939	a0.45	16	2.8
Montana Power	1912	1935	1.68	30	5.6
Niagara Share	1929	1935	a0.29	15	1.9
Prentice-Hall	1929	1933	0.74	43	1.8
Puget Sound Power & Light	1912	1943	1.82	30	6.1
Reynolds Metals	1928	1942	0.85	18	3.3
Riegel Textile	1946	1946	0.80	17	4.7
Stop & Shop	1925	1936	0.90	24	3.7
Tobin Packing	1942	1943	0.55	14	4.3
Walgreen Co.	1909	1933	1.00	25	4.0
Wometco Enterprises	1925	1936	0.44	21	2.1

40 TO 49 YEARS

	Year Incor-porated	*Dividends Paid Since*	*Dividends Total 1971*	*Recent Price*	**Yield*
Abbott Laboratories	1900	1929	$1.10	66	1.7%
Adams-Mills	1928	1928	0.20	12	1.7
American Can	1901	1923	2.20	35	6.3
Anchor Hocking	1928	1929	1.00	32	3.1
Archer-Daniels-Midland	1925	1927	1.00	37	2.7
Beneficial Corp.	1929	1929	1.07	45	2.4
Chicago Rivet & Machine	1927	1932	1.80	24	6.7
Columbus & So. Ohio Elec.	1906	1926	1.80	28	6.6
Continental Can	1913	1923	1.60	32	5.0
Credithrift Financial	1927	1930	0.70½	23	3.1
Family Finance	1927	1929	0.55	12	3.3
Federated Department Store	1929	1929	1.00	52	1.9
Honeywell Inc.	1927	1928	1.30	131	1.0
Keebler Company	1927	1928	0.70	29	2.4
Kraftco Corp.	1925	1924	1.70	45	3.8
Lone Star Gas	1926	1926	1.30	27	5.0
Macy (R. H.)	1919	1927	1.00	47	2.1
New Process	1924	1931	0.60	68	0.9
Philip Morris	1919	1928	1.20	72	2.0
Quaker State Oil	1931	1931	0.80	60	1.3
Safeway Stores	1926	1927	1.30	36	3.6
Universal Leaf Tobacco	1918	1927	1.50	31	4.8

50 YEARS OR MORE

Airco Inc.	1915	1917	$0.80	21	3.8%
Allied Chemical	1920	1921	1.20	29	4.1
American Brands	1904	1905	2.20	42	5.2
American Electric Pwr.	1906	1910	1.70	30	5.8
American Home Products	1928	1919	1.70	87	2.0
American Tel. & Tel.	1880	1881	2.60	46	5.7
Atlantic City Electric	1907	1919	1.36	23	6.1
Baltimore Gas & Electric	1906	1910	1.82	32	5.9
Borden Inc.	1899	1899	1.20	28	4.3
Boston Edison	1886	1890	2.33	39	6.1
Burroughs Corp.	1886	1895	0.60	150	0.4
Chesebrough-Pond's	1880	1883	1.04	58	1.8
Cincinnati Gas & Electric	1837	1853	1.56	27	5.8
C.I.T. Financial	1924	1921	1.90	50	4.0
Cleveland Electric Illum.	1892	1900	2.24	38	6.0
Coca-Cola Co.	1886	1893	1.58	117	1.3
Combustion Engineering	1912	1912	1.35	61	2.3
Commonwealth Edison	1887	1890	2.20	39	5.6
Consolidated Edison	1884	1885	1.80	27	6.7
Consumers Power	1910	1913	2.00	31	6.5
Conwood Co.	1900	1903	1.90	33	5.8
Corning Glass	1875	1881	3.25	187	1.7
CPC International	1906	1920	1.70	33	5.2
Dayton Power & Light	1911	1919	1.64½	26	6.4
Detroit Edison	1903	1909	1.40	21	6.7
Diamond International	1881	1882	1.80	41	4.4
Du Pont	1903	1904	5.00	146	3.4
Eastman Kodak	1901	1902	1.32	97	1.4
Gen'l Amer. Transportation	1916	1919	1.60	52	3.0
General Cigar	1906	1909	1.20	26	4.6
General Electric	1892	1899	1.35	63	2.2
General Foods	1922	1922	1.40	35	4.0
Gillette Co.	1901	1906	1.40	41	3.4
Grant (W. T.)	1906	1907	1.50	47	3.2
Heller (Walter E.) Int'l	1919	1920	0.68	30	2.5
Helme Products	1911	1912	s0.55	20	2.0
Hercules, Inc.	1912	1913	1.20	53	2.3
Household Finance	1925	1917	1.20	55	2.2
Interco Inc.	1911	1913	1.20	49	2.4
Int'l Business Machines	1911	1916	5.20	341	1.5
Kansas Gas & Electric	1909	1922	1.44	25	5.8
Kresge (S. S.)	1912	1913	0.48½	95	0.5
Kroger Co.	1902	1902	$1.30	33	3.9
Liggett & Myers	1911	1912	2.50	57	4.4
MacAndrews & Forbes	1902	1903	s0.20	13	1.5
May Dept. Stores	1910	1911	1.60	52	3.1
McIntyre Porcupine	1911	1917	0.80	77	–
Melville Shoe	1916	1916	0.80	61	1.3
Midwest Oil	1911	1920	3.00	114	2.6
Nabisco, Inc.	1898	1899	2.20	57	3.9
National Fuel Gas	1902	1903	1.68	25	7.0
National-Standard	1907	1915	0.75	35	2.0
National Steel	1929	1907	2.50	44	5.7
New England Tel. & Tel.	1883	1886	2.36	35	7.7
NL Industries	1891	1906	1.00	14	7.1
Norfolk & Western	1896	1901	5.00	77	6.4
Oklahoma Gas & Electric	1902	1908	1.24	26	4.9
Owens-Illinois, Inc.	1907	1907	1.35	45	3.0
Pacific Gas & Electric	1905	1919	1.60½	32	5.1
Pacific Lighting	1886	1909	1.60	25	6.4
Pfizer Inc.	1900	1900	0.65	41	1.5
Philadelphia Electric	1902	1902	1.64	24	6.8
Procter & Gamble	1890	1891	1.45	77	1.9
Public Service Co. (Colo.)	1906	1907	1.12	24	4.7
Public Service Elec. & Gas	1903	1907	1.64	27	6.1
Reynolds (R. J.) Industries	1899	1900	2.40	60	4.0
San Diego Gas & Electric	1905	1909	1.08	21	5.1
Southern California Edison	1909	1910	1.50	30	5.2
Standard Oil (Calif.)	1911	1912	2.80	59	4.7
Standard Oil (N. J.)	1882	1882	3.80	76	5.0
Sterling Drug	1901	1902	0.83	47	1.8
Tampa Electric	1899	1900	0.80	26	3.1
UGI Corporation	1882	1885	1.28	23	5.6
Union Carbide	1917	1917	2.00	42	5.6
Union Oil of California	1890	1916	1.60	35	4.6
Union Pacific Corp.	1897	1900	2.00	61	3.3
Upjohn Company	1909	1909	1.60	71	2.3
U.S. Gypsum	1901	1920	1.50	31	4.8
U. S. Tobacco	1911	1912	1.20	40	3.0
USM Corp.	1899	1905	1.17	15	2.7
Washington Gas Light	1866	1852	1.80	25	7.2
Westvaco Corp.	1899	1899	1.05	21	5.0
Woolworth (F. W.)	1911	1912	1.20	46	2.6
Wrigley (Wm.) Jr.	1910	1913	5.00	138	3.6

*Based on indicated rate or 1971 payments. a-Income. s-Plus stock.

MEDIAN YIELD ON DIVIDEND-PAYING COMMON STOCKS
LISTED ON THE NEW YORK STOCK EXCHANGE AT YEAR END

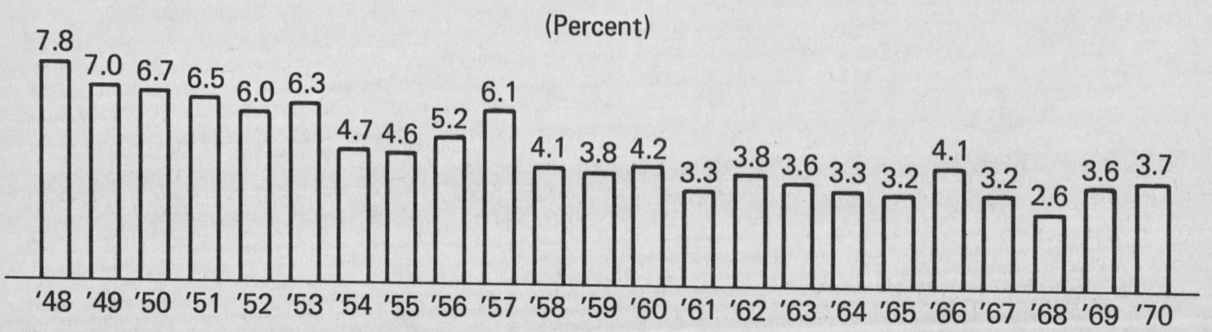

As will be developed later, this is but a representative handful.

In this search for high income, combined with better-than-average quality, it sometimes helps to break down the field into industries and then concentrate on some areas which may at the moment be out of favor either with the "gilt-edge" seekers or the general populace for one reason or another. Often this is the best method of discovering "sleepers"—those securities which go along year after year turning in a good performance dividend-wise but lacking the wide appeal, say, of the electronic or jet engine or nuclear stocks.

Home building has been disappointing in the last few years, although overall construction has been carried on at a near-record rate. Some of our highest investment quality stocks are included in this field. For example: Flintkote (dividends every year since 1934); Johns Manville (1935); National Gypsum (1939); U.S. Gypsum (1919).

A mark of a country's standard of living is its communications system. There is none better in all the world, and profiting from this inherent desire and need of people and companies to talk to each other are American Telephone & Telegraph (dividends every year since 1881); General Telephone & Electronics (1936); International Telephone (1951); and Western Union (1950), to name only the largest and best known.

Whatever may be one's personal feelings about buying on time, there can be little doubt that many of our comforts have been purchased that way by a large portion of our citizenry.

Over the years, the use of credit in buying everything from automobiles to TV sets and trips to Europe, has gone steadily higher. Here are a half dozen of the leaders in the fields which have been so successful that they have been able to maintain annual dividends for anywhere from twenty-five to more than forty years: Beneficial Corp. (dividends since 1929); C.I.T. Financial (1921); Household Finance (1917).

The farm problem will always be with us. But so will some of the leading farm equipment makers. Good yields are obtainable from this division, which includes such leaders as Allis-Chalmers (a steady dividend payer since 1936) and International Harvester (1910).

WHAT ABOUT THE RAILS?

It has long been considered sophisticated in certain investment circles to sneer at the railroad securities. "You don't invest in railroad stocks, you speculate in them," is the snappy verdict. Yet Lefferts could have done much worse—incomewise—than to hold railroad stocks during the last decade despite the tremendous growth in air travel and the government subsidization of practically all the railroads' competitors.

Today, many railroads are still doing a good job—not only in transport, but in providing income for investors. This despite the fact that the overall rail picture is far from encouraging. Taxes, outmoded labor regulations and unfair allocation of commuter responsibilities have brought the industry to a crisis. The overall situation, in fact, is so bad that many observers feel it can only improve.

If the Federal and state governments can be forced to modernize regulations to the point where the railroads can operate as a twentieth-century business, the tremendous technical progress made by the roads will begin to bear fruit in increased efficiency and higher earnings.

Certainly modern railroad managerial thinking has displayed a flexibility in planning which hitherto has been associated only with much younger industries.

Given advantage of updated tax and rate regulation, the railroads can be expected to roll for years. It is difficult to visualize a nation 3,000 miles across without a top-notch heavy transport industry.

When the turn will come in the fortunes of the carriers is a matter of guesswork. In the meantime, the careful investor—giving weight to areas served, type of traffic, balance sheet (and especially debt) position, can get some generous yields, assuming he can take the risk which goes with an old industry in modern-day transition. For those seeking relatively good yield with high safety from the railroad industry, there are also the guaranteed railroad stocks.

This is a little-known area of investment, generally restricted to sophisticated professional investors and money managers.

The typical guaranteed railroad stock represents a proprietary interest in a strategically located rail property leased for a long term of years to a large operating railroad system. It offers a safety of return corresponding with that of the guarantor railroad's funded debt, or mortgages. Pricewise it is unusually stable.

It cannot be stressed too much that the safety factor is dependent 100 per cent on the financial strength of the large railroad leasing and guaranteeing the payments on the stock of the leased line. Here are some examples of yields obtainable:

Mobile & Birmingham RR. $4 Preferred
  Lessee; Southern Railway Company
  Quoted 44 bid, 48 asked, yielding 8.34%
Southern Ry.-Mobile & Ohio. 4% Stock Tr. Ctfs.
  Lessee; Southern Railway Company
  Quoted 44 bid, 48 asked, yielding 8.34%
Carolina Clinchfield & Ohio Ry. $5
  Lessees; Atl. Coast Line RR. and L & N RRs.
  Quoted 82 bid, 83 asked, yielding 6.02%
Nashville & Decatur RR. $1.875
  Lessee; Louisville & Nashville RR.
  Quoted 23 bid, 25 asked, yielding 7.50%
Dayton & Michigan RR. $4 PFD.
  Lessee; Baltimore & Ohio RR.
  Quoted 40 bid, 44 asked, yielding 9.10%
Dayton & Michigan RR. $1.75 Common
  Lessee; Baltimore & Ohio RR.
  Quoted 17 bid, 20 asked, yielding 8.75%
North Carolina RR. $7
  Lessee; Southern Railway Co.
  Quoted 97 bid, 101 asked, yielding 6.93%

Wheeling & Lake Erie RR. $5.75
Lessee; N.Y. Chicago & St. Louis RR.
Quoted 86 bid, 88 asked, yielding 6.53%

A $25,000 INCOME PORTFOLIO
(as suggested in *Financial World* magazine January 1972)

Shares		*Price*	*Cost*	**Income*
50	American Brands	43	$ 2,150	$ 110.00
50	American Tel. & Tel.	46	2,300	130.00
75	Columbus & Southern Ohio Electric	28	2,100	138.00
75	Consol. Natural Gas	30	2,250	146.25
100	Diversified Mtge Investors	28	2,800	246.00
40	General Motors	81	3,240	136.00
40	Procter & Gamble	77	3,080	60.00
50	Sherwin-Williams	47	2,350	100.00
50	Standard Oil (Indiana)	69	3,450	119.60
75	Tenneco, Ind.	26	1,950	99.00
	Totals		$25,670	$1,284.85
	Yield			5.0%

*Indicated annual rate.

WHAT CAN YOUR MONEY EARN?

In mid-February 1972, *Financial World* magazine presented this tabulation of what one can expect from his investment capital:

Industrial common stocks	2.70%
Dow Jones transportation stocks	2.95
91-day Treasury bills	3.20
Dow Jones industrial stocks	3.45
6-month Treasury bills	3.70
Commercial bank savings	4.00
Savings banks	5.00
Savings and loans	5.00
Municipal bonds	5.35
Series E & H savings bonds	5.50
U.S. Treasury bonds	5.70
Dow Jones utility stocks	5.70
Certificates of deposit	6.00
Preferred stocks	6.60
Corporate bonds AAA-rated	7.15
New AA-rated utilities	7.40
Residential mortgages	7.50
Corporate bonds A-rated	7.65
Corporate bonds BBB-rated	8.15

As will be noted, the yield on the leased line's stock is largely determined by the financial standing of the guarantor road. Even so, within these limitations, it can be seen that generous yields are obtainable even in today's high stock markets.

The railroad equipment maker stocks have also been neglected to the point where they yield a higher return than the market average.

It has been fashionable to label the steel business a feast or famine business and forthwith dismiss it from the society of sophisticated investments. But this snap judgment, as in the case of the rails, fails to take into consideration the fact that the steel industry is a vastly improved business over what it was a quarter century ago.

In evaluating the modern steel industry, too little thought has been given to the fact that steady improvement of and addition of facilities have brought an increase in demand. Notwithstanding strikes, heavy foreign competition, decline in operations and heavy amortization charge for new plant, many of the leading steel producers are still showing yields of around 5 per cent and even more on their common.

Utility stocks have for decades been considered "orphans and widows" investments. This reputation is well deserved. A comparison of the long-term price trend of the utility averages with those of the industrial and railroad industries will show the utilities to be sober movers indeed. But what is the in-and-out speculator's poison may well be the long-term investor's steak, or, at least, pot roast.

Putting aside for the purpose of this discussion the wild gyrations of the top-heavy holding companies in the '20s (which weren't really utilities at all, but gambling devices), the utility industry is a logical hunting ground for the retirement planner. Its important plants have an enviable record for consistent dividend payments. In fact, their safety record earns many of them representation as safety stocks as well as high income producers.

It is true that unless you select a company which serves an area growing faster than the national rate, you may not get much market action for your money.

But the dividend checks should come in with comforting regularity.

The utility division is a large one and—for the investor—possesses the additional advantage of being geographic in nature. An adult investor who has lived most of his life in Baltimore, or Milwaukee, or Tucson should, by the time he's ready to invest his retirement money, have a pretty good idea of whether he is living in a growth area, a stabilized, or a declining one.

Since most utilities automatically get all the business generated in their areas, the future of any public utility is pretty well tied to the future of its particular bailiwick. It is for this reason that the common stocks of companies located in areas believed to have reached or passed maturity (the New England States are—mistakenly or otherwise—often given as an example) sell at prices which yield a good deal more than those servicing a fast-growing suburban and industrial area.

Obviously, over the years, the latter growth utilities may prove to be a far better investment than the higher yielding stocks of mature companies. But that's something for you to decide, depending on whether you need your income soon, or twenty years from now.

A relatively recent addition to the utility field are the natural gas utility companies which have been extending their pipelines throughout the country. As of the present writing, it is true, these companies are under heavy governmental regulation. They will, of course, continue under Federal control. But even so, they are here to stay as investments.

The textile industry has been in the investor doghouse so long that its disfavor seems almost chronic. Even professionals in the industry will wave you off, saying "Keep away. The only time we can be sure of making money is during wartime shortages. The rest of the time this is a cutthroat, low-profit business."

Undoubtedly, some of the companies have proved poor investments. But that's no reason for Lefferts to write off the entire industry as unworthy of his consideration. We shall continue to wear clothes, sleep between sheets and use fabrics in our homes and automobiles. And textile managements have proved just as capable as the next ones in research in keeping up with, or, in fact, fashioning public demand. Many of them are now in the process of learning you can't supply 1972 markets with 1890 mills. Forced to learn this lesson, just as the rails were forced to modernize, the better managed textile companies should prove investor-worthy once again.

In any event there are enough important companies in the field to merit any investor's spending a few hours looking over their records.

For centuries we have accepted water as a commodity about as free as the air. Now we are learning that not only is pure air hard to come by but that adequate water supplies are a matter of increasing concern.

Twenty years from now, the United States will require more than 500 billion gallons of water a day for farmers, industry and for thirsty consumers. A couple of years ago that figure was actually only 209 billion.

It would do well, then, for the forward-looking investor to consider the profits which may be derived from providing the ever-growing need for water.

Much of the supply, it is true, is now in the hands of municipal and other governmental agencies. But it is also true that 30 per cent of all water enterprises in the United States are in private hands. Many of these are locally and closely owned, so that there is very little trading in their securities.

But there are some substantial companies whose stocks are traded. The top holding companies in the industry include the giant—American Water Works—drawing income from more than sixty water companies in sixteen states. General Waterworks serves about 160 communities in seventeen states and Citizens Utilities Co. of Stamford serves five states.

YIELDS ON THE AMEX

Although the American Stock Exchange (Amex) is generally considered to list less seasoned issues than the New York Stock Exchange, it still has its complement of issues which have established a record of dividend payments. Here are 61 issues listed on the Amex representing a broad spectrum of industry which have paid dividends continuously for 10 years or more and which, as of late 1971 prices, were yielding at least 5 per cent.

	Number of Consecutive Years Dividends Have Been Paid	*% Yield*
Alan Wood Steel	24	7.6
American Petrofina	24	5.1
American Realty Trust	10	11.6
Arkansas Louisiana Gas	19	5.7
Atlas Consolidated Mining	12	10.5
Baldwin Securities	21	5.6
Canadian Intl. Power	11	8.2
Castle (A.M.) & Co.	38	5.5
Chicago Rivet & Machine	40	7.7
City Gas of Florida	12	5.6
Community Public Service	36	6.2
Creole Petroleum	37	11.7
Domtar Ltd.	26	5.7
Electrographic Corp.	37	6.2
Epko Shoes	26	5.0
Fabien Corp.	18	5.1
First Union R.E. Eq. & M.I.	10	7.0
Gorin Stores	25	7.0
Gorman-Rupp Co.	36	5.2
Greit Realty Trust	10	9.1
Gross Telecasting	16	6.1
Hanover Shoe Inc.	16	5.2
Hoskins Mfg.	38	7.7
Investors Funding Corp.	17	7.1
Knott Hotels	36	5.1
Lehigh Press	10	5.5
Louisiana General Service	13	5.7
Maine Public Service	28	7.3
Means (F.W.) & Co.	44	5.8
Mirro Aluminum	70	5.5
Mount Vernon Mills	26	5.9
National Realty Investors	10	6.7
Newcor Inc.	35	8.0
Ohio Brass	38	6.6
O'okiep Copper	26	11.4
O'Sullivan Corp.	12	7.3
Pacific Northwest Bell Tel.	11	7.0
Penn. R.E. Inv. Tr.	10	7.2
Philippine Long Distance Tel.	19	10.2
Pittsburgh-Des Moines Steel	37	6.2
Pratt & Lambert	67	6.3
Presidential Realty (Cl. A)	11	6.6
Presidential Realty (Cl. B)	11	6.9
Preston Mines, Ltd.	11	5.3
Providence Gas Co.	123	7.1
Real Estate Invest. Tr. of Amer.	85	8.0
Reliance Insurance	114	5.3
Remington Arms	36	7.5
Rockaway Corp.	43	5.5
San Carlos Milling	31	14.1
Sinclair Venezuelan Oil	14	9.9
Star Supermarkets	20	5.1
Tasty Baking (Cl. A)	57	5.9
Thorofare Markets	29	5.9
U.S. Realty Investments	11	9.2
Utah-Idaho Sugar	31	6.0
Voplex Corp.	38	5.6
Vulcan, Inc.	26	6.3
Washington R.E. Invest. Tr.	10	8.4
Whippany Paper Board	11	7.7
Whiting Corp.	32	6.7

–Source: Standard & Poor's Inc.

SOME QUESTIONS AND ANSWERS

Q. *Would my $20,000 savings earn more for me if invested in common or preferred shares? I know nothing about investments and fear losing my money. How does common stock serve as a hedge against inflation? Does the dividend increase automatically as the value of money declines? I can't understand when the owner of common shares receives the "income per share" shown on financial statements.*

A. It is possible today to get a return of 5 to more than 7 per cent from stocks and bonds. However—except for U.S. Treasury issues—there is no guaranty of the safety of your principal that is equivalent to the one you now have if your savings institutions are insured by the FDIC or the FSLIC.

Common shares tend to offset inflation, since corporation sales and earnings, in dollars, tend to rise when the buying power of the dollar goes down. And frequently dividends rise, too. There is nothing automatic about it, however. A company may well suffer lower sales and earnings and pay out smaller dividends during a period of inflation.

The owner of common stock never receives the "income per share." A company's board of directors decides what it will pay out in dividends. Obviously, a solvent company does not pay out all it earns, any more than a prudent person spends his full salary.

Preferred-share dividends, in practically all cases, are fixed—hence offer no inflation protection.

Q. *I have modest savings I would like to invest in a nonliquid asset. What are some that will yield 6 per cent? Would buying a house and renting it out for income be considered a nonliquid asset? What about an annuity? I am a woman of 44.*

A. Liquidity in an investment is a relative matter. If you have money in a bank, you can walk in and draw it out immediately. That's 100 per cent liquidity. Government bonds and other high-grade, actively traded securities are almost as liquid.

At the other end of the scale, $1,000 invested in an antique chest or rare book would be a much less liquid investment. You might not be able to sell in a day. A desirable house would, I suppose, rank somewhere in between.

An annuity bought at age 44 to begin providing monthly income when you retire, say, at 60, is liquid until that time, since you may cash it in, make certain changes, etc. But once you begin drawing benefits on a lifetime contract, with no payments certain, it is no longer liquid, since you can't draw out any balances or change the terms. Short of that or an irrevocable trust fund, I can't think of any 100 per cent nonliquid investments.

Generally, the only time you can't get at money (which is what nonliquidity means) is after you have either (1) given it away for good or (2) contracted irrevocably for its disposition.

I'd go slow on that buying-and-renting bit. It might not prove a 100 per cent safe hiding place and it could be a headache.

Q. *I intend to travel. Is it possible to turn my securities over to a bank and have the dividends sent directly to my account? I would like to keep control of the buying and selling.*

A. Commercial banks will provide you with a form which you can send to a corporation, instructing it to pay your dividends directly to the bank. Whether you turn the securities over to the bank or keep them in your own vault is immaterial. Either way you retain trading control.

Q. *I bought 100 A.T.&T. on May 10. I still have not received the certificates or the July 1 dividend. Is the broker responsible? Should he pay me interest for 30 days on dividends not received by the 10th? Also, if I decide to sell, shouldn't I have the certificate in my possession?*

A. You are entitled to the July 1 quarterly payment since you bought the stock well in advance of the May 26 "ex-dividend" date. The dividend may have been credited to your account at the brokerage firm, since the stock may have still been in its name on the ex-dividend date. Also, at the time of purchase, did you tell your broker you wanted the stock issued in your name? Finally, I don't think you're going to get very far with that interest bit. Unless you are an active customer, holding that stock for you and receiving and crediting the dividends to your account is pretty much of a nuisance to your broker.

You don't have to have the certificate in your possession in order to sell. In fact, it's simpler if the broker holds it in his vault.

Q. *Acting on a friend's advice, we bought 25 shares of Washington Gas Light at $77.50. Since then it has split 2 for 1, and we have 50 shares selling at around $28. We realize it was a big mistake for retired people to have bought such expensive stock. Should we sell?*

A. Utility shares have been depressed for about a year—so your only "mistake" was in buying some shares which happened to decline in price. You have a lot of sophisticated company. All this, however, does *not* indicate that you should sell out now, even though the shares are depressed.

Washington Gas Light is a B-plus equity which, at today's market, is yielding about 7.1 per cent. Further, the company has paid dividends without interruption since 1852. If anything, I'd say it's the type of stock a retired couple should have.

I'd vote to hold the shares for good income and for price recovery when the money market and the stock market sober up.

Q. *I plan to retire in 3 years. I now hold A.T.&T., Cleveland Electric Illuminating, du Pont, General Electric, General Motors, Illinois Central, Goodyear Tire, Gulf Oil, U.S. Steel, Union Electric. What do you think of switching out of this list and into higher-income stocks?*

A. That is exactly what you will have to do—*after* you retire.

Some of your finest issues are low yielders. But, if you have held them any length of time you undoubtedly have profits on them. There would be no point to taking that profit now, paying a capital-gains tax increased by your earnings, and switching into stocks providing income—which you will not need for awhile.

Time enough to do some yield arithmetic, take your profit and reinvest in income stocks in the first year in which you will have no taxable earnings.

Q. *We plan to retire in 2 years and will need more than our pension to live on. We have substantial amounts of A.T.&T. and New England Electric, on which we have a profit. We would have to pay a sizable gains tax if we sold in order to convert into bonds. Is there any way the stock could be switched into bonds without paying a tax?*

A. If you sell stock on which you have a profit you must report a capital gain, no matter what you subsequently do with the money. Frankly, I don't see why you have to do anything.

1. Retirement is 2 years off. Why take any capital gains now when your income-tax bracket is higher than it will be after you retire?

2. What's wrong with keeping the shares you have? A.T.&T. yields nearly 6 per cent at current market, and New England Electric better than 6. Certainly there is no reason to toss these out for the sake of bonds—especially since you will want some inflation protection in retirement, too.

The issues you have suit you to a T until retirement and may well be perfect for your needs after retirement. If you had a substantial loss in stocks ill suited to retirement needs, I'd urge you to take that loss early enough so that you can use it to reduce your earned-income tax burden. But just the reverse is true in your case. So why fret?

Q. *We are interested in income for retirement. We own our home, some vacant lots, and nearly 500 shares of Union Oil. We realize the dividend is low, but feel it is secure.*

A. The question of holding vacant land is always difficult to discuss since some land may be in an area on the verge of great expansion whereas other parcels may have little potential.

It would seem to me, however, that retired folks cannot afford to hold vacant land unless (1) they have no need of additional current income, or (2) they have good reason to feel they can double their money on it in a year or two.

As to your nearly $25,000 investment in Union Oil: There can be little argument that your investment is "secure." Union Oil holds an A-minus rating, can boast of a handsome earnings record and has paid a dividend without fail for the last half-century. But the fact remains that the stock is a growth situation rather than a generous retirement-income provider.

Elsewhere, your money could be bringing in 7 per cent and even a trifle better.

Q. *We are in our late 50s and thinking of retiring this fall on a generous pension. We hold 100 A.T.&T., 20 du Pont, 60 General Electric, 20 General Motors, 28 IBM, 40 Sears and 20 Standard Oil of N.J., on which we have a profit of about $11,000. Should we sell out and buy a mutual fund?*

A. Do nothing until next year when your tax bracket drops. Furthermore, you may find after you retire that you won't be so hard pressed for income as to force liquidation of these good growth stocks. Since you will both be short of 60, you may find that accepting, say, a 3 per cent return from a stock that can give you both growth and inflation protection will prove far more comfortable than you now expect. In any event, don't subject yourself now to a capital-gains tax based on your earned income when your retirement tax bracket will be much lower next year.

Q. *I sold United Corp. on February 17 and was told that I was not entitled to the March dividend check. How come? I've owned the stock for 17 years and feel I should get* some *of the dividend.*

A. That dividend went to the investor who owned your shares at the close of business March 7. (It went "ex dividend" the next morning, March 8.) Since you sold it on February 17, you are not entitled to the dividend. There is no "sharing" of a dividend. Either you own the stock on the proper date and get the entire dividend or you get nothing. Interest on bonds is prorated according to the time owned; dividends on stock are not.

Q. *By next month we shall both be retired. We have $53,000 in savings, own our home and odd lots of more than 650 shares of Pacific Gas & Electric, Pacific Light, A.T.&T., General Telephone & Electronics, Southern Pacific, Pacific Power & Light, International Harvester, Sante Fe, General Motors and Pacific Gas & Electric preferred. Should I sell and invest in tax-exempt municipals? Invest in higher-yield stocks?*

A. This is an excellent list. I would make no changes except for reasons of higher income. Certainly there would be no point to switching your high yielders—General Motors, Pacific Light, and Pacific Power & Light.

Q. *We are retired on $411 a month, own our home and have about $3,000 in government bonds and savings. We recently contracted to buy $1,500 worth of a shopping center security—$200 down and $50 a month—but have since become dubious about it. Might it take too long to realize any return on our investment?*

A. It doesn't sound right to me, although I must admit I can find nothing on the enterprise itself. However, whether it is sound or not, I can't see it as an investment for a couple retired on about $400 a month.

I don't understand the arrangement. What is this $200 down and $50 a month going to get you? Stock? If so, at what price? It will take you more than 2 years to complete the $1,500 payments. Is the stock to remain price-fixed during that time? If so, it implies there will be no public market, which, in turn, indicates that you may have trouble getting your money out if you want to terminate the deal. I would urge you to have this deal fully explained to you by some disinterested party who knows something about it. The details you give me are far too sketchy.

(Incidentally, if your bonds are E bonds, they should be switched into Hs for additional current income.)

Q. *I have recently retired at 60, with $14,000 in savings and $9,000 in E bonds. I find I must cash about $25 worth of bonds a week. I've been reading about inflation. What would you advise?*

A. Inflation is only one of your problems. Today you can get about 7½ per cent from good-grade bond investments. I don't know what your savings are bringing in, but E bonds grow at the rate of 5½ per cent. Taking that $9,000 investment alone—there's no way you can get $25 a week out of it. Putting the $9,000 into an annuity would get you about half that, at your age. An investment in income securities would bring much less, although that would provide some inflation protection. I don't think you can avoid dipping into capital.

Q. *We plan to retire soon. We have savings which pay us 5 per cent. Should we buy a mutual fund or income stocks?*

A. I can't say, because I don't know whether:

This savings account is your only income-producing asset, or whether you have others;

You are 60 or 80. It makes a difference in figuring on inflation;

You are talking of $5,000 or $100,000. If it is $5,000 it should be left where it is. If it's $50,000 or $100,000 (and if you are young enough to have to face up to inflation), perhaps half, or even more, should be in stocks—and high-yield bonds.

Q. *We will retire soon. Our money is now invested in savings certificates paying 5 per cent. We need all the income we can get. Should we buy common shares in order to hedge against inflation, although, we understand, stocks yield only about 3 per cent or less and are not absolutely safe? Are there good bonds that yield 5 per cent or more?*

A. If you want to hedge against inflation, common shares, real estate, rare works of art, jewelry, etc., are the accepted media.

There is a long list of good to high-grade common shares which yield 5 per cent at market, and even a trifle more.

I don't know what you mean by "absolutely safe" (loss of income? loss of capital?), but I can assure you *no* investment is safe from all financial hazards. Your savings certificates, for example, may be insured by a government agency and are, therefore, safe from the point of view of your getting back the number of dollars you invested. But there is no guaranty that the dollars you get back will buy as much as those you put in. Inflation has been constantly nibbling away at their purchasing power.

In the same vein, there are scores of high-grade rail and utility bonds which yield above 7 per cent. Any broker can list a few dozen for you. There would be little cause for worry about the safety of the number of dollars invested. But, as in the case of money in banks, there is no hedge against inflation.

Q. *I am 54, retired from the Army and employed. We live comfortably. I now hold some utility, rail and electronic stocks and have $15,000 more to invest. I don't know whether I should buy for maximum dividends or for growth. Some extra dividends would be welcome.*

A. This is a popular question—and has no definite answer. I suppose one could reply to you by asking: "How welcome?"

The growth potential scale goes from zero to 100. And so does the income scale. A 7% bond due, or callable, in the next few years and selling around par, I suppose, would score about 100% on the income scale and about zero on the growth potential scale.

A new electronics stock paying no dividend would score zero on the income scale but, at least in the eye of the beholder, could rate 100% on the growth scale.

In practical application you will find that one scale is the reverse of the other. If you mark off the income scale from left to right, zero to 100, you'll find that the growth scale can be superimposed on it with the readings running from 100 to zero.

Now, somewhere along this scale you must take your stand, giving up some income in the hopes of some growth, and vice versa.

You say you are living "comfortably," but more income would be welcome.

If it would be welcome enough for you to face up to higher income taxes and the corresponding loss of growth potential, then you lean more toward income than toward growth. In other words, do you want more of your investment goodies now, or in future?

One word of caution:

If you buy an investment-grade steel, rail, auto, tobacco stock which has been paying dividends for 40 or 50 years without interruption and which has earnings comfortably covering dividend requirements you can be relatively certain of getting a dividend.

Growth is a far less tangible item. In fact—despite even years of growth history, there is never any guaranty that history will repeat. It's your money and your needs—so you'll have to make the decision.

Q. *I differ with you on stock yields. If I bought 100 shares of a stock at $23 and am getting $250 a year in dividends I'm getting better than 10% on my investment even though today's buyer, paying $50 a share, earns only 5%. You can't convince me otherwise.*

A. O.K. I'll agree with you if you sell me your 100 shares for $2,300, which is the value you're setting on them.

Q. *How would I obtain information on a large oil company in which I own stock?*

A. There are various sources of corporate information: Standard & Poor's, Fitch, Moody's—to name three of the large statistical organizations. You will find their volumes in brokerage firms and in many large public libraries.

Then, too, there is the company itself, which sends you quarterly reports, annual reports plus proxy statements. And finally, if you are a shareholder, there's no reason you can't write to the executives of the company directly.

Q. *It's my feeling that a reasonable degree of income can be expected from growth stocks only after a period of five to ten years. I need immediate income, if possible. Do you have any suggestions for stocks that will yield income in relatively short time?*

A. Growth stocks often remain growth stocks not only for five years, but for decades. They are preferred investments for those seeking capital gain, *not* generous current income.

If you want income *now*, you should turn to securities that pay out generous interest or dividends—now. These include good quality corporate bonds, which today yield over 7%; common stocks of sound utilities, rails, manufacturing companies yielding around 5%.

I don't know what "relatively short time" is. If you speculate you can double, or lose, your money in a few weeks. If you aim for solid growth you must carry your risk over a longer period of time. But if you want income, now, why not concentrate on securities which are doing that sort of job?

Q. *I've been offered a 25% return in six months for a $2,500 investment.*

A. That's no investment, that's a license to steal. I don't want to hear about it.

Q. *You wrote that a man who bought 100 shares of a stock at 23, received 50 shares more as a stock dividend, and is now getting $240 a year in dividends receives a yield of only 4.8%. Actually, his return is over 10%. My broker tried to give me the same rigmarole.*

A. Now you're trying to give me some rigmarole.

The stock is now selling at a price of 33½. Right?

So the man owns 150 shares of stock today worth about $5,000. Right?

His investment today brings in $240 a year. Right?

Take 4.8% of $5,000 and you get $240. Right?

Q. *A mortgage company in my town offers 8 to 10% interest on money invested with it. What would you advise?*

A. I don't know the mortgage company—which is evidently a local concern—so can offer no opinion on it. I *do* know that your local utility company, which enjoys an "AA" rating for its bonds, pays 7¼%.

Q. *I'm 41, looking to invest $10,000 for greater growth than an insured savings account, but with no more risk.*

A. You can't have it both ways. If you are looking for growth, you must assume risk. Seeking growth means peering into the future. I don't know of any 100% safe way of doing that. If you insist that $10,000 always be there when you want it then you'll just have to keep it in insured savings.

10 Let Mutual Fund "George" Do Your Investing

In investing, as well as in gardening, home maintenance, auto repairs, there are two schools of thought:

"Do it yourself," or–

"Let George do it"–"George" being a professional gardener, plumber, auto mechanic–or investment company.

Every investor must decide early in the game of building capital whether he is going to do the job himself, or farm it out to a professional. The bases for his decision are many:

Has he the time to invest? A man spending long hours in a doctor's office, or running a pharmacy, or a restaurant may well not have the time also to study corporate reports, follow various industries in particular or the overall economy in general.

Has he the ability? A man may be a successful salesman, a veteran airplane pilot or a highly skilled and highly paid tool designer, but not be proficient in reading financial studies.

Has he the temperament? He may be a leading actor, or a famous surgeon or head of the police bomb squad, but not have the nerve to invest counter to the popular trend or to withstand the shattering experience of seeing his hard-won dollars melt away under a hysterical selling wave on the stock market.

This is not to say that a man may not start on a do-it-yourself program and later–frankly evaluating his lack of success–turn the job over to a professional. Many do. Or he may start with a professional and, after years of experience, may decide he can do a better job himself. In no other field is the old saying "You pay your money and you take your choice" more applicable.

The professionals we are talking about here are the investment companies. They are the most popular pros today, managing a total of somewhere around 75 billion dollars for several million investors, large and small.

Investment companies come in all sizes–ranging from a few hundred thousand dollars in assets to nearly 3 billion. They aim at growth of capital, or income, or various combinations of both.

They are divided, according to their method of operation, into the older, but far fewer, "closed-end" investment companies and the far larger group of "open-end" mutual funds which today control about 57 billion dollars of investments for both small and large individual investors, pension funds, institutions.

Whether they are large or small, open-end or closed-end, the basic appeals of all investment companies lie first in professional management, and second in diversification–a spreading of risk among one hundred or more corporations' securities, a form of insurance which is, practically speaking, out of the reach of most small investors.

The older closed-end investment funds have only recently set up a trade association–the Association of Closed-End Investment Companies–with offices at 330 Madison Avenue, New York City 10017.

Their stock is traded, in most cases, on the New York Stock Exchange and you acquire–or sell–shares in exactly the same way you would buy or sell shares of U.S. Steel or General Motors.

Members of the association and their addresses are:

Adams Express, 48 Wall Street, New York City 10005; American European Securities, 368 Center Street, Southport, Conn. 06490; American General Bond fund, 3910 Keswick Rd., Baltimore, Md. 21211; American Research and Development Corp., 200 Berkeley Street, Boston, Mass. 02116;

Baker, Fentress, 208 South LaSalle Street, Chicago, Ill. 60604; Bancroft Convertible Fund, 660 Madison Avenue, New York City 10021; Carriers & General Corp., 1 Wall Street, New York City 10005; Central Securities, 375 Park Avenue, New York City 10022; Diebold Venture Capital, 480 Park Avenue, New York 10022; Dominick Fund, 30 Broad Street, New York City 10004;

General American Investors, 60 Broad Street, New York City 10004; International Holdings Corp., 1 State Street, New York City 10004; John Hancock, Investors, 200 Berkeley Street, Boston, Mass. 02116; Lehman Corp., 1 South William Street, New York City 10004;

Madison Fund, 501 Farmers Bank Building, Wilmington, Del. 19801; National Aviation Corp., 630 Fifth Avenue, New York City 10020; Niagara Share Corp., 70 Niagara Street, Buffalo, N.Y. 14202; Overseas Securities Co., 100 Wall Street, New York City 10005; Petroleum Corp. of America, 48 Wall Street, New York City 10005; SMC Investment Corp., 1888 Century Park East, Los Angeles, Calif. 90067; Standard

Shares, 40 Wall Street, New York City 10005; Surveyor Fund, 90 Broad Street, New York City 10004;

Tri-Continental Corp., 65 Broadway, New York City 10006; United Corp., 250 Park Avenue, New York City 10017; U.S. & Foreign Securities, 767 Fifth Avenue, New York City 10022; Value Line Development Capital Corp., 5 E. 44th Street, New York City 10017.

Then there are the more than 550 mutual funds, or open-end companies, so-called because their capitalization is open—they create and sell shares whenever you want them, buy them back and retire the shares whenever you want to cash in your chips. In other words, you join by turning over your funds to the company and getting newly created shares which represent your pro rata shares of the entire fund; you bow out by turning the shares back to the company for cash.

These mutuals are classified according to their general purpose.

For example, among the larger funds dedicated to growth of capital are Chemical Fund, Dreyfus, Enterprise, Fidelity Capital, Fidelity Trend, Investors Variable, Keystone S-4, Massachusetts Investors, National Investors, T. Rowe Price Putnam Growth, Technology Fund, United Accumulative.

Among the larger funds aiming at a combination of capital growth and income are Fidelity Fund, Fundamental Investors, Investment Co. of America, Investors Stock Fund, Massachusetts Investors Trust, One William Street, Putnam Investors Fund, State Street Investment, United Income, Affiliated, American Mutual, Broad Street Investing, Dividend Shares, Group Securities Common, National Securities Stock.

Then there is a group of "balanced" mutual funds that invest in both stocks and bonds with the aim of providing income and stability of capital. Among the largest are the Axe-Houghton Fund B, Boston Fund, Eaton & Howard Balanced, Investors Mutual, George Putnam, Wellington.

Then, too, there are funds devoted to investment in life insurance and bank stocks, in Canadian or other foreign issues, and finally, among the latest additions to this long roster, the dual-purpose funds which will be discussed later in this chapter.

In all, nearly 57 billion dollars are now invested in these funds, representing the holdings in about 9 million individual shareholder accounts. Who are these investors who have decided to "let George do it"? About two-thirds are men, one-third women. More than two-thirds are married, and the largest age group is around the fifty-year mark. Almost a third of these investors are professionals, with the next largest group coming from executives and administrative workers.

The 1960s were good years for the mutual fund business. Between 1959 and the end of 1968, the number of shareholder accounts rose from 4.3 million to an estimated 9.0 million, and net assets expanded from $15.8 billion to $52.7 billion. By early 1972, assets passed the $56 billion mark.

In response to queries of why they chose the mutual fund route for investing, more than 75 per cent of investors gave professional management as their prime reason. Diversification of investment was the next important consideration, followed by the mutual funds' provisions for automatic reinvestment of dividends and capital gains, the convenience of purchasing the shares on a regular program, the ease of redemption, the convenience of receiving a single dividend check from their invested funds and the level withdrawal plan—especially for those who have retired.

Investment company data is readily available.

The *closed-end* companies' histories are recorded in all the standard manuals, in exactly the same way that past earnings and dividends and price levels of Chrysler Corp. and American Can are reported. Most of these issues are traded on the stock exchanges, and their day-to-day price fluctuations are easily followed.

The mutual funds are reported on by several special agencies which do an admirable job. These are *Investment Companies*, by Wiesenberger Services, 1 New York Plaza, New York City 10004; *The Mutual Fund Directory* published by the Investment Dealer's Digest, 150 Broadway, New York City; Kalb-Voorhis summary, 27 William Street, New York City; Johnson's Investment Company, *Charts; Fundscope Magazine*, Century City, California; Arthur Lipper Corp., 140 Broadway, New York City, as well as others.

You can look them over at your bank or broker's office or in the library.

Quotations are carried daily by many newspapers.

Public information center for the industry is The Investment Company Institute at 1775 K Street N.W., Washington D.C. 20006.

No matter what may be your program or your particular problem, every investor can, by scanning the list of investment companies, find a half dozen which will meet his requirements.

Naturally, the value of the individual investment company varies with the individual investor, according to the amount of money he has to invest, the length of time before he has to call upon this money for support and his own ability to acquire data upon which to base an investment program.

Young Morse—starting his program at an early age—could, if he wished, achieve moderate diversification on his own by buying at intervals small blocks of stocks in various industries. He has the time to study new industries and new corporations as they develop and invest in them whenever he becomes satisfied they are going to work out and become an important part of his future. If he makes any mistakes, he will have time to correct his course. If he himself has professional knowledge of, say, the chemical industry, or has a high-level job which brings him into daily contact with the industry, he might well then make his own decisions and pick his own companies for investment.

But if neither his training nor his work give him a special edge in following any industry he wants to invest in, and if he hasn't the ability to dig out the facts on his own, he might better leave the decision to funds which specialize in the field and can afford the expert technicians and financial analysts needed to keep abreast of scientific and financial developments.

If he should decide that peering into the future is a job he'd best leave to experts, young Morse will find a wide choice of open-end companies which concentrate almost entirely on growth industries.

Obviously he must prepare himself for little current income from some of these funds. Such funds pay only a small dividend because their holdings are concentrated mainly in young, growth-type businesses which plow back most of their earnings and pay out few, if any, dividends. This is characteristic of mutual funds that have substantial portions of their money invested in the young electronic, automation, chemical, atomic energy companies. Their chief rewards are in long-time growth of capital.

FUNDS FOR EVERY INDUSTRY

There are growth funds covering almost every industry which may attract Morse's fancy.

Chemical Fund, for example, is an open-end fund that concentrates its investments in companies in which the science and technology of chemistry play an important role.

If Morse feels that we are just now in the early stages of the miraculous age of chemistry he would naturally look over the prospectus of this company which in a decade has more than trebled its asset value. An investment in such a fund, for example, would give Morse participation in the shares of fifty or more leading chemical, drug and pharmaceutical, glass, oil and miscellaneous related corporations.

EASY-TO-GET INFORMATION

There are dozens more of these special funds. The slightest sign that you are interested will bring you complete prospectuses, records, past history and buying terms from almost any brokerage firm.

In every one of these instances, Morse can satisfy his desire to look toward the future. In addition, he has the consolation of knowing that even if he doesn't know the difference between U-235 and a downdraft carburetor his money is being managed by people who do.

Obviously, spreading his bet on the future among a hundred different companies will be far less profitable than if he could select the "General Electric" of the atomic energy field of 1995. But—by the same token—there will be far less risk of winding up with the kind of wallpaper which today is all that remains of the hundreds of electronic and auto companies which never made the grade.

Quinn, only a few years away from retirement, may have an entirely different approach to the use of investment companies. He wants a high degree of safety, with as much income as he can get. In this context, diversification is also an important consideration.

And bearing in mind that the higher the yield the higher the risk, and vice versa, he can find plenty of funds from which to make a choice.

Some open-end companies, in fact, have several series of funds, according to the goals and risks involved. Thus the investor has the opportunity to pick the fund which will closely parallel his own investment aims.

The "National" family of funds distributed by National Securities & Research Corporation, exemplifies a mutual fund organization designed for varying investment objectives. They have combined assets of over $1 billion and include the National Securities series of funds managed by National Securities & Research Corporation, Fairfield Fund, which is managed by a subsidiary company, Fairmont Advisory Service, Inc., and Capital Trinity Fund, managed by Stateside Asset Management Corp.

Shareowners of each of the funds have the privilege of modifying their investment program, whenever necessary, by converting to any of the other funds in the group with an objective better suited to their current needs. There is no sales charge for this exchange—the only cost is a $5 clerical fee. Purchases of any or all of the funds also may be lumped together by one investor to earn commission discounts available on larger investments. The National family includes:

National Growth Fund— seeks long-term growth of capital and emphasizes quality investments. During 1971 dividends of 16 cents per share and a capital gain distribution of 25 cents per share were paid. Its adjusted net asset value per share advanced 16 per cent during 1971. An assumed investment of $10,000 made on January 1, 1957, with reinvestment of all dividends and capital gain distributions, would have been worth $37,236 on December 31, 1971. A similar investment made 20 years ago on January 1, 1952, would have been worth $91,126, and one made 25 years ago $164,638. Total net assets at the start of 1972 were $303 million.

National Stock Fund—seeks a combination of reasonable capital appreciation possibilities and relatively good income. During 1971 dividends of 33 cents per share and a capital gain distribution of 17 cents per share were paid. Its adjusted net asset value per share advanced 5.1 per cent during 1971. The dual nature of the fund's goal is reflected in the results of an assumed $10,000 investment made on January 1, 1957. In the period ended December 31, 1971, a total of $9,897 in quarterly dividends and $9,905 of capital gains would have been automatically reinvested, and the account would have had an end value of $26,352. A similar investment made 20 years ago on January 1, 1952, with reinvestment of $27,139 in quarterly dividends and $25,419 of capital gains, would have been worth $62,044, and one made 25 years ago, with reinvestment of $46,867 in quarterly dividends and $40,977 of capital gains, would have been worth $98,279. Total net assets at the start of 1972 were $343 million.

National Dividend Fund—pursues an aggressive approach in seeking high current yield possibilities. During 1971 dividends of 21 cents per share and a capital gain distribution of 10 cents per share were paid. Its adjusted net asset value per share advanced 10.4 per cent during 1971. An assumed investment of $10,000 made on January 1, 1957, with reinvestment of $11,721 in quarterly dividends and $8,541 of capital gains, would have been worth $27,108 on December 31, 1971. A similar investment made 20 years ago on January 1, 1952 would have been worth $54,495 and one made 25 years ago, $88,849. Total net assets at the start of 1972 were $107 million.

National Income Fund–follows a balanced approach for income, investing in bonds, preferred and common stocks selected for relatively generous yields with a reasonable expectation of continuing such payments. Its adjusted net asset value per share advanced 12 per cent during 1971. An assumed investment of $10,000 made on January 1, 1957 with reinvestment of all dividends and capital gain distributions, would have been worth $26,057 on December 31, 1971. A similar investment made 20 years ago on January 1, 1952, would have been worth $47,435 and one made 25 years ago, $68,603. During 1971 dividends of 28 cents per share and a capital gain distribution of 6 cents per share were paid. Total net assets at the start of 1972 were $85 million.

National Securities & Research Corporation was the first mutual fund company to offer investors the ability to insure their investments against loss of paid-in capital. The insurance premium is not paid out of pocket but is automatically deducted from the shareowner's dividends before they are reinvested, and this amount, as well as the initial sales charge, is also included as part of the guaranteed coverage. This feature was available in over 30 states at the start of 1972. The insurance may be increased at any time to "lock in" profits if the shares rise in value. The two funds in the National family currently offering this feature are:

Fairfield Fund: is an aggressive capital appreciation fund which uses venturesome tactics, including leverage and technical analysis and assumes higher risks in an all-out, single-minded quest for growth. During 1971 dividends of 12 cents per share were paid, and its adjusted net asset value per share increased 18.9 per cent. Fairfield first became registered as a mutual fund on May 13, 1960, and an assumed $10,000 investment made on that date, reinvesting all dividends and capital gain distributions, would have been worth $28,-519 on December 31, 1971. At the start of 1972 total net assets of Fairfield were $54 million.

Capital Trinity Fund: began operations early in 1971. In seeking capital growth it emphasizes small to medium-sized emerging growth companies which are believed to have the managerial and financial resources to produce superior profits. The portfolio is relatively concentrated–only 34 issues were held at the start of 1972.

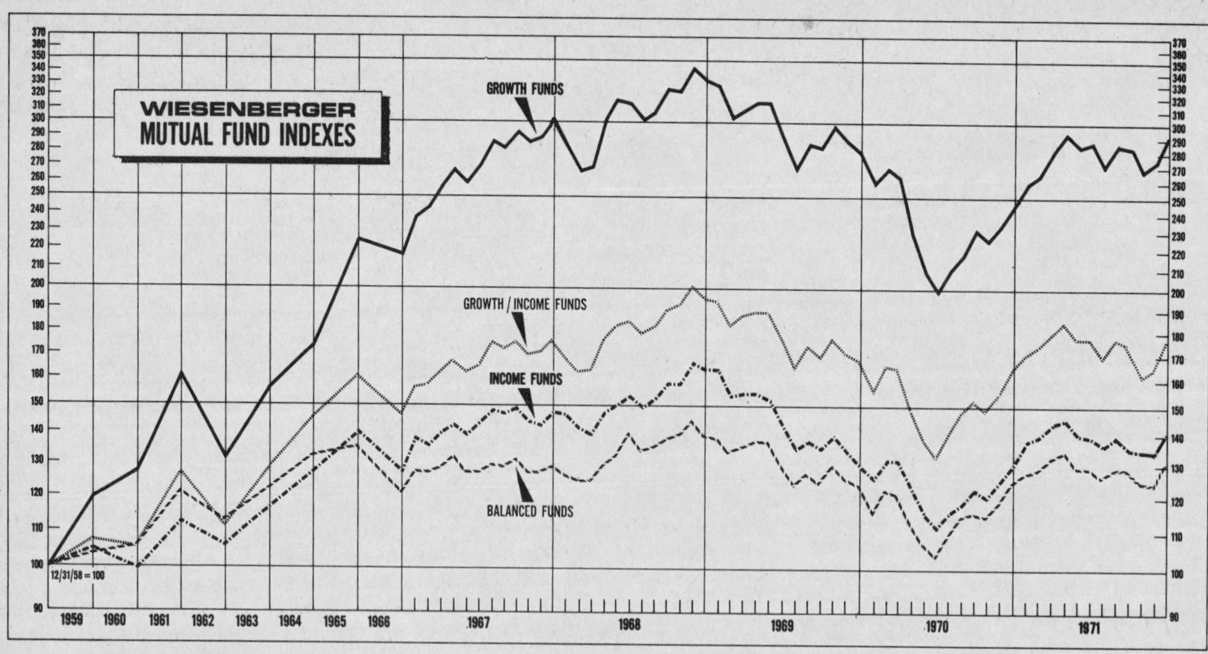

How various types of mutual funds have fared over the years.

The National family of funds is only one of many such groups.

If Quinn were to look at the Value Line Funds, he might, for example, leave Value Line Fund—which has as its primary objective capital growth "with regular income important but of secondary consideration"—to Morse, but find the Value Line Income Fund exactly to his liking. Its objective is a level of income "as high and as dependable as possible in keeping with sound investment principles and the investment outlook."

As noted before, there are hundreds of funds. Obviously, all are out to make money by varying combinations of the principles of investment—growth, income, safety. Morse can make his decision pretty much on the basis of the fund's avowed aims and its portfolio. If it is a growth fund specializing in an industry which he feels is headed for better days, he can reasonably assume that it will employ experts in the field who should be able to select appropriate subjects for investment. He will have to go pretty much on that faith, for most of these new era funds have only a few years' history on which to base judgment of their ability.

The older Quinn and Lefferts have a far larger field from which to make a selection and a longer history upon which to base their decisions. But that doesn't make their job much easier, nor does it reduce risk by very much.

It must always be remembered that an investment in a mutual fund's shares is an investment in the stock market. And the stock market is *never* without risk.

While it is true that the professional management and wide investment diversification provided by mutual funds do tend to reduce risk, this is only a generalization.

When the stock market went into a precipitous decline in 1969, most mutual funds suffered precipitous declines, too. In fact, The Arthur Lipper Corp.'s analysis of mutual fund performance showed that the mutual fund average decline for 1969 was 14.38 per cent, only slightly less than the 15.19 per cent drop in the Dow Jones industrial averages, and exceeded the 10.20 per cent drop suffered by the Standard & Poor's 425-stock average and 12.51 per cent decline of the New York Stock Exchange composite index.

These are *average* figures. Since the decline took place just when many of the newer, smaller growth funds were going all out to make "big scores," mutual fund declines of 20, 30 and even 40 per cent in that single year were not unknown. A new generation of mutual fund managers were learning the oft-repeated lesson that the higher the gains sought, the more the risk assumed. And their avid followers learned their lesson right along with the managers.

In fact, many funds continued to experience losses throughout 1970, even though the general stock market had bottomed out at midyear and finished December with slight gains. As against a Dow Jones advance of 4.82 per cent for 1970, the average mutual fund decline was 9.12 per cent.

By the time the recovery of late 1971 set in, many mutual fund managers had reorganized and "de-risked" their portfolio positions sufficiently to take advantage of the general market upturn.

Both mutual fund managers and mutual fund investors have learned painful lessons since the start of 1969. An entire crop of "go-go" fund managers have been wiped out and, to the credit of the industry, it can be said that the bulk of today's mutual funds are operating much closer to the "prudent man" rule, which was one of the founding precepts, than they were a few years ago. Long-term, this must be viewed as a constructive step, and one which increases the value of mutual fund investment for the average unsophisticated small investor who has neither the time to search out nor the ability to analyze investment opportunities.

It must be remembered, however, that in most mutual funds (with the outstanding exception of the recently formed bond funds), an important portion of the investor's ultimate reward comes in the form of market gains.

In the matter of judging income, therefore, it must be constantly emphasized that the yield of most investment companies—both closed-end and mutual fund—usually includes profits from securities transactions as well as dividends received. In other words, you receive payments from the investment company which are made up of both current income from investments plus your share of any profits the managers may have made on the purchases and sales of securities. This latter portion of your income is doubly welcome, since it is taxable only as a long-term capital gain, which means at only half your normal rate. *But*, it must also be borne in mind constantly that this portion of the income is highly speculative, depending entirely as it does on (1) your fund manager's ability to make profits in stock market dealings, and (2) even more important, the existence of a favorable, rising stock market.

In other words, an investment in an investment company—open- or closed-end—should not be made on the basis of its last fifteen years' achievements. With practically no exceptions, they were all good. The next fifteen years may be a far different matter, and that's when the company's objectives and, above all, its management will be of the utmost importance.

You will hear a common criticism of both closed- and open-end funds: *They don't do any better than the market averages!*

This may well be true of the investment industry as a whole.

But the fallacy lies in the offhand assumption that the "averages"—Dow Jones, Standard & Poor's or what have you—represent merely a willy-nilly, aimless sort of wandering of prices, a movement entirely without professional influence.

Nothing could be further from the truth!

The leading stock market averages are, in the main, made up of the prices of representative stocks which are very much in the line of sight of the nation's (and the world's) most sophisticated professional investors. Not just anyone can do as well as the averages. If you or any fund do as well as the averages, it's because you are doing some highly professional thinking.

To sum up: Arguments have been going on for nearly 50 years as to the value, as to the desirability, of investing via mutual funds rather than selecting one's own portfolio. With hundreds of different funds in the field, directed by hundreds of different managements it should be apparent that any valid decision, good for all time, will never be reached.

In recent years, mutual funds have suffered reverses in exactly the same way nonprofessional small investors and giant brokerage houses have.

The Investment Company Institute, which is the national organization for mutual funds, publishes a bimonthly *Forum* which is obviously designed to help the industry put its best foot forward.

Still, a recent study has some validity. Based on the annual average performance of all the funds listed by Wiesenberger's Investment Companies, here are the results of $9,150 ($10,000 less $850 in commissions) invested in this "average" mutual fund at the start of 1950. The figures include reinvestment of all dividends and capital gains:

Year	*Initial Investment: $10,000**	*% Change*	*Gain*	*Loss*
1950	$11,163	+22	$ 2,013	
1951	12,726	+14	1,563	
1952	14,126	+11	1,400	
1953	14,168	+ 0.3	42	
1954	19,977	+41	5,809	
1955	23,373	+17	3,396	
1956	25,009	+ 7	1,636	
1957	22,508	−10		$ 2,501
1958	31,061	+38	8,552	
1959	34,788	+12	3,727	
1960	35,831	+ 3	1,043	
1961	46,580	+30	10,749	
1962	40,525	−13		6,055
1963	47,820	+18	7,295	
1964	54,037	+13	6,217	
1965	65,385	+21	11,348	
1966	62,116	− 5		3,269
1967	83,857	+35	21,741	
1968	98,113	+17	14,256	
1969	85,358	−13		12,755
1970	79,383	− 7		5,975
1971	95,021	+19.7	15,638	
			$116,425	$30,555

Total Gains $85,021

Strictly for comparison, a $10,000 savings deposit made at the same time and compounded annually at 5 per cent would have grown to $29,256.

You will hear criticism of high mutual fund selling commissions (in cases where commissions are charged). And they are high—running to as much as 8½ to 9 per cent. However, the industry is highly competitive, so we must assume that selling costs are, also.

But when we talk of the small investor, it may become meaningless to carp about 8½ per cent mutual fund commissions or "loads" and annual fees of ½ of 1 per cent or less. Because the fact of the matter is that even in a period of almost constantly rising security prices, the ordinary small investor often comes nowhere near keeping step with the Dow Jones Industrial Index or any other market yardstick. In fact, it is often just during a period of booming prices that the novice (and, *let's be frank about it*, careless and greedy) investor gets taken in by a flood of blue sky financing which generally accompanies a rising stock market. In other words, why talk about an 8½ per cent load when many a small investor left to his own speculative devices can wind up losing 100 per cent of his money?

In conclusion, the mutual funds are by no means a panacea for every financial ill, nor even the best possible medicine. But they do fulfill a tremendous need, as witness their phenomenal growth in a comparatively short space of time. They do provide, *at a price*, diversification, professional management and regular, habit-forming saving-investing on a favorable dollar averaging basis.

Some plans, in addition, offer low-cost, declining balance term insurance which guarantees that the program will be completed for the investor's estate if anything happens to him. Those who can use more insurance should certainly look into this feature.

COST OF BUYING INTO INVESTMENT COMPANIES

The shares of most closed-end investment companies are traded on the stock exchanges. Some are traded over-the-counter. In either case you will pay a commission computed in exactly the same way that your commission would be figured in buying shares of any industrial corporation.

You buy most mutual funds through brokerage offices or through selling organizations set up to handle a series of funds or one fund. Commission costs will vary, starting as high as 8½ to 9 per cent of the total cost of the shares for small investments to half that amount or even less for sums running into the tens of thousands of dollars. Each fund has its own schedule of fees.

You can tell at a glance what the maximum fee is by checking the price of the fund in the special list of mutual fund quotations carried by many newspapers and financial publications. The fund will be listed thus:

	Bid	*Asked*
XYZ Fund	$11.34	$12.26

That signifies that the fund's asset value per share (its total assets divided by the number of shares outstanding) stood at $11.34 per share on this day. The asked price is the price you'd pay per share. The 92-cent difference represents the commission cost per share which, in this case, comes to 8.1 per cent. Another fund might be listed $13.12 bid, $14.00 asked, the 88-cent difference here representing a commission of about 6.7 per cent.

Some funds have a compulsory front-load system which consumes up to 50 per cent of the first thirteen monthly payments to prepay commissions for the entire life of the plan, and thus penalizes heavily anyone embarking on a ten-year investment program and dropping out before completion. (If you need pressure to keep on saving, this may be for you, but if your earnings record is haphazard, avoid it.)

THE NO-LOAD FUNDS

However, there are about 150 mutual funds with total assets of about 2 billion dollars, which charge no sales commission—very simply, because they have no salesmen or sales organization. Most of these funds grew out of investment advisory services which originally managed the investment of large sums for individuals, but were prevailed upon by smaller investors to open their services to them, also.

If you want to buy any of these mutual funds *you must take the initiative.* While these funds also do some of the modest, low-pressure advertising allowed the mutual fund industry, any inquiry on your part will not be followed up by a salesman, *because there are none.* If you don't follow up your initial query, there's no deal.

Some of the better-known of these funds include American Investors; deVegh; Dodge & Cox; Energy; Guardian Mutual; Johnston; Loomis-Sayles; Mutual Shares; Nassau; Nelson; Newton; One William St.; Penn Square; T. Rowe Price; Scudder, Stevens & Clark; Stein, Roe & Farnham.

You can always spot a no-load (no commission) fund merely by running your finger down the mutual funds list in any financial publication: the "bid" and "asked" price will be identical. For example:

	Bid	*Asked*
ABC Fund	$16.94	$16.94

Since no-load funds are likely to be far less advertised than the usual, commission-charging funds, and since they do not employ salesmen who will come out and present the story of the fund to you, it may be helpful if we list their names and addresses so that you may do your own investigating.

Remember: the no-load fund in a way is a sort of self-service market. If you don't walk in and sell yourself on the item, no one will be there to sell it to you. You must make the first move and all subsequent moves as well.

Following is a list of mutual funds which charge no sales commission (or, in a few cases, a low fee of up to 3 per cent) as published early this year by the No-Load Mutual Fund Association, 375 Park Avenue South, New York City 10022 (those charging a "low-load" fee of up to 3 per cent are marked by an asterisk):

	Objective	*Founded*
The Acorn Fund, Inc. 1 First National Plaza Chicago, Ill. 60670	Capital Appreciation	1970
Afortress Fund, Inc. 8 Pennell Road Village of Lima, Pa. 19060	Long Term Capital Growth	1971
Afuture Fund, Inc. 8 Pennell Road Village of Lima, Pa. 19060	Growth	1968
*Age Fund, Inc. 155 Bovet Road San Mateo, Calif. 94402	Growth	
*Leon B. Allen Fund, Inc. 120 Broadway New York, N.Y. 10005	Long Term Capital Appreciation	1952
*Alliance Growth Fund, Inc. Box 1032 Wall Street Station New York, N.Y.	Growth	1969
American Enterprise Fund 50 Broad Street New York, N.Y. 10004	Growth	1958
American General Growth Fund, Inc. Post Office Box 1931 Houston, Tex. 77001	Capital Growth	1964
American Investment Counseling Fund, Inc. 615 South Flower Street Los Angeles, Calif. 90017	Capital Growth	1965
American Investors Fund, Inc. 88 Field Point Road Greenwich, Conn. 06830	Capital Appreciation	1957
American Union Investment Fund, Inc. 1100 West Wells Street Milwaukee, Wisc. 53203	Long Term Growth & Income	1970
Aragon Fund, Inc. 170 4th Avenue Nashville, Tenn. 37201	Growth & Income	1970
Argonaut Fund, Inc. 1415 First Nat'l Bank Bldg. San Diego, Calif. 92101	Capital Appreciation	1968
*Atlantic Fund For Investment In U.S. Government Securities 110 Wall Street New York, N.Y.	Growth	1960
Armstrong Associates, Inc. 3200 First Nat'l Bank Bldg. Dallas, Tex. 75202	Long Term Capital Growth	1967
B.A.I. Fund, Inc. 666 Fifth Avenue New York, N.Y. 10019	Growth of Capital	1969
David L. Babson Investment Fund, Inc. 301 West Eleventh St. Kansas City, Mo. 64105	Capital Growth & Income	1959
Bank Stock Fund, Ltd. Tejon at Colorado Ave. Post Office Box 367 Colorado Springs, Colo. 80901	Capital Appreciation	1970
Barclay Fund, Inc. 30 Broad Street New York, N.Y. 10004	Capital Appreciation	1968
Beacon Investment Fund 1107 Bethlehem Pike Flourtown, Pa. 19031	Growth	

	Objective	Founded
Beacon Hill Mutual Fund, Inc. 75 Federal Street Boston, Mass. 02110	Long Term Growth	1964
Berger Kent Special Fund 102 Greenwich Greenwich, Conn.	Capital Appreciation	1968
Bernstein-Macaulay Special Fund, Inc. 767 Fifth Avenue New York, N.Y. 10022	Growth	1964
Berkley Dean Special Fund, Inc. 1345 Ave. of the Americas New York, N.Y. 10019	Capital Appreciation	1969
Bridges Investment Fund, Inc. 8401 West Dodge Road Omaha, Neb. 68114	Growth & Income	1963
Brown Institutional Fund, Inc. 915 Fort Street, Suite 1100 Honolulu, Hawaii 96813	Long Term Growth	1967
The Burnham Fund, Inc. 60 Broad Street New York, N.Y. 10004	Capital Appreciation	1969
California Venture Fund, Inc. 611 W. Sixth St. Los Angeles, Calif. 90017	Aggressive Growth	1969
Chesapeake Fund, Inc. 527 St. Paul Place Post Office Box 297 Baltimore, Md. 21203	Growth & Income	1970
Columbia Growth Fund, Inc. 621 S.W. Morrison Street Portland, Ore. 97205	Capital Appreciation	1967
Columbia Investors Fund, Inc. 621 S.W. Morrison Street Portland, Ore. 97205	Growth & Income	1967
Companion Fund, Inc. 900 Cottage Grove Rd. Bloomfield, Conn. 06002	Growth	1969
Compustrend Fund, Inc. 22 N. Front Street Memphis, Tenn. 38103	Capital Growth	1970
Concord Fund, Inc. 366 Madison Ave. New York, N.Y. 10017	Capital Appreciation	1949
Continental Mutual Investment Fund, Inc. 480 E. Woodrow Wilson St. Jackson, Miss. 39201	Long-Term Capital Appreciation	1959
Consultant's Mutual Investments, Inc. 211 South Broad St. Philadelphia, Pa. 19107	Growth	1962
Convertible Leverage Fund 1309 Highland Avenue Abington, Pa. 19001	Capital Appreciation	1970
Convertible Securities Mutual Fund 1309 Highland Avenue Abington, Pa. 19001	Growth & Income	
The Davidge Fund 1747 Pennsylvania Ave. N.W. Washington, D.C. 20006	Capital Appreciation	1969
Decathlon Fund, Inc. American Bank Bldg. Rm. 322 Portland, Ore. 97205	Long-Term Growth	1967
de Vegh Mutual Fund, Inc. 20 Exchange Place New York, N.Y. 10005	Capital Growth	1950
*Dern's Selected Fund, Inc. 134 Evergreen Place East Orange, N.J. 07018	Long Term Capital Growth	1969
Dodge & Cox Balanced Fund 3500 Crocker Plaza San Francisco, Calif. 94104	Income, Protection, Growth	1931
Dodge & Cox Stock Fund 3500 Crocker Plaza San Francisco, Calif. 94104	Long Term Growth & Income	1964
Doll Fund, Inc. Thackery Lane Mendham, N.J. 07945	Capital Appreciation	1968
Drexel Equity Fund, Inc. 1500 Walnut Street Philadelphia, Pa. 19101	Capital Appreciation	1961
Drexel Hedge Fund, Inc. 1500 Walnut Street Philadelphia, Pa. 19101	Capital Appreciation	1969
Drexel Investment Fund, Inc. 1500 Walnut Street Philadelphia, Pa. 19101	Capital Appreciation	1968
East/West Fund, Inc. 9301 Wilshire Blvd. Beverly Hills, Calif. 90210	Capital Appreciation	1970
Edie Special Growth Fund, Inc. 530 Fifth Ave. New York, N.Y. 10036	Capital Appreciation	1969
Edie Special Institutional Fund, Inc. 530 Fifth Avenue New York, N.Y. 10036	Capital Appreciation	1969
Eldorado Fund, Inc. 18158 Westover St. Southfield, Mich. 48075	Capital Appreciation	1970
Elfun Trusts 570 Lexington Avenue New York, N.Y. 10022	Growth	
Endowments, Inc. P.O. Box 7650 San Francisco, Calif. 94120	Growth	1969
Energy Fund, Inc. 120 Broadway New York, N.Y.	Long Term Capital Growth	1952
Farm Bureau Mutual Fund, Inc. 1000 Merchandise Mart Chicago, Ill. 60654	Long Term Capital & Income	1965
*First Multi Fund of America 60 E. 42nd St. New York, N.Y.	Long Term Capital Growth	1965

	Objective	*Founded*
First Spectrum Fund, Inc. 230 Park Avenue New York, N.Y. 10017	Long Term Capital Growth	1971
The 44 Wall Street Fund, Inc. 150 Broadway New York, N.Y. 10038	Capital Appreciation	1969
Fund for Mutual Depositors Inc. 200 Park Avenue New York, N.Y. 10017	Growth	1969
*Fund for U.S. Government Securities, Inc. 421 Seventh Avenue Pittsburgh, Pa. 15219	Income	1969
Fund of the West, Inc. 500 Union Street Seattle, Wash. 98101	Capital Appreciation	1969
*Fundex, Inc. 245 Park Avenue New York, N.Y. 10017	Capital Appreciation	1967
*The Fundpack 382 Miracle Mile Coral Gables, Fla. 33134	Capital Growth	1970
*GAC Growth Fund, Inc. 1040 Bayview Drive Fort Lauderdale, Fla. 33306	Growth	1969
*Garrison Growth Fund 50 Broadway New York, N.Y. 10004	Growth	1971
General Securities, Inc. 133 S. Seventh St. Minneapolis, Minn. 55402	Long Term Gains & Security	1951
*Gibraltar Growth Fund Post Office Box 7171 2455 E. Sunrise Blvd. Fort Lauderdale, Fla. 33304	Capital Appreciation	1967
Samuel Greenfield Fund, Inc. 25 Broad Street New York, N.Y. 10004	Capital Appreciation	1966
Growth Industry Shares, Inc. 135 S. LaSalle Street Chicago, Ill. 60603	Growth	1946
Guardian Mutual Fund, Inc. 120 Broadway New York, N.Y. 10005	Capital Growth & Income	1950
Hartwell & Campbell Fund, Inc. 345 Park Avenue New York, N.Y. 10022	Capital Appreciation	1965
Hartwell & Campbell Leverage Fund, Inc. 345 Park Avenue New York, N.Y. 10022	Capital Appreciation	1968
Hedberg & Gordon Fund, Inc. 111 N. Broad Street Philadelphia, Pa. 19107	Capital Appreciation	1952
*The Herold Fund, Inc. 35 Mason St. Greenwich, Conn. 06830	Capital Appreciation	1967

	Objective	*Founded*
The Hornblower Equity Fund, Inc. 8 Hanover Street New York, N.Y. 10004	Long Term Capital Growth	1969
The Hornblower Growth Fund, Inc. 8 Hanover Street New York, N.Y. 10004	Capital Appreciation	1969
Hyperion Fund, Inc. 126 Barker Street Mt. Kisco, N.Y. 10549	Capital Growth	1970
Incentive Fund, Inc. 3142 Wilshire Blvd. Los Angeles, Calif. 90005	Growth	1969
Interfund, Inc. 23 148th Avenue S.E. Bellevue, Wash. 98007	Capital Appreciation	1970
Investment Guidance Fund, Inc. Investment Plaza Cleveland, Ohio 44114	Capital Appreciation	1968
Investment/Indicators Fund c/o First Commander Corp. 120 Montgomery Street San Francisco, Calif. 94104	Capital Appreciation	1967
*Istel Fund, Inc. 345 Park Avenue New York, N.Y. 10022	Capital Appreciation	1953
Ivy Fund, Inc. 155 Berkeley Street Boston, Mass. 02116	Capital Growth	1960
Ithaca Growth Fund 100 Fairview Square Ithaca, N.Y. 14850	Capital Appreciation	1969
Janus Fund, Inc. 6780 E. Hampden Ave. Denver, Colo. 80222	Capital Appreciation	1970
The Johnson Mutual Fund, Inc. 460 Park Avenue New York, N.Y. 10022	Growth	1949
Josten Growth Fund Box 1386 Minneapolis, Minn. 55440	Growth	
LaSalle Fund, Inc. 135 S. LaSalle Street Chicago, Ill. 60603	Long Term Capital Appreciation	1971
League Investment Fund, Inc. 15600 Providence Drive Southfield, Mich.	Capital Growth	1971
Loomis-Sayles Canadian & International Fund, Ltd. Post Office Box 45 Toronto-Dominion Centre Toronto, Ontario, Canada	Growth	1959
Loomis-Sayles Capital Development Fund Post Office Box 499 Back Bay Annex Boston, Mass. 02117	Capital Growth	1960

	Objective	Founded
Loomis-Sayles Mutual Fund, Inc. c/o NE LESCO 501 Boylston Street Boston, Mass. 02117	Long Term Growth, Income & Protection	1929
Mairs & Power Growth Fund, Inc. West 2062 First National Bank Building St. Paul, Minn. 55101	Capital	1958
Mairs & Power Income Fund, Inc. West 2062 First National Bank Building St. Paul, Minn. 55101	Income	1961
Market Growth Fund 431 Fifth Avenue New York, N.Y. 10016	Capital Appreciation	1964
Mates Investment Fund, Inc. 1700 Broadway New York, N.Y. 10019	Long Term Capital Appreciation	1967
Mathers Fund, Inc. 1 First National Plaza Chicago, Ill. 60670	Capital Appreciation	1965
The Medici Fund, Inc. 120 Broadway New York, N.Y. 10005	Capital Appreciation	1968
Mediterranean Fund, Inc. 1578 Northway Mall Pittsburgh, Pa. 15237	Long Term Growth	1967
Moody's Capital Fund, Inc. 28 Park Place New York, N.Y. 10007	Diversified	1967
Moody's Fund, Inc. 28 Park Place New York, N.Y. 10007	Diversified	1966
Mutual Shares Corporation 200 East 42nd St. New York, N.Y. 10017	Short Term Capital Gains, & Income	1949
Mutual Trust 4901 Main Street Kansas City, Mo. 64112	Capital Growth, Income & Security	1944
Naess & Thomas Special Fund, Inc. 201 North Charles Street Baltimore, Md. 21201	Capital Appreciation	1960
The Nassau Fund Post Office Box 629 1 Palmer Square Princeton, N.J. 08540	Appreciation & Income	1957
National Industries Fund, Inc. 1880 Century Park E. Los Angeles, Calif. 90067	Capital Growth & Income	1958
*NEA Mutual Fund, Inc. 1156 15th Street N.W. Room 915 Washington, D.C. 20005	Long Term Growth	1964
Nelson Fund, Inc. 345 Park Avenue New York, N.Y. 10022	Growth	1955

	Objective	Founded
Nicholas Strong Fund, Inc. 312 East Wisconsin Avenue Milwaukee, Wis. 53202	Capital Appreciation	1969
No-Load Selected Fund, Inc. 1133 Chain Bridge Road McClean, Va. 22101	Long Term Capital Growth	1971
Northeast Investors Trust 50 Congress Street Boston, Mass. 02109	Income	1950
O'Neil Fund 3450 Wilshire Blvd. Los Angeles, Calif. 90005	Capital Appreciation	1965
Oceanographic Fund, Inc. 15 Exchange Place Jersey City, N.J.	Capital Appreciation	1968
The One William Street Fund, Inc. One William Street New York, N.Y. 10004	Capital Growth & Income	1958
*Old Dominion Investors 110 Bank Street Suffolk, Va. 23434	Income & Growth	1951
Pax World Fund, Inc. 224 State Street Portsmouth, N.H. 03801	Income	1971
PDI Fund, Inc. 2 Overhill Road Scarsdale, N.Y. 10583	Growth	1970
Penn Mutual Equity Fund, Inc. 530 Walnut Street Philadelphia, Pa. 19105	Capital	1958
Penn Square Mutual Fund 451 Penn Square Reading, Pa. 19603	Capital Appreciation	1958
Pennsylvania Mutual Fund, Inc. 431 Fifth Avenue New York, N.Y. 10016	Capital Appreciation	1962
Pension Equity Fund, Inc. 41 New York Plaza New York, N.Y. 10004	Capital Appreciation	1961
Pine Street Fund, Inc. 20 Exchange Place New York, N.Y. 10005	Growth & Income	1949
Platt, Tschudy, Norton Fund, Inc. 600 Dain Tower Minneapolis, Minn. 55402	Capital Appreciation	1971
Pro Fund, Inc. Valley Forge Colony Bldg. Valley Forge, Pa. 19481	Growth	1967
Professional Portfolio Fund, Inc. Post Office Box 208 Honolulu, Hawaii 96810	Growth	1963
Prudential Fund of Boston, Inc. 50 Congress Street Boston, Mass. 02109	Growth, Income & Security	1949

	Objective	*Founded*
Redmond Growth Fund, Inc. 1750 Pennsylvania Avenue N.W. Washington, D.C.	Capital Appreciation	1970
Rittenhouse Fund 2 Penn Center Plaza Philadelphia, Pa. 19102	Diversified	1948
The Rochester Fund, Inc. 31 E. Main Street Rochester, N.Y. 14614	Long Term Growth	1968
Rowe Price New Era Fund, Inc. 1 Charles Center Baltimore, Md. 21201	Growth	1969
Rowe Price New Horizons Fund, Inc. 1 Charles Center Baltimore, Md. 21201	Capital Appreciation	1960
Rowe Price Growth Stock Fund, Inc. 1 Charles Center Baltimore, Md. 21201	Long Term Growth	1950
Sagittarius Fund, Inc. 375 Park Avenue New York, N.Y. 10022	Capital Appreciation	1966
Scudder Development Fund 345 Park Avenue New York, N.Y. 10022	Long Term Capital Growth	1971
Scudder Special Fund, Inc. 345 Park Avenue New York, N.Y. 10022	Capital Appreciation	1956
Scudder, Stevens & Clark Balanced Fund, Inc. 10 Post Office Square Boston, Mass. 02109	Conservation, Income & Long Term Growth	1929
Scudder, Stevens & Clark Common Stock Fund, Inc. 10 Post Office Square Boston, Mass. 02109	Capital Growth & Income	1929
Sequoia Fund, Inc. 1 New York Plaza New York, N.Y. 10004	Capital Growth	1970
Shamrock Fund 1800 East Bridgegate Westlake Village, Calif. 94015	Capital Appreciation	1969
Shasta Fund, Inc. Montchanin, Del. 19710	Capital Appreciation	1970
Sherman Dean Fund, Inc. 140 Broadway New York, N.Y. 10005	Capital Appreciation	1968
Shearson Capital Fund, Inc. 14 Wall Street New York, N.Y. 10005	Growth	
Smith, Barney Equity Fund 1345 Avenue of the Americas New York, N.Y. 10005	Capital Appreciation	1968
Social Dimensions Fund 431 Fifth Avenue New York, N.Y. 10016		1971

	Objective	*Founded*
State Farm Growth Fund 112 E. Washington Street Bloomington, Ill. 61701	Growth	1967
State Farm Income Fund, Inc. 112 E. Washington Street Bloomington, Ill. 61701	Income	1967
State Street Investment Corp. 225 Franklin Street Boston, Mass. 02110	Growth	1924
Steadman Associated Fund 919 18th Street N.W. Washington, D.C. 20006	Income	1939
Stein Roe & Farnham Balanced Fund, Inc. 150 S. Wacker Drive Chicago, Ill. 60606	Protection, Growth & Income	1949
Stein Roe & Farnham Capital Opportunities Fund, Inc. 150 S. Wacker Drive Chicago, Ill. 60606	Long Term Capital Appreciation	1954
Stein Roe & Farnham Stock Fund, Inc. 150 S. Wacker Drive Chicago, Ill. 60606	Capital Growth	1958
S & P Counselors Fund, Inc. 1775 Broadway New York, N.Y. 10018	Capital Appreciation	1969
Torrence Equity Fund, Inc. 1775 Broadway New York, N.Y. 10019	Capital Appreciation	1969
Tudor Hedge Fund 120 Broadway New York, N.Y. 10005	Capital Appreciation	1968
United Services Fund, Inc. 115 E. Wright Blvd. Universal City, Tex. 78148	Capital Appreciation	1970
USAA Capital Growth Fund, Inc. 4119 Broadway San Antonio, Tex. 78215	Long Term Capital Growth	1971
Variable Stock Fund, Inc. Ninth & Main Street Richmond, Va. 23219	Growth	1957
Wade Fund, Inc. 63 S. Main Street Memphis, Tenn. 38103	Growth	1949
Washington Investment Network, Inc. 1001 Connecticut Avenue Washington, D.C. 20036	Capital Appreciation	1969
Weingarten Equity Fund, Inc. 331 Madison Avenue New York, N.Y. 10017	Capital Appreciation	1967
Western Venture Fund, Ltd. 106-10235 124th Street Edmonton 40, Alberta, Canada	Growth	1971
The Willow Fund, Inc. 1 Chase Manhattan Plaza New York, N.Y. 10005	Long Term Capital Appreciation	1970

	Objective	Founded
The Wilshire Fund, Inc. 3700 Wilshire Blvd. Los Angeles, Calif. 90005	Growth	1960
*C. M. Whipple Fund The 532 Building Rt. 38 & Hollywood Avenue Cherry Hill, N.J. 08034	Long Term Capital Growth	1967
Worth Fund, Inc. 4400 N. High Street Columbus, Ohio 43214	Long Term Growth	1957
W. S. & W. Fund, Inc. 20 Exchange Place New York, N.Y. 10005	Growth of Capital	1968

The existence of these two types of mutual funds side by side—one charging sales commissions of as much as 9 per cent and the other zero—may at first seem strange. But a moment's reflection will provide you with similar situations in life insurance, retailing and many other areas where one may either go in for self-service or pay a fee to be sold.

No conclusion as to the value or potential value of a long-term mutual fund investment can be drawn from the fact that one fund charges 8½ per cent commission and another charges no commission at all. The commission should not be your determining factor. It is paid for *selling* the fund, *not* for managing it.

Almost all mutual funds, whether they charge sales commissions or not, do take an annual management fee, running up to about ½ of 1 per cent of assets.

Addresses of most investment companies, as well as other pertinent information, may be obtained from The Investment Company Institute, 1775 K Street N.W., Washington D.C. 20006.

THE DUAL PURPOSE FUNDS

Early in 1967 a new type of investment fund came to market—the dual purpose fund.

Dual funds are closed-end investment companies established with two classes of stock. One class is called the "preferred" or "income" stock. Its holders receive all dividend income after deduction of operating expenses. Dividends, of course, vary, but a minimal annual return—in some cases around 6%—is promised and if that amount is not paid out in any one year, the shortage becomes a claim against future years, somewhat in the form of a cumulative preferred corporate share. The funds have a specified life, often about 15 years. These same preferred shares are also given first claim against the assets of the fund up to the amount of their original purchase price, plus unpaid dividends, if any.

The other class of stock is called "capital shares." These receive no income dividends during the life of the fund, have all capital gains reinvested and are entitled to all assets of the fund at termination—after satisfaction of the preferred, or income, shareholders' claims.

Thus, this new type of fund offers an inducement to Investor A, seeking current income, as well as to Investor B, interested in capital growth by diverting to each the proceeds of $2 at work in his chosen field for each $1 originally invested.

The investor interested in income receives the dividend income earned by $2 of capital for every $1 he put into the fund, but gives up any hope of growth. The investor interested in growth enjoys the efforts of $2 invested for every $1 he puts in, but gives up any claim on current income. Of course, this leverage, in the case of the capital shares, can work either way.

A year is too short a time to evaluate any medium of investment. While the dual funds have been hailed as still another product for the investment market "department store," there is not too much agreement on how well they have fared so far.

They may well satisfy your needs for growth or income, but—as is the case with all investments—should not be bought merely on the basis of their label. Only a reputable, experienced broker who knows your investment needs can advise you.

Remember, too, that since these are closed-end companies, you buy and sell your shares on the exchanges or in the over-the-counter market. There is no fixed "bid" or "asked" price, as is determined daily by open-end mutuals.

Among the leading dual purpose investment funds are:

American DualVest Fund—Haywood Management, 25 Broad St., New York City 10005

Gemini Fund—Wellington Management Co., 1630 Locust St., Philadelphia, Pa. 19103

Income & Capital Shares—John P. Chase, Inc., 535 Boylston St., Boston, Mass. 92116

Leverage Fund of Boston—Vance, Sanders & Co., 111 Devonshire St., Boston, Mass. 02109

Scudder Duo-Vest Fund—Scudder, Stevens & Clark, 10 Post Office Square, Boston, Mass. 02109

Hemisphere Fund—Tsai Management & Research Corp., 680 Fifth Ave., New York, N.Y. 10019

Putnam Duo Fund—Putnam Management Co., 265 Franklin St., Boston, Mass. 02110

MUTUAL FUND SELLING

Most funds—perhaps 85 per cent of those in business—are sold via salesmen. The salesman may work for a distributing organization handling one or more funds or he may be a representative of a brokerage firm. In any event, his business is to sell. And selling can often mean high pressure.

There is nothing illegal or immoral about high-pressure selling, per se. If it weren't for aggressive selling, far too many of us would be without life insurance protection, savings bonds, and other necessities of our financial life.

But it does mean that the process of buying a mutual fund is bound to be far different from investing in American Can or Zenith Radio. When you go into your brokerage firm to discuss one of the latter, your broker can afford to be impartial about the matter. There is no reason for him to favor one or the other except as one or the other may best suit your investment book. Commission rates are the same for buying either.

But if you express interest in a mutual fund, you must expect him to try to sell you the fund, or one of the funds, which his brokerage firm handles.

It is up to you, then, to decide whether the fund or funds he is selling best suit your needs. This is not easy. But, fortunately, there is *never* any rush to buy a mutual fund. Such an investment is a long-time proposition, at least ten years long and often designed for life. Mutual fund shares cannot double overnight. So you will suffer no great financial harm if you take another week or month to decide.

Whatever you do, *do not* allow yourself to be stampeded into buying a fund "by next Monday night" because you would then become an owner in time to share in a "big" capital gains distribution. All you will accomplish by this display of haste is to receive a $1.85 capital gains distribution, for example, which in reality is only a return of your own money, since the asset value of the fund will drop by $1.85 at the same time. Furthermore, you will have to pay a tax on that money, even though you had just turned it over to the fund only a short time before. If you have a choice, buy a mutual fund *after* the capital gains distribution has reduced the price of the stock.

INCOME vs. CAPITAL GAINS

If you are a young man looking for capital gain, select a growth-type fund—one invested in growth-type securities—aviation, electronics, chemicals, life insurance, synthetics, etc., etc.

If you are approaching retirement and will soon need income, consider only funds which are aimed at providing maximum income—funds which concentrate their investments in coppers, rails, utilities, cyclical manufacturing concerns, etc., etc.

Don't let a salesman talk you into a growth-type fund with the argument that his fund has been successful in rolling up large annual capital gains, so dividend income is not important. Capital gains are welcome, but dividend income is steadier.

If you are only six years from retirement, there isn't much point to your now initiating a ten-year monthly payment program, especially if 50 per cent of your first 12 or 13 payments will be used to prepay part of the commissions for the entire ten-year period. Unless you have money to spare in retirement you may not be able to continue the investment—and those prepaid commissions will be wasted.

Don't be overly impressed by a killing any particular fund made in the past year or in the past five or ten years. That's history. You're buying the future.

There are a few criteria anyone can apply to purchase of mutual funds.

While there is no law against investing in a fund created last year, you obviously have not got the history of management performance to go on that you have in a fund formed back in the '30s or '40s.

THE "GO-GO" FUNDS

The last few years have seen the creation of literally hundreds of small mutual funds—mostly aimed at high performance and dedicated to taking considerable risk in new corporate ventures for the sake of turning up a high percentage gain in assets.

In many cases, these new funds succeeded. Gains of 50, 60 and 100% in a single year were not unknown. It seemed that the "go-go" spirit which had been felt in dress, in dancing, in "jet set" activities had also infiltrated the field of finance. As often happens, the public flocked to the "go-go" funds. They became the darling of the glamour-seeking mutual fund investor.

For awhile, it seemed, the new funds had discovered a new principle of finance: take big risks in new, unproven companies—often in stock which was not yet qualified for public sale. The tide was with the "go-go" funds. The general market-wide interest in glamour stocks helped—especially as it made the more modest gains of the old-line, much larger mutuals seem Rip Van Winklish.

Then two things happened:

1. As the new funds' success attracted millions of dollars from eager investors who wanted to get in on the action, the funds' pace slackened. Reason: It simply is not as easy to find 50 hot investment or speculative situations into which one can put $50 million as it was to find 5 hot situations for investment of only $5 million.

2. The entire glamour market cooled off and the old-line blue chip stocks (held in large amounts by the longer-established mutual funds) began to reassert themselves.

The net result has been that the small, new, go-go funds, which scored sensational gains in 1967, closed 1968 with gains of 5, 10 and 15% and even with slight losses. In 1969 and 1970 they suffered much heavier losses. In 1971 these funds recovered and continued to improve into 1972.

The debate over the 1967–68 "go-go" mutual fund craze will continue for years in financial circles. They did prove a few arguments: 1) that a smaller fund can move faster and climb faster than a big, ponderous, $1½ billion or more fund (but if the smaller fund's success continues and it attracts billions in new funds, too, it no longer remains a small fund); 2) that "live," enterprising management can always find profitable investment opportunities, which is another way of saying that many of the large, old-line fund managements had not been doing as well as perhaps they might have.

Some important points that were *not* proved: The "go-go" fund is not the wave of the future; it did not set the pace for the entire mutual fund industry; its wheeling-dealing tactics are not adaptable to large funds and, in fact, may violate the spirit of the broad mutual fund ideal.

To give the "go-go" managements their due, they did

liven up the mutual fund scene. In fact, their experience may lead managements of bigger funds to try harder. But it does not follow that a "go-go" fund is every investor's dish any more than a low-slung sports car is every motorist's ideal vehicle.

BUY FUNDS FOR KEEPS

Take your time. And when you go in, try to go in for keeps. Don't let another salesman talk you into selling out your fund and buying his. Commission costs can be extremely high. Mutual fund shares are not for trading.

Many fund organizations will allow you to transfer from their growth fund to their income fund for a nominal fee, $5.

Many funds provide life insurance with their monthly acquisition program at extremely low rates. This is valuable but in no way to be confused with lifetime insurance. It is in the form of declining balance term insurance and assures the completion of your investment program should you die before the entire plan is paid up. That's worth considering. But don't let an eager mutual fund salesman talk you into canceling your life insurance policy and substituting this form of mutual fund coverage. In a ten-year $50-a-month program, the protection in mutual fund insurance is $5,950 during the first month, but only $50 in the last month of the tenth year. Thereafter, zero.

ONCE YOU'VE BEGUN THE PROGRAM

Ten years is a long time to look ahead. Investment, as well as other programs begun with enthusiasm, may begin to pall and, in fact, become an unbearable drain.

If you find yourself in such a bind—don't panic!

Whatever you do—don't just say the heck with it and walk away, giving up your prepaid commissions as well as other privileges.

Talk it over with your fund salesman. The mutual fund wants to keep you investing and will offer several alternatives.

You can cut the amount of the plan. Or better yet, you can stretch out the payment period so that instead of $50 a month, for example, you might make a payment every second, or every third month. In fact, in time of emergency, you can keep a mutual fund plan alive by making only one payment a year.

MUTUAL FUNDS AS RETIREMENT INCOME PROVIDERS

To this point we have dwelt more on the problem of differentiating among the various types of mutual funds and on their acquisition than on the use the retired person may make of them.

Once you have completed your ten-year acquisition program you may adopt one of several courses:

You may make no further payments, but allow dividends and/or capital gains to be reinvested in acquiring further shares;

You may take your dividends and capital gains in cash;

You may set up a level withdrawal plan which will give you so many dollars a month to live on;

You may redeem, cash in your shares.

The level withdrawal plan is one of the more interesting, fairly recent developments in mutual fund investing. It makes the mutual fund a handy device for financing retirement. It works this way:

Most funds in which you have $10,000 invested (one or two set the level at $5,000) will allow you to make a regular monthly withdrawal from the fund, measured in dollars or shares.

The widely accepted rule of thumb for this level withdrawal program—which can be so helpful in financing retirement—is that $50 a month can be withdrawn from a $10,000 investment, beginning around retirement age, with little danger that the investor will run out of money in his lifetime.

To make this payment, the fund will redeem enough of your shares every month to provide a payment of $50. Then, when it declares its dividends and capital gains, it will repurchase shares.

A well-run income-type fund, one can generally hope, will generate enough dividends and capital gains to at least keep your investment stake fairly level—offsetting your withdrawals with quarterly and annual reinvestments of the dividends and capital gains. Some funds, in fact, can boast that over various periods of time they have actually been able to increase the $10,000 investment, all the while paying out $50 a month to the investor. In some cases, and at other times, it would not be surprising if the $50 monthly withdrawal cut into assets a bit.

In any event, this plan—while a sensible one for retired folk—is *not a guaranteed annuity!*

You are drawing $50 a month from an equity investment. And equities may go up or down. But—to repeat—this particular rule of thumb has worked well in the past. But don't let anyone talk you into drawing, say, $100 monthly from $10,000. Yields of 12 per cent a year are not easy to come by.

As noted above, the monthly withdrawal may be set at a fixed number of dollars a month, or expressed in terms of shares.

If, let us assume, your mutual fund asset value now stands at $10 a share, you might ask the fund to sell five shares a month and send the proceeds to you. Naturally, if the price goes to $11, you will be getting $55; if it falls to $9, you will get only $45. If you need exactly $50 a month—this is no plan for you.

But if your budget can stand some slight variation from month to month, then the share plan works out slightly better over the years since you will not find yourself having to sell more shares when the price is low and fewer when the price is up—the reverse of the dollar averaging plan which is often so advantageous in buying mutual funds.

SOME QUESTIONS AND ANSWERS

Q. *Is $10,000 the minimum required for a mutual-fund annuity? I work for an organization which has no pension fund. Is it possible for me to invest a small amount in a mutual fund and gradually build up the payments over the years?*

A. Mutual funds don't offer annuities. These are offered by life insurance companies and by various religious and charitable institutions. An annuity, basically, is a *contract* that guarantees a monthly, quarterly, or annual income for life, or even longer.

Mutual funds *do* offer monthly withdrawal plans, and most do fix a minimum investment of $10,000, although some will set up a program for $5,000. The $10,000 plan, generally, will provide a check for $50 a month. There is *no* guaranty of how long this will last. Given good management and good markets, a fund could pay $50 a month out of $10,000 forever and even increase the value of the investment. Or, over a period of years, the $50 payments might wipe out the investment. Or anything in between. Such a plan is *not* an annuity. It is a system for drawing a regular monthly check with the hope that the fund can generate enough earnings to keep the $10,000 intact, or even increase it.

You can invest as little as $10 a month in some mutual funds. There is no top limit, so you can increase that payment any time you like.

Q. *I am in my mid-30s and am considering a growth-type mutual fund, starting with $500 and adding $500 a year thereafter. My broker suggested that I wait 3 weeks to a month, as the market is too unstable at this time.*

A. If you intend to invest several thousand dollars regularly over the next 10 or more years, it seems to me you're straining at a gnat to worry about getting the best market for your initial $500. I'm sure that broker has your best interests at heart. But in the two weeks since you've written your letter, the market has risen about 3 per cent. I don't think that's earth-shaking, but it does, it seems to me, indicate that it does little good to try to con the stock market.

Your idea is a good one. Get started, carry it through and "damn the torpedoes."

Q. *I invested $2,000 in a mutual fund which charged 8 per cent commission. Isn't that high? Would it be better for me to buy government bonds? I'm 54 and hope to retire at 62.*

A. If you divide the difference between the bid and asked price (which represents the sales charge) by the bid price you'll find your commission works out to about 9 per cent–all of which you could have determined before you made the investment, thus saving yourself the surprise.

Mutual-fund commissions run anywhere from zero to about 9 per cent. I don't think that has much to do with the desirability of your investment.

Government bonds–Treasuries or savings bonds–can play a role in most investment portfolios. But if you are trying to build capital for retirement, you need equities.

Q. *I'm interested in a mutual fund which has gone up and down with the market. But I have noticed that total assets have increased very fast in the last 7 years.*

A. Most mutual funds go up and down with the stock market. In fact, a good fund will pretty much keep step with the market. Growth of total assets may mean that the fund has been successful in attracting new investors (through aggressive salesmanship), or it may mean that its managers have been extremely skillful in the market, or both.

A far closer check on a fund's investment progress is the growth of assets *per share*.

Q. *Some years ago, when I was in the Army, I began a mutual-fund program for $20 a month. I didn't miss the money then, but after my discharge my financial condition was not very sound. I had to discontinue payments, even though much of the commission had been paid. I'm now able to invest $40 monthly. What would you suggest?*

A. Going back to that fund and discovering just where you stand. Funds are eager to see programs carried through to conclusion. I'm sure you can arrange something which will give you benefit of those prepaid commissions.

Q. *The manager of a local Stock Exchange member firm has urged us to buy two $10,000 blocks of mutual funds to help meet retirement income needs about 10 years hence. He is very enthusiastic about this combination, and this raises certain reservations in my mind. Does his firm make more by pushing these particular funds? What about no-load funds? I know they exist but am not familiar with them.*

A. If you're 10 years from retirement you surely have run into salesmen before. When you walk into an auto salesroom, you expect the salesman to push the make of car his firm handles. (Business would be in a sad state if he didn't.)

Most large brokerage firms specialize in several funds. I don't think there's anything sinister about that. Furthermore, sales commissions run about the same for most "load" funds.

No-load funds have no salesmen–therefore, no commission is charged (their "bid" and "asked" quotes are alike). It's up to you to make the advances. And you do that by writing to the funds directly. Many are members of the Investment Company Institute, 1775 K Street, N.W., Washington D.C. 20006, and you can get their addresses there, as well as in the earlier pages of this chapter.

Q. *I've been approached by a fund salesman who tells me that a voluntary program with his fund requires a minimum of $300 to start and $50 minimum thereafter. Is this customary?*

A. There is no "customary" figure. Some funds require $500 as an initial purchase and a minimum of $100 for subsequent purchases; others set the figures at $250 and $25; some ask only $25 initially and $10 thereafter; some have no minimum for either initial or subsequent purchases. There is no hard-and-fast rule. All that I would caution about is that you investigate the custodial charges, too. Sometimes you will find that the bookkeeping fees work out to a very high percentage on an extremely low payment plan. If that's so, you might do better to make less frequent payments of larger amounts.

Q. *I buy mutual-fund shares and reinvest income and capital gains. Do I pay a commission on this reinvestment? If I do, I'd like to quit and switch to another fund.*

A. Practically all funds reinvest capital gains at "asset value"—which means no commission. About half the funds do charge a commission for reinvestment of dividend income; the other don't. Neither case justifies switching.

Q. *Six years ago I invested $5,900 in 1,241 shares of a mutual fund. With reinvestment of income and capital gains I now hold 1,677 shares. I receive about 32 cents a shares. Should I sell out? I also hold 1,488 shares of another fund which pays 9 cents in dividends and 24 cents in capital gains. Is it worth holding? Should I buy Pacific Gas & Electric 6% preferred?*

A. You leave me completely in the dark by failing to give the name of the funds or even the prices at which they sell.

The Pacific Gas preferreds are all rated "double A" and yield 6 to 6½ per cent. But I have no way of knowing whether that is more or less than you are now getting.

Q. *Since each shareholder must pay a capital-gains tax on a mutual fund's distribution from realized gains, isn't it true that a person who buys shares in a fund which has substantial unrealized gains automatically buys a tax liability?*

A. Yes. But having said that, I don't know what you can do about it.

Let's review the situation first:

You buy 100 shares of XYZ mutual fund, paying an asset price of $12.50 a share (in addition to commissions, if any, which have no part in this discussion). Let's say that $2.50 of that $12.50 represents accumulated long-term gains on stock already in the portfolio. During the course of the year, the fund takes $1 of this gain by selling some securities on which it has profits. The $1 a share gain ($100 on your 100 shares) is distributed to you and you pay a tax of, say, 11 per cent (half your 22 per cent tax bracket). So you are paying out $11 taxes on a profit which you actually didn't enjoy, since that gain was already included in the price of the stock when you bought it. In other words, you were repaid $1 a share of your own money (and this $1 was then deducted from the asset value of the shares), but you had to pay a tax on it, nevertheless.

I repeat, I don't know what you can, or should, do about it. If you buy into a successful operation, you have to pay for that success—and capital gains are a stamp of success. Certainly you wouldn't want to avoid a fund because it has made profits. You wouldn't want to invest in a loser merely to escape paying taxes.

I do want to point out, however, that this is one more argument for not jumping into a fund with, say, $12,500, just because one fine morning you suddenly decide you must own stocks. If you buy into a mutual fund over a 10-year period, you not only get the advantage of dollar averaging, but certainly would also avoid, as you put it, buying a large accumulated tax liability.

One other observation is appropriate: Frequently I get mutual-fund queries from readers who ask an early reply because they must buy the fund shares "by next Tuesday" in order to get the capital-gain distribution. It should be obvious from the above that it's wisest to buy a mutual fund immediately *after* a capital gains distribution and not just before it.

Q. *Five years ago my broker persuaded me to buy a growth fund. I invested $5,000. Today it is worth $7,000. Now he is urging me to sell out and put the $7,000 into another, "hot" fund. Should I make the switch or sign up on a 10-year plan with the second fund? I'm 45.*

A. If he's so keen on hot funds, why didn't he recommend the second fund 5 years ago? It was hotter then, relatively speaking, than it is today.

I'd vote no. You've paid about $450 to acquire the first fund. It would cost you about that much to switch to the second. There's nothing really wrong with either fund. If you have funds to invest over the next 10 years, there's no reason why you can't let the first $5,000 fund stand and sign up on a monthly plan with the second. This chasing around from one fund to another just because one company enjoys an outstanding record in any one year can be expensive and futile.

Q. *I am a widow with 5 years to retirement, when I shall have income from annuities and pensions. As a hedge against inflation I should like to invest $150 a month from present salary. Is it too late for me to buy mutual funds?*

A. It is not too late for you to buy mutual funds, but you should not sign up for a 10-year "front-load" plan since you may not be able to continue payments after you retire.

However, you could buy mutual-fund shares under a voluntary plan which does not require prepayment of commissions or commit you for any length of time.

Q. *I have a mutual fund plan which will be completed this month. All dividends and capital gains over the last ten years have been reinvested. Should I cash it in or wait for higher prices?*

A. You don't have to do anything with it.

I'm sure that the fund will list the various options you have when you make your final payment.

Q. *Can a person who has been declined life insurance on an individual basis obtain mutual fund life insurance protection?*

A. He may.

This is an important matter and, as in many such questions, can't be given a simple yes or no answer.

Many mutual funds (mostly, contractual front-loads, but including some which sell voluntary programs and some which charge no commissions) offer a form of de-

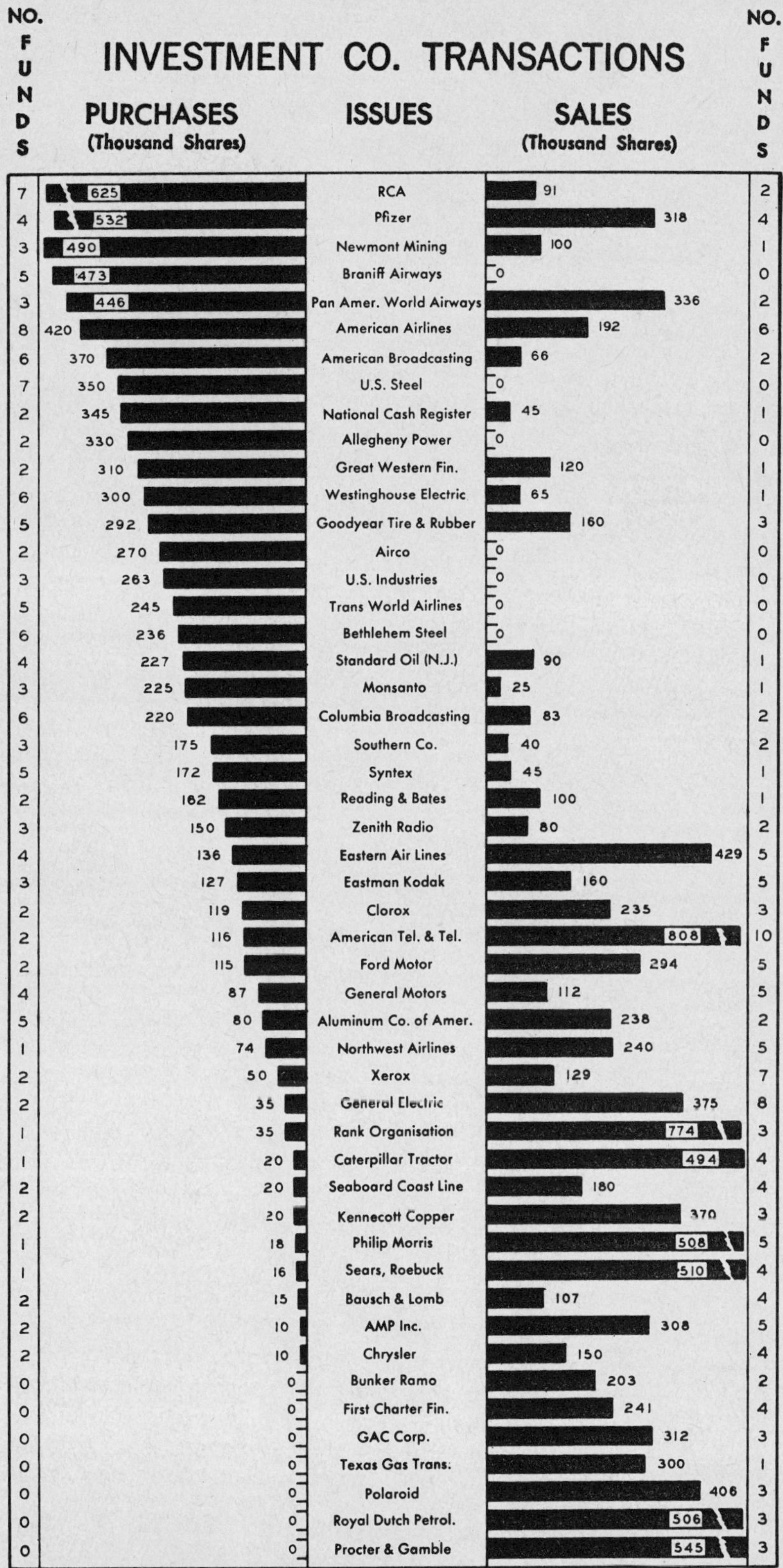

—from Standard & Poor's The Outlook

clining balance life insurance which guarantees completion of the plan for the benefit of his estate should the investor die before the program has been completed.

This should be clearly understood. It is *not* a life insurance policy. It does *not* guarantee any fixed amount of money.

If an investor agrees to put $50 a month into a mutual fund plus insurance, for 10 years, and dies after having made 35 payments, the insurance company will immediately complete the program by making the balance of the 120 payments–in other words, by buying $4,250 worth of stock. The beneficiary then receives a completed program. There is *no way* of knowing ahead of time what such a plan would be worth in dollars.

The $1,750 put in by the investor himself may be worth $3,000 at his death, or $750 or $1,500. So if the widow were to cash in her completed plan immediately she could get $7,250, or $5,000 or $5,750.

But the plan does offer valuable protection at a modest cost.

Premium costs vary, generally run upwards from 50 cents per month per unpaid $1,000. That means the investor's monthly insurance costs decline as the number of his monthly payments into the fund increase. Since this is group insurance, all ages pay the same rate.

In most cases, an investor seeking mutual fund insurance will be asked to fill out a medical questionnaire. If this indicates some health problems, he may be required to pass a physical examination. The examination may also be required automatically of any one who is above a certain age or is investing large amounts.

A person who has some health problem may be accepted for insurance at an increased rate, say 75 cents per month for $1,000 as against 50 cents.

Some companies are more lenient than others. Some will accept people above 60 years of age, others may not.

All I can say to anyone who wants to combine some life insurance protection with his mutual fund is: shop around. If you have insurance problems, it may well be worth it.

Q. *We own several hundred shares of one fund and a smaller amount of a second. The first, which sells for about $9.50, paid out 48 cents in dividends and 44 cents in capital gains–a total of 92 cents–last year while the second, which sells for about $15.25, paid out 37 and 50 cents, a total of only 87 cents. How do you account for the fact that one distributes a total of nearly 10 per cent while the second distributes less than 6%. I asked my broker, but he couldn't explain. I could sell the second at a profit and put the proceeds into the first.*

A. Comparing mutual fund performances can be tricky –and when you do so on the basis of one year's results you are using far too narrow a base.

Fund A, it's true distributed 92 cents last year and, as of the day your letter was received, had asset value of $9.43 a share. But if you look back over the last ten years you will find that its advantage over Fund B is far from clear. During that period, the first fund has risen only about $2 in asset value, a gain of about 27%, whereas the second has risen from about $8.25 to about $15.25, or a rise of about 85%.

So if you were to add long term gain to annual payout you could make quite a case for Fund B.

Also, fund goals vary. One may aim at aggressive growth and assume all the risks necessary thereto. A second may offer a higher degree of safety. It would be unfair to compare the two on the same basis.

Q. *We have about $5,000 invested in A.T.&T., Commonwealth Edison, North American Car, National Biscuit, National Distillers, American Machine & Foundry, Northeast Utilities (all common) and some Arkansas Louisiana Gas preferred. Income is our goal. It has been suggested that we sell out everything and put the money into a mutual fund.*

A. It sounds like a pat answer. All your stocks are fair to good quality. Some–such as Arkansas Louisiana Gas and Northeast Utilities–are yielding 5% or more. I see no reason for selling out anything paying you a good return and then paying another commission to reinvest the money in an income type mutual fund.

Some of your lower yielders could be sold and the proceeds put into a mutual or into a high yield common or preferred.

Q. *I am a resident physician, married to a school teacher. I have 2 more years of training, to be followed by two years of military service before I can open an office. We have $10,000 in E bonds. Should my goal be to invest in short term or long term mutual funds, individual issues, or to retain the savings bonds?*

A. Four years is long enough to try for capital gain.

Certainly, it's long enough to have inflation enter into the cost of operating a doctor's office.

I don't know what the level of the stock market will be four years from today, but I think you'd be justified in putting some of this money into good grade common stocks. The balance could be kept in bonds as an emergency fund.

There are no "short-term" mutual funds. A mutual fund investment, almost by definition, is long term, and the longer the better.

Q. *Where do I get a list of no-load mutual funds, and their addresses?*

A. The same place you find load funds–in the newspaper listings. If you see a fund listed: "bid, $17.10; asked $17.10" or "bid, $15.28; asked, $15.28" you're looking at a no-load fund. If the fund is quoted: "bid, $7.11; asked, $7.78," you're looking at a "load" or sales commission fund, and the 67-cent difference between the bid and the asked prices represents that sales fee.

Most funds are members of the Investment Company Institute, 1775 K Street N.W., Washington, D.C. 20006, and you can get addresses there. Also, see earlier pages of this chapter.

Q. *I notice you told a widow that you wouldn't advise switching stocks earning 5 or 6% into a mutual fund. I bought $3,000 worth of a fund in April 1964. Today it's* *worth $4,655. That seems to me much more than a puny 5 to 6% annual interest rate.*

A. It is. But the 5 to 6% can be obtained regularly, with little risk. The widow can count on it to help pay grocery, rent and clothing bills.

Evidently you didn't need any income from your capital, so you could take a chance at capital gain—and when I use the word "chance" I mean just that. The dictionary defines chance as "something that happens unpredictably." And the synonyms given are "luck" and "risk."

Q. *I'm planning to put $10,000 into a mutual fund and withdrawing $100 a month. The statement the fund showed me indicated that during the last ten years the fund would have grown to $14,000 after withdrawing $100 a month.*

A. I have absolutely no quarrel with the figures. I'm sure this reputable fund is reporting the facts. But what can't be put into a printed statement is the fund's experiences in the next decade. Generally, a $50-a-month withdrawal is suggested from a $10,000 investment.

Q. *I don't understand no-load mutual funds. Certainly you must pay for the service some way.*

A. You pay for the services of a no-load fund in exactly the same way you pay for the services of a fund charging commission: by paying a management fee based on total assets of the fund. It generally comes to a fraction of 1 per cent. This fee is charged by BOTH "load" and "no-load" funds.

The commission fee charged by load funds is paid to the salesmen and distributing companies involved in selling you the shares. Since no-load funds do not have salesmen or selling organizations (you buy the shares directly from the fund) there is no selling commission. It's as simple as that.

Q. *I have $1,000 invested in a mutual fund but have always felt the commission charges are too high. I would like to get into a fund which charges no sales commission, or possibly a fund that sells at a discount.*

A. That commission fee may or may not have been too high. But what has that got to do with selling the fund now? That fee has already been paid, and it's paid only once.

There are mutual funds which have no salesmen, therefore charge no commission.

There are also *closed-end* investment companies (not mutuals) which are traded on the exchanges and which you buy and sell by paying regular stock exchange commissions.

Some do sell at a discount from asset value but as I have pointed out many times that means very little, if anything.

Q. *I bought a mutual fund several years ago and have been very disappointed with its growth. Should I sell out?*

A. The fund you bought is a balanced fund—with large holdings of bonds as well as common stocks. If you want growth, you're in the wrong fund. Yours is designed to provide income and stability.

The time to find out what you're buying is BEFORE you put your name to the dotted line.

Q. *I was suddenly widowed a year ago. Should I put all my assets into mutual funds?*

A. It depends upon what those assets are earning for you now. It might be they are in good real estate, or good common stocks and bonds yielding 5 to 7%. In that case, the answer would be no.

Q. *I'm told certain mutual funds offer free life insurance.*

A. Many mutual funds offer declining balance term insurance with their investment plans. Costs are generally quite low. You may include it in your plan, or not—as you choose. But if you do you must pay for it.

OWNERSHIP OF MUTUAL FUNDS BY INCOME, AGE AND EDUCATION

	% of All U.S. Households	
Total Family Income	*Aware of Funds*	*Own Funds*
Under $8,000	16.8	2.4
$8,000-$9,999	28.4	6.2
10,000-14,999	41.4	11.7
15,000-24,999	50.0	17.9
25,000 or more	70.0	30.0
Age		
Under 30	39.4	5.8
30-34	37.5	10.7
35-44	37.6	9.4
45-54	33.6	10.7
55-64	23.4	7.5
65 over	13.8	4.1
Education		
Grade School	5.1	.6
Some High School	15.9	1.9
High School Complete	26.5	6.6
Some College	59.5	14.3
College Complete	67.4	21.7
Post Graduate	88.6	28.6

Q. *I am buying a mutual fund at the rate of $100 a month. Are the monthly commissions deductible on my annual income tax report?*

A. The commission paid out to acquire any equity is added to the cost of the equity. The commission you expend each year is *not* deductible on your annual income tax reports. Instead, it goes into the price of the stock.

When you sell, your taxable capital gain is reduced by the amount of the buying commission (and selling commission, if any). If you sell at a loss, this loss—which is a deduction—is thus increased by the amount of commissions.

Q. *I am 21, will join the armed forces in September for a 4-year term. I would like to put $25 a month into a mutual fund. My father feels I will be strapping myself in case of an emergency and also feels I will not have enough money to start a mutual fund. This fund allows me to miss a monthly payment without penalty. Also, I can sell the stock at any time. I have $1,000 in the bank and some savings bonds.*

A. I think your plan is a good one. It will enable you to build a common stock portfolio indirectly, by merely sending your money in to a fund organization and "leaving the investing" to them.

The type of program you set up is, of course, solely up to you. If you sign up for a contractual, front-load plan you will be expected to send in your $25 every month (although all funds will listen to reason if a payment is skipped–especially in the case of an investor in the armed services).

Many funds also offer voluntary programs–which means there is no contractual agreement binding you to a monthly payment.

All funds, of course, allow you to sell your stock (redeem your shares) at any time–at the current asset value–although if you sell out a contractual "front-load" plan you will lose prepaid commissions. (Half the first 12 or 13 monthly payments are used to prepay commissions, not buy stock, and you don't get these commissions back if you quit before the plan is completed.)

Many plans also offer low cost declining balance term insurance. So you might consider that feature, too. I am sending you an information sheet on mutual funds.

I think your father is unnecessarily concerned.

You have enough money to start a plan, and enough to maintain it. (In fact, a somewhat larger monthly payment would reduce your overhead charges percentagewise. While a lot of fuss has been kicked up by the SEC and others over the mutual fund industry's selling practices and charges, the unconscionably high custodial fees and bookkeeping charges are being swept under the rug. On a small monthly payment they can amount to as much as 3%.)

But, charges or not, I think the plan is basically a sound one. It will give you a regular "painless" investment program for 4 years and could prove the basis for a sound lifetime plan.

Q. *I own some mutual fund shares. I have always paid taxes on annual capital gains distributions. My broker insists that I do not need to report capital gains distributions from mutual funds until I actually sell the shares.*

A. That's his story; but you had better not get stuck with it.

Mutual fund capital gains distributions are taxable as received. And that holds whether you spend the money on a new car or reinvest it in additional shares of the fund.

The capital gain you report when you sell your shares is the amount you receive over and above the total amount you invested. (And in that amount invested you should include all reinvested dividends and capital gains.)

There are two types of gain involved:

The first is the trading profit the fund has taken during the year and passed on to you–to be spent or reinvested. That's taxable in the year received. The second is the profit you make when you cash in your investment, turn in your shares for redemption. That, of course, becomes a tax liability only when you sell shares at a profit.

Q. *Why are capital gains distributions deducted from the price of a mutual fund share? My investment seems to get nowhere.*

A. If a fund distributes $1 in capital gains it has made in stock market transactions during the course of the year, that $1 is no longer in the fund. Since the bid price of a fund is the sum total of its assets divided by the number of shares outstanding the price must reflect this distribution. You can't have the same $1 in your pocket as well as in your fund.

If you reinvest the $1 in additional shares you have more shares, but that doesn't alter the fact that the distribution was made. The $1 is now back in the fund, but there are more shares outstanding.

By your own figures, your $7,000 investment over the last three years is now worth $8,600. It's not a sensational advance, but, then, you invested in a conservative income fund and this performance is just about in line with the group.

Q. *Why does one closed-end investment company sell at a premium (over net asset value) and another at a discount?*

A. Because investors think that one company does more with its assets than the other.

Q. *We began investing in a mutual fund a few years ago and now find we can't continue. Can we quit?*

A. You can always quit. You didn't sign any binding contract. Whether you SHOULD quit is another matter.

If you have a front-load–contractual–program (one which deducts 50% of your first 12 monthly payments to prepay commissions for the entire 10-year plan) you're going to lose money by quitting now. If this is the case, you ought to discuss your problem with the agent and see whether you can't keep the plan alive (and get some use out of those prepaid commissions) by stretching out your payments.

If it is a voluntary fund plan (which deducts the same commission from each payment) then, of course, you lose nothing by quitting.

Q. *How do I go about getting information on a mutual fund without dealing with a broker?*

A. By asking the fund directly for its prospectus. You can get its address from the Investment Company Institute, 1775 K Street N.W., Washington, D.C. 20006. The Institute sells nothing. It is the national information center for the investment-company industry.

Q. *I've been considering investing in a mutual fund which has been suspended for a while. When sale of shares is once more permitted, will the inflow of money cause the price to rise or drop?*

A. Purchases or sales of a mutual fund's shares have no effect on the price of those shares. The mutual fund prices its shares by dividing its total assets by the number of shares outstanding. If it has $10 million in investments and one million shares outstanding, the asset price is $10 a share. If you buy 100 shares, you add $1,000 in cash to the $10 million so that the asset value of the fund is now $10,001,000 and it has 1,000,100 shares outstanding.

The asset value is still $10. The same process–in reverse–takes place when you redeem your shares.

Q. *You recently wrote that mutuals generally don't yield 5% income, but that income is generally around the 1 to 3% level. This is hard to understand. We received 32 cents in dividend income and 69 cents in capital gains per share from our fund in 1968, which, to my way of figuring, works out to about 10% on the present value of the stock. Aren't capital gains as useful to the investor as dividend income?*

A. As a matter of fact, capital gains are more useful since they are generally long-term gains and therefore taxable at only one-half the rate you pay on dividend income.

However, the mutual fund industry's policy–going back to the basic Investment Company Act of 1940–holds that only dividends may be counted in the income computation. Capital gains are excluded.

I agree that if you are retired and receive $1.01 a share in both income and gains, you can spend all of it, but the fact remains that they are not exactly alike, if only because the capital gains portion is much more "iffy" than the income portion.

If you look back at your fund's records you'll find that in poor market years, the capital gains distribution was less than half of what you received for 1968, whereas the dividend record was far more stable. Also, you must realize that your fund today is selling at only a few cents a share above the level of 10 years ago. It's been a good milch cow, but hasn't won any glamour prizes. I'm not knocking it. I'm just trying to tell it as it is.

Q. *Could you please send me a prospectus on a mutual fund?*

A. I don't have any, but a request to the Investment Company Institute, 1775 K Street N.W., Washington, D.C. 20006, will bring you the address of the fund, and a note to the fund will bring you all the information you desire.

Q. *Last month I completed a $15-a-month, 10-year mutual fund plan. My stock is now worth $3,000. Should I withdraw the money and reinvest elsewhere?*

A. Not necessarily. The fund has shown an ability to grow and also pay out roughly 5% a year in total gains and dividend income. As an equity investment it serves as a hedge against inflation. Do you need one? The only other income you mention is dollar-fixed. If, however, another $60 a year is necessary–at the expense of giving up inflation protection–the $3,000 could go into high-grade utility bonds.

Q. *I own some closed-end investment companies and am pleased with their performance. However, I'm puzzled by the fact that few of the directors are substantial shareholders.*

A. I don't think one can make much of a case for or against large ownership positions by directors–of any corporation. A much-sought-after director might well be on the board of quite a few corporations. It would be unrealistic to expect that he could hold large blocks of all the companies.

Q. *Suppose I have $20,000 invested in 1,000 shares of a mutual fund. I receive in one year $800 in capital gain and $400 in dividend income. I reinvest both in 60 additional shares, and pay a tax on both gain and income. Is my tax cost for the 1,060 shares I now hold $20,000 plus my Federal and state income taxes?*

A. No. Your tax cost for the 1,060 shares is your original $20,000 plus the $1,200 gain and income on which you paid taxes, or $21,200. The $1,200 you reinvested is as much your money as was the original $20,000.

Q. *A few years ago we put about $7,000 into a mutual fund. We haven't gotten the growth we expected. Should we switch?*

A. Just how much growth did you expect from a fund which is income-oriented and substantially invested in bonds?

SHAREOWNERS OF FUNDS AND CORPORATIONS

(By Size of Metropolitan Area)

	MUTUAL FUNDS		*ALL PUBLIC CORPS.*	
Size of Metro Area (Total Population)	*Share-owners (000's)*	*Percent of Total*	*Share-owners (000's)*	*Percent of Total*
1,000,000 or more	4,032.2	47.7	14,647.0	47.5
750,000 to 999,999	358.6	4.3	1,733.0	5.6
500,000 to 749,999	577.5	6.8	2,290.0	7.4
250,000 to 499,999	653.2	7.7	2,679.0	8.7
100,000 to 249,999	594.2	7.0	2,064.0	6.7
Less than 100,000	71.1	.9	286.0	.9
ALL METRO AREAS	6,286.8	74.4	23,699.0	76.8
NON-METRO AREAS	2,126.9	25.2	6,913.0	22.5
TOTAL U.S.	8,413.7	99.6	30,612.0	99.3
U.S. Territories, Possessions, & Foreign	36.3	.4	238.0	.7
	8,450.0	100.0	30,850.0	100.0

INDIVIDUAL MUTUAL FUND SHAREOWNERS

(Selected States)

State	*Shareowners (000's)*	*Male (%)*	*Female (%)*
California	1,517.6	47.2	52.8
New York	667.2	49.7	50.3
Pennsylvania	515.4	44.8	55.2
Illinois	439.1	48.6	51.4
Florida	414.0	44.2	55.8
Ohio	329.4	48.7	51.3
Massachusetts	329.3	49.5	50.5
Michigan	329.3	47.7	52.3
All other	3,908.7	48.7	51.3
Total	8,450.0	48.0	52.0

Your question—rephrased into more popular terms—would read like this: "A few years ago we bought a five-ton truck. We carry a lot of baggage, but we can't get the speed our friends are getting out of their sports cars."

There are more than 500 mutual funds. Their goals range all the way from all-out growth to conservative income; their investments, all the way from exotic, young 21st century companies to large portfolios of "AAA" quality utility bonds. Yet for some reason or other most of the letters I receive concerning mutuals reveal no appreciation of this wide variation in make-up.

When you are approached by a mutual fund salesman—or when you approach a no-load mutual fund that has no salesman—your first job is to determine just what sort of fund you're talking about.

If you are a young person interested in building capital, consider only those funds aimed at growth. If you are on the verge of retirement and want safety and income, consider the income and balanced funds. But don't rush in and buy one type and then complain because you didn't get the service the other type is offering.

The Wiesenberger listing of mutual funds has no fewer than a dozen different categories of funds. I'll grant you that the lines of demarcation are arbitrary. But at least you can get a general idea of what you are going in for. If you see a growth fund that distributes about 0.1% in dividend income, don't buy it in haste and then regret at leisure that you're not getting big dividend checks. Conversely, if you go to the other end of the scale, as you did, and buy a fund which is so heavily invested in income stocks and bonds that it can pay out 4.7% in dividends, don't complain that it hasn't performed like a "go-go" fund.

And these points hold true whether you are considering a load fund or one that charges no sales commission.

Q. *I'm a young retiree with substantial amounts in savings at 5 per cent and a mutual fund. I'm being clobbered by inflation. Should I sell out the mutual fund and buy common shares?*

A. The mutual fund is about 95 per cent invested in common shares already.

Q. *About two years ago I bought 200 shares of a mutual fund at $13.62 a share. I now realize it is a load fund. Would I lose money if I sold out? What would you suggest as an income type of investment when I retire? I'm now 49.*

A. I don't see much point to yelling ouch so long after you've been bitten.

When you say you "now realize it is a load fund" all you're doing is confessing that you did not look before you leaped. It takes no trick to determine whether a fund charges a commission. The price listing tells you that. If the bid is $16.05 and the asked price $17.59, you should know that the commission is the difference, or $1.54 per share. If the bid and asked are both $12.15, there is no commission. It is a no-load fund.

Now as to your particular investment. Current bid is $16.05 so your 200 shares are worth $3,210 as against the $2,724 you paid in. Considering the rough market of the last two years I'd call that pretty good and see no reason why a person of 49 should turn up her nose at such a performance.

As to retirement income—let's wait and see what's being offered in the year 1985. Maybe by that time stocks will once more be offering more than bonds. Who knows? Why borrow worries ahead of time? Right now your job is to build capital.

Q. *I must buy some mutual fund shares in three days. Please let me know as soon as you can.*

A. It should be obvious that going through channels, your answer can't get back to you in so short a time. Furthermore, you should resent—and refuse to be influenced by—any such "hurry-up" investment recommendations.

I can't think of any good reason why any mutual fund must be bought within the next three days (except, of course, the agent's rush to collect his commissions).

Q. *I'm a tax consultant. Will you please tell your readers to keep strict account of every dollar they pay for their mutual fund shares* plus *every dollar of dividends and capital gains they reinvest to accumulate additional shares? This is all needed to determine their capital gain or loss.*

A. I've done so many times and I'm glad to do it again.

Q. *A few years ago a broker talked me into selling some stock and buying $32,000 worth of a mutual fund for the monthly income. I got $230 a month, but my investment has dropped in value. I'm afraid I won't have any left.*

A. The fund is one of the better-managed mutuals and if you just had to pull all your money into it at the peak of the stock market I suppose you're lucky it was one of these better ones.

Your trouble is that you've been taking about 8¾ per cent out of the fund—far too much for the market experience of the last few years. It is a growth fund, and if it doesn't make stock market profits it doesn't have much to pay out, since its regular dividend income runs a bit less than 1½ per cent (which is not out of line for growth funds).

I'd say you ought to stay with it (its price has already improved since your letter). But you'll have to cut down your monthly withdrawal to somewhere around a more logical $175 a month.

Q. *I have a substantial investment in a mutual fund which refused to distribute any capital gains in 1971. We rely on those distributions for income. The fund claims it is doing us a tax favor. We can't see it. Should we sell out?*

A. The fund—as did many funds—suffered capital losses in 1970. Last year, it made some capital gains but these were not sufficient to offset all the 1970 losses.

If the fund had distributed the 1971 gains, the investor would have had to pay full income tax rates on the distribution rather than the much lower (generally one-half) long-term capital gains tax rate. So it held on to the gains in order to reduce the shareholders' tax burden.

That doesn't help you, of course, with the problem of buying lamb chops.

But there is a way out—in fact, two ways:

1. Sell a few of the shares to raise the money you need. Even if you have a profit on the shares you will pay only the lower long-term capital gains tax on that profit. Thus you would be paying no more tax than if you had received a normal capital gains distribution, and your overall investment picture would not be affected.

2. If the fund has a related income-type fund to which you can switch your shares for an additional fee of, say, $5, do so and get yourself into the more comfortable position of depending more on dividend income and less on chancy capital gains.

Q. *I own shares in six different funds. They must be tied in to some brokerage firms. One fund sells a number of stock issues and another of the funds I own buys the same stocks—both paying commissions.*

A. Differences of opinion are what make horse races—and investing. Each fund may have had a good reason for its particular action.

Q. *We are considering long-range investment in mutual funds. Would you consider a no-load fund or one of the established funds?*

A. I don't get this question at all. Many no-load funds are longer established than many funds charging a commission. I think the only method of deciding between two funds is their announced goal and their success in having achieved it.

Q. *I am a young married man with one child. Our combined earnings enable us to save about $150 to $300 a month. I've been thinking of mutual funds but hate to pay 8 to 9 per cent commission and refuse to get into a contract arrangement.*

A. So don't. You can buy just about every mutual fund on a voluntary (non-contractual) basis. And if you don't want to pay selling commissions, select one of the many no-load funds.

Q. *We've been upset by the fact that our $50 monthly withdrawal from a mutual fund has forced the sale of 90 of our 590 shares.*

A. Your 590 shares were worth about $7,000. Even in "good market" times, drawing $600 a year from a $7,000 mutual fund investment is frowned on—even by fund managements. You should reduce your withdrawals by at least one-third. You're expecting too much.

Q. *I'm 47 with some money in a bond fund and another $5,000 to invest for retirement income at age 62. The broker suggests putting another $5,000 into this fund.*

A. I don't see why a man of 47 should lock his money into an income bond fund 15 years before he is going to require the income. This money should be in stocks, which, you could hope, would help you offset inflation over the next 15 years. Time enough for bonds when you retire.

Q. *Please explain the difference between load growth mutual funds and no-load mutual funds. I have $10,000 to invest.*

A. A no-load (no commission) fund has no salesmen and therefore charges no sales commission. If you don't write the fund and ask them for a purchase form, nothing happens.

And if you put the entire $10,000 into any fund on one fine day, don't write me later and complain that you bought at the top of the market. There's no reason you can't spread that investment over a year or even more—whether you buy a load or no-load fund.

11 How to Live With a Bear Market

Longfellow, it seems, also wrote about the stock market:

> "Into each life some rain must fall,
> Some days must be dark and dreary."

The avid stock market speculator feels that a rising market is a "good" market; that a falling bear market is an insult, an invasion of his rights and an attack on his personal fortunes. Not so.

There are few hard-and-fast laws in the stock market—but constant fluctuation is one of them. And this may mean not only fluctuations from transaction to transaction, from hour to hour and from day to day, but from month to month and even year to year. If you look back over the modern history of prices on the New York Stock Exchange, you will see relatively few periods when stock prices remained unchanged for long periods of time. And this is not difficult to understand.

The stock market, after all, both predicts the future and reacts to current events. As a barometer of the future, it attempts to forecast the state of business and the overall economy, not only at home, but around the world. As a thermometer it reacts to current events: economic, governmental, diplomatic; local and worldwide. And it also measures speculative fevers and current financial "styles." These fevers and styles (the favoring of bowling shares over utilities, or electronics over cements) may run on for months and years, or may change suddenly after a short run.

Sometimes the change is based on facts—a turn for the better or worse in the earnings of a particular industry; basic changes in the overall economy, dislocations in the political or international area; wars; peace; discovery of new products or processes; discoveries in outer space or beneath the ocean's surface.

Often the change is psychological and originates mainly in the collective thinking of traders and investors. Within the last few decades there have been particular speculative fevers which have boosted the prices—at one time or another—of bowling, boating, life insurance, electronic stocks. Sometimes these fevers have run on for months and even a year or two; sometimes they were broken within a matter of a few months. But whatever the time period involved, there have always been those traders who sensed the turn first and those traders who were still buying the stocks months after the sophisticated traders had taken their profits and run.

Sometimes the reasons for the ending of an overall bull market are slow in emerging. And again some buyers continue to take on stock long after others have discerned the storm clouds gathering and have sold out.

These "bull" (rising) and "bear" (falling) markets have persisted for various lengths of time, depending—in many instances—on the length of time internal market pressures (in either direction) have been building up, and—in some instances—on outside influences, such as wars and peace.

There are no hard-and-fast definitions of what constitutes a bear market or a bull market. It all depends upon how short or long a trend you want to dignify by calling it a "market." For example, over the last generation, the lows in the Dow-Jones industrial averages were reached in 1932 at a reading of 41.22. If one insisted on taking the long view, one could argue that we have been in a bull market ever since. The averages were 41.22 then; they have touched 1,000 since.

Or one could, with a bit more reason, break down the gyrations of the market since that dark day in 1932 into more than a half-dozen bull and bear markets.

From that discouraging July day in 1932 until the spring of 1937, a period of fifty-five months, the market rose 371 per cent. From the spring of 1937 until 1938—almost exactly one year later the market fell 49 per cent. This was followed, in order, by:

- a 7-month rise of 60 per cent; a 5-month fall of 23 per cent;
- a 5-month advance of 28 per cent; a 31-month drop of 40 per cent;
- a 49-month rise of 128 per cent; a 36-month fall of 24 per cent;
- a 43-month rise of 83 per cent; an 8-month fall of 14 per cent;
- a 31-month rise of 106 per cent; a 19-month fall of 21 per cent;
- a 26-month rise of 66 per cent; a 10-month fall of 18 per cent;
- a 13-month rise of 30 per cent; a 7-month fall of 27 per cent;
- a 43-month rise of 86 per cent (which lasted until February, 1966 and carried the Dow Jones averages to an all-time peak of 1001.11).
- a precipitous decline to below the 750 level in the fall of 1966;

- a steady rise to 950 by the summer of 1967;
- a drop back to the 820 level by spring, 1968;
- a recovery to within a few points of 1000 level by late 1968;
- a decline which carried through all of 1969 and into mid-1970, by which time 35 per cent of the market values (as measured by the Dow Jones) had been wiped out;
- a 50 per cent recovery into the spring of 1971, once more achieving the 950 level in the industrial averages;
- a subsequent drop to the 800 level by late November, of 1971 followed by a rise almost as dramatic to above the 950 level by mid-1972.

A few generalizations emerge from such a history:

1. A bear market's fall is generally more precipitous than the preceding rise.

2. A bear market generally is of shorter duration than the preceding bull market. (The single exception in the list above—the 31-month decline of 40 per cent which ran from September 1939 to April 1942 reflected the steadily worsening position of the Allies in World War II. When the tide of war turned in that latter year, the stock market took off on one of its longest bull sessions.)

3. If you draw a line through the middle of any long-term stock market price range you will discover that this long-term trend is upward, irrespective of the anguish you may suffer while one of your issues drops from 88 to 54.

In fact, at no time during the above chronological history was the percentage lost in a bear market as large as the amount which had been tacked on in the preceding bull market. (Even if we include the Big Crash of 1929, we find that the percentage price drop from September 1929 to July 1932 was 88 per cent, whereas the ground gained in the previous six-year bull market had been 338 per cent.)

There is no stock market law which guarantees that this comforting experience will continue in force. But there is substantial economic reasoning behind the expectation that it will. And this reasoning is best expressed in the one phrase: long-time inflation.

There may have been periods in our history when a dollar bought more one year than it had in the previous year. But where this has been true, the experience has been a short-term and infrequent one.

The hard, cold fact is that over the years the dollar continues to lose purchasing power. It takes steadily more and more dollars to buy a ship, or a pair of shoes, or a package of sealing wax as the years pass. The price of anything—ships, shoes, sealing wax; an ice cream cone or the family sedan—goes steadily higher, expressed in dollars. So do the prices of factories, raw materials, inventories—and the selling prices of their products—and so do their sales volume and their profit margin and their profit expressed in terms of dollars. And also the selling price of a share of stock which represents part ownership of that factory and its products and its profits. That's long-term inflation in the stock market.

And the continued expectation of inflation is the informal guaranty that regardless of how much stocks have fallen in the last three months, six months or thirty-six months, regardless of the current events which are depressing common stock prices, it's a safe bet (based on past performances) that five years from now, the stock market will be higher.

One lives, then, with a bear market pretty much as one lives with the common cold—except that in the latter case one knows that, treated or untreated, it is likely to run its course in twenty-one days.

It is impossible to tell how long a bear market will take to run its course. But history pretty much convinces us that after it has run its course, stock prices will achieve still higher levels.

This is not to say that a bear market represents a "do nothing" period for the investor.

While he may not go in for the short selling by which speculators or professional traders will attempt to make profits on the decline, the long-term investor may well take advantage of the harsher light cast by a bear market to recast his portfolio, eliminate issues he may have bought in the flush of the previous bull market fever, search out bargains in the solid companies.

The traditional bear market generally offers unusual opportunities for the last pursuit.

A wild bull market may come a cropper because some speculative issues have not proved as successful as some speculators hoped. But a bear market is no respecter of quality—and quality issues as well as overblown speculative stocks will frequently come down in price at the same time. The natural tendency of the short-term market player is to become insulted during a bear market, to turn his back on it and, licking his financial wounds, declare "that's enough of that game. I'm never going back there again." But the experienced investor knows that bear markets represent far greater long-time investment opportunities than bull markets; that the very discouragement which leads the amateur market player to dump his stocks regardless of quality or price is the very factor which is putting bargain price tags on a long list of worthwhile issues.

The ideal investor position in a bear market, of course, is to have gotten out before prices began to slide. But bear market signals are not that distinct. It is not at all unusual for even long-term market experts and professional investors to remain fully invested in the same issues.

The investor takes his losses on his errors (admitting one's mistakes is a virtue in investing as well as in other pursuits), and reinvests his money in higher quality securities now available at much lower prices.

Living successfully with a bear market means upgrading one's portfolio; weeding out errors; replacing them with better quality issues which will share in the recovery that has always followed bear markets.

SOME QUESTIONS AND ANSWERS

Q. *A few years ago a broker recommended I buy a cement company stock at about 14. It is now currently* *around 11, even though it is earning more than $1 a share. How come? Do you think I should buy more for growth and income?*

A. Cement shares have been in the doghouse for several years—overcapacity and resulting pressure on prices for cement have been the chief reasons. Some analysts are now predicting a turn for the better in this group. It could be so; certainly, it is long overdue. Your company, which serves the Midwest, has shown some slight uptrend in earnings, although I don't think many cements are generally considered growth stocks. However, there isn't much question about income. Cement stocks today pay anywhere from 5 to 6 per cent.

Q. *I held Northwestern Utility shares for more than a year. I now have a paper loss of one to 5 points, depending upon daily price changes. Should I sell out?*

A. I am not much good at guessing market trends, but I'd be reluctant to sell out good-quality utilities at this point, basing my decision merely on the fact that this division of the market has been depressed for some time while all the play has been going to the glamour issues. Market fashions change—sooner or later.

Q. *We are a young couple, self-employed, in our 30s, with 2 small children. Currently we have about $1,800 in RCA, Holiday Inns, Ipco Hospital Supply and Sperry Rand. We had a profit of about $500 until the market began to slide in fear of inflation and a tax increase. We could, from time to time, invest several hundred dollars. Is this a good time? Can you offer any encouragement to people such as ourselves in these worrisome times?*

A. If I may be permitted to adopt a crotchety-old-uncle tone of voice, I can assure you that in the past 50 years (except for the false complacency of the mid-Twenties) we have always had "worrisome times"—certainly as far as securities prices are concerned.

One of the few basic laws of the stock market is that of change. The market is always reacting to something. And very often the way it reacts is determined more by where it is at that moment and where it has come from than by the stimulus itself. In other words, event A, at one stage of the market, may bring a rally; at another time—if the market has gotten a bit top-heavy—it may bring an opposite reaction. And sometimes it may react violently even without outside stimulus—like a child who gets cranky merely because he's overtired.

Now as to your particular picture: I don't think the melting away of part or all your $500 profit means the end of your investment world. All of us have our bad days. I don't know whether the market will go still lower next week, next month, or next year, but I'd venture a guess that by the time you need this money for college tuitions or retirement you'll have a handsome gain.

Is this a good time to invest? If you have a few hundred dollars to invest in growth stocks, the answer is yes.

Your program, it seems to me, is to continue investing all through your capital-building years—low market or high market.

The only other suggestion I would make is that since you are self-employed you ought to explore the possibility of income-tax savings under the Keogh Bill. This may require setting up some formal program, or a mutual-fund plan, or some annual investment in U.S. retirement bonds. But there's no point in losing that tax credit.

Q. *Some time back, I wanted to sell most of my stocks. But my broker insisted business was good and that the issues would go higher. I didn't sell. Now the portfolio is $30,000 lower. Should I sell? Among stocks held are Am. Bosch, Ampex, Carrier, Chrysler, Ford, Gamble, Goodrich, Interlake, North American Aviation, Parke Davis, Radio Corp., Southern Pacific, Stauffer, Timken, Union Oil, United Air Lines.*

A. You now know what I mean when I say, "Uneasy lies the head that owns a buck."

If you hide it under the mattress, it may be stolen, destroyed by fire; it earns no interest and loses buying power every year. If you invest it in insured savings or savings bonds, you're sure of your capital, and today can get a generous return; but you are still vulnerable to the inroads of inflation. If you put it into stocks—as you did—you must be prepared to see your investment swept from time to time by tidal waves of selling which can wipe out substantial hunks of its value.

What you are asking me is: "How does one live with a bear market?"

I think there are a dozen answers, ranging all the way from "Sell everything and head for the hills," to "Hedge, sell half and keep half" to "Do nothing—hold everything." Then, there are those who would have you take your profits but dig in and hold your losers. That could be dangerous. And, vice versa, keep the good ones and take your licking on the losers. Also, sell growth stocks and hold on to the defensive issues.

A great deal, it seems to me, depends upon your own particular investment situation.

If you had planned to retire this fall, for example, I'd say you missed the boat in not at least getting out of your glamour issues this spring and putting the proceeds into generous income Treasuries, insured certificates of deposit, etc.

If you are a young man, or a man who is still 5 to 10 years from retirement (in other words, a man who is still in his capital-building years) I suppose you can console yourself with the reasonable promise that 10 years from now this list should be worth more than it is today, or even higher than it was during its past peaks. Such reasoning would justify your sitting tight and holding everything.

A broker or investment advisor can give you his opinion, but it is no more than that; the final decision must be made by you alone, and must reflect your confidence (or lack of it), your resources, your responsibilities and most certainly the number of years remaining before you must turn from stressing capital gain to emphasizing safety of capital and income.

All these are variable factors, and when you get right down to the wire, it's up to you to weigh them all and make your own decision.

No one can tell you for certain whether the market is

going lower or not; and if it does go lower, how much lower, and when it will turn.

Q. *I don't understand how the Dow Jones average can advance 8 points when the gains in the day's "selected stocks" run from ½ to 2½ points.*

A. There is no connection between the two sets of figures. In the first place, I don't know what your listing includes as "selected stocks." Most likely, they are the day's most active stocks, which may or may not be in the Dow Jones industrial average list.

Secondly, the Dow Jones industrial average is arrived at by adding up the market prices of the 30 stocks in that average and dividing the total (as of this moment) by 1.661.

Q. *For more than a decade I have been investing in four stocks under the exchange's monthly investment plan–RCA, American Can, Goodyear and Gulf Oil. I invested a total of $14,590 plus just under $10,000 in dividends received. Market value is now above $32,000. Comments please? I plan to retire in five years.*

A. I think it's a better than fair record considering that you didn't catch any of the fast-moving glamour stocks. And also that over the last six years the old-line blue chip division of the stock market has done very little ground-gaining.

I would continue dollar averaging right up to retirement, although I think you could broaden your portfolio a bit, including one or two of the top-quality rails, utilities, foods and building shares.

Q. *I've been dabbling in the market for years and managed to make money. But I don't agree with you that the decline of 100 shares of stock from 40 to 30 indicates a loss of $1,000–if you don't sell. I don't. I've traded Union Pacific, for example, several times and made money–just refusing to sell out when I have a loss.*

A. The question of whether you have a loss until you sell is somewhat like the old philosophical question: Does a tree falling in a distant forest, far from human habitation, make a noise? I say it does, even if no person hears it.

However, the important factor in your argument is that you restrict yourself to quality. In the last 15 years, Union Pacific has followed an upward zig-zag course and if you didn't sell out during declines you were doing the right thing.

The chief danger in your philosophy is that it is also followed by people who take flyers in $5 or $10 new issues and then hang on for 20 years while the stock languishes around $1.25 a share and even lower. They refuse to admit they made a mistake; they refuse to admit they have a loss, even though the chances of that particular promoter's darling recovering are practically nil.

When you buy a quality issue, such as Union Pacific, for example, you have good reason to believe it's going to be around for a long time and will profit from a comeback in its industry or in the market.

Signposts on the way to an investment accident: "I told the broker I wanted to buy a stock selling under $50, because I could then buy 100 shares." . . . "I didn't want a growth stock to be held for a long period of time, but something I could buy and sell even daily or weekly." "From now on I'm going to sell whenever a stock goes down 2 points." . . . "I figure the stock will go up 30 points in two years."

Q. *Many writers on investments, including yourself, seem to stress buying and holding quality stocks. I went into the market at the 1970 low and made money in short-term trading even though my broker advised against it. The doubts he raised–and the high short-term gains taxes I was paying–tended to change my mind so I went long-term, only to see much of my profit melt away in late 1971. Doesn't there come a time in a market which goes up and down, as at present, when it is foolish to try to invest long-term? Shouldn't one be flexible?*

A. Let's try to take these points one at a time:

1. I do, in most cases, urge long-term holding of quality stocks, even though I realize that many corporations do suffer ups and downs in profits and interruptions in growth. I admit it's an elementary approach (somewhat like saying everyone should eat a balanced diet and get 7 hours sleep).

But I feel I must adhere to it because the only alternative is expert analysis of the general market and of every corporation in which you own stock–an approach which is beyond the reach of most investors and, for that fact, often escapes professional analysts whose interpretations and forecasts have proved many times to be wide of the mark.

There is no question but that a long-term investor even in, for example, such high-quality issues as IBM and Eastman Kodak could have doubled his profits if he could have sold out at every top and bought back in at every bottom of the last 15 years. But for that you have to be the seventh son of a seventh son.

2. Wandering into the stock market at the mid-1970 low turned out to be a brilliant maneuver, regardless of whether you did so because of instinct or because a rich uncle just happened to leave you speculating money then.

3. That broker who warned you against in-and-out trading, whether he was proved right or wrong at that particular moment, is a rarity.

4. Your being caught in the late 1971 market downturn was pretty much of a piece with your having stepped into the market at the 1970 low.

Your letter asking "why don't I sell out everything now" just happens to carry the date on which the late 1971 rally (we now know) got started and which has since boosted market averages about 15 to 20 per cent and has recovered all the late 1971 losses. So if you followed your inclination and sold out in late November, you now understand what I mean about how difficult it is to trade stocks and catch market savings.

5. The stock market goes up and down "at present," it has done so in the past, and will do so in the future. A stock market–very much like the tide–does not stand still. The only problem is that (unlike the tides) the up and down movements generally don't become clearly apparent until you can use hindsight.

Now as to the bottom line:

Is it best to be flexible and sell stocks, even good stocks, some time? Yes.

Will it prove more rewarding than long-term investment? Yes—*if* you can pick the turns.

And how do you pick the turns? That's what the ball game is all about. It's a subject that fills library shelves. It's a skill that sometimes appears only after years of experience in evaluating market cycles and, most important, understanding the human emotions that control them.

The decision must be yours.

HOW TRADING "STYLES" CHANGE

Stock market trader fashions change constantly, not unlike the fashions in women's clothing. Here are two lists, the first showing the most actively traded stocks on the New York Stock Exchange in 1971, and the second, the most actively traded in 1970. Note that high activity is no guide to a stock's desirability as a vehicle for capital gains. In several instances, stocks that were the traders' delight in 1970 lost ground and closed lower by the end of 1971.

1971 VOLUME LEADERS

	Share Volume in Hundreds	*Price Range*	*Closing Price*
1. American Tel. & Tel.	322,319	53⅞–40¾	44¾
2. Occidental Petroleum	269,388	22¾– 9⅞	11⅞
3. Federal Nat'l Mortgage	231,641	100 –55	98¼
4. Pan Amer. World Airways	215,332	20¼– 9½	15¼
5. Texaco Incorporated	211,579	39⅝–29⅝	34⅜
6. Gulf Oil Corporation	193,524	34 –24¼	28⅞
7. Chrysler Corporation	190,887	33⅜–24½	28⅝
8. Greyhound Corporation	181,998	25½–15⅞	21
9. Telex Corporation	181,923	22⅜– 7¾	12
10. Eastern Air Lines	177,517	28⅞–14⅜	22⅝
Total	2,176,108		

"MOST ACTIVE" STOCKS IN '70

	Share Volume in Hundreds	*Price Range*	*Closing Price*
1. Telex Corporation	386,749	31⅞– 9⅛	16⅝
2. Occidental Petroleum	257,209	26⅝–13⅛	18½
3. American Tel. & Tel.	234,198	53⅞–40⅜	48⅞
4. Chrysler Corporation	180,859	35¾–16⅛	28
5. Xerox Corporation	179,743	115¾–65¼	86½
6. Texaco Incorporated	178,892	35¼–24	34⅞
7. University Computing	158,934	99⅜–13¼	21⅝
8. Standard Oil (N.J.)	153,427	73⅜–49⅞	73⅜
9. Gulf Oil Corporation	153,122	32⅝–21¾	32⅜
10. Natomas Company	153,047	67⅞–13⅛	54⅝
Total	2,036,180		

Q. *We owned stock in one company which was taken over by another corporation with each of our shares receiving 0.050984 shares of the second firm's preferred and 0.0260279 shares of its common. I agreed to the deal but did not authorize any sale of my stock. However, I received only 4 shares of common, plus checks for sales of a fractional share of the preferred and a fractional share of the common. How come?*

A. Evidently you did not have enough original shares to receive a full share of the preferred and 5 shares of the common of the merged company. So they sent you a check for the fractional share of the preferred and for the fractional share of common left over after getting your 4 shares.

You say you did not authorize a sale, but I think you will find that if you read carefully the letters and forms you received at the time of the exchange you will see a note to the effect that if you don't signify your intentions of buying enough additional fractions of shares to round out your holdings, the company will undertake to sell your fractional shares without brokerage fee. This was done.

I admit that these letters can be pretty confusing. I guess legal requirements make them so. But the fact is that the action taken was perfectly proper.

And, if it's any consolation to you, you're money ahead on the deal. Both preferred and common have gone lower since the deal was made. So if you want to own more shares, you can buy them cheaper today than at the time of the exchange.

Q. *I have some United Industrial preferred. Should I convert into the common?*

A. Why? The preferred (as of the date of your letter) was worth $8.50 a share. If you turned it in, you'd get one-half of a share of common selling at $15. The preferred pays dividends of 42½ cents a year; the common, 30 cents.

Now explain to me why you would want to turn in $8.50 worth of stock paying 42½ cents a year for one-half share of a $15 issue, paying 30 cents?

It seems to me that if an investor goes in for convertible issues, he ought to make sure he understands the conversion feature. Otherwise, what's the point?

Q. *When is the best time to convert Madison Fund preferred?*

A. I don't know that there is any "best time" for the long-term investor to convert. If you are interested in current income, the common is more rewarding since it distributes capital gains in addition to dividend income. If that's what you want you shouldn't be in the preferred in the first place.

The preferred holder gets income of about 4¼% on current market price, but enjoys a steady rise in his conversion privilege every year, since the conversion rate is stepped up to take into account the capital gains distributions on the common. This increase in conversion rate ultimately will work out as a long-term capital gain which he need take only when his tax load is lightest.

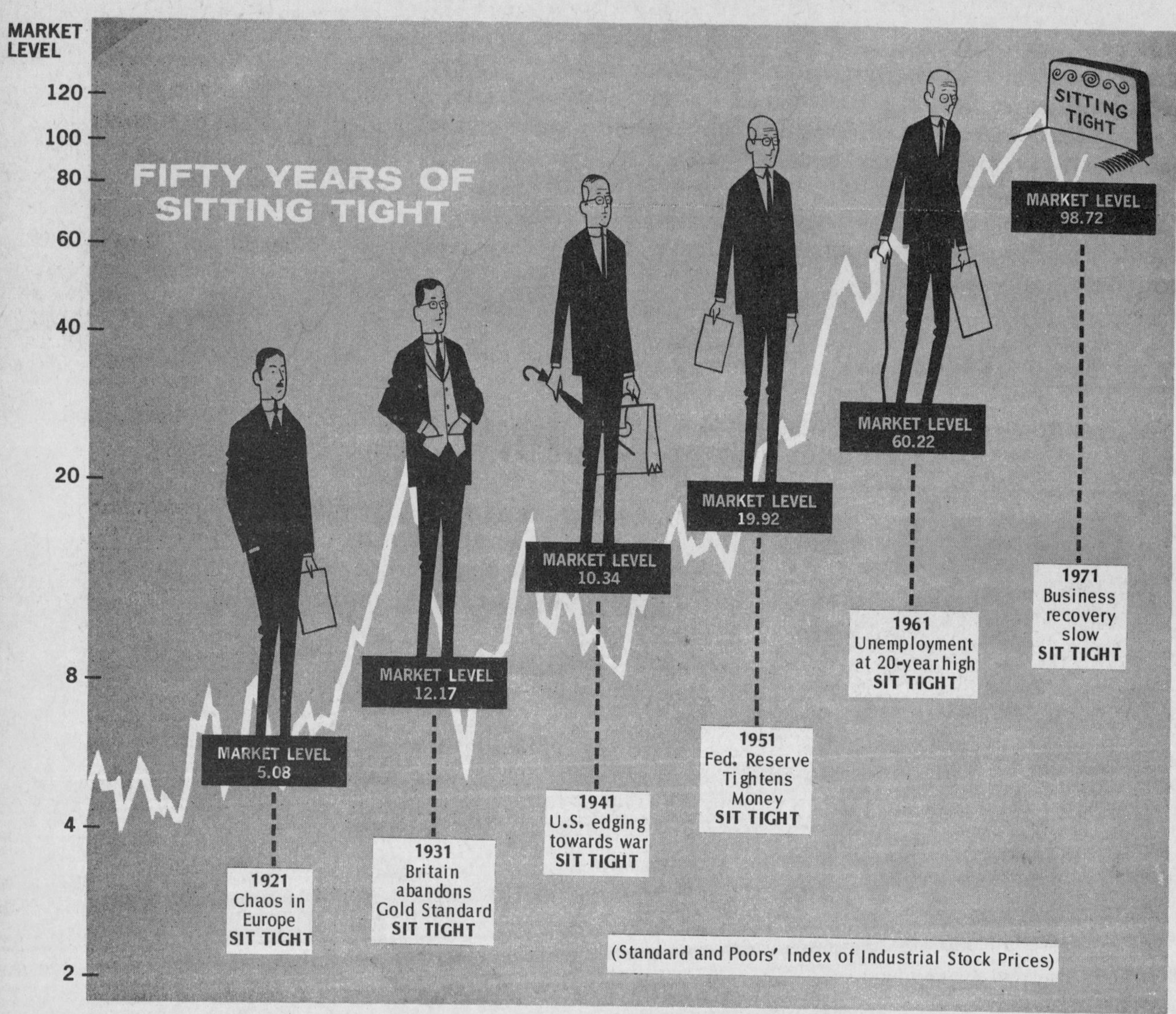

A cartoon published in Brevits, a Vance, Sanders publication, showing the futility of delaying investments until the "time is right." A famous Boston financial editor once wrote: "The investor who takes the attitude he will not invest until he can see the outlook clearly had better dig a hole and bury his money here and now. There is a risk in any investment at any time. And there is a risk in liquid position because of the steady erosion of fixed dollars due to inflation."

Q. *I have 100 General Motors $3.75 preferred for which I paid 92¼ in May, 1963. I've been advised to sell out and reinvest elsewhere. Do you agree?*

A. It depends. At current prices, the stock is yielding around 6.3%, with the $3.75 dividend protected, last year, by earnings of $215! So much for safety.

If you could use the loss to reduce income taxes (although there's no point to establishing the loss so early in the year) you might consider selling and putting the proceeds into good quality utility bonds yielding around 7%. If your tax bill does not present any problems, I'd be reluctant to go through the expense of selling and then of buying other securities merely for the income gain on a $6,500 investment.

Q. *I have 12 shares of Central Illinois P.S. preferred. Would it be wise to sell them because I get only 4%? I need income.*

A. The dividend rate on the Central Illinois P.S. preferred is 4%, but the yield to you on your money now is around 8%. At a recent price around 50, the $4 dividend works out to that generous figure. Coming from an AA quality cumulative preferred stock, with the dividend protected at least 12 times over by recent earnings, this is a fine return.

Q. *I hold Beneficial Corp. common, $4.30 convertible preferred, and the $4.50 preferred. On the latter, I inadvertently let the conversion deadline slip by without converting, and the issue is now down to around $61. Should I hold it in hopes of it reaching a higher level? The $4.30 preferred is convertible into 2.1 common until 1977. (I'm 78. Will I be around in 1977?) I won't bother to ask your advice on the common which I will hold for its yield.*

A. Letting that conversion deadline slip by proved costly. The $4.50 preferred sold as high as 120 in 1966 when it was still convertible. Now it's down to half that. However, it now yields a generous 6.8% from a well-protected dividend which, it seems to me, makes it perfect for your needs. I'd hold.

Second: The $4.30 preferred will benefit from any improvement in the common until 1977.

Any good quality preferred, convertible or not, can reach a higher price level if interest rates come down.

Third. You say you're not going to ask me about the common, but I'm going to tell you, anyway. At current market, it yields about 2.5%—by far the lowest of your holdings in this company. Since you already hold an option on any rise in the common via the $4.30 convertible preferred, I can't make any case for a man of 78 holding the common for a 2.5% yield—certainly not when high grade utility bonds are yielding 7%, plus.

Q. *Could you suggest some good utility preferreds that yield 7 per cent? My broker says he has none.*

A. Almost every large utility company has preferred issues outstanding which yield a fraction either side of 7 per cent: Commonwealth Edison, Consolidated Edison, Detroit Edison, Public Service Electric & Gas, Pacific Gas & Electric, San Diego Gas & Electric, Southern California Edison—and many, many more.

Tell him to go through his preferred stock lists.

Q. *In the "bid and asked" table in my paper I find quotations for stocks not traded that day. For instance: "Illinois Power $8.24 pf, bid 57, asked 57½." Does it really pay that much in dividends, and if so, why doesn't it sell much higher?*

A. You've been misled, evidently, by a typographical error. The figures are correct, but there should be no dollar sign in front of that "8.24." The stock you mention does *not* pay $8.24 in dividends but 8.24 per cent of $50 par value. So the actual cash payment is $4.12 a year, which at a bid price of 57 for the shares works out to a yield of about 7.2 per cent.

Incidentally, that isn't a bad yield from a stock rated AA, even if it isn't $8.24.

Q. *I'm 57, interested in building capital. Should I switch out of an A quality preferred stock in the hope of profiting by a rising market?*

A. An A quality utility preferred would rise mainly if interest rates fall. If you are playing for a rise in the stock market, it will have to be in some common issue—or a convertible or debenture convertible into common.

Q. *I've been considering buying some recently issued preferreds paying dividends well above 9 per cent.*

A. O.K., but make sure you understand just what return you are getting and what loss you may suffer if the shares are called in and paid off at a price below what you are now paying for them.

For example, if you pay $120 a share for a preferred issue paying a dividend of $9.44 a year, you are not getting 9.44 per cent on your money, but closer to 7.8 per cent. Furthermore, if the issuer exercises his right to redeem the shares at $110, you can see where you will have to sustain a loss.

However, all these factors are taken into consideration in the present market price, which means this particular issue is in line with other income-type securities. Just be sure you understand them.

12 Preferreds—The Safety Stocks

Safety is one of the three important ingredients of any investment program, sharing with income and growth the attention of all forward-looking, prudent investors.

We might as well begin by making it crystal clear that there is no 100 per cent "safe" investment. Even if the number of dollars invested is guaranteed by the U.S. Government or one of its agencies, there can be no guaranty of the long-term purchasing power of those dollars. If one invests in equities as a means of hedging against inflation, he must, of course, be prepared to weather market upsets.

But even though 100 per cent safety is unattainable, that is no reason investors should not attempt to approach that goal. The preferred stock is one of the best known vehicles for this endeavor.

A preferred share, as well as the common, represents ownership of a corporation.

The preferred share is junior, or subordinate, to any debt the company owes, but it comes ahead of the common in its claim upon the company for its fixed dividend and, in case of dissolution—forced or otherwise—for assets.

The designation "preferred," of course, should not be accepted as a blanket endorsement of quality. The preferred of Company A may be distinctly inferior in investment quality to the common shares of Company B—not only in safety of principal but in dividend return and in possibility of price appreciation. But when considering the securities of *any one company*, it may be safely assumed that unless otherwise specified, the preferred ranks ahead of the common in event of bankruptcy, liquidation or sale, and in the year-to-year claim on a stated amount of dividends.

Naturally, the investor in high level preferreds must give up something for this prior position. Generally, he forsakes any possibility of higher dividends in time of prosperity (thus giving up any protection against inflation) in return for the assurance that in times of depression he will get his money before the common gets anything. Furthermore, some preferred stocks are tabbed with a price—the call price—at which the issuing company may redeem the shares at its option. Obviously, such a call price acts as a damper on rising quotations. If a preferred may be called in at $108, it isn't likely that a prudent investor is going to get caught paying $120 for it. And even if there is no such call price, preferreds—by their very nature—are inclined to market stodginess, with, in the main, little opportunity for capital gain.

Furthermore, since it does offer a fixed dividend, the market price of a preferred share is linked inversely with current interest rates—the going price for money. In this respect, preferred stock is similar to a bond, which also offers a fixed return to the investor.

A $4 dividend preferred stock issued at $100 a share when interest rates were in the 4% area cannot be expected to continue to sell at $100 when interest rates—as they have at the present writing—have risen to 7% and higher. The preferred must then settle until it finds the level at which the $4 annual dividend represents a return of 7%. That would mean a market price of around $58 a share.

It is for this reason that during an advancing market for common stocks many top quality preferreds may touch new lows.

But for the investor looking for safety these drawbacks are secondary to the substantial advantages in income and safety the preferred share possesses, plus some other features he may shop for.

These additional features, which may be found singly, or in various combinations, are:

Convertibility. The owner of this type of preferred has the right, at any time it is to his advantage, to convert his preferred into a stated number of common shares. Thus, if his company enters on a period of successful growth and expansion of earnings, he may elect to give up the safety of his preferred and take instead common shares when their price or dividend rate will give him more for his original investment than he could get by remaining with the preferred. Or, he may elect to take his capital gain by selling the preferred, since the rise in the common will most always be reflected in higher prices for the preferred.

Cumulative preferred. This type possesses an added safety feature which says that if by any chance the preferred dividend is omitted for any period, it accumulates as a claim of the stockholder against the company and must be paid off before the dividends may be paid on the common.

The preferred stock is the sober citizen of the equity field and as such rarely attracts speculative following, or makes newspaper headlines. But those are two characteristics of little importance to a man seeking safe, generous income.

Investors in preferred shares, however, should realize that these securities—unlike common shares—are most often callable, i.e., redeemable by the issuing corporation at fixed prices. In recent years, when money rates soared to new all-time highs, some utilities issued preferred shares yielding 8 and 9 per cent and even a trifle more. These yields, of course, are attractive, but the investor should realize that if and when the company can get capital at lower interest costs, it will call in these preferreds and issue new ones with lower dividend rates.

So if you are attracted to a preferred stock which pays a 9.15 per cent dividend, you may also find that it is selling at a premium price—well above the price level at which the company has the right to retire that preferred share. In such a case you must reduce the attractiveness of the high current yield by the drop in market price to the nearest date on which the shares may be retired at that lower price.

Basically, preferreds are divided into two main groups: those which are not convertible into common shares and those which are convertible.

The nonconvertible preferreds may also enjoy cumulative dividend features and, in a few rare but fast-disappearing instances, the participatory right to increased dividends once the common stockholders receive a certain amount.

Nonconvertible preferreds are interesting mainly because of their generous yield. Here is a sample list of the yields available from good-quality industrial preferreds early in 1972:

	Rate	Call Price	Market	Current Yield
Allied Stores	4%	100	55 -6½	7.08
Aluminum Co. of Amer.	$3.75	100	52½-3¼	7.04
Armour	$4.75	102	64 -5	7.31
Armstrong Cork	$3.75	102.75	56 -7½	6.52
Atlantic Richfield	3¾%	101½	55¼-6½	6.64
Carrier Corp.	4½%	50	33½-6	6.25
Celanese	4½%	100	62¾-3¼	7.11
Colgate Palmolive	$3.50	100	55 -½	6.31
Continental Can	$4.25	110	64¼-6	6.44
Control Data	4½%	100	58½-9½	7.56
Crown Zellerbach	$4.20	102½	61½-2	6.77
Du Pont	$3.50	102	56 -¼	6.22
Du Pont	$4.50	120	71½-2	6.25
General Motors	$3.75	101	59 -⅜	6.32
General Motors	$5.00	120	81⅛-½	6.13
General Tire	$5.00	100.50	69½-71	7.04
Getty Oil	$1.20	25	19 -⅜	6.19
Grant (W. T.)	3¾%	100	54 -6½	6.64
Inmont.	4½	105	57 -8¼	7.73
International Paper	$4.00	105	58 -9	6.78
Intl. Tel. & Tel.	$5.50	105	77½-8½	7.01
Kaiser Alum. & Chem.	4¾%	51½	36½-7½	6.33
Koppers Co.	4%	107¾	60 -¾	6.58
Liggett & Myers	7%	N.C.	102 -3	6.80
Macy (R.H.) "A"	4¼%	107.50	60½-1¾	6.88
Melville Shoe "B"	$4.00	100	62 -3	6.35
National Distillers	4¼%	101	67¼-8	6.25
National Distillers	4½%	50	32¾-3¼	6.77
Natl. Gypsum	$4.50	103	72½-3½	6.12
Philip Morris	3.90%	100¾	61 -2½	6.24
Philip Morris	4%	105.50	63 -5	6.15
Radio Corp. of America	$3.50	100	53 -4¼	6.45
Reynolds Metals	4¾%	51½	36¼-7	6.42
Southern Railway	5%	20	15 -¼	6.56
Standard Brands	$3.50	100	57¾-8¼	6.01
Stand. Oil (Ohio) "A"	3¾%	100	62 -3½	5.91
Tri-Continental	$2.50	55	37½-8	6.58
Uniroyal Inc.	8%	N.C.	106 -7	7.48
U.S. Plywood-Champion	$5.50	105	74 -5	7.33
U. S. M. Corp.	6%	N.C.	19 -½	7.69
Westinghouse Elec.	3.80%	101	61 -2	6.13

N.C.–noncallable.

PUBLIC UTILITY PREFERREDS

	Rate	Market	Current Yield
Appalachian Power	8.12%	107 -8	7.52
Baltimore Gas & Elec.	7.88%	105½-7	7.36
Boston Edison	8.88%	112⅝-13¼	7.84
Carolina Pr. & Lt.	$7.95	104½-6	7.50
Cincinnati G. & E.	9.30%	116 -¼	8.00
Cleveland Electric	$7.40	102½-3	7.18
Conn. Lt. & Pr.	$3.80	51¾-2⅛	7.24
Comw. Edison	$2.00	27⅜-	7.21
Consolidated Edison	8.30%	105 -6	7.83
Consumers Power	$7.45	103¾-4½	7.13
Dallas Pr. & Lt.	$6.84	95½-7	7.05
Dayton Pr. & Lt.	7.48%	102½-3½	7.23
Delmarva Pr. & Lt.	7.88%	105½-6½	7.40
Detroit Edison	7.45%	102¾-3½	7.20
Duke Power	8.70%	111½-12¾	7.72
Duke Power	8.20%	108½-9	7.52
Illinois Power	8.24%	56 -½	7.29
Indiana & Michigan	7.76%	104 -5	7.39
Jersey Central Pr. Lt.	8.00%	102½-3½	7.73
Kansas City Pr. & Lt.	7.72%	104½-5½	7.32
Long Island Ltg.	8.12%	106 -8	7.52
Niagara Mohawk Power	4.85%	67¼-¾	7.16
Northern States Power	$4.11	58 -9½	6.91
Northern States Power	$7.84	106 -7	7.33
Ohio Edison	4.56%	65 -7½	6.76
Ohio Power	7.60%	102 -¾	7.40
Pacific Gas & Elec.	4.80%	16¾-7¼	6.96
Pacific Lighting	$4.50	60½-1¾	7.29
Penn Power & Light	8.60%	111½-12½	7.64
Philadelphia Elec.	7.85%	105 -½	7.44
Potomac Electric Pr.	$4.04	52¼-3	7.62
Potomac Electric Pr.	$4.50	57⅛-¼	7.86
Pub. Svc. Elec. & Gas	9.62%	119 -½	8.15
Pub. Svc. Elec. & Gas	7.40%	103¼-4	7.12
Sou. Calif. Edison	5.80%	20⅝-⅞	6.95
Sou. Calif. Edison	8.70%	111½-13	7.70
Tenneco #	4.90%	73 -5	6.53
Texas Power & Light	$7.24	100¾-1¼	(a)
Union Elec.	$8.00	100 -1½	7.88
Virginia Elec. & Power	$7.45	103 -½	7.20
Virginia Elec. & Power	$8.84	114 -15	7.69
Wisconsin Electric Pr.	8.90%	111 -12	7.95

Thus far, we have been seeking mainly increased safety. We have examined straight preferreds—which merely rank ahead of the common in claims on earnings and assets.

CONVERTIBLE PREFERREDS

Now we consider another preferred stock feature—the privilege of conversion. This clause gives the holder of the preferred stock the right to convert his shares into a fixed number of common if the fortunes of the company should improve to such a point that the price of the common would climb to a point which would make this transfer profitable; or, even if he doesn't convert, to profit by a capital gain in his stock, sparked by a rise in the underlying common.

Curiously enough, this privilege of conversion at once makes the otherwise stodgy preferred a highly desirable security for those who would otherwise be inclined to ignore the preferred with its fixed dividend. It would make such a security interesting even to young Morse since, as a convertible preferred holder, he not only holds a prior claim to dividends, but retains the privilege of profiting by any rise in the company's common stock.

The following list gives numerous examples of these convertible preferreds. There are literally hundreds of these issues outstanding. Some possess the additional right of accumulating any unpaid dividends; some do not. But all give their holder the right of converting into common any time it may be to his advantage.

You will notice in this list several issues selling at prices which bring their yield down to below 4 per cent and even lower. These market prices are in many cases determined not by the yield but by the value of the conversion privilege.

Here is the list. It will be seen at a glance that the choice is wide. Where the common stock has not yet risen to the conversion level, many of these convertible preferreds still offer excellent returns:

Issue and Dividend	*Common Shares per 1 Share of Preferred*	*Common Price*	*Convertible Preferred Price*	*Current Yield of Preferred*
Amer. Metal Clim. $5.25	2.43	30	92	5.69%
Am. Waterworks $1.44	1.3	13	22	6.62
Ashland Oil $2.40	2.0	27	56	4.28
Beneficial Finance $4.30	2.1	39	95	4.50
CIT Financial $5.50	2.5	47	115	4.78
Columbia Broadcasting $1	0.7	53	37	2.78
Cons. Edison 6%	3.09	26	80	6.85
Emerson Electric $0.90	0.7	85	59	1.53
Flintkote $2.25	1.1	28	41	5.48
Flintkote $4.50	2.7	28	83	5.45
Gen. Telephone $2	0.9	31	36	5.55
Int'l. Tel, & Tel. $4.00	3.1	62	190	2.11
Int'l. Utilities $1.25	0.8	49	39	3.18
Kaiser Aluminum $4.13	1.7	21	58	7.15
Kidde $2.20	2.1	33	68	3.23
Marcor $2	2.0	30	62	3.25
McGraw Hill $1.20	1.6	18	28	4.22
Radio Corp. $4	2.1	42	98	4.08
Reynolds Metal $4.50	2.0	19	66	6.81
Sante Fe Ind. $0.50	0.3	32	10	5.26
Scovill Mfg. $2.50	2.44	28	69	3.64
Sun Oil $2.25	0.8	49	44	5.11
Tenneco $5.50	3.7	25	95	5.80
Textron $2.08	1.1	35	44	4.74
Western Union $4.60	1.9	48	95	4.84
Western Union $4.90	2.27	48	110	4.45

NON-CALLABLE PREFERREDS

Finally, a word on the relatively rare noncallable preferred. There aren't many of these around, and it's easy to see why.

A corporation now issuing a preferred on which—because of high interest rates—it must promise to pay a high dividend obviously will want to protect itself if, in the future, it can retire the issue and replace it with one costing it less in dividends. As a result, recently issued preferreds are callable.

However, here are some of the few non-callable issues still outstanding. Their attractiveness lies in the fact they may be considered a "perpetual" investment. In cases where quality .is good they will move conversely to the trend of interest rates. That is, when money rates are falling, the prices of these non-callable preferreds will rise—and vice versa. In early 1972 the preferred market was in the "vice versa" stage.

The following short list names some of these "perpetual" investments, giving their investment rating (mostly "AA" and "A"), their price early in 1972, and their yield:

American Can 7% (A)	26	6.6%
Kansas City Southern 4%	14	6.9%
Liggett & Myers 7% (A)	102	6.8%
Pacific Gas & Electric 6% (AA)	21	6.9%
Pacific Gas & Electric 5½% (AA)	19	7.1%
Pacific Gas & Electric 5% (AA)	17	7.1%
(other P.G. & E. preferreds are callable)		
Southern California Edison 5% (AA)	26	6.0%
(other Southern California Edison issues are callable)		
Southern California Gas 6% (AA)	21	7.1%
Uniroyal 8% (BBB)	106	7.5%

An explanation for the relatively lower return on the Southern California Edison 5% preferred is the fact that the issue is a participating preferred—one of the few remaining of that rare breed. A participating preferred is entitled not only to the stated dividend, but to a "bonus" dividend if earnings or other conditions are favorable. Over the years, Southern California Edison 5s have enjoyed increases in dividend payments.

A high quality non-callable preferred ranks pretty close to a perpetual bond. The only way you can make a stock market profit on the investment is to buy when money rates are high (and the price of the preferred therefore depressed) and sell when money rates drop (and the market price of the preferred rises).

But they are always a pretty good source of income, generally with dividends well protected by earnings; and can be bought with far smaller amounts of money than are required to buy bonds. Furthermore, they pay dividends quarterly (instead of semiannual interest payments as in the case of bonds).

SOME QUESTIONS AND ANSWERS

Q. *How risk-free are 6 and 7 per cent preferred stocks? What is the difference between a debenture and a preferred stock?*

A. A preferred yielding 6 or 7 per cent, all other things being equal, is riskier than one yielding 4½ to 5 per cent and less risky than one yielding 8 per cent.

A debenture represents debt of a corporation. It is a bond issue and the owner of the bond is a creditor. A preferred share is part of the capital of the company. Its holder is a part owner of the company.

If you are asking about relative safety of the two, there is no flat answer. A debenture ranks higher on the safety list than a preferred *of the same company*, but I'd much rather own the preferreds of some companies than the debentures of others.

Q. *Frequently you recommend preferred shares for income. My wife inherited 10 shares of Southwestern Electric Power 5 per cent preferred. We tried to sell them, but couldn't find a bid.*

A. There is a market for your stock—although an inactive one.

Your problem is that you have a few shares of an extremely small issue—only 75,000 shares. Further complicating matters is the fact that you hold what is called an "old money" preferred: one that offers only 60.20837 per cent exemption on dividends to certain large institutional investors—corporations and, in recent years, savings banks and insurance companies. Most preferreds today offer a tax exemption of 85 per cent to corporate investors.

Since these institutional investors are a large factor in the preferred market, there would be less interest in a preferred such as yours offering only 60 per cent tax exemption than in a "new money" preferred offering 85 per cent.

By the same token, however, your type of issue should be more attractive to individual investors, since you don't have to compete with large institutional buyers.

Any individual considering good-quality utility preferreds for generous income would do well to look into this matter of "new money" vs. "old money" preferreds. All things being equal, you can get a better return from an "old money" preferred, since the prices of these issues aren't supported as well by corporate bidders. You can see this all spelled out in Moody's public utility manual.

While we're on the subject, it is only fair to point out that there are wide differences of opinion on the desirability of *any* preferreds for the individual investor, since he can claim neither the 60 per cent nor the 85 per cent tax exemption.

Several brokers and analysts have written to point out that in many cases an individual can get a better yield from a corporation's bonds (on which interest there is no tax exemption for anyone) than on the preferreds.

Their arguments are well taken. If you are considering the preferred of a corporation, it won't hurt to look a step higher and see what the same firm's bonds are yielding.

There are other factors to be considered, too: bonds generally come in $1,000 amounts and pay interest twice a year; preferreds are lower-priced, pay dividends 4 times a year.

Talk it over with your broker and make the investment most comfortable for yourself.

Q. *I've noticed that many A- and AA-rated bonds are*

yielding above 7 per cent. The same is true of preferreds. If money rates should go even higher, these issues could fall to a price level which would yield 8 per cent. A second purchase could then be made to bring one's average to over a 7 per cent yield.

A. There can be no doubt that, on a yield basis, bonds and preferreds are providing generous income today. One reason is that all money rates are high, so high-quality bonds must sell on a comparable basis. Another reason is that inflation fears are rampant, and long-term investors are wary about putting their money into these issues, which yield a fixed return and thus cannot combat inflation.

So prices have been under further pressure, which translates into higher yields. The lower the market price of a bond paying $50 a year, the higher its yield.

I don't know whether money rates will go much higher or not. If business continues to ease a bit, it could be argued that money rates would rest here and not go higher. But certainly there is more reason to include some bonds and preferreds in income portfolios today than there has been for years.

Q. *We have some Wisconsin Power & Light 4½% preferred. Should we convert it into common stock of the same company?*

A. You can't "convert" this preferred into common–it's not a convertible preferred. You would have to sell the preferred through a broker and buy the common in the same way.

Now–should you? That depends. The 4½ per cent preferred, as of the moment, is selling at 63 and pays a dividend of $4.50. That works out to a yield of about 7.1 per cent on your investment. The common sells at 23 and pays $1.40. Yield: around 6%.

Wisconsin P. & L. common has an excellent rating–A minus. The company has shown a steady earning rise in recent years on the common, so it qualifies as a growth utility. The preferred, of course, is even safer. But the preferred dividend is fixed at $4.50, whereas the common dividend has risen in the last dozen years.

The preferred market price will always be determined, to a large extent, by the going rates for money; the common–which has about doubled in price in the last dozen years–will reflect the company's ability to increase earnings and dividends.

13 Convertible Debentures—Growth Potential with Bond Security

We have stressed constantly in this book that any form of investment means putting money out at risk. In the preceding chapter we discussed the role the preferred share can play in reducing that risk. The purpose of this chapter is to go a step further.

In a corporate setup, bonds and debentures represent debt and the holders of these securities are creditors of the company, rather than shareholders. As creditors, they enjoy first call on assets in case of liquidation, first call on earnings in payment of interest due them.

From the point of view of safety of principal and certainty of income, the position of the bond and debenture holder ranks considerably ahead of the preferred and common stockholders *of that same* corporation. As is customary, the creditors must give up something in return for this added safety. First, they give up any real chance for capital growth, since their loan to the enterprise is fixed at a certain number of dollars to be repaid them at a specified date. Secondly, they give up any right to share in the prosperity of the company, since the income they receive for lending their money is likewise fixed. It may not go down in bad times, but neither does it rise in any period of prosperity.

But there is a way of having this security without giving up the chance to share in future growth. This two-way security is the convertible debenture, a bond which, at the holder's option—and with certain time limits—may be converted into a fixed number of common shares of the company.

It is this option which provides the yeast in an otherwise fixed bond investment.

If, in times of corporate prosperity, the common stock rises, the convertible debenture will advance also since, once the stock passes the stated conversion price, the bond moves in step with the market price of a certain number of common shares.

In times of economic uncertainty, or poor business for the corporation, the debenture holder has a bondholder's claim on earnings for payment of interest due him, a bondholder's claim on assets if, by any chance, the company were to be liquidated or go into bankruptcy. His investment position is protected by the fact that he is a bondholder with a fixed claim on earnings and assets.

This does *NOT* mean that a convertible bond cannot go down in price, or that it may not turn out to be a poor investment.

If the stock does not approach or pass the conversion price the convertible bond must make its way in the open market primarily as a bond, with the conversion feature only a far-off dream. And its life as a bond is subject to as many dangers as any other bond: the company itself may not be doing well; even more importantly, interest rates may have risen to a level which leaves the bond's 4½ or 4¾ or 5% coupon uninteresting. This was true in the spring of 1969 when even top quality creditors were paying 7% and more for money.

A convertible bond of a company whose stock was languishing far below the conversion price then had to "go it alone"—as a bond. And if it had, let us say, a 5% coupon it most likely could not command a price anywhere near its par level of 100, but would reasonably be expected to sell in the mid-70s where the $50 a year interest it pays would work out to above 6½% on the invested money.

The convertible bond is an interesting, if sophisticated, investment instrument. It is *NOT* fool-proof. You *CAN* lose money on it. But it does have the downside risk of a bond and the upside potential of a common share. The investor's job is, then, either to learn enough about the specific instrument to evaluate it himself or to get expert aid from his broker.

There are hundreds of convertible debentures. In some cases, the price of the common is high enough to put a premium on the bond even though its yield is relatively low. In other cases, the price of the common is currently so far below the level at which conversion would be profitable that the debenture sells primarily as an interest-bearing bond, but still with the chance that some day its conversion privilege may become valuable. To sum up, there are:

Convertible debentures which sell at a high price and yield little because the common stock's value has lifted the cost of the debentures.

Convertible debentures which are selling at a relatively low price because their conversion privilege is only a hope.

Debentures which sell at a high premium over their investment value; debentures which sell at a high premium over their conversion value.

A list of some of the outstanding convertible debentures is included in this chapter.

As in the selection of every security, the investor must make his own decision: high yield, high quality, nearby conversion, far-off conversion. A few warnings and truths, however, will not be amiss.

A convertible debenture selling above par (generally $1,000) because the common stock into which it is convertible has risen in price is, of course, more vulnerable than a debenture which is selling strictly on its value as a bond. In other words, the S. S. Kresge 5s of 1995 bond quotation (see bond list) could easily drop if the common stock were to go into a drastic decline while the Vanadium Corp. bond is more likely to be immune to the common stock decline since its conversion privilege is rather vague at this point, anyway.

Another factor should be mentioned as a warning—the call price.

Unlike common stocks, most bonds—straight as well as convertible—may be called in and paid off by the issuing corporation at a price fixed in the indenture. Usually, this call price is par, 100, or a few points above. If a convertible bond is called in for redemption at 102 at a time it is selling on the open market at 180, the owner would be forced to sell it or convert it into common shares before the deadline set for such conversion. If he failed to do so he might find himself receiving $1,020 for a bond which only a few days before was selling at $1,800.

Convertible bonds must be watched. And this is especially true if you own the bond in bearer form—that is, not registered in your name. An issuing corporation has no information on who owns its bearer bonds. It can do no more than advertise the fact it is calling in the bonds. If you don't spot the advertisement, or don't have it brought to your attention, you may sustain a sharp loss. Investors who hold registered bearer bonds are, of course, notified by the corporation of any action affecting the bond.

If you buy convertible debentures at prices above their call price, you must bear in mind that a sharp drop in money rates, making a refunding operation possible and profitable for the issuing corporation, may well result in your bonds being called at a time when the common is not selling high enough to convert profitably.

Secondly, an investor in convertible debentures must be careful to note the length of time his option has to run.

Take the Allegheny Ludlum 4 per cent convertible debentures of 1981. Each $1,000 bond is convertible into 19.23 shares of common until maturity in 1981.

On the other hand, United Aircraft has a 5³/₈ per cent bond which doesn't mature until 1988. *But*—the conversion privilege runs out in 1973.

There is still another type of warning sign which must be observed.

El Paso Natural Gas has a 4½ per cent convertible debenture outstanding which does not mature until 1993. The conversion option also runs until 1993. *But*—on Feb. 1, 1979, the value of the conversion privilege will decline. Currently the bond may be exchanged for 43.99 shares of El Paso Natural Gas common. After Feb. 1, 1979, the number of shares which may be claimed will be reduced. Whenever there is a change in the conversion option, it is always toward a lower number of shares. As a result, the holders of El Paso Natural Gas, as they approach Feb. 1, 1979, will have to evaluate their position in terms of how much the conversion privilege will be reduced after that date.

Convertible debentures are an interesting, sophisticated and complicated investment. They may well deserve a place in your portfolio. But be sure you understand what you're buying before you invest your money.

Following is a list of many convertible debentures traded on the N. Y. and American Stock Exchanges from the Kalb, Voorhis & Co. "Convertible Fact Finder," one of the financial industry's definitive lists of convertibles. The coupon is that carried by the bond. The second column of figures gives you the year in which the bond matures, the third the year in which the conversion privilege expires. "No. of shares" refers to the number of shares which can be claimed by turning in one $1,000 convertible debenture.

Company	*Coupon Rate %*	*Year Due*	*Year Exp.*	*No. of Shares*	*Stock Price $*	*Bond Price %*	*Current Bond Yield %*	*Yield To Maturity (Approx.) %*
AMF Inc	4¼	81	81	16.84	55.87	106	3.99	3.40
APL Corp	5¾	88	88	36.90	23.37	101	5.67	5.60
ARA Services	4⅝	96	96	6.58	160.00	133	3.47	2.74
A-T-O	4⅜	87	87	17.09	11.62	56	7.74	9.96
Air Reduction Co	3⅞	87	87	32.00	22.50	87	4.43	5.04
Alaska Airlines	6⅞	87	87	108.00	8.50	90	7.64	8.00
Alaska Interstate	6.000	96	96	38.46	25.25	108	5.53	5.36
Alexanders	5½	96	96	31.01	18.25	85	6.47	6.77
Alison Mortgage Inv	7.000	90	90	52.67	27.75	140	5.00	3.96
Allegheny Airlines	5¾	93	93	43.17	20.12	97	5.90	5.95
Allegheny Ludlum	4.000	81	81	19.23	20.62	75	5.33	7.73
Allen Electric	6.000	87	87	33.75	20.12	88	6.82	7.31

Allied Artists	8¾	90	90	222.22	5.50	121	7.23	6.73
Allied Stores	4½	81	81	35.71	34.62	123	3.66	1.87
Allied Stores	4½	92	92	22.47	34.62	86	5.19	5.59
Allied Supermkts	5¾	87	87	64.77	7.75	73	7.88	8.98
Aluminum Co of Amer	5¼	91	91	11.76	44.75	85	6.12	6.55
Amerace Esna Corp	5.000	92	92	27.03	26.50	84B	5.89	6.33
American Air Filter	6.000	90	90	18.87	78.87	150	4.00	2.53
American Airlines	4¼	92	80	22.60	45.75	112	3.78	3.39
Amer Broadcasting Co	5.000	93	93	23.08	60.25	137	3.64	2.68
Amer Century Mtge	7.000	90	90	47.62	26.87	124	5.65	4.97
Amer Century Mtge	6¾	91	91	35.71	26.87	93	7.22	7.38
Amer Export Ind	5¼	93	93	17.54	7.87	49	10.55	11.69
Amer Hoist & Derrick	4¾	92	92	62.02	11.75	84	5.65	6.13
Amer Hoist & Derrick	5½	93	93	46.51	11.75	78	7.03	7.57
Amer Motor Inns	5½	91	91	31.25	31.75	109	5.05	4.77
Amer Safety Equip	5¾	83	83	80.58	11.00	100	5.75	5.75
Amfac Inc	5¼	94	94	22.90	38.37	106	4.94	4.79
Ampex Corp	5½	94	94	21.74	9.00	54	10.05	10.95
APCO Oil Corp	5.000	88	88	32.49	23.00	86	5.81	6.38
Arlans Dept Stores	6.000	94	94	36.36	5.25	63	9.52	10.21
Arlen Realty & Dev	5.000	86	86	52.63	22.75	123	4.07	3.00
Armstrong Rubber	4½	87	87	19.60	43.37	94	4.76	5.01
Ashland Oil	4¾	93	93	20.00	27.50	83	5.72	6.19
AVCO Corp	5½	93	93	18.52	18.75	74	7.43	8.04
Bangor Punta	8¼	94	94	18.87	14.62	92	8.97	9.09
Bank of California	6½	96	96	33.20	28.50	108	5.99	5.84
Bank of New York	6¼	94	94	26.67	40.12	114	5.46	5.15
Bartell Media	6½	88	88	66.12	7.00	69	9.40	10.43
Baxter Laboratories	4.000	87	87	57.97	37.37	214B	1.86	
Baxter Laboratories	4¾	90	90	25.97	37.37	115	4.13	3.61
Baxter Laboratories	4⅜	91	91	26.32	37.37	115	3.79	3.29
Becton Dickenson	4⅛	88	88	20.00	38.87	101	4.08	4.04
Becton Dickenson	5.000	89	89	14.81	38.87	94	5.29	5.48
Beech Aircraft	4¾	93	93	21.92	22.00	71	6.69	7.48
Belco Petroleum	4¾	88	88	18.09	21.00	71	6.64	7.84
Belden Corp	8.000	90	90	40.00	25.25	110B	7.27	7.03
Bell Ind	6¾	84	84	109.59	6.25	86	7.78	8.47
Berkey Photo	5¾	86	86	50.45	17.62	102	5.64	5.54
Big Three Ind	5¾	90	90	26.60	45.62	127	4.53	3.69
Black & Decker	4.000	92	92	32.14	86.37	276B	1.45	
Bobbie Brooks	5¼	81	81	28.71	17.50	84	6.25	7.64
Booth Computer	5¾	88	88	21.72	15.12	67	8.58	9.83
Brunswick Corp	4½	81	81	19.74	45.62	98	4.59	4.77
Budd Co	5⅞	94	94	45.45	16.00	90	6.47	6.67
Bulova Watch	6.000	90	90	26.20	17.37	85B	7.06	7.53
Burlington Ind	5.000	91	91	25.64	36.50	107	4.65	4.42
Burroughs Corp	4⅝	94	94	6.29	167.00	124	3.73	3.11
Buttes Gas & Oil	5½	88	88	40.47	19.37	91	5.99	6.30
Cablecom-General	6½	90	90	67.78	17.37	119	5.44	4.86
Cabot Cabot & Forbes	6¾	91	91	47.62	28.75	135	4.98	4.05
Carrier Corp	5⅛	89	89	23.81	47.75	127	4.02	3.07
Castle & Cooke	5⅜	94	94	28.51	20.00	87	6.18	6.49
CECO Corp	4¾	88	88	26.67	34.00	98	4.85	4.92
Celanese	4.000	90	90	10.47	65.37	88	4.51	4.95
Cenco Instruments	5.000	96	96	21.50	52.87	122	4.10	3.64
Central Hudson Gas	5¾	78	78	34.48	24.12	96B	5.99	6.57

Cessna Aircraft	3⅞	92	92	35.29	30.25	108	3.59	3.33
Chadbourn Inc	6½	89	89	75.00	4.00	64	10.16	11.30
Chase Manhattan	4⅞	93	93	18.18	53.25	106	4.60	4.43
Chase Manhattan Bank	6½	96	96	17.39	53.25	111	5.82	5.61
Chase Manhattan Mtge	6¾	90	90	38.10	55.12	204	3.30	.67
Chase Manhattan Mtge	6½	96	96	18.18	55.12	107	6.07	5.94
Chelsea Industries	5¼	93	93	31.91	17.12	76	6.91	7.50
Chemical Bank	5.000	93	93	13.51	54.37	93	5.38	5.56
Chemical N Y	5½	96	96	13.51	54.37	97	5.64	5.69
Chock Full O Nuts	4½	81	81	37.91	10.00	75	6.00	8.37
Chris Craft Ind	6.000	89	89	50.18	6.62	65	9.23	10.42
City Investing	7½	90	90	60.61	19.62	131	5.73	4.94
Cluett Peabody	4¼	84	84	48.38	22.87	111B	3.81	3.12
Coburn Corp	5½	87	87	36.17	6.87	59B	9.32	11.09
Collins Radio	4⅞	87	87	13.79	16.50	64	7.56	9.33
Columbia Pictures	5¾	94	94	32.65	12.50	68	8.42	9.08
Columbia Pictures	4¾	87	87	42.83	12.50	74	6.42	7.64
Commercial Solvents	4½	91	91	14.71	26.62	68	6.62	7.70
Commonwealth Oil	4¼	92	92	37.50	16.25	77	5.52	6.26
Computer Sciences	6.000	94	94	37.04	7.87	58	10.34	11.11
Condec Corp	5.000	93	93	43.84	12.62	66	7.58	8.46
Condec Corp	7¾	96	96	111.11	12.62	135	5.74	5.21
Connecticut Gen Mtge	6¾	90	90	45.45	30.00	133B	5.08	4.13
Connecticut Gen Mtge	6.000	96	96	30.77	30.00	102	5.85	5.80
Continental Airlines	3½	92	92	27.43	23.37	74	4.68	5.60
Continental Mtge Inv	6¼	90	90	44.94	13.62	88	7.10	7.47
Continental Tel	5¼	86	86	38.83	21.12	103	5.10	4.95
Cooper Laboratories	7½	91	91	45.45	31.87	143	5.23	4.15
Copperweld Steel	5.000	79	79	35.71	25.50	98	5.08	5.23
Crane Co	5.000	93	93	20.00	48.50	101	4.93	4.88
Crocker National Co	5¾	96	96	22.73	33.75	99	5.76	5.77
Crowell Collier	4.000	92	92	38.94	12.62	68	5.84	6.90
Crystal Oil Co	7.000	84	84	86.58	10.12	98	7.11	7.18
DCA Development	6.000	88	88	40.00	9.25	67	8.96	10.18
DPA Inc	6¾	85	85	71.43	5.37	75	8.94	10.20
DPF	5½	87	87	25.62	11.25	61	9.02	10.70
DWG Corp	5½	87	87	102.99	6.50	83	6.59	7.27
Data Products	5¾	95	95	43.48	6.37	59	9.75	10.50
Dayco Corp	5¾	94	94	30.00	20.87	82	7.01	7.42
Dayco Corp	6.000	94	94	33.33	20.87	88B	6.81	7.07
Dayco Corp	6¼	96	96	46.24	20.87	103	6.07	6.01
Dearborn-Storm	5¼	88	88	41.55	21.37	100	5.25	5.25
Del Monte Corp	5¼	94	94	25.64	25.50	88	5.97	6.26
Development Corp Amer	5.000	96	96	29.41	34.50	105	4.76	4.65
Di Giorgio Corp	5¾	93	93	58.82	16.25	106	5.42	5.27
Dillingham Corp	5½	94	94	31.25	13.37	75	7.33	7.91
Disney Walt	4¾	96	96	7.85	165.00	137	3.47	2.67
Diversified Ind	5⅞	93	93	33.33	7.00	63	9.33	10.17
Duplan Corp	5½	94	94	20.96	19.50	75	7.28	7.85
Duro-Test Corp	5¾	92	92	62.34	12.87	89B	6.46	6.74
E G & G Inc	3½	87	87	21.62	25.75	73	4.79	6.27
Eastern Air Dev	8.000	88	88	105.00	11.25	114	7.00	6.56
Eastern Air Lines	5.000	92	92	20.00	26.12	71	6.98	7.78
Eastern Air Lines	4¾	93	93	29.41	26.12	93	5.09	5.28
Echlin Manufacturing	5¼	91	91	18.91	65.00	124B	4.23	3.52
Eckerd Jack	4¾	88	88	80.13	27.87	220	2.16	
El Paso Natural Gas	6.000	93	93	43.99	19.62	98	6.12	6.17
El Paso Natural Gas	8½	95	95	56.00	19.62	122	6.97	6.63
Electronic Assist	6½	85	85	125.00	5.75	85	7.65	8.39
Electrospace	5½	83	83	32.01	21.50	86	6.40	7.30

Elgin National Ind	6⅞	82	82	71.11	6.00	69B	9.89	11.98
Elgin National Ind	6¾	88	88	51.30	6.00	66	10.23	11.32
Equitable Life Mtge	6¾	90	90	38.10	28.75	105	6.40	6.24
Equity Funding Corp	5½	91	91	27.21	38.75	116	4.72	4.25
Essex International	5⅜	96	96	21.00	48.75	108	4.94	4.76
Esterline Corp	6¼	95	95	27.03	13.25	75	8.28	8.73
Evans Products	6¼	94	94	45.54	24.00	117	5.32	4.95
Extendicare Inc	6.000	89	89	34.25	27.50	105	5.69	5.49
FMC Corp	4¼	92	92	24.10	25.50	76	5.59	6.36
Fairchild Industries	4⅜	92	92	41.03	12.75	68	6.36	7.38
Farah Mfg	5.000	94	94	26.58	25.87	88	5.65	5.94
Fedders Corp	5.000	96	96	20.00	42.87	106	4.71	4.58
Federal National Mortge	4⅜	96	96	12.74	98.37	125	3.49	2.91
Fibreboard Corp	4¾	93	93	32.00	22.75	92B	5.16	5.37
Fidelity Mtge Inv	7¾	85	85	47.06	26.87	123	6.30	5.36
Filmways Inc	6.000	88	88	41.99	7.00	69B	8.63	9.82
First Mortgage Inv	6¾	85	85	41.67	25.50	103B	6.55	6.40
Fischer & Porter	6.000	86	86	60.98	22.00	144B	4.15	2.39
Fischer & Porter	5½	87	87	32.87	22.00	91	6.01	6.36
Fisher Foods	6½	94	94	33.33	19.37	93	6.99	7.13
Foremost-McKesson	6.000	94	94	32.62	27.50	106	5.62	5.47
Forest City Ent	5⅝	88	88	40.00	26.50	107	5.26	5.00
Franklin Realty	7.000	89	89	100.00	9.25	94B	7.45	7.62
Frontier Airlines	6.000	92	92	58.04	6.37	65	9.16	9.97
Fruehauf Corp	5½	94	94	21.62	38.62	100	5.47	5.46
Fuqua Industries Inc	7⅝	95	95	80.00	23.50	188	4.06	2.62
GAC Corp	5⅞	94	94	20.00	13.00	62	9.44	10.21
General Instrument	4¼	85	85	32.49	25.37	90	4.72	5.27
General Instruments	5.000	92	92	14.93	25.37	72	6.89	7.66
Genl Mortgage Inv	8.000	90	90	95.24	10.50	104	7.69	7.59
General Tel & Elec	4.000	90	90	20.00	30.75	76	5.21	6.15
General Tel & Elec	5.000	92	92	20.58	30.75	85	5.88	6.30
General Tel & Elec	6¼	96	96	29.74	30.75	107	5.84	5.71
Georgia Pacific	5¾	94	94	18.46	45.50	107	5.34	5.17
Georgia Pacific	5¼	96	96	15.19	45.50	96	5.47	5.55
Giddings & Lewis	4⅝	87	87	27.50	13.37	76B	6.03	7.12
Gordon Jewelry	5.000	88	88	34.48	29.25	107B	4.67	4.39
Grace W R & Co	4¼	90	90	16.48	29.75	73	5.82	6.88
Grace W R & Co	6½	96	96	33.76	29.75	110	5.88	5.70
Granite Management	6.000	87	87	26.77	9.25	65	9.23	10.61
Grant W T	4¾	96	96	13.70	41.00	83	5.72	6.10
Gray Mfg	5¼	82	82	45.62	13.37	80	6.56	8.10
Great Northern Nek	4¼	91	91	17.70	47.62	96	4.43	4.56
Green Giant	4¼	92	92	22.73	29.37	79	5.36	6.03
Greyhound Computer	6.000	86	86	43.48	10.12	76	7.89	9.00
Greyhound Corp	6½	90	90	54.42	21.12	116	5.59	5.10
Grolier Inc	4¼	87	87	25.32	24.00	78	5.45	6.50
Grow Chemical	5¼	87	87	57.60	12.50	82	6.40	7.18
Grumman Aircraft	4¼	92	92	22.99	18.37	65	6.54	7.65
Gulf & Western Ind	5¼	87	87	22.94	34.37	90	5.83	6.27
Gulf & Western Ind	5½	93	93	17.64	34.37	79	6.92	7.42
Gulf & Western Ind A	5¼	87	87	22.94	34.37	90	5.82	6.25
Gulf Life Holding Co	5½	91	91	22.22	46.62	115	4.76	4.31
Gulf Resources	6¼	91	91	71.43	7.00	74	8.45	9.15
Hammermill Paper	5.000	94	94	25.00	17.00	75B	6.62	7.23
Heitman Mortgage	8.000	91	91	100.00	14.12	140	5.71	4.76
Helmrich & Payne	5.000	87	87	36.67	28.75	112	4.43	3.90
Heublein Inc	5¾	94	94	23.67	53.50	141	4.08	3.18
HI-G Inc	6.000	88	88	32.15	5.75	51	11.76	13.44
Hilton Hotels	5½	95	95	16.39	55.87	111B	4.95	4.70

Hoerner Waldorf	5.000	94	94	29.85	29.87	99B	5.05	5.07
Host International	$5\frac{1}{4}$	94	94	23.67	40.00	106B	4.95	4.80
Houston Light & Pwr	$5\frac{1}{2}$	85	85	22.73	43.25	116B	4.74	3.91
Howmet Corp	$4\frac{1}{2}$	92	92	24.66	15.75	69	6.52	7.48
Illustrated World En	$7\frac{1}{2}$	91	91	111.11	10.25	119	6.26	5.77
Indian Head	$5\frac{1}{2}$	93	93	25.97	29.12	94	5.85	6.00
Instrument Systems	6.000	77	77	27.03	7.12	77	7.72	12.02
Instrument Systems	7.000	91	91	83.33	7.12	82	8.54	8.99
Intl Minerals & Chem	4.000	91	91	19.01	18.75	63	6.30	7.69
Interstate Stores	4.000	92	92	22.78	11.62	55	7.21	8.68
IPCO Hospital Supply	$5\frac{1}{4}$	89	89	31.82	17.50	83	6.33	6.98
ITEL Corp	7.000	95	95	54.05	10.50	81	8.64	8.96
ITEL Corp	8.000	96	96	66.67	10.50	92	8.67	8.78
Jervis Corp	$5\frac{3}{8}$	82	82	54.95	12.37	80	6.70	8.28
Kaufman & Broad Inc	6.000	95	95	37.38	43.62	162	3.68	2.48
Kerr McGee	$3\frac{3}{4}$	92	92	22.22	39.87	98	3.82	3.87
Kirsch Co	6.000	95	95	30.83	47.50	146B	4.11	3.17
Kresge S S	5.000	95	95	18.69	98.75	186	2.69	.88
LTV Electrosystems	$4\frac{1}{2}$	92	92	41.67	6.25	52	8.65	10.12
Leisure Technology	$6\frac{3}{4}$	96	96	41.67	20.62	96	7.01	7.07
Libby McNeil & Libby	5.000	89	89	61.63	6.75	66	7.55	8.90
Liberty Leasing	$8\frac{1}{2}$	90	90	142.86	7.25	111	7.66	7.40
Litton Industries	$3\frac{1}{2}$	87	87	25.00	25.00	79	4.40	5.51
Lockheed Aircraft	$4\frac{1}{4}$	92	92	13.79	11.87	45	9.44	11.18
Lone Star Ind	$5\frac{1}{8}$	93	93	38.46	25.00	107	4.78	4.59
Lucky Stores	5.000	93	93	100.00	20.50	200	2.50	.17
Lundy Electronics	$6\frac{1}{2}$	88	88	26.85	12.50	66	9.85	11.07
MacDonald E F	6.000	87	87	81.43	5.87	73	8.22	9.35
Macke Co	$4\frac{7}{8}$	92	92	58.39	15.00	93B	5.21	5.40
Macy R H	$4\frac{1}{4}$	90	90	33.33	43.87	142	2.99	1.59
Macy R H	5.000	92	92	27.78	43.87	122B	4.10	3.49
Madison Sq Garden	$6\frac{1}{4}$	87	87	146.00	3.87	84	7.44	8.05
Marcor Inc	5.000	96	96	24.69	30.37	99	5.03	5.03
Marinduque Mining	6.000	88	88	22.32	18.50	72	8.33	9.33
Martin Marietta	6.000	94	94	37.74	22.25	99	6.05	6.07
Maryland Cup	$5\frac{1}{8}$	94	94	19.25	32.50	91B	5.60	5.81
Masco Corp	$5\frac{3}{8}$	94	94	40.00	37.50	145B	3.71	2.69
Massmutual Mtge & Rlty	$6\frac{3}{4}$	90	90	47.62	29.87	138	4.89	3.86
Massmutual Mtge & Rlty	$6\frac{1}{4}$	91	91	29.85	29.87	98	6.38	6.43
McCory Corp	$6\frac{1}{2}$	92	92	33.33	28.50	105	6.15	6.01
McDonalds Corp	$4\frac{1}{2}$	96	96	14.18	90.00	141	3.18	2.27
McDonnel Douglas	$4\frac{3}{4}$	91	91	25.20	39.00	107	4.43	4.21
McGraw-Hill	$3\frac{7}{8}$	92	92	16.00	17.62	65	5.89	7.09
Medusa Portland	$5\frac{3}{4}$	88	88	28.57	44.37	127	4.53	3.53
Melville Shoe	$4\frac{7}{8}$	96	96	15.62	66.62	118B	4.11	3.71
Memorex Corp	$5\frac{1}{4}$	90	90	7.02	34.37	58	8.97	10.37
Metro-Goldwyn-Mayer	5.000	93	93	21.28	21.00	68	7.30	8.13
Miles Laboratories	$5\frac{1}{4}$	94	94	15.38	50.25	98	5.32	5.35
Mohawk Airlines	6.000	93	93	76.92	5.62	63		
Mohawk Data Sciences	$5\frac{1}{2}$	94	94	11.70	20.62	69	7.97	8.63
Mony Mortgage Inv	7.000	90	90	90.91	12.62	110	6.36	6.08
National Bellas Hess	6.000	84	84	97.56	4.00	67B	8.96	10.86
National Can	5.000	93	93	32.13	16.00	82	6.04	6.49
Natl Cash Register	6.000	95	85	15.38	32.25	94	6.35	6.46
National City Lines	$5\frac{1}{2}$	88	88	36.36	25.50	100	5.50	5.50
National City Lines	$6\frac{1}{2}$	91	91	36.36	25.50	111B	5.86	5.56
National Distillers	$4\frac{1}{2}$	92	92	38.83	16.87	80	5.59	6.19
National General	4.000	93	93	20.62	27.87	68	5.88	6.86
National Health Ent	$8\frac{1}{2}$	86	86	200.00	5.12	110	7.73	7.36
National Homes	$4\frac{3}{4}$	96	96	24.10	27.37	92B	5.14	5.30

National Industries	5¾	88	88	42.50	8.37	67	8.52	9.73
Natl Medical Ent	6¾	96	96	24.69	39.62	108	6.25	6.11
Newberry J J	6½	94	94	33.33	20.37	85	7.60	7.88
Newhall Land	6.000	95	95	24.39	21.75	87	6.88	7.14
North Amer Phillips	4.000	92	82	17.24	32.50	74	5.34	6.19
North Amer Rockwell	4¼	91	91	21.74	35.25	87	4.84	5.28
Northeast Airlines	6½	86	86	40.00	5.75	75	8.67	9.76
Northrop Corp	4¾	87	87	20.00	24.12	79	5.99	6.96
Nowstn Mut Life Rlty	6.000	91	91	47.62	26.00	119	5.04	4.50
Nytronics Inc	6½	83	83	59.21	2.37	37		
OKC Corp	5¾	88	88	41.67	22.00	100	5.75	5.75
Oak Electro/Netics	4⅜	87	87	28.84	15.62	65	6.73	8.55
Occidental Petroleum	7½	96	96	50.00	12.75	90	8.33	8.47
Offshore Co	5.000	92	92	26.67	30.50	95	5.26	5.40
Ogden Corp	5.000	93	93	20.00	17.62	68	7.30	8.13
Oneida Ltd	5½	88	88	34.19	18.62	82	6.71	7.39
Otis Elevator	6½	95	95	21.51	39.50	106	6.10	5.98
Owens-Illinois	4½	92	92	16.95	47.25	95	4.70	4.83
Ozark Air Lines	5¼	86	86	129.03	10.12	132	3.98	2.57
Ozark Air Lines	6¾	88	88	115.53	10.12	116	5.82	5.25
Pan Am World Air	4⅞	79	79	133.33	15.75	206	2.37	
Pan Am World Air	4½	84	84	68.38	15.75	109	4.10	3.49
Pan Am World Air	4½	86	86	28.70	15.75	64	7.00	8.96
Pan Am World Air	5¼	89	89	34.61	15.75	74	7.05	8.02
Papercraft Corp	5¼	94	94	28.68	36.25	110	4.77	4.53
Parker-Hannifin	4.000	92	92	13.15	46.75	75B	5.33	6.15
Penn-Dixie Cement	5.000	82	82	34.81	10.37	70	7.08	9.44
Pennsylvania Eng	5.000	93	93	102.56	3.00	54	9.26	10.36
Pennzoil United	5¼	96	96	26.14	20.50	85	6.14	6.44
Pepsico Inc	4¾	96	96	15.75	72.00	132	3.58	2.88
Permaneer Corp	5¼	89	89	32.79	14.25	66	7.92	9.23
Philip Morris	6.000	94	94	36.04	76.00	266	2.26	
Phillips-Van Heusen	5¼	94	94	35.56	25.00	100	5.25	5.25
Phoenix Steel	6.000	87	87	86.66	3.75	54	11.11	12.94
Pillsbury Co	4¾	89	89	17.24	53.12	104	4.55	4.37
Purex Corp Ltd	4⅞	94	94	28.71	21.62	85	5.71	6.10
RCA Corp	4½	92	92	16.95	42.50	91	4.95	5.22
Ralston Purina	4⅞	92	92	37.74	38.50	145	3.36	2.17
Ramada Inns	8.000	95	95	127.00	19.50	247	3.24	.97
Ramada Inns	5.000	96	96	53.33	19.50	120	4.15	3.72
Rapid American	5¾	77	77	47.06	20.00	109	5.23	3.54
Reading & Bates	5½	88	88	34.32	30.37	112	4.91	4.47
Reeves Brothers	4.000	91	91	26.19	36.00	93B	4.28	4.51
Revere Copper	5½	92	92	29.41	15.37	78	7.05	7.62
Reynolds Metals	4½	91	91	16.41	19.12	67	6.69	7.84
Rheingold Corp	6½	94	94	33.33	23.87	102	6.34	6.29
Riegel Textile	5.000	93	93	22.99	19.75	71	7.04	7.83
Roblin Industries	6½	84	84	74.77	7.25	80	8.13	9.31
Rochester Telephone	4¾	94	94	21.74	45.00	107B	4.44	4.25
Rockwood Computer	7.000	83	83	15.43	6.12	54	12.96	15.81
Rockwood Computer	5¼	87	87	32.00	6.12	50B	10.34	12.51
Rohr Ind	5¼	86	86	39.11	20.50	95	5.53	5.75
Rust Craft Greeting	5¼	96	96	40.00	27.00	117B	4.47	4.10
Ryan Homes	6.000	91	91	32.79	29.00	107	5.58	5.37
SCM Corp	5½	88	88	21.50	18.12	77	7.10	8.00
Sanders Associates	5.000	92	92	14.93	17.75	66	7.58	8.52

Sanitas Services	9.000	90	90	125.00	8.75	118	7.61	7.20
Santa Fe Ind	6¼	98	88	31.25	32.50	111	5.63	5.45
Santa Fe Intl	5½	87	87	31.58	39.62	131	4.18	2.97
Seaboard World Air	5.000	86	86	37.50	16.12	80	6.23	7.26
Seatrain Lines	6.000	94	94	36.36	13.37	75	8.00	8.49
Sherwin Williams	6¼	95	95	21.74	46.50	111	5.61	5.37
Skil Corp	5.000	92	92	25.00	29.50	92	5.43	5.66
Sola Basic	4½	92	92	45.11	18.25	90	5.00	5.31
Sonderling Broadcast	5¼	88	88	24.13	27.87	84	6.23	6.85
Southern Calif Ed	3⅛	80	80	22.99	26.75	77	4.02	6.59
Sprague Electric	4¼	92	92	21.98	10.37	54	7.87	9.30
Standard Internation	5.000	87	87	59.77	19.12	115B	4.35	3.71
Std Oil of Indiana	5.000	96	96	14.18	67.62	111	4.50	4.26
Std Prudential	6½	90	90	66.67	12.50	94	6.91	7.09
State Mutual Inv	6¾	91	91	47.62	24.75	115	5.87	5.46
Stauffer Chemical	4½	91	91	18.69	39.75	85B	5.29	5.80
Stevens J P	4.000	90	90	17.72	29.75	69	5.80	7.05
Storer Broadcast	4½	86	86	19.61	34.75	79	5.69	6.85
Sundstrand Corp	5.000	93	93	14.08	32.75	73	6.85	7.58
Sunshine Mining	6½	89	89	51.39	10.75	92	7.05	7.30
Surveyor Fund	5.000	84	84	121.61	6.12	91	5.49	6.06
Susquehanna Corp	5½	88	88	30.63	12.00	68	8.09	9.34
Sutro Mortgage Inv	6¾	91	91	50.00	20.25	98	6.87	6.92
Talcott Natl	6.000	94	94	37.04	20.25	90	6.67	6.88
Tappan Co	5½	94	94	32.26	37.87	123	4.47	3.93
Teledyne Inc	3½	92	92	19.08	25.75	68	5.09	6.23
Tesoro Petroleum	5¼	89	89	26.25	45.75	123	4.27	3.44
Texfi Industries	4¾	96	96	17.54	25.87	71	6.69	7.30
Tidewater Marine Svc	5¾	91	91	32.26	30.50	111	5.18	4.87
Trane Co	4.000	92	92	13.89	71.25	104	3.85	3.72
Trans-Lux Corp	5.000	87	87	71.12	12.12	94	5.32	5.58
Trans World Airlines	4.000	92	92	11.97	49.00	74	5.37	6.24
Trans World Airlines	5.000	94	94	18.52	49.00	100	5.00	5.00
TYCO Laboratories	5⅞	88	88	16.40	16.75	70	8.39	9.59
Tyler Corp	5.000	93	93	27.40	29.00	93	5.37	5.54
Union Corp	6.000	88	88	63.33	15.62	106	5.66	5.44
Union Corp	7.000	89	89	90.91	15.62	145	4.82	3.53
Union Pacific Corp	4¾	99	99	17.50	61.87	112	4.22	3.98
Uniroyal Inc	5½	96	96	39.40	19.75	98	5.61	5.65
United Aircraft	4½	88	73	30.00	34.62	105	4.25	4.01
United Aircraft	5⅜	91	76	11.85	34.62	77	6.91	7.57
United Aircraft	4½	92	77	10.00	34.62	65	6.87	7.92
United Brands	5½	94	94	18.18	12.75	64	8.49	9.29
United Merchants	4.000	90	90	29.20	28.37	83	4.78	5.39
United Nuclear	5.000	88	88	25.97	14.87	73	6.78	7.93
U S Financial	5½	91	91	21.20	37.25	95	5.79	5.94
US Realty Inv	5¾	89	89	39.60	19.75	75	7.67	8.55
US Smelting & Ref	5¾	93	93	14.85	26.50	73	7.88	8.53
United Utilities	5.000	93	93	35.71	18.75	88	5.64	5.95
University Computing	7¼	95	95	22.08	20.50	79	9.15	9.48
Vendo Corp	4½	80	80	21.51	14.37	75	5.98	8.66
Vernitron Corp	5¾	82	82	49.31	6.00	62B	9.27	12.23
Virginia Elec & Pwr	3⅝	86	86	28.67	18.75	72	5.03	6.69
Walgreen Co	5½	91	91	31.00	26.75	98	5.57	5.61
Wallace Murray	6½	91	91	45.45	21.50	107	6.07	5.88
Jim Walter Corp	5¾	91	91	23.81	35.37	103	5.58	5.49

Wean United	5½	93	93	41.67	7.62	57	9.63	10.64
Welded Tube Co	8.000	78	78	142.86	7.25	114	6.99	5.30
Westates Petroleum	6½	87	87	191.57	4.12	99	6.57	6.60
Western Air Lines	5¼	93	93	29.93	43.37	131	4.00	3.19
Western Union	7¼	95	95	26.85	48.50	135	5.37	4.76
White Consolidated	5½	92	92	37.01	22.00	99	5.53	5.54
White Motor	5¼	93	93	18.35	29.37	86	6.10	6.47
Whittaker Corp	4½	88	88	21.24	12.87	64	7.03	8.65
Wickes Corp	5⅛	94	94	18.85	44.75	103B	4.98	4.90
Will Ross	5¼	89	89	18.96	47.50	111	4.73	4.34
Williams Co	5.650	91	91	20.00	45.87	113	4.98	4.58
Wilshire Oil	6.000	95	95	141.84	6.50	100	6.00	6.00
Witco Chemical	4½	93	93	20.00	27.00	79	5.68	6.26
Wometco Enterprises	5½	94	94	43.10	23.62	108	5.09	4.90
Work Wear	4¾	85	85	70.18	16.62	114	4.15	3.42
Wyle Laboratories	5¼	88	88	43.96	5.50	54	9.63	11.45
Xerox Corp	6.000	95	95	10.87	133.75	166	3.61	2.35
Zapata Corp	4¾	88	88	18.87	34.25	82	5.79	6.59
Zapata Corp B	4¾	88	88	18.87	34.25	81	5.86	6.70
Zapata Corp C	4¾	88	88	18.87	34.25	82	5.79	6.55
Zayre Corp	5¾	94	94	25.00	32.50	101	5.67	5.64

SOME QUESTIONS AND ANSWERS

Q. *I own some convertible debentures and have just been informed that the bonds were called last spring. Why did I receive no notice at the time? I have thereby lost a lot of money, since the conversion rate was highly favorable to the bondholders.*

A. I must emphasize once more that when you hold a bearer bond it is up to you to keep yourself informed of any redemptions, conversion changes, etc. Even though your bond has a number, there is no way for the issuing company to know who holds it, since it may be transferred like cash and with no report on the transfer made either to the issuer or to the bank acting as trustee.

This is a difficult situation for all concerned. You, as a bearer-bond holder, are in limbo. There is no clear path of communication between you and the borrowing corporation. Usually it is required that notice of redemption be published in a New York City paper. Sometimes if there has been a heavy regional sale of the bonds, say, in the Northwest or the Southeast, papers in that area will be used to advertise the redemption. But if you live in a small town, you're quite likely to miss the notice.

I have no other solution than these suggestions:

1. Buy registered bonds. The company then sends you an interest check every 6 months and knows exactly where you are.

2. If you insist on bearer bonds, leave them with your broker, where, as a client, your bond lists will be checked against redemptions. (I don't know that the brokers will thank me for this.)

Q. *I hold convertible debentures: Pan American 4⅞s, of '79 and Pan American 4½s of '84. Should I hold them or convert into stock?*

A. The Pan American debentures and common move so widely in price from day to day that it is impractical to attempt a similar example. But I'm sure that if on any given day you work out the market values of the bonds and the market values of the common into which they are convertible (into 133.33 common shares for the 4⅞s and into 68.38 shares for the 4½s) you will find that you have more market value in the bonds than in the common.

As a rule, it does not pay to convert debentures into common because the bond usually sells at least a slight premium over the value of the stock so obtained. If you want to hold Pan Am common, sell your bonds on the open market and buy the stock.

Q. *I'd like to buy some convertible bonds. I've been told that so long as the market remains stable they can't go below their par value.*

A. I'm afraid you've been brainwashed by the current frenzy over convertibles. Convertible bonds not only can go below par, but have done so–and not only in stable (or falling) markets, but in rising markets, as well.

A glance through a list of such issues will show many below par today and including such well-known corporate names as Air Reduction, Celanese, Chock Full O' Nuts, Northrop, Pan American, TWA.

Q. *I'm looking for maximum income, with as much safety as I can get. Would you suggest convertible debentures?*

A. As a class, no.

A convertible debenture, in addition to offering a fixed return, gives you the right to convert into the common stock of the corporation.

If that conversion privilege is worth anything (that is, if the price of the stock is anywhere near the conversion point) you can't expect to get that privilege for nothing. You pay for it in lower interest rates as contrasted with nonconvertible bonds of the same quality.

Q. *I'm disappointed in your reply to my question about*

convertible debentures. I had asked you about transferring funds from 5 and 5¼% savings certificates into convertibles, but when I studied some of the examples you gave, I discovered that the yield is no better, and in some cases less that 5%. Do you really think it wise to switch out of insured savings and accept a smaller return in a risk investment?

A. Your arithmetic is perfect, but you've completely lost sight of the original question. The basic reason for going from savings in dollars, or in dollar-fixed (straight, nonconvertible) bonds into common stocks (or senior issues convertible into common) is NOT to obtain a higher yield on your money. You rarely can.

The chief reason for making such a switch is that you 1) fear inflation and 2) are hoping for capital gain.

Therefore, before you make such a switch you must ask yourself which you want more: the safety of the number of dollars invested in savings or high-grade straight bonds, or the inflation protection and capital gain one hopes for in equity investments.

I made NO suggestion that you make ANY switch. I merely pointed out what the alternatives are. It's now up to you to decide whether you fear the shrinkage of your dollar's purchasing power more than you fear a market decline in the price of convertible issues.

I am NOT a salesman pushing savings accounts, bonds, common shares, or convertibles. I am NOT a doctor who tells his patient: "Either follow this regimen or I'll put you into the hospital where you'll be forced to do as I say."

I'm merely trying to set forth the various choices available to an investor—somewhat like, I suppose, an industrial exhibition hall where many different products are displayed, but where no selling takes place.

Q. *I have just recently become interested in the potential offered by convertible debentures. If a person is interested in a common stock of a company which also has convertible debentures outstanding, why wouldn't it be a good idea to buy the bond and then convert to common stock when the common rises?*

A. I have frequently mentioned the potential in convertibles, but have also warned that they are a sophisticated investment and must be approached cautiously.

A convertible debenture does have defensive strength and also appreciation potential, IF you buy it "right."

If you buy a 5% convertible debenture selling, for example, at 180 ($1,800 per $1,000 debenture) because it is convertible into 60 shares of common currently selling around 30, then you are to all intents and purposes buying the common and must expect that any prolonged decline in the common would be reflected in a similar decline in the bond.

The bond's defensive values would not come into play until it got down to the price at which the $50 a year interest payment became attractive. And in this market that might not be until the bond fell to the 70s. So, you see, a convertible debenture can be risky, too.

If you pay $900 for a 5% debenture which carries the option of conversion into 20 shares of stock now selling at 18 (and showing no signs of ever being able to reach 50) then you are, to all intents and purposes, buying a straight 5% bond. Your downside risk, of course, is measured by the quality of the bond and the going interest rates. Your appreciation potential is nebulous.

If you find a company you like with a convertible debenture selling not too far above its straight investment value (that is, its value as a straight bond—without a conversion privilege) and also selling not too far above its conversion value, then you should consider it as an alternative to buying the stock. But it does not necessarily follow that buying just any bond will eliminate or even reduce risk.

Incidentally, if the common should rise, a convertible debenture will rise too. It is rarely necessary to convert into the common to take your profits.

Q. *What is the difference between interest and yield on a bond? On a stock?*

A. A bond may be listed as carrying a 5% coupon, thus: "ABC" 5% debentures due in 14 years. So it pays $50 a year in *interest.* But it sells at 80% of par, or $800. So the *current yield* is $50 divided by $800, or 6¼%. But it will be paid off at par, $1,000. So, adding the $200 gain in price to the 6¼% current yield gives you a *yield to maturity* of 7.37%.

A stock paying an annual dividend of $2 and selling for $40 a share yields 5% ($2 divided by $40). Since a stock has no maturity, there is no yield to maturity.

Q. *Why does a company's 5½% convertible bond sell at 85 while its 3½% convertible preferred sells at 167?*

A. Because the bond represents the right to convert to stock at 58½ and the preferred, at under 25.

Q. *Should one convert a convertible preferred into common if the common sells for more than the preferred but pays fewer dividends? If both are at the same price, but the common yields less? Is there time allowed to convert the preferred if the company decides to call in the issue?*

A. The relative market prices of the preferred and common cannot be evaluated in making a conversion decision unless you tell me whether the preferred is convertible into one share of common, five shares, or one-half a share. If the common yields less, why not continue to hold the preferred?

You *ARE* notified if the issuing corporation decides to call in the preferred. You then either sell the preferred for cash or convert into common, depending upon which works out better for you.

Q. *If I own a convertible bond which may be exchanged for 500 shares of stock, may I make the exchange any time? Could I then sell the 500 shares and make a profit if it is trading at more than $2 a share?*

A. Yes, unless there is some time restriction on the conversion. However, if you may convert, and the stock is selling about $2, you'll find the bond is also selling above $1,000—so you can get just as much or more gain by selling the bond, without bothering to convert.

Q. *On the advice of my broker who said I could get an income of 7½ per cent and also make some money on them, I paid par for $5,000 convertible bonds of an oil* *company. They since have fallen to 80 and I'm worried.*

A. When you step down in quality, you must be prepared to take a bit of worry with your income. A rate of 7½ per cent is high for a convertible bond.

The bonds are rated BB by Standard & Poor's and Ba by Moody–which is the same thing–the fifth grade down from the top in the quality scale.

The bond is convertible into 50 shares of stock. The stock is volatile, so you must expect some relatively wide price movements. When the stock was up around 20, the bond's price enjoyed the support of the common stock market. Now that the common has fallen, the bond has lost some ground, since its rating evidently does not justify a price of 100 for the bond without the support of a nearby conversion into the common.

Q. *How would I go about selecting convertible bonds and convertible preferreds as part of a portfolio aimed at high safety and high return and still have some value as a hedge against inflation?*

A. You're not going to be able to touch both bases at the same time. High return and high safety *never* go together.

A convertible debenture or preferred, by its very nature, can't be expected to yield as much as a straight bond or straight preferred of the same quality. (You don't get the conversion feature for nothing.)

The more immediate the value of the conversion feature, the less you must generally expect in income; the more distant the chances of profiting by the conversion feature, the higher the yield.

There are literally hundreds of convertible debentures and preferreds. Since every investment in this area would involve the simultaneous juggling of yield, quality and conversion features, I suggest you sit down with your broker and have him explain some choices which would best suit your individual book–depending on your age, goals, ability to assume risk.

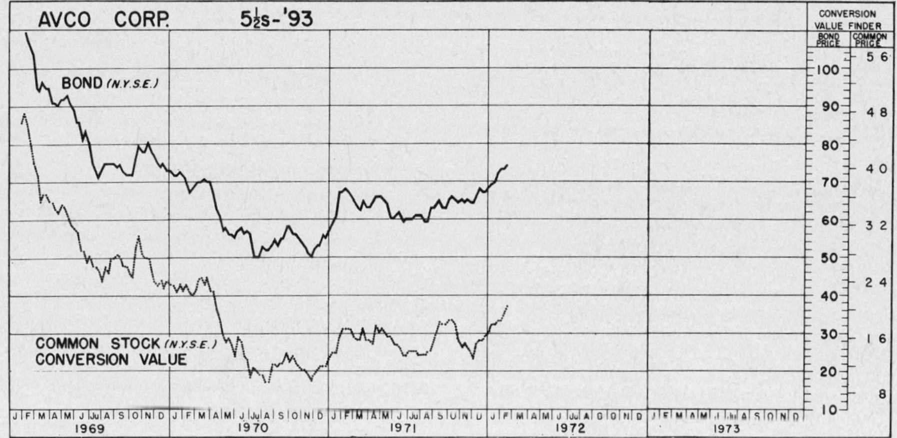

Convertible debentures are complicated investment instruments, since they are evaluated not only as a debenture (a bond) but as an option to claim common shares. Avco Corp. has outstanding a 5½% convertible debenture due in 1993. Until that date it may be exchanged for 18.52 shares of common stock. Late in February, 1972, the bond was selling at 73 and the common shares at 18½. Since 18.52 shares of a stock selling at 18½ are worth only about $345, the market price of 73 ($730) for each debenture represents a premium of 115% over the conversion value and must be considered, therefore, as representing investors' hopes that the common price will some day rise to the level where it will bolster the market price of the bond.

14 Corporate Bonds as a Conservative Investment Base

Bonds—historically the most conservative of the corporate securities family—actually have had a checkered career in this century.

During the early 1900s, bonds still retained the aura of solidarity and respectability they had enjoyed for centuries. Railroad, utility, and corporate bonds were the foundation of the solid citizen's investment portfolio. They stood for wealth—solid, continuing, dependable, impregnable wealth.

But then came the Big Depression, and millions upon millions of dollars' worth of railroad bonds—which had served as the backbone of the investment bond market—went into the bankruptcy courts and emerged sadly shrunken in value and often translated in form into the far lowlier common shares and even into mere options to buy common shares. Utility bonds—especially those of the holding companies which had mushroomed during the '20s—followed the same course.

The public's confidence in and respect for bonds were badly shaken.

Adding further injury to bonds' prestige was the accelerated rate of inflation which accompanied the fighting of two world wars and the subsequent series of "police" episodes around the world. Even gilt-edged bonds, it seems, were proving no match for the violently changing national and international economies and no defense against the steadily declining purchase power of the dollar.

For a bond, by its very nature, is of no help in withstanding inflation.

What is its nature?

A bond is a certificate of debt—a mortgage.

If you buy a $1,000 bond—whether issued by the U.S. Treasury or by the ABC automobile company or the XYZ railroad—you have merely lent your $1,000 to the government or to the corporation for a specified number of years at a fixed rate of annual interest.

The chances of getting your annual interest—and your $1,000 back at the end of the loan period—vary directly with the credit standing of the borrower. If the U.S. Treasury is the borrower, there can be no doubts about either principal or interest. As you go down the quality ladder, you assume higher and higher risks from lower and lower quality borrowers, in return, generally, for higher interest rates.

But whether you have a top or bottom grade bond, these points should be made clear:

A bond is a fixed-dollar debt investment. It is *not* a growth security. It is a loan of dollars to be repaid in the same number of dollars regardless of what happens to the dollar's purchasing power during the years the loan remains outstanding. You lend $1,000; you expect to get $1,000 back—and no more.

The bond does not give the investor an ownership position in a company (which is the position of the preferred and common shareholders). It does *not* promise you more interest or more principal repaid if the company prospers. And you have a right to expect no less than what is promised even if the company is not a huge success.

You remain—all through the life of the bond—a *creditor* of the corporation. The corporation is obligated only to pay you interest (generally in semi-annual installments) and to repay you the principal borrowed at maturity. (Common and preferred shares have no maturity—they are generally perpetual certificates.)

But the bond's obligations to you as an investor, while limited, do take precedence over the corporation's responsibilities to its shareholders. As a bondholder, you hold a mortgage on the corporation. Your interest must be paid before any dividends are paid to the shareholders. At the termination of the loan (at the bond's maturity date) you must be paid off or you can take your claim to court. If the bond does not offer any opportunity to get rich (as is implied in an investment in common shares) at least it does promise to give you a seat at the head of the corporation table when it comes to dishing out earnings and to safeguarding the money you've invested.

And so today—even with inflation and a wide and growing interest in common share ownership—bonds are enjoying an active market. The reason is, chiefly, this:

> With money rates so high as to yield more than 7 per cent from high grade corporate bonds (as against an average yield of about 3 per cent from stocks in the Dow Jones industrial averages), bond interest had become far more rewarding that it had been for many decades.

U.S. Treasury issues set the pace with yields up to 6½ per cent, and other government agencies, such as the Federal

The bond market is a highly-sophisticated field of investment. It is watched–"to 3 decimal places"–continually by some of the sharpest investment minds. It is only natural, then, that yields obtainable from bonds should, as a rule, move in close relationship to each other. The greater the risk, the higher the yield; the lower the risk, the lower the yield. The above chart indicates the spread in yield between the top quality issues, as exemplified by U.S. and state governments and highest grade corporates and the significantly higher yield obtainable when quality is lower.

Home Loan Bank, topped that with yields going up to even a shade higher.

Top quality corporate issues, including some of the nation's finest utilities, have recently floated new bond issues yielding 7 per cent and more–just about the highest rates in a century.

For investors interested in safety of principal, in terms of the number of dollars invested–and in generous income more than in aggressive growth of capital–the bond market today offers advantages this generation of investors has never before known.

A bond, however, is not as simple an instrument as, for example, a share of common stock.

A bond's ability to provide income is measured on two different yardsticks:

1. The coupon (the interest rate set forth on the face of the certificate);
2. The yield (the rate of return you get, based on the amount of money invested).

An example:

ABC Co. has a bond issue, due in 20 years, which carries a coupon of 4¾ per cent.

That coupon designation means that the bond will pay 4¾ per cent of $1,000 (the face value of the bond) in annual interest. Now, 4¾ per cent of $1,000 works out to $47.50. This will be paid the investor in two semiannual installments of $23.75 each. So–the bond provides interest income of $47.50 cash each year.

But the *yield* on the money invested is far different. In fact, there are two different yields to be computed on the basis of money invested.

One is the *current* yield–the annual return to you on the actual amount of money invested. Since the bond sold at 75 (75% of the face value of $1,000) or $750, a return of $47.50 cash on $750 invested works out to a current, annual, return of 6.33 per cent.

But that isn't all.

There is a built-in gain in this investment owing to the fact that the bond you buy now for $750 will be paid off at $1,000 by 1992–if not sooner. So, in addition to the $47.50 a year, you can count on a $250 capital gain. Prorating this gain over the 20 years to maturity gives you a total return on your investment–to maturity–of 7.05 per cent. And what's more, that $250 capital gain will be taxable only as a long-term capital gain, which means, generally, at half your regular income tax bracket.

So the three indices to the rewards provided by this one bond are as follows:

1. A 4¾ per cent coupon, or $47.50 cash each year;
2. In terms of the $750 invested, a current yield on your investment of 6.33 per cent;
3. A yield to maturity, which includes the long-term capital gain, brings this figure to 7.05 per cent.

It should be apparent that bond interest computations can be complicated.

Furthermore, the question of higher current income as

against a higher "yield to maturity" is one which should be taken into consideration and evaluated against the background of the individual investor's needs and tax status.

Does he need maximum cash money coming in now, or because of a high income tax bracket, would it be better for him in the long run to accept a lower coupon bond and take his profits in a lower-taxed capital gain?

For example, if he feels he wants more income now, he might do better to pass up the ABC 4¾s and put his money into a recently issued XYZ utility bond selling at par ($1,000) and yielding 7½ per cent, or $75 a year.

As the old adage puts it: You pay your money and take your choice.

And, as of early 1972, there were plenty of desirable choices in the bond market. Yields as high as have been seen in a century were being offered by some of the nation's leading corporations as seen in these Salomon Brothers offering sheets:

CORPORATE BONDS

Long Term Industrials

	Coupon	Maturity	Price	Yield to Maturity
Standard Oil Calif. S.F. Deb.	4⅜	'83	82	6.65
Texas Co. Deb.	3⅝	'83	76¼	6.70
Borg Warner S.F. Deb.	5½	'92	86⅞	6.70
Shell Oil Co. S.F. Deb.	4⅝	'86	81¾	6.60
Corn Products Co. S.F. Deb.	5¾	'92	89	6.75
Sears Roebuck Co. S.F. Deb.	6⅜	'93	95½	6.78
Sears Roebuck Co. S.F. Deb.	8⅝	'95	110¾	7.63
Shell Oil Co. S.F. Deb.	8½	'00	110¼	7.61
Sun Oil Co. S.F. Deb.	4⅝	'90	78	6.70
Pitts Plate Glass S.F. Deb.	5⅝	'91	87½	6.80
Bendix Corp. S.F. Deb.	6⅝	'92	94½	7.15
Cities Service Co. S.F. Deb.	6⅝	'99	94⅜	7.09
Cities Service Co. S.F. Deb.	7.65	'01	103½	7.36
Con'l Can S.F. Deb.	5⅛	'85	85.67	6.75
Diamond Shamrock S.F. Deb.	7¾	'94	103½	7.43
Goodyear Tire & Rubber S.F. Deb.	8.60	'95	109½	7.73
Inland Steel 1st Mtge.	6½	'92	93.15	7.15
Hanna Mining S.F. Deb.	4¾	'90	77	6.95
Morton Norwich S.F. Deb.	8⅞	'95	109¾	7.95
National Cash Register S.F. Deb.	7.70	'94	103¾	7.35
Owens Illinois Glass	3¾	'88	71	6.70
Owens Illinois S.F. Deb.	7⅝	'01	104½	7.25
Reynolds Ind. S.F. Deb.	7⅜	'01	101¾	7.23
Westinghouse Elec. S.F. Deb.	8⅝	'95	110¼	7.68
Weyerhaeuser Co. S.F. Deb.	8⅝	'00	110¼	7.23
U.S. Steel Sub. Deb.	4⅝	'96	68¼	7.50
General Tel. & Elec. S.F.Deb.	6¼	'91	89	7.30
Spiegel Inc. Deb.	5¼	'83	81.60	7.75
Pullman Inc. S.F. Deb.	5⅞	'97	83	7.37

SHORT TERM INDUSTRIALS

	Rate	Maturity	Price	Yield to Maturity
International Bank S.F. Deb.	3⅜	'75	93¼	5.65
General Foods Notes	8¾	'75	108½	5.91
Cities Service Co. Notes	7	'78	102	6.58
Honeywell Finance Deb.	7	'78	101¼	6.76
May Dept. Store S.F. Deb.	3¼	'78	84¼	6.50
Seagram & Son Notes	7½	'78	103½	6.81
Union Oil Calif. Deb.	8¼	'76	107¼	6.55
Swift & Co. Deb.	7⅜	'78	102¾	6.81
Food Fair S.F. Deb.	3⅜	'74	93⅝	6.15
Manufacturers Hanover Trust Notes	6½	'79	99¼	6.63
Commercial Credit Co. Notes	3⅝	'76	89.35	6.75
Commercial Credit Notes	6⅞	'77	100¾	6.69
Ford Motor Credit Notes	6⅞	'78	100¾	6.72
General Motors Accept Co. Deb.	3⅝	'75	92	6.18

FINANCE COMPANIES

	Rate	Maturity	Price	Yield to Maturity
Associates Inv. Co. Deb.	4½	'83	75⅜	7.75
Associates Inv. Co. Deb.	4⅝	'85	75	7.68
Beneficial Finance Co. Deb.	4.45	'88	73⅞	7.20
Beneficial Finance Co. Deb.	4⅞	'81	84⅝	7.15
Borg Warner Accept. S.F. Deb.	7⅞	'91	102½	7.63
C.I.T. Finc'l	4½	'84	78	7.20
C.I.T. Finc'l Deb.	5⅛	'80	87½	7.23
Clark Equip. Cr. Deb.	7.85	'91	102	7.65
Commercial Credit Co. Notes	4½	'85	75½	7.40
Deere Credit Co. Deb.	5	'90	76	7.39
Ford Motor Co. Credit S.F. Deb.	8⅞	'90	110	7.84
General Motors Accept Co. Deb.	4⅝	'82	82⅛	7.05
Sears Roebuck Accept. Deb.	5	'82	84¾	7.10

BANKS

	Rate	Maturity	Price	Yield to Maturity
Morgan Guaranty Cap Notes	5	'92	81	6.75
Lincoln First Group	6¼	'92	88.4	7.35
United Calif. Bk. Cap Notes	4½	'90	72⅝	7.25
Wells Fargo Bank Cap Notes	4½	'89	73¾	7.15

PUBLIC UTILITY BONDS

	Coupon	Maturity	Call Price	Bid Price	Yield to Maturity
Alabama Pr.	8½	11/2001	107.87	104½-5½	8.01
Baltimore G & E	7¼	4/15/2001	107.75	98½-9½	7.18
Boston Edison	6⅞	11/98	107.29	95¾-6¾	7.20
Boston Edison	8⅛	5/15/2001	109.54	105⅛-6⅛	7.55
Buffalo Niag. El.	2¾	11/75	100.81	88½-9⅛	6.05
Cincinnati G. & E.	2¾	10/75	100.75	88½-9½	6.00
Cincinnati G. & E.	8⅝	12/2000	109.44	109 -10	7.75
Cleveland El. Il.	7⅛	1/15/90	107.65	97½-8½	7.28
Columbia Gas	4⅜	11/87-72	102.85	73¾-7¾	7.05
Columbia Gas	6¼	10/91-72	105.85	89 -90	7.20
Columbia Gas	7	10/93-72	107.00	94¾-5¾	7.40
Columbia Gas	8⅜	3/96	108.875	105½-6½	7.77
Columbia Gas	8¾	4/95	108.40	107½-8½	7.87
Columbia Gas	9⅛	10/95	108.875	109 -10	8.30

Commonwealth Ed.	3	2/77	101.375	84⅞-5⅞	6.35
Commonwealth Ed.	3¾	3/88	102.57	68 -9	7.00
Commonwealth Ed.	4⅝	3/90	102.87	74½-5½	7.05
Commonwealth Ed.	5¼	3/96	105.60	78¼-9¼	7.05
Commonwealth Ed.	5¾	12/96	104.96	83⅜-4⅜	7.10
Commonwealth Ed.	6⅜	10/98	106.49	89⅞-90⅞	7.15
Commonwealth Ed.	6¾	7/98	106.60	93¾-4¾	7.20
Commonwealth Ed.	7½	1/2001	108.10	101 -2	7.33
Cons. Edison N.Y.	2¾	6/72	100.17	98½-9¼	5.25
Cons. Edison N.Y.	3⅜	12/85	101.94	62¾-3¾	7.65
Cons. Edison N.Y.	4⅜	12/92	104.17	65 -6	7.65
Cons. Edison N.Y.	5	1/96	104.79	70 -1	7.65
Cons. Gas Balt.	2⅞	4/81	102.15	71 -2	7.00
Cons. Nat. Gas	4⅜	4/88	102.92	73¼-4¼	7.05
Cons. Nat. Gas	4¾	9/90	104.11	75¼-6¼	7.05
Cons. Nat. Gas	8⅜	5/96	108.64	107 -8	7.64
Consumers Power	2⅞	9/75	101.25	88¾-9¾	6.00
Consumers Power	3¼	2/90	102.82	60⅞-1⅞	7.00
Consumers Power	4⅝	12/90	103.04	73⅞-4⅞	7.05
Consumers Power	5⅞	8/96	106.34	84⅞-5⅞	7.10
Consumers Power	6⅝	10/98	107.08	92⅛-3⅛	7.20
Consumers Power	8⅛	8/2001	106.50	105¾-6¾	7.55
Consumers Power	8⅝	11/2000	109.44	108¾-9¾	7.77
Dayton Pr. & Lt.	8⅛	8/2001	106.55	105¼-6¾	7.57
Dallas Pr. & Lt.	4½	2/89	104.70	73½-4½	7.10
Dallas Pr. & Lt.	5⅜	2/97	106.65	79⅜-80⅜	7.05
Detroit Edison	6	12/96	108.00	85¾-6¾	7.15
Detroit Edison	6.40	10/98	106.15	90 -1	7.15
Detroit Edison	7	6/15/76	100.00	100¼-1	6.74
Detroit Edison	8⅛	6/15/2001	106.10	105¼-6¼	7.50
Duke Power	3	1/75	100.60	90¾-1¾	6.00
Duke Power	5⅜	4/97	106.38	78⅞-9⅞	7.10
Duke Power	4¼	8/92	103.63	68¾-9¾	7.05
Duke Power	6⅜	2/98	107.38	89⅜-90⅜	7.20
Duke Power	7	2/99	108.00	96 -7	7.25
Duke Power	7½	3/2001	108.50	100¾-1	7.41
Duke Power	8	9/99	108.21	105 -6	7.48
Duke Power	8⅝	8/2000	108.36	108⅜-9⅜	7.80
Duquesne Light	5¼	2/97	105.44	80 -1	7.05
Duquesne Light	7	1/99	106.99	96 -7	7.25
Duquesne Light	7⅞	3/2001	108.38	103¾-4¾	7.47
Florida Pwr. Corp.	4¼	5/92	103.52	69 -½	7.05
Florida Pwr. Corp.	7	11/98	108.90	96 -7	7.26
Florida Pr. & Lt.	4½	8/92	103.97	70¾-1¾	7.05
Florida Pr. & Lt.	4⅝	3/95	105.16	72 -3	7.00
Florida Pr. & Lt.	7¾	9/01	107.88	102¼-3	7.50
Florida Pr. & Lt.	6	12/96	106.38	84¾-5¾	7.25
Florida Pr. & Lt.	7	12/98	108.53	95 -6	7.34
Georgia Power	6⅝	9/98	106.64	91⅝-2⅝	7.25
Georgia Power	8⅛	6/2001	108.41	105¼-6¼	7.60
Georgia Power	7⅜	3/2001	108.38	99 -¾	7.40
Houston Lt. & Pr.	5¼	1/97	106.50	78 -9	7.05
Long Island Ltg.	4⅝	6/94	104.65	71¾-2¾	7.05
Long Island Ltg.	7¼	4/2001	109.11	97½-8½	7.38
Mich. Cons. Gas.	5⅞	6/91	105.43	83⅜-4⅜	7.40
Mich. Wisc. P.L.	4⅞	6/15/84	104.27	79¼-80¼	7.30
Mich. Wisc. P.L.	5¾	4/15/86	106.08	85⅜-6⅜	7.30
Natural Gas P.L.	4¾	11/85	103.22	76⅞-7⅞	7.30
New York St. E. & G.	6¼	9/97	107.45	88 -9	7.20
Niag. Mohawk Pr.	3⅞	6/88	103.26	66⅝-7⅝	7.30
Niag. Mohawk Pr.	6¼	8/97	106.69	83⅞-4⅞	7.45
Nor. Ind. P.S.	8⅛	5/2001	110.13	105 -6	7.61
Nor. Nat. Gas	5⅞	5/87	104.64	85⅝-6⅝	7.34
Nor. Nat. Gas	7¼	5/88	105.27	97⅛-9⅛	7.45
Nor. Nat. Gas	9½	11/90	109.50	108½-9½	8.49
No. Nat. Gas	8	5/91	107.50	101⅜-2⅜	7.75
Nor. Sts. Pr.	6¾	5/98	106.06	93¾-4¾	7.20
Nor. Sts. Pr.	8	3/2001	109.50	104½-5½	7.53
Nor. Sts. Pr.	8¼	6/2001	109.00	106½-7½	7.61
Nor. Sts. Pr.	9¼	12/99	109.42	109¼-10¼	8.30
Ohio Edison	8⅜	6/2001	108.41	106½-7½	7.72
Ohio Power	5	1/96	105.59	72¾-3¾	7.35
Pacific G. & E.	2¾	6/81	101.00	69½-70½	7.05
Pacific G. & E.	3⅛	12/84	102.00	67¼-8¼	6.90
Pacific G. & E.	4¼	6/95	103.71	68 -9	6.95
Pacific G. & E.	4⅝	6/97	104.64	71 -2	7.00
Pacific G. & E.	5¾	12/98	105.01	82⅞-3⅞	7.10
Pacific G. & E.	6⅞	12/99	107.09	94½-5½	7.25
Pacific G. & E.	7½	6/2001	107.58	100 -¾	7.44
Pacific G. & E.	8	6/1/2003	109.50	104½-5½	7.54
Pacific G. & E.	8⅝	6/2002	109.14	108½-9½	7.80
Pacific G. & E.	8⅞	12/2002	109.67	110¼-11¼	7.90
Pacific Pr. & Lt.	4⅝	10/94	103.67	65¾-6¾	7.75
Panhandle E.P.L.	5¾	2/87	104.54	84⅞-5⅞	7.30
Panhandle E.P.L.	8⅝	11/90	108.38	104 -6	8.00
Penn. Pr. & Lt.	7¼	2/2001	108.48	97¼-8¼	7.39
Pennzoil United	8⅜	3/96	108.63	103½-4½	7.95
Phila. Elec.	3¾	5/88	103.80	67⅛-8⅛	7.05
Phila. Elec.	4½	5/94	104.50	70 -1	7.10
Phila. Elec.	6½	3/93	105.70	91½-2½	7.20
Phila. Elec.	8¼	8/96	107.00	104⅜-5⅜	7.75
Pub. Svc. El. & G.	7	6/98	107.98	96 -7	7.26
Pub. Svc. El. & G.	7¾	8/15/96	106.14	101¼-2¼	7.55
Pub. Svc. El. & G.	8⅜	5/15/2001	108.98	106½-8	7.68
Pub. Svc. El. & G.	9⅛	3/2000	110.06	111 -½	8.08
Pub. Svc. Indiana	7⅝	1/2001	108.51	100½-1½	7.50
So. Calif. Ed.	4¼	2/15/82	101.88	78½-9½	7.15
So. Calif. Ed.	4⅜	3/89	103.10	92¼-3¼	7.10
So. Calif. Ed.	5¼	5/15/91	104.16	79¼-80¼	7.15
So. Calif. Ed.	5⅞	5/15/92	105.93	85 -6	7.20
So. Calif. Ed.	7⅛	1/15/94	107.22	97 -8	7.30
So. Calif. Ed.	8⅛	10/15/94	107.79	104½-5½	7.61
Tenn. Gas Trans.	5⅜	1/86	104.33	81⅝-2⅝	7.40
Texas East. Tr.	4¾	10/84	103.25	76¾-7¾	7.50
Texas East. Tr.	8.90	2/1/91	108.90	105 -7	8.27
Texas East. Tr.	10½	5/90	109.95	112 -13½	8.98
Texas Gas Trans.	9½	4/90	108.59	108½-10	8.41
Texas Pr. & Lt.	5½	2/97	105.82	80⅜-1⅜	7.10
Texas Pr. & Lt.	7⅛	2/2001	109.32	96⅞-7⅞	7.30
Texas Pr. & Lt.	8⅞	9/2000	110.20	111¼-12¼	7.80
Transcont'l P.L.	5	12/82	102.75	81¾-2¾	7.30
Transcont'l P.L.	6¾	5/88	105.40	92⅜-3⅜	7.45
Union Elec.	4½	4/95	104.10	69⅝-70⅝	7.10
Union Elec.	7⅝	4/2001	109.47	100½-1½	7.50
Virginia El. & Pr.	5⅛	2/97	104.64	76 -7	7.10
Virginia El. & Pr.	6⅞	12/97	107.02	94⅝-5⅝	7.25
Virginia El. & Pr.	7⅜	3/2001	108.90	99 -¾	7.40
Virginia El. & Pr.	8⅞	9/2000	108.75	110⅛-11⅛	7.85
Wisc. Elec. Pr.	7¼	4/99	106.77	97½-8½	7.38

It would be a disservice to the reader to close this chapter without repeating warnings which every bond investor should bear in mind:

The bond market is a far more sophisticated marketplace than that for common shares.

Many of the bonds mentioned here—and hundreds more—are listed on the leading exchanges. But, in general, by far the largest part of bond trading takes place "over-the-counter"—directly between brokers. So it will pay to go to a broker who is a bond expert.

Furthermore, there are many complicated features of a bond which are not apparent from its listing on the market. These can be determined only with the help of a bond trader or by studying them in the financial manuals.

A bond investor should not only acquaint himself with the quality of the bond, its price, coupon, current yield and yield to maturity, but also be informed on the provisions for its redemption, either at maturity or at various periods in advance of that date—at the option of the company. He should know whether the bond is a "first mortgage" or subordinate to a long list of other mortgages. In other words, just how far up toward the head of the table does he really sit?

It would be dangerous indeed for an investor to run his

finger down the yield list and decide: "This looks like a bargain, that's for me."

However, for the first time in many years, it should be reiterated, bonds do deserve consideration for a place in the portfolio of many investors—especially those investors who are more interested in generous income and safety of principal than in attempting to increase their capital.

And those investors who seek to combine bond safety and income with tax exemption benefits would do well to consider the municipal bond securities discussed in Chapter 17.

SOME QUESTIONS AND ANSWERS

Q. *What are C.D.s? Which are the best to buy? Must they be held for a specific period of time? Do rates differ? What is the highest rate you know of? Are they better than growth mutual funds?*

A. A certificate of deposit (C.D.) is a time deposit under which you place $1,000, $5,000 or whatever the sum may be on deposit with a bank for a specified period of time. In some cases you may withdraw your money before the period expires, but you will then suffer a cut in interest rate.

Rates vary according to amounts of money involved, issuing banks, and length of time of the deposit.

You can't compare a C.D. and a mutual-fund investment. One is a deposit of a specified number of dollars at a specified rate for a specified length of time. The mutual fund represents an investment in the ownership of up to a hundred different corporations.

Q. *What's the proper way to compute interest on savings? I suppose the bank is right, but how can one be sure?*

A. There are scores of different systems for figuring savings-bank interest, and different banks use different systems—especially when you take into account any deposits and withdrawals you may make within the interest period.

A simple example would run thus:

If your bank pays 4 per cent interest compounded quarterly, $1,000 on deposit during the months July, August and September will earn 1 per cent, or $10. So at the end of the quarter you would have $1,010 in the bank. At the end of the next quarter you would have $1,020.10 —1 per cent of $1,010 ($10.10)—added to your previous principal.

Now, when you complicate this by depositing $10 a week during July and August and withdrawing $50 in mid-September to pay some bills, you'd better rely on the bank's computers.

Q. *We are retired with a long list of blue chip stocks and some mutual funds and slightly more than 2 dozen bond issues—each ranging in size from $1,000 to $10,000. Would you suggest culling out a few items—just to reduce bookkeeping? I've been thinking of making a contribution to the Salvation Army.*

A. There's no quarreling with your list of stocks or bonds. If you have sufficient income there is no reason to do anything. If you want more income you should consider selling some of your low yielders—such as Sears and Pfizer—as suitable as they would be in a young man's growth-oriented portfolio. The proceeds could go into preferreds and bonds.

However, you seem to be comfortable, so there is no pressure to do anything.

One point: if you are going to make any contributions, do so in the form of shares on which you have large capital gains. Don't sell the stock in order to raise cash for the contributions, because you will have to pay a capital gains tax.

As to reducing the number of issues to ease the bookkeeping task: I grant you that a lot of $1,000 and $2,000 bond holdings are a nuisance, but if they are in registered form—which brings you a check every six months—the headache is mostly on the side of the paying agents. (Going into your bank vault to clip a coupon every two weeks could be a nuisance.) I'd go slow on eliminating any small bond holdings. Commission costs could be high and the bonds are all excellent quality and well-suited to your needs.

Q. *I am a single woman in a high tax bracket. Retirement may be a few years off. Where should I put additional funds? I already own mutual funds.*

A. If you are not inclined to put more money into low-yield, aggressive growth stocks, buy short-term tax-exempt bonds which will come due when you retire.

Q. *Wouldn't it be better for me to invest $25,500 in 8 per cent bonds rather than pay off a 25-year 7½ per cent mortgage? The income from the bonds would just about meet mortgage payments—$2,286 a year—and at the end of that time, I'd have my $25,500 intact. I'm 32—if age is important.*

A. I'd say it's very important. A person only 32, and facing up to decades of inflation, would do far better to have his money invested in equities (not bonds) and to owe a fixed amount of dollars, as in a mortgage, for the next 25 years. And that's without doing *any* arithmetic.

Even on a straight mathematical basis, you're overlooking a few points. You'll get closer to 7¼–7½ per cent than 8 on top-quality corporate bonds today. So you would have to add several hundred dollars a year to the bond income to meet that mortgage payment.

Even more important: at the end of the 25 years you'd have the $25,500—as you point out. But it would have cost you $47,150 in total payments. So that $25,500 by then would have cost you about $22,000 ($57,000 minus the fact you would have a mortgage-free house).

Q. *Are there any bonds which remain outstanding forever?*

A. A bond represents a debt, and by definition a debt becomes due some time. If it didn't come due it would actually be part of the permanent capital of the corporation—which would make it equity.

The only exceptions which come to mind right now are the Canadian Pacific 4% perpetual "debenture stock" and the Canadian government perpetual 3s. Undoubtedly, there are others.

Q. *I don't know what you mean by good-grade bonds. At 51, I have $10,000 to invest and want to protect my future as much as possible.*

A. Grading a bond is not much different from grading any other investment, or other piece of property, for that matter. You may say you have a "good" car and someone else may say he has a better one. There are a dozen grades of bonds in the Standard & Poor's rating system, for example, and 9 in the Moody's. The bottom three in the S. & P. list relate to bonds which are in default.

In general, these ratings range downward from the AAA quality at the top, which afford maximum protection as to interest and principal. As you go down the list, the risk and the yield increase. A broker can help you find the niche which suits you best.

The question which remains uppermost, as far as I am concerned, however, is whether you, at 51, are "protecting your future as much as possible" by considering bonds at all. A good-grade bond will offer semi-annual interest and repayment of principal without too much worry. But it won't protect you against inflation, nor is it a favorite vehicle for capital gain.

Q. *I notice you frequently mention common stocks of companies with generous dividend records. That's O.K. But I wonder why you don't mention the bonds of good companies which are now selling at a deep discount—say, the A. T. & T. 3¼s. Don't you think some of these offer a good return and will some day be worth par?*

A. There is considerable justice in what you say. Bonds have been in the investment "doghouse" for years—and still are. As a result, bond portfolios have shown marked losses and balanced mutual funds—which hold substantial amounts of bonds—have been among the most disappointing performers in an industry which has become extremely performance minded.

There are, as you say, many good-to-top-quality bonds which are today selling at deep discounts. The A. T. & T. 3¼s you mention are a triple-A (top) quality bond, but as this is written are languishing around 67 ($670 per $1,000 bond).

The reason is simple: A $1,000 mortgage paying $32.50 today is not worth $1,000 in a money market chock full of $1,000 bonds yielding over $70 (7% plus).

Now—should you buy the A. T. & T. 3¼s, due 1984?

It depends upon what you want your investment money to do for you.

If you want the most income you can get—right now—you can do much better if you buy other bonds, selling around par.

It's true, of course, that the 3¼s will climb from their present 67 to 100 by 1984, when they become due (if they are not called in at a higher price before then). So you can also safely count on a long-term capital gain of 33 points ($330 per bond) in, at most, 17 years. And this gain will be taxable only at one-half your regular income tax rates.

So if you prefer lower current yield, plus a long-term capital gain, your course is clear.

You could have, or course, gone even further, and mentioned bonds selling at 50 cents on the dollar (and even less). But here I would warn you that the bond market is an extremely sophisticated area—dominated to a large extent by specialists. So don't go way out looking for bargains.

Q. *What are the pros and cons of investing in stocks vs. bonds? What rule of thumb is there for balancing savings and investments?*

A. When you buy a share of stock you become part owner of the business, a "partner" in its gains or losses. When you invest in a bond, you are lending the corporation $1,000 and all you can expect to get back is the $1,000, plus annual interest. You don't share in any higher profits, but your risk of loss is far less.

There is no fixed ratio for savings *vs.* investments. Savings come first—to the amount which leaves you feeling that you can cope with emergencies. Thereafter you invest in securities: for growth, for income.

Q. *I've noticed frequent articles and brokerage advertisements proclaiming the advantages of owning bonds. In the last six months I've tried several times to get information, but brokers have steered me away from bonds into common shares. It has been almost impossible to find out what bonds are selling for and what commission charges are. Some time ago, anticipating lower interest rates, I bought some Commonwealth Edison 5¾s of 1996, paying $1,057 a bond, but no commission. It's been difficult to get quotes, but recently I discovered they are down below par. Why the drop when there has been only a slight change in the economy? It seems I was overcharged.*

A. There has been a lot of talk about bonds—and with good reason.

Bond yields today are just about the highest they've been in many decades. Yields of around 7½% are obtainable from good-grade issues. A person seeking generous income—and not too fearful of inflation (either because of age or because of other resources), should certainly look into bonds as a means of beefing up his income from securities.

Brokers may encourage you to buy bonds, or may not—depending upon the nature of their business and your needs.

Bond quotes are often not as readily available as are those of the leading blue chip common stocks. In the first place, public interest in bonds is far less than it is in stocks. Secondly, many bonds are not traded on the exchanges, but over the counter—between brokers who shop around over the telephone.

Also if you are buying a single $1,000 bond, you can't expect to pay as low a price as though you were buying 50 or 100 bonds. The bond market is not a penny ante market, but one used to a large degree by big institutional investors. For the same reason, commissions will vary—anywhere from $5.00, or even a bit more, for a single $1,000 bond to a fraction of that on a large order.

Now as to your specific experience:

When you bought, you expected lower interest rates.

If your diagnosis had proved correct, bond prices would have risen since they move inversely to interest rates. But you were wrong—as were many far more sophisticated, professional investors. So your bond declined in price.

Did you overpay? I can't tell. The Standard & Poor's bond guide notes that this issue touched a 1967 high of 105¼ ($1,052.50).

Did you get away without paying a commission? Not likely. You paid either a commission or a brokerage markup.

What to do now? Nothing. Assuming you were looking for a good bond paying a generous yield, you have it.

If you were trying to play the bond market, you guessed wrong—at least for the time being.

But if I have to make a guess, it would be that sometime within the next five, ten years bond prices paid today will appear to be bargains.

Q. *I am an heir to a rather large six-figure estate. I notice you mentioned that there are certain U.S. Treasury issues which sell at a discount but are acceptable at par in payment of Federal estate taxes. What are the restrictions on my buying enough of these to pay the estate tax?*

A. The only restriction is that taxes are paid by the estate, not by the heirs. The official regulation on the use of these particular bonds reads:

"Redeemable at par and accrued interest to date of payment, at any time, upon the death of the owner, at the option of the duly constituted representative of the owner's estate, provided that the entire proceeds of redemption are applied to payment of Federal estate taxes due from the deceased owner's estate."

So, it seems clear to me, that the bonds must be in the estate itself at the time of death. Talk this over with your benefactor's tax attorney or accountant.

There are about two dozen Treasury issues which qualify for this use. Any bond dealer can give you the full list.

Q. *I've been advised to buy General Telephone tax-exempt bonds for 7½ per cent income.*

A. Your advice was garbled in transmission. Private corporation bonds do not pay tax-exempt interest.

Q. *You've written that losing a bearer-form bond, Treasury or corporate, can be a "disaster." My Treasury notes are in a safe-deposit box, but since a bill was signed last spring which would replace them if lost or stolen, I feel I can keep them at home, the same as I do with E bonds. You ought to correct your statement.*

A. There is nothing for me to correct. I warn you again that if you lose a bearer bond you've bought yourself a peck of trouble.

The bill you refer to—Public Law 9219—did go into effect last May 27. All it changed was to make possible the reimbursement by the Treasury for any of its bonds lost or stolen *before maturity*. (Before passage of the bill, such securities were paid off within a week *after* maturity.)

But—all other provisions qualifying one for reimbursement remain the same. And these provisions include proof of loss *plus* an indemnity bond *plus* yards of red tape.

Indemnity bonds for lost or stolen securities are expensive items. Large banks and brokerage firms of course carry blanket insurance for all the securities they handle. But I'd hate to have to go shopping for a $5,000 indemnity bond to cover the loss of a bearer bond—Treasury or corporate—and then have to follow through with all the red tape required.

I repeat: This law in which you are so mistakenly placing your trust *does not* reduce any of the risk in owning bearer security. It merely makes possible earlier replacement of the security, but *only* if all other requirements are met—and it is these requirements (same as before passage of the bill) which make the loss of a bearer security a "disaster" for anyone but an institutional investor with big insurance coverage and a staff of legal experts to follow through.

Lost or stolen E bonds, it is true, can be replaced with considerably less effort. (Of course, they aren't in bearer form in the first place.)

But *don't take any chances with bearer securities*, or, for that matter, any securities. Keep them in a safe place, preferably a bank vault. And if you have to transmit them anywhere by mail, be sure you use registered mail and, to make doubly sure, send along any required endorsement in a separate envelope by using a bond or stock "power" blank.

Q. *You say that fixed income bonds are not a hedge against inflation. I wish to differ. If you were to buy a 5% bond due 1988 for around 60 you would be receiving more than 8% in interest PLUS $400 appreciation to par, 100, in 19 years.*

A. I don't deny that there are bargains in discount bonds available today. But, as in the case of most bargains, you should look to the risk involved.

In today's money market, high-grade bonds are yielding about 7%, a most generous figure and just about the best in a century. However, that does NOT mean the laws of finance have been repealed.

When you find an 8.3% current yield, as you point out, a $400 appreciation to maturity (bringing the return to maturity to around 9½%), you should look to the safety of your investment.

Standard & Poor's rates the bond "B," which is six grades down from the top in a field of eight covering bonds which are paying their interest. The company's erratic earnings record may be another factor. Whatever you do, never delude yourself into thinking you've found a "sleeper." If Wall Street demands a 9½% yield from one bond on the same day it will buy others for a 7% yield, you can be sure there's a reason.

The $400 appreciation to maturity value is something else again. However, if you are banking on that, you ought to lift your sights to better quality bonds—to issues of companies you can feel certain will honor their obligations when the bond matures. You will find quality bonds selling in the 60s, although in most cases the coupon is 3 or 3½% and not 5, which means their yield to maturity is somewhere around the 7% bracket being offered by new issues.

Now you also have to ask yourself whether your $600 growing to $1,000 in 1988 is really going to help you keep abreast of inflation. Would you care to make a guess as to what a refrigerator or TV set or automobile will cost in 1988?

INFLATION AND BOND INVESTMENTS

Back in the days when "sound as a dollar" was widely accepted as a standard of stability, high-grade bonds—which are evidences of debt as expressed in terms of dollars—provided the foundation (if not the entire structure) of many conservative portfolios.

The increasing inflationary pressures of recent years, however, has changed all that. High-grade bonds remain as "safe" as they were, but safety no longer can fulfill all the requirements of a viable investment program. The certainty of having the $1,000 you lent a corporation in 1972 returned to you as $1,000 in the year 1997 is no longer sufficient reward, because it is generally accepted that the $1,000 you get back in 1997 will buy far less than the $1,000 you are lending today. As a result, bond yields have had to be increased to well above that offered by common shares in order to attract investors willing to hold fixed-dollar amount securities.

A study by *Financial World* magazine shows how over the last three-quarters of a century the once conservative bond investor has demanded, and gotten, higher rewards for his investment in terms of annual yield to the point where recent comparisons show highest-grade corporate bonds yielding twice as much as common shares. The figures are for market low points since before the start of the century.

Date	*Stock Yield*	*Bond Yield*
August 1896	6.46%	5.19%
June 1900	5.14	4.50
November 1903	7.91	4.64
November 1907	7.63	5.12
October 1911	5.77	4.60
October 1914	6.05	5.03
December 1917	11.44	5.42
August 1921	6.02	6.04
October 1923	5.74	5.25
June 1932	9.35	5.43
April 1938	4.50	3.32
May 1942	7.91	2.86
June 1949	7.19	2.69
September 1953	6.20	3.26
December 1957	4.50	3.81
October 1960	3.50	4.30
June 1962	3.72	4.27
October 1966	3.68	5.36
March 1968	3.17	6.00
November 1969	3.12	7.29

Q. *Late last year I sold $2,000 Treasury Bonds. The quote I saw in the paper was close to 75, but I got 73½. Was that an error?*

A. I can't check on the quotes, but I must warn you that when you sell only two bonds (especially Treasury issues) you can't hope to get anywhere near the quoted market.

Q. *Would you please send me a formula for figuring a bond's yield to maturity.*

A. Basically, you arrive at a rule-of-thumb answer (in the case of a bond selling at discount) by adding the annual average price appreciation to par. You divide that total by the average price of the bond to par—that is, today's market price, plus 100 (par), divided by two.

In the case of a bond selling at a premium you subtract from the annual interest the average annual amount the bond will decline to par. You divide that by the average price of the bond to par: today's price plus 100, divided by two.

I warn you: This will get you only an approximate answer which will be disputed as too little or too much and as applying only to short-term, rather than long-term, bonds, and bring up a lot of other arguments. But you did ask.

Q. *Please send me a list of recently issued bonds that would prove a solid, long-term income source.*

A. New bond issues are coming out daily.

What an investor must stress even more than the name of the issuing corporation is the credit rating of the bond—AAA, AA, A and so on.

But just as an example of what I mean, here are some new issues—as this is written, yielding about 7¼ per cent:

AAA rating: N.Y. Telephone 7⅜s of 2011; Bell Telephone of Pennsylvania 7⅛s of 2012; Baltimore Gas & Electric 7⅛s of 2002; Texas Electric 7⅛s of 2002;

AA rating: Public Service of Indiana 7s of 2002; Oklahoma Gas & Electric 7⅛s of 2002; Philadelphia Electric 7⅜s of 2001;

A rating: South Carolina Electric & Gas 7¼s of 2002; Central Telephone of Illinois 7½s of 1996; General Telephone of Indiana 7½s of 2001; Pennsylvania Electric 7⅞s of 2001.

Q. *You wrote that a 6 per cent bond now selling at 83 and due in 1992 yields 7.66 per cent to maturity. I figure about 8.25 per cent.*

A. You were correct in combining the annual interest and the annual average gain to par at maturity in order to arrive at the investor's total reward. But you made an error in dividing by today's cost of 83 as though that figure would be the price of the bond from now until 1992.

As maturity approaches, that market price will rise. You'd have come closer to the truth (and even then it is only an approximation) if you had used 91½ as a divisor (the average between 83 and the final maturity price of 100).

Q. *Whenever I call my broker at a large firm about buying high-grade corporate bonds he always suggests new issues in the sale of which his company has an interest.*

A. There's nothing wrong with that. If his firm is a member of an underwriting or selling group now offering a new bond issue which meets your quality requirements there is no reason why you shouldn't buy that bond and save the commissions.

Q. *How can a yield to maturity be below current yield?*

A. Easy. If a 9⅝ per cent bond, due in 1995, is selling at 110½, its current yield is 8.71 per cent ($96.25 divided by 110½). But the yield to maturity is only 8.57 since the current income must be decreased by the erosion of the 10½ point premium by 1995, when the bond will be paid off at 100.

Q. *We are retired, and hold such bonds as Lone Star Gas 9¾s and Pacific Tel & Tel 8¾s. Should we sell these at premium prices, take the profits, and reinvest in other bonds?*

A. You do have some healthy profits, but that doesn't necessarily indicate you should take them. The bond market—which is closely controlled by money rates and credit ratings—generally does not offer "bargains," which is another way of saying that it's difficult to take a profit and then replace the securities with a "better buy" in an equivalent quality bond.

At a recent price of 114, the Lone Star Gas 9¾s yield about 8.57 per cent current and 8.38 per cent to maturity. (Of course, a call before maturity would reduce that latter yield considerably.) The Pacific Tels yield 7.95 current and 7.88 per cent to maturity.

If you were to take your profits, and reinvest in more recent issues you could, of course, buy them much closer to par, leaving you—on sale of five bonds each—about $1,200 free cash (before taxes). But you would have to reinvest the $10,000 for a yield of only about 7¼ per cent—to get the same quality.

If I knew now that money rates would be at 6 per cent or even less when your bonds first become callable (and would, therefore be retired at prices below present market levels) I would say sell now and reinvest, even for a lower coupon. But I don't know. Meanwhile you are getting a handsome return from a high-quality bond.

Q. *I owe $12,000, which must be paid back in 1974. What would be the safest way to invest this money?*

A. In either an insured savings account or in a U.S. Treasury bond coming due nearest the day you must repay the $12,000.

Q. *Recently you said a yield of 7 per cent from a municipal bond issue "is on the high side." I've always felt that municipal bonds should not give any reason for concern. Is there any doubt that I may not receive the face value of the bond when due in 1986? Or that I won't continue to collect interest at the rate of 7½ per cent? My broker says I can sell the bond at any time prior to maturity and that the selling price won't vary more than $30 either way. True? Why is the safety of a municipal bond threatened as the yield increases?*

A. Municipal bond prices (and therefore their yields) can vary from day to day. (That is also true of most securities.)

However, I think it is fair to say that a yield of 7½ per cent from a tax-exempt bond would indicate quality below the best—perhaps Baa—as against the top ratings of Aaa, Aa, A.

You don't name the bond, and I wouldn't discuss it specifically even if you did. All I can say is that bond ratings are set by experts who put the highest rating on the bond they feel offers the least risk of getting your money back at maturity and the least risk of default on semi-annual interest. From there on down they attempt to evaluate the increasing risk. Therefore:

1. All that one can say is that the risk in your Baa bond is greater than in a triple-A bond.
2. Ditto for the chances of failing to collect interest.
3. I don't know where that broker got the idea that price fluctuations between now and 1986 will be limited to only 3 points—$30 a bond—but even without knowing the specific bond, I'd say that's pretty loose talk.
4. The safety of any bond is not threatened as the yield increases. It's the other way around: Price drops and yield increases as safety is threatened.

My mail indicates that interest in tax-exempt (municipal) bonds is increasing algebraically—which is only natural as income time approaches and tax rates rise. I think any person in a 30 per cent-or-above income tax bracket seeking income from bonds should by all means consider tax-exempt bonds.

As a class, they have enjoyed a high record of safety. But that does *not* mean all rules of securities quality and risk have been rescinded. Quality still carries a higher price. All securities fluctuate in price.

Your only course is to have an expert evaluate the degree of risk you are assuming.

15 E Bonds—A Tax-Favored Investment

In the darkening days of the late 1930s—as war clouds gathered over both Europe and the Far East—our government began to enlist the aid of its citizens in financing military preparedness by selling defense bonds. When war finally erupted and the United States was drawn into it by the attack on Pearl Harbor, the bonds were used to raise funds for financing the conflict.

These government savings bonds have carried a long list of designations—defense bonds, war bonds, A, B, C, D, F, G, J, K and most recently E, H and U.S. savings notes called "freedom shares." But their purposes were, and have remained, the same:

To enlist the citizens' financial aid in financing defense efforts;

To combat inflation by diverting the increased money supply which always accompanies wars—"hot" or "cold"—toward investment and away from price competition in the open market for too few goods and services.

The public has responded. Millions of our citizens have purchased many billions of dollars' worth of these bonds over the years, and they still retain more than 55 billion dollars of them, nearly all the later in the E and H series.

The savings bond, by and large, is not a sophisticated investment. It carries with it no hope of making a killing or doubling your money overnight. Its interest-earning ability has moved up from an initial 2.9 per cent for the earliest E bonds to a current 5½ per cent when held to maturity—5 years and 10 months for E's and 10 years for H's.

However, the interest rate has been only part of the story.

Far more important to the investor has been:

1. The 100 per cent safety of his dollar investment: Savings bonds are a direct obligation of the U.S. Government and are thus the safest investment in the world.
2. The income tax benefits: The bonds are exempt from local or state income taxes. And Federal tax on the annual accrued interest on the E bonds may either be paid annually or it may be deferred until the bonds mature or are redeemed by the investor. In the more than thirty years since the current series was first offered, the Treasury has extended the maturity of the E bonds so that an investor who first began buying them in 1941 could still have all his capital invested, plus accrued interest, intact—undiminished by annual income tax payments. Although it has not been officially announced, it's a safe bet that an investor in E bonds will be able to carry his bonds for many more years, continuing to defer the accrued tax liability until such time, in retirement, as he moves into a lower income tax bracket, or is released by exemptions from paying any income taxes at all.

   U.S. savings notes of "freedom shares" sold from May 1967 through June 1970 have been granted a 10-year extension beyond their initial 4½-year term. The interest rate paid in extension will be the savings banks rate prevailing at the time they enter the extension period.
3. The ease of investment. E bonds are sold at most banks. There is no commission involved in either their purchase or redemption. Even more important has been the growing success of the payroll deduction program under which an employee authorizes his employer to deduct X number of dollars a week or a month from his pay check to be applied to the regular purchase of bonds.
4. The bonds' high liquidity. After a short waiting period (two months for E bonds and six months in the case of H bonds) the investments may be cashed in at any bank or branch of the Federal Reserve Bank. The investor knows, to the penny, what he will receive since the bonds are not traded on the open market and are not subject to price fluctuation. The value of each bond at any time during its original maturity period is given in a table printed on the back of the certificate. Values of bonds in periods of extended maturities are listed in tables issued by the Treasury's Bureau of the Public Debt.
5. The case of safekeeping. The bonds are not negotiable, so there is little danger of losing them through theft. Since they are registered in the owner's name, they can be easily replaced in case of loss by fire or theft, or by being mutilated or destroyed. No matter what the cause, the Treasury will replace them free of charge.

All these factors have accounted for the savings bond's popularity, but perhaps the most significant—for the average investor—has been the bond's ability to provide a safe, long-term haven for funds which do not add to the investor's tax liability during his period of capital accumulation, when he is most likely to be in his highest income brackets.

The single investor with $8,000 to $10,000 of taxable income is in the 25 per cent income tax bracket. For him, $1,000 invested in a savings account paying 5 per cent, means $50 a year income, subject to $12.50 in taxes, or a net increment to his funds of $37.50.

The same $1,000 in E bonds, now growing at the rate of 5½ per cent a year, would earn $55 a year, with the entire $55 remaining to his credit since he need not declare the interest as part of his taxable income until he decides to cash in the bonds—which most likely will come at a time when his income-tax liability is much lower or nonexistent.

This means that a man buying E bonds during his working years continues to build up his assets year after year with nothing taken out for tax payments. He arrives at retirement with none of his capital diminished by tax payments.

If it suits the investor's tax book, he may, of course, report his annual liability on his savings bonds' increment. This option may be found desirable in the case of bonds being accumulated in a child's name for his education. Until the annual interest accrual on the bonds reaches $750, the youngster is subject to no tax. This means that more than $13,000 can be accumulated to a youngster's credit, a tax report filed every year listing the total annual accruals, no tax paid—and yet one wipes out any tax liability when the bonds are ultimately cashed to pay college tuition.

The decision on whether to report annual interest on E bonds or to merely ignore the annual increment until the bonds are finally cashed is one which each investor must make for himself after doing some arithmetic on his current tax liability and on what he can forecast will be his tax liability when he finally turns to the bonds accumulated for retirement or other income.

The only savings bonds now being sold are the E and H.

All the bonds are identical from the point of view of safety.

The E's earn at the rate of 5½ per cent a year when held to maturity; the H's pay out that amount, by semiannual check.

When an investor has finished with accumulating capital and turns to it for income he may convert his E bonds into H bonds without expense, without any diminution of capital and *without paying any income taxes* on the past accruals in the E bonds.

This tax liability is not forgiven, it is merely deferred—until such time as the H bonds are redeemed. Since the Treasury has steadily extended the maturity of the H bonds, also, it is a safe bet that an investor will be able to hold them as long as he likes.

Semiannual interest payments received by H bond holders are subject to Federal income taxes. (There are no state income taxes involved in any government savings bonds—at any time.)

Thus, an investor who has accumulated $25,000 worth of E Bonds and converts them into H bonds will receive—on the average, over the lifetime of the H bonds—$1,375 a year. All this income is subject to Federal income taxes.

Even this tax burden, however, may be reduced.

If, instead of switching his $25,000 worth of E's into H's, he merely cashes in about $1,375 worth of E bonds each year (which is 5½ per cent of his total investment) only the interest accrual included in the $1,375 worth of bonds cashed will be subject to taxes. In the case of bonds held only six years, this gain would be about one-third of the total. Thus, in his case, only about $460 of his income would be subject to Federal income taxes. And the bonds remaining in his portfolio would grow sufficiently during the ensuing year to keep his total investment at the $25,000 level.

To sum up: U.S. savings bonds are not a glamour investment and should never be mentioned in the same breath with common stocks, which might gain 4 points in a single stock market session (or lose 4 points). But they have earned over the years a niche in the portfolio of most prudent citizens. And for good reasons:

They are 100 per cent safe.

They do not fluctuate in price, but grow in value—or pay out income—at a fixed rate.

They provide a much-needed tax shelter during the years an investor accumulating capital is most likely to be heavily burdened by income taxes.

They are subject to no local or state taxes at any time.

They may be easily acquired (painlessly acquired, in fact, through payroll deduction); easily kept; easily redeemed when necessary.

They provide an anti-inflationary method for financing government budget needs.

SOME QUESTIONS AND ANSWERS

Q. *I am confused about the interest on Series E savings ings bonds. Some time ago I cashed 2 bonds, issued in the same month but 1 year apart. I found that the younger bond was worth more than the older one. The bank officer said it frequently happened.*

A. He's right. Because of frequent changes in interest rates on savings bonds, these quirks do occur.

If you are going to cash any substantial amount of bonds you should avail yourselves of 2 guides:

1. "Tables of Redemption Values for U.S. Savings Bonds," which may be obtained from the Superintendent of Documents, Washington, D.C. 20402, for 15 cents, and

2. "Offerings of U.S. Savings Bonds, Series E," Treasury Dept. Circular 653, which you can obtain free at Federal Reserve Banks.

The first gives you current values for all E bonds; the second gives you growth rates and, interestingly, the interest rate at which bonds grow from any period to maturity.

Q. *Is there any reason to hold H bonds at 5½ per cent when savings banks are paying 6 per cent on savings certificates?*

A. Yes.

1. If you acquired the H bonds by exchanging E's on which you had considerable gain, cashing in the H's would make you liable to income taxes on the accrued gains in the E's. It's quite possible that if this gain is large enough and if your tax bracket is high enough, you would be left with an amount of capital which, invested at 6 per cent, would yield less than you now get from the H's paying 5½ per cent.

2. The H bonds represent a government contract which says the U.S. will pay you 5½ per cent over the lifetime of the bonds and for any extended maturity period (and I think this is merely another way of saying many, many years). Money in savings institutions now earns 5 and even a trifle higher. They once paid a lot less. They may do so again.

Q. *I turned in some savings stamps for my daughter and received an E bond due in 5 years and 10 months. But the bonds I am buying on payroll deduction say 7 years and 11 months to maturity.*

A. Your employer is merely using up some old forms. All E bonds sold since June 1, 1970 mature in 5 years and 10 months.

Q. *We hope to retire in 5 to 7 years. All our reserves are now in E or H bonds and in bank certificates–a total of about $33,000. We don't want income now, but will need income when we retire. We have about $2,000 or $3,000 to invest in the next 5 years. Should we switch our E bonds to other forms of investment?*

A. I think you ought to have some funds in common shares. Currently you are tied entirely to dollars. However, I can't see redeeming the E bonds, since they are earning 5½ per cent with tax deferred until after you retire. I don't know your tax bracket, but even in the lower brackets the E bond investment makes sense. (If you don't want income, why the H bonds?)

I'd allocate any new investable funds into commons. In addition you might cut into cash a bit.

Q. *I am 80, holding bonds worth about $3,500. I never reported any interest income. But now I read in the tax blanks that I should report interest. What do I do now?*

A. You've read the tax blank incorrectly. It's true you must report interest received (or credited to your accounts in a savings institution). But annual interest growth on E bonds *need* not be reported annually, and no tax need be paid on it until you cash in the bonds.

If you are 80 and could use some income, it seems to me you ought to cash some of those bonds every year and use the money to meet living costs.

If you cash in about 5½ per cent of them every year you won't even cut into your investment. And your tax liability will be negligible.

Q. *I've bought, and held, a $100 E bond every month since 1952. Now that I am retired, I find I do not need to draw on this money. What should I do with them? It seems an imposition to ask a bank to exchange all these E's and H's. Do they charge a fee?*

A. If you don't need the income from these bonds, you must decide what job you do want the money to undertake.

If you want to retain the funds merely as a backstop for yourself, there's no need to do anything. Hold the E's. If you want to build capital for your heirs, the bonds could be redeemed and the money put into growth stock. This, of course, would necessitate your paying a substantial tax on the accrued interest.

I don't see any point to switching to H's, since the H bond is identical with the E except that the H pays interest semiannually, and you say you don't need the income.

It's no imposition on anyone to swap E's for H's. Ask your bank or the Federal Reserve Bank of your district for form PD3253. There are no fees.

Q. *Some time ago you mentioned that certain U.S. Treasury bond issues, then selling at a discount, would be acceptable at par in payment of inheritance taxes. I have some E bonds bought 20 years ago. Would they qualify?*

A. No. Savings bonds–E, H, "freedom shares"–do not qualify.

The bonds you have reference to are about two dozen in number and include Treasury bonds, notes and certificates–the 3½s due in Nov. 1998; the 3s of Feb. '95; the 4s of Feb. '93; the 4⅛s of May '94; the 4¼s of Aug. '92, and so on.

They are acceptable at face value in payment of Federal estate taxes due from the owner's estate.

So anyone interested in helping his heirs pay his estate taxes at 70 to 85 cents on the dollar should look into these.

Q. *We are an elderly retired couple who have about $20,000 in E bonds, plus some money in bank shares as a long-term investment. Is this wise?*

A. If you need income you must do something with the E bonds. Either cash in about $1,000 worth a year or convert all the E's to H's and begin drawing about that much in average annual interest income. Either way you'll have some money coming in to help meet living expenses.

If your bank shares are yielding close to 5 per cent, O.K.; otherwise the money should be shifted to better dividend-paying issues.

Q. *What are the merits and pitfalls of selling a $10,000 H bond and using the money to buy Treasury issues at maximum margin?*

A. H bonds yield 5½ per cent; Treasuries yield 6 and more.

Question 1: Were these H bonds acquired by exchanging E's? If so, how much accrued gain was included in the E's–all of which gain becomes taxable when you redeem the H's?

Question 2: What's your goal? The switch will not increase your security and it may not increase your net income if there is a large taxable gain included in that H bond figure.

I'm left with the impression that your intention is to speculate in Treasury bonds. This indicates you think interest rates are going lower (so that bond prices will rise). Maybe you're right; maybe you're wrong.

One fact: While you're waiting for a rise in the price of the Treasuries, you must be prepared to lose money on the interest you will have to pay on your margin loan.

Q. *Would U.S. Treasury bonds and notes be preferable to bank deposits? Why does the yield on these issues vary so much? I understand they are as negotiable as a dollar bill; if lost or destroyed or stolen, your capital is gone.*

A. Treasury bonds and notes fluctuate in price; bank deposits do not. Which do you want? Coupons on outstanding Treasury issues range all the way from $2^1/_2$ to $7^3/_4$ per cent. Their *yields to maturity* (coupon rate divided by market price, plus appreciation to maturity) run from around 2 to 7 per cent.

Any bond—Treasury or corporate (but not savings)—may be owned in bearer form, which, as you say, can be as dangerous as carrying around a $1,000 bill.

Q. *I begin my 74th year next month and am concerned about preserving my estate. I estimate inheritance taxes will take $40,000, which will have to be raised by liquidation of common stocks. I am concerned about the market's course. It seems to me that some of my assets should be so invested as to make liquidation possible when common stocks are threatened by unfavorable economic conditions.*

A. I agree with you, not only against the background of today's stock market, but in any market.

Actually, this may be a problem in finance, but—as is often the case—the goal is comfort and freedom from worry rather than an additional dollar of estate or an additional percentage point in yield.

However, at age 74, with a comfortable estate, and with more concern for conserving that estate than enhancing it, I should think you could buy yourself ease of mind by switching out of more volatile stocks and into Treasury bonds, today still yielding close to highest rate over the last 45 years.

Furthermore, you can reduce that inheritance-tax bite by selecting any of a couple dozen U.S. Treasury issues that are now selling at a deep discount from par ($1,000) but are acceptable at par in payment of inheritance taxes.

Whether the market goes lower or turns around and climbs, I would certainly vote for some Treasuries in your case.

Q. *We are elderly people, living on our investments. We've become jittery over holding too much in common stocks and have been thinking of buying Treasury bonds for a yield of close to 6 per cent. These would increase our income. Is this wise?*

A. In the circumstances you outline, I'd never say no to investing in Treasuries for a 6 per cent-plus return.

Q. *Please send me a list of government bonds that can be bought and sold. I'm afraid to put my funds into stocks.*

A. U.S. Treasury issues are listed daily in many newspapers. There are bonds, notes and certificates, as well as issues of government agencies. All these are negotiable—can be bought and sold daily.

What confuses me is your implied intention to buy and sell government issues. I want to warn you that this is a highly sophisticated field in which millions of dollars worth of bonds are traded back and forth in 32nds of a point.

If you want to own Treasury bonds because you fear stocks—fine. Buy some, put them in your strongbox, and enjoy income of around 6 per cent on your money from the world's safest investment. But if you think you can become a hotshot government-bond trader in one easy lesson, forget it.

Q. *Please explain the meaning of "quotations in 32nds of a point" and also "$2^1/_2$s, 3s, 4s," etc.*

A. You're referring to the market for U.S. Treasury bonds and notes, as well as quotations for government-agency bonds—all negotiable.

A point in a bond is 1 per cent of par. In a $1,000 bond, that would mean $10 per point. Thus, if U.S. Treasury $3^3/_8$s are quoted 99.16 bid, it means 99 and $^{16}/_{32}$nds, or $99^1/_2$, or $995.0 per $1,000 bond. If the price were 99.8, it would mean 99 and $^8/_{32}$nds or $99^1/_4$, or $992.50 per $1,000 bond.

The "s" following the interest rate is merely a way of referring to the bonds—thus, the 4s of Feb. 1993. A more complete description would be, "Treasury bond maturing February, 1993, and paying 4 per cent interest, $40 a year."

Q. *I am a "youngish" widow barely managing to get along on social security plus income from E bonds and savings. Would you please suggest some securities investments for income? Also, I'd like to buy some growth stock for my five infant grandsons.*

A. If you're "barely managing," it's time you put those E bonds to work bringing in current income. Right now, they merely GROW at the rate of $5^1/_2$% a year—and you need cash coming in NOW. Either cash in $5^1/_2$% worth of them a year or—if the tax bite isn't too serious—cash them all in and reinvest in quality stocks today.

It seems that one simply can't do enough explaining about savings bonds. With more than $55 billions held by millions of Americans, you'd think that some of the basic conditions would be generally known. But readers still complain that they are starving with thousands of dollars in E bonds "paying" $5^1/_2$ per cent.

As clearly as I can put it:

E bonds *do not pay anything!* They *grow* at the rate of $5^1/_2$ per cent when held to their new 5 years and 10 months maturity. You may own $100,000 worth of E bonds but still won't get a dollar of current income from them to spend at the grocery.

H bonds *do* pay interest every 6 months via a check from the Treasury. The rate of interest is $5^1/_2$ per cent when held to maturity—10 years.

If you need more current income you have no capital

to put into growth stocks for youngsters to enjoy 15 years from now.

I admit it's none of my business, but this diverting of funds from the necessary and immediate job they should be doing is one of my pet peeves–and I'll have no part in it.

Q. *Are there U.S. guaranteed bonds yielding 6% or more and are they as safe as E bonds?*

A. Yes–to both questions. There is a long list of U.S. Treasury bonds, notes and certificates as well as some government agency bonds which today yield around the 6% mark. Since the government stands behind them as it does behind E bonds, their safety is unquestionable. Interest from these bonds, of course, is taxable, whereas the tax on growth in E bonds is deferred.

Q. *My wife and I have passed our 72nd birthdays. We own a few E bonds. Would we have to pay a tax on the accrued interest in these bonds if we cash them? Would this affect our Social Security benefits?*

A. Interest accrued on E bonds is considered *taxable income* when the bonds are cashed. So are dividends and interest. But that does *NOT* mean you *AUTOMATICALLY* are subject to income taxes. To become subject to tax, your total taxable income (and this does *NOT* include Social Security) must exceed your exemptions.

I don't know what other income you have, but I don't think you'd have any tax to worry about unless your taxable income exceeds $4,000. In any event, you'd have to be in quite a high income tax bracket to justify continuing to hold E bonds when you are 72. That's when you should derive current income from your assets, not merely watch them grow.

Cashing the E bonds would *NOT* affect your Social Security benefits.

Q. *I took some E bonds into my bank to have them exchanged for H bonds. The bank used the wrong form and cashed the bonds. Now I find I am faced with income taxes on the accrued interest. What is the proper form?*

A. If you wanted H bonds (thus delaying the tax liability on the past gain in value of the Es) and got cash instead, you should demand a rescinding of the transaction. Either get the bank to do it or write to the nearest Federal Reserve Bank and explain what happened.

Anyone desiring to turn in E bonds for H bonds–in order to begin receiving semiannual interest payments–should insist on using Form PD 3253 ABC (as revised September, 1971).

Another word of warning: After you have switched to H bonds, don't become disillusioned by that first semiannual check. It will be at the annual rate of only 3.7 per cent. However, the return steps up in the second six months so that the first year income averages out at 4.49 per cent; the next four years will bring you 5.4 per cent interest and in the last five years (of the 10-year maturity), the payment rate will be 6 per cent. It all averages out–over the 10 years–to 5½ per cent.

And you will get a flat 5½ per cent rate if you hold the H bonds beyond the first 10-year period.

All H bonds have been extended, are "alive" and paying out interest.

Q. *We are retired at age 60 because of my husband's illness, and need more income; we have $30,000 in savings, $10,000 in a 6 per cent bank certificate and $10,000 in E bonds.*

A. If you need more income you can't hold E bonds. I thought that had been made clear here time and time again. Exchange the Es for H bonds, which pay you interest twice a year, or redeem them–if your tax bracket isn't too high–and put the money into recently issued utility bonds yielding 7¼ per cent.

Q. *I'm retired, but still in a fairly high tax bracket. Assets are substantially in cash and E bonds. I've been thinking of cashing in the Es and buying some tax-exempt bonds.*

A. The tax-exempt bonds would be O.K. But I'd approach the investment from another angle.

Let the Es stand as an emergency fund and use the cash to buy the bonds. You're paying taxes on the savings interest now, so why not switch that into the tax-exempt bracket. The tax liability on the growth in the Es is deferred anyway.

Q. *When an E bond purchased for $18.75 reaches maturity value of $25, is that $25 treated as though it's used to buy a new bond? When one converts Es to H bonds to get maximum return should they be turned in monthly?*

A. An E bond purchased for $18.75 continues to grow in its same form for so long as you hold it. All E bonds issued since May 1, 1941 are still growing, in their original form.

You may exchange E bonds for H bonds and begin receiving interest checks every six months. There is some slight variation in growing power of E bonds, but I don't see how you can do much maneuvering, since the minimum denomination for H bonds is $500. I'd be inclined to turn in the whole ball of wax and begin receiving income as soon as possible.

Q. *I suppose there are many people, like ourselves, who have been acquiring E bonds ever since they came out in 1941 and have paid no income tax on the accrued annual interest. Was that a mistake? Have these maturities been extended? What advantage would there be in exchanging Es for H bonds?*

A. Most people do *not* annually declare, or pay income taxes on, the interest earned by E bonds. That is their privilege. They are deferring the tax until such time as they cash in the bonds. Their reasoning, in most cases, is that their income tax bracket is higher during the years they are buying the E bonds than it will be in retirement, when they cash in the bonds. That sounds sensible to me.

Or they may figure on exchanging the E bonds for H bonds when they retire, in order to receive semiannual interest checks, and still delay the tax liability on the interest accrued in the E bonds. That is sound reasoning, too.

One of the big selling points for E bonds is that they

represent a handy way to build an emergency nest egg during your working years and yet pay no tax, at that time, on the interest being accrued.

However, an E bond holder *may* elect to declare the annual interest earned by his E bonds and pay income taxes on that interest every April 15. That is also his privilege. But I don't see the point unless his tax bracket during his acquisition years is as low as it's likely to be in retirement.

There is one other case where annual payments are desirable: when infants or young children are given E bonds as gifts, it would pay the parents to file a report for the child declaring that annual interest. Since the child probably does not pay income taxes anyway (the interest earned by a modest amount of bonds would not be sufficient to lift him into even the lowest tax bracket) the child by reporting would thereby work off this long-term tax liability at no expense.

All E and H bond maturities have been extended.

The only advantage of H bonds over E bonds is that the former pay out semiannual interest while the latter merely increase in value.

16 Retirement Day—Before and After

Retirement—financially speaking—means asking your money to work for you for the remainder of your life just as you worked for it during all your years of capital accumulation.

It's the cut-off date on which you stop "putting" and begin "taking."

The profound social, personal, psychological changes which take place upon retirement we leave to others. Here we talk only of money—capital—and how it can be put to work rewarding its owner with worry-free income, which certainly is one of the prerequisites of a comfortable retirement.

Retirement planning, as we have pointed out before in this volume, ideally should begin with the first pay check. Thereafter there really is little change in goal or, for that matter, procedures for many years. One merely continues to build capital the best he can—by saving, by investing for growth, by plowing back profits, etc., etc., etc. The goal is simply this: to arrive at "R" Day with as much capital as possible to be put to work bringing in income.

However, there are subtle changes in emphasis as the years pass and "R" Day approaches. The young man, as we have pointed out earlier, can take many changes in his capital accumulation that the person in his middle or late 50s would do well to avoid. As the time for recouping losses becomes less so should the degree of risk which may bring on such losses.

But the change still remains a matter of degree. Whereas a young man in his late 20s would be justified in speculating on a new $5 stock just issued by an electronics or chemical company with no earnings record, the older man would do well to bank on established electronic and chemical companies for his capital gains.

For those who are carrying on a gradual investment plan, this slight change in emphasis should not be too difficult, calling for merely an upgrading in investment grade of new issues acquired. Those who are going along with a portfolio accumulated mostly in earlier years might consider switching out of more speculative into less speculative types of issues.

However, this does not mean that actual retirement budgeting should be anticipated too far in advance. Too many investors—and these include to a large degree those "orderly" people who like to have everything set ahead of time—are tempted to switch into income stocks a year and even two years before they will actually need retirement income. (Just as in many cases they are tempted to begin buying retirement homes in more amenable climates long before they will be in position to inhabit these homes. The dangers of such a move will be discussed in the chapter on housing.)

The person who switches from growth into income stocks a year or two or three before he needs income for retirement is likely to do himself financial harm on at least two fronts.

If he has been a successful investor in growth issues over the years we can assume that his stocks today show him a gain—long term, it's true, but a gain nevertheless.

For every $1,000 in profit he takes by selling growth stocks, he must pay taxes on at least $500. It is reasonable to assume that as he approaches retirement he is at or near his lifetime peak in earnings, and tax bracket. Let's assume he's in the 40 per cent income tax bracket. So taking his $1,000 gain then costs him at least $200 in cold cash turned over to Uncle Sam.

If he waited until after he has retired (in fact, after he has been unemployed a full tax year), we can assume that his income tax bracket, if he is subject to any tax at all, will be much lower. Call it 19 per cent. So, if he waits until he's retired and his tax bracket has dropped, his cash tax payment on his $1,000 gain will thus be only $95. If he and his wife, both entitled to double personal exemptions at age 65—plus other senior citizen benefits—drop out of the taxpaying category entirely, the entire $1,000 capital gain may go scot free of taxes.

This is only one part of the total saving.

If he over-eagerly switches to income stocks, say, two years before retirement, he also subjects himself unnecessarily to taxes on increased dividends received from income-type stocks, which, we must assume, are larger than the taxable income he would have received if he had continued to hold on to the growth stocks. Finally, of course, he passes up for a year or two whatever capital gain potential remained in his original growth stocks.

So, though "Be prepared" is a tried and true Boy Scout motto, too early emphasis on it by a person planning for retirement can be expensive.

The ideal solution would be to combine the switch from growth to income-type securities with as much tax savings as are possible to obtain from the situation. This, of course, requires some careful reckoning.

Investor A has a portfolio of 2 dozen growth stocks. All show him profits over his original cost. He is now in his last few years of employment as a skilled mechanic or professional and paying a substantial income tax. His logical program, then, would be to do nothing until his income tax bracket drops in retirement. If he retires as of Jan. 1, the solution is easy. The ensuing year is the one in which he may begin to take his profit on growth stocks and switch the proceeds to income securities. If he doesn't quit until July 1, it might well be that his first six months' earnings are enough to continue him in a high tax bracket. So he can't do much switching, if any, until the next tax year.

Investor B, approaching retirement, has two dozen growth stocks, also, but about six of them show losses. Assuming he is taking no taxable gains during the last few years of employment, he must then schedule his sale of these depressed growth issues so that he can deduct $1,000 of loss each year from his earnings and thus get the most benefit from his securities losses. It wouldn't do for him to wait until after he retires to take his losses because his tax savings then will be much less, assuming he is in any tax bracket at all.

Now both Investors A and B go into retirement with gains on their growth stocks. The logical move is to sell out, take their gain, and switch the proceeds into income securities.

However, this does not mean the entire portfolio should be switched on the first Monday after the start of the non-earning year. It might just happen that the gains are so large that even without taxable income, the investor would find himself in a substantial tax bracket merely by virtue of these stock market gains. So moderation–preceded by a little pencil work–is in order.

If substantial amounts are involved, it would be far better to spread the switching from growth to income over a few years, or even more, if necessary, in order to see to it that the gain in any one year is not large enough to cause undue tax hardships. Certainly if the investor is fortunate enough to go into retirement with a substantial portfolio of securities, he should also be in position to "get by" comfortably without at once switching 100% of his portfolio into income producers.

Once the tax course is set, the retiring investor has another hurdle to get over: sentiment, which may be best described as the Auld Lang Syne approach to portfolio management. No financial scene observer has greater respect for the capital-building powers of International Business Machines and Eastman Kodak–to name only two–than the present writer. Fortunes have been built for investors by these and similar growth stocks.

But by their very nature, growth stocks are not generous cash income providers. And cash income, coming in every month with the regularity of the calendar, is what most retired people need.

So even though these issues may have been your portfolio's best performers for the last 30 years, you should say goodbye to them if your need from now on is generous cash income.

Two misconceptions often get in the way of this necessary portfolio switching: poor arithmetic and tax misinformation.

The poor arithmetic takes the form of figuring present investment yield on the basis of the original cost thirty years ago.

Too many investors insist on arguing that the $400 stock they own today, which pays $4 a year in dividends, is giving them a return of 8% because they bought the stock at $50 a share 25 years ago.

This is fallacious reasoning which does considerable damage to the pocketbook. The fact that the investor was clever enough to pick out that investment 25 years ago when it was selling at $50 a share has nothing whatsoever to do with his investment TODAY. Today he has $400 invested, not $50. And $400 invested at 5% can bring in $20 a year, and not the $4 he is currently getting.

But then, to carry his error a step further, he argues: "Yes, but what about taxes? I'd have to pay 25% of my $350 profit to Uncle Sam, so I wouldn't have as much left to invest."

In the first place, the tax on long term capital gains never was a flat 25% for most investors but a tax at 50% of regular income-tax rate. So if the retired investor is in, say, the 19% bracket, only half his $350-a-share gain is taxable. He thus winds up paying a tax of 19% on $175, or, to put it another way, a tax of 9½% on the $350 gain –NOT 25%.

Finally, we have Investor C who, more conservative in nature, has held a portfolio of retirement stocks through most of the years. He now approaches retirement and feels he should make some changes, especially because some of his stocks have gone down in price. They have failed him, he feels, and he wants to part company.

For example, he may have paid $50 for a steel stock ten years ago which is now selling at $40. It's been a "bad" stock and he wants to get shut of it, and take his loss.

If he can take advantage of the tax loss and replace the issue with another income producer, he may be justified in selling out. But before he does so he should figure out his current yield on the stock.

The fact that the market price is down $10 a share has no bearing on the fact that the stock is still paying, for example, $2.25 in annual dividends, or better than 5½% on his *present* investment, with the dividend well protected by earnings.

In other words, pique at seeing his stock go down instead of up is no substitute for doing some arithmetic. In retirement, he will be basically concerned with stable income and if the steel stock provides that he must shut his eyes to the fact it hasn't gone up in price. It may not have been the best investment for him 25 years ago, but it merits retention in his portfolio once "R" Day arrives.

Except in those cases where extreme wealth make retirement income of little concern, a retiree's thinking should be concerned with evaluating what he now owns and what it can do for him in making his retirement years comfortable.

A DIVIDEND CHECK EVERY MONTH

It is possible to receive a dividend check every month merely by buying as few as three different stock issues, each of which pay quarterly dividends in different quarters. Following is a list of well-known companies arranged according to their dividend-paying months. One stock from each group would assure a monthly dividend check–every month. The list is by no means all-inclusive, but presented here merely as an example of how retirement income can be conveniently arranged:

Companies paying dividends in JANUARY, APRIL, JULY and OCTOBER: American Telephone & Telegraph, CPC International, Middle South Utilities, Northern States Power, Pacific Gas & Electric, Household Finance, Duquesne Light, Family Finance, Marcor, General Electric, CIT Financial, Union Pacific, Allied Stores, Philip Morris, Otis, Portland General Electric, Southern California Edison, New England Electric, Mountain States Tel. & Tel., Campbell Soup.

Companies paying dividends in FEBRUARY, MAY, AUGUST and NOVEMBER: Abbott Laboratories, Boston Edison, California Water, Consumers Power, N. Y. State Electric & Gas, Pacific Lighting, Caterpillar Tractor, Commonwealth Edison, American Can, Columbia Gas, Illinois Power, Union Oil, Stone & Webster, Chase Manhattan, Borg-Warner, American Natural Gas.

Companies paying dividends in MARCH, JUNE, SEPTEMBER and DECEMBER: Chesapeake & Ohio, Liggett & Myers, Niagara Mohawk, American Brands, Philips Petroleum, Sinclair Oil, Inland Steel, Arizona Public Service, Northern Indiana Public Service, General Foods, Shell Oil, Reynolds Industries, NL Industries, Norfolk & Western, Public Service Electric & Gas, Mobil, Con Edison, General Motors, Owens-Illinois Glass, Int'l Nickel, New England Tel. & Tel., Chesebrough-Pond's.

SOME QUESTIONS AND ANSWERS

Q. *I'm about to retire this year and will have to live quite economically. I'd like advice on some safe, fair-yield investments which would protect me from income taxes.*

A. There is at least one field open to you–although you should first determine whether you want to venture into it. If you are going to live on a tight budget, it may be that the tax bite is more feared than actual.

You can get around 5% today from tax-exempt bonds issued by states, cities, and their various water, bridge, tunnel, education, highway authorities.

However, do not make any commitments in this field until you are sure you will have an income tax problem, because–as is the case with everything in finance–you don't get the exemption for nothing. And the price you pay–in reduced yield–may be much higher than your retirement budget will warrant.

The difference in yield between high-grade, taxable corporate bonds and high-grade, tax-free municipal bonds is about 30%. If your tax bracket is below 30% you may be biting off your income to spite the tax collector.

Q. *As I head toward retirement, I've been experimenting with fairly speculative stocks as a means of producing capital gains on which I can live. I organized a small club and we've kept pretty much fully invested–possibly a mistake. Using charts, we have done well.*

A. I see nothing wrong with an investment club speculating–just so long as all the members agree on that course. But I can't see speculating for retirement income. Nor can I understand how an investment club can be used to provide retirement income.

Q. *I have $40,000 in a savings account. Instead of taking it out and risking it in stocks or bonds, or using it to buy an annuity–which might not leave anything for my heirs–why can't I withdraw a certain amount every year?*

A. You can.

About 6 years ago, the Bowery Savings Bank–the country's largest–originated a plan which enables depositors to withdraw a certain amount monthly from savings. The amount, of course, depends upon the size of the account, the number of years withdrawals are to be made, or–as an alternative–the amount of withdrawal possible without cutting into principal. Many other banks around the country have since set up these programs.

You don't give me your age, but taking your $40,000 savings account–and assuming interest at the rate of 5% a year, compounded quarterly–you could:

withdraw $300 a month for 16 years and 1 month, at the end of which time your $40,000 plus $18,006 in interest would be exhausted; or

withdraw $500 a month for 8 years, at which time your $40,000 plus $8,461 interest earned would be exhausted; or

withdraw $165.28 a month "forever," leaving the $40,000 intact for your heirs.

If your deposit balance today were a more modest $15,000 you could:

withdraw $100 a month for 19 years and 5 months; or $200 a month for 7 years and 5 months; or $61.98 a month without cutting into capital.

Which of these plans would be best only you, of course, can tell. It all depends upon how long you intend to live, how much you are interested in leaving an estate and whether you will have other resources to fall back on if you live longer than your capital.

Q. *I wish to take issue with your ideas that "as an investor grows older he should switch to peace-of-mind stocks," and that "an elderly person has no business in ANY speculative stocks." Over the last 15 years, an investor would have been a big loser following your plan. My point is that conservatism is no longer a refuge for the old. If the market in the next ten years does what it did in the last ten your advice is a disservice. I'll take a capital gain rather than hold a bunch of conservative stocks.*

A. I'll also take a capital gain any day (especially if it's long term) in preference to even a generous dividend from a conservative stock.

The trick, if you're retired and living off limited investments, is to be able to take capital gains with the regularity required to meet food, clothing and shelter bills. In some markets, that isn't so easy.

You say—correctly—that the stock market of the last ten years has not been as rewarding to holders of "peace of mind" stocks as it has been to those who've taken chances in, say, new computer, oceanographic, leasing and conglomerate securities. But, you must admit, you're taking advantage of 20/20 hindsight.

You'll also have to admit that there were frequent intervals during the last decade when retired investors depending primarily upon capital gains for income would have had no gains. Glance back at the charts of any of our leading growth companies and you'll see what I mean. And don't forget that during the months (and even years) that prices were declining, there were little or no dividends coming in.

Also keep in mind that if you depend upon a program of steady liquidation of growth stocks to finance your retirement and have to sell some shares during a market slump you have to sell more shares in order to receive the required proceeds. This works out to a reverse of the dollar-averaging system which has often proved successful in ACQUIRING stocks.

Our difference of opinion is not financial, but chiefly psychological.

I assume, from your letterhead, that you are a skilled, highly paid professional, in your capital-building years. Your philosophy is, therefore, 100% correct—for you.

But I also receive thousands of letters from retired people, many living on pensions with only modest capital funds to provide a few extras. I think they are entitled to the comfort of a generous dividend check every quarter or an interest check every six months.

When you are 68, a "sure dime" is often far more comforting than a "risky dollar." The hope that a speculative stock will pay off handsomely in 1977 seems far less important than a dividend check in hand today.

And finally, if you study the records of even conservative blue chips which have not scored sensational market gains during the last decade you will find that dividend increases have been generous, often exceeding the rise in the cost of living. Such inflation protection is not to be taken lightly when one is living on income from investments.

I won't argue any further except to make one point:

When I reply to an elderly person living on limited means my first concern is to get him as much income as he can get without too much worry.

I am NOT even interested in suggesting how he can try for 25% capital appreciation by assuming the risk of losing 25%, or even 10% of his funds, a loss which he can no longer replace through earnings. If that's a disservice, I plead guilty.

Q. *What course of investment action would you recommend for a man in his mid-50s, no dependents, who would like to retire as early as possible. I now have substantial long-term gains on my portfolio. I would like best possible income with security: no need to leave an estate.*

A. Your first step would be to take stock of your total assets. You can, today, count on a return either side of 5%, with inflation protection. If that would yield enough to live at a satisfactory level, the money should be put into good quality common shares, stressing utilities, sound rails and manufacturing issues.

The fact that you have gains on stocks now held does not necessarily indicate that the issues should be sold. If the companies are still good and the *current* yield (not the yield based on your original cost) is still around 5%, then perhaps the shares should be held.

Until you are much older, the questions of whether or not you want to leave an estate is academic. Unless you have so much money that you can invade principal with impunity, you must plan, for at least 10 to 15 years, on offsetting inflation with income from equities or senior securities convertible into common shares.

When you get into the 65-70 range you may consider diverting some of your funds to a lifetime annuity.

Q. *I have just retired, at age 61, on pension of $125 a week. We have about $10,000 in E bonds and savings of about $9,000. I think it's high time I took the plunge and invested in stocks.*

A. I have no desire to engage in semantics, but that word "plunge," left undefined, can do, and has done, a lot of harm.

During your working lifetime you have patiently built up $19,000 in savings. I'm sure you considered this a conservative program and the very antithesis of "plunging." (It wasn't, exactly. In fact—you were speculating on the dollar's ability to maintain its strength and thus help support you in retirement, and lost. But that's water over the dam.)

Plunging, in finance, means wild speculation in hopes

of a quick profit. That's the last thing you should consider doing now. There's enough risk in buying any security without adding unnecessary risk by buying volatile issues in the hopes of a quick gain. It's important that you remove the "plunging" idea from your mind before considering any retirement investments.

What you now want is to put your money to work for the long term bringing in fair income (perhaps not much more than you are now getting in savings interest) but with some hope that the shares you buy will help offset inflation. After all, your pension will be fixed and you no longer will have a boss to go to with the argument that your salary is not enough to meet steadily rising living costs.

Buy–and hold–quality issues.

The E bonds should be (1) redeemed, and the money invested to bring in current income; (2) switched to H's; or (3) cashed in at the rate of around $550 worth a year, to provide spendable income without cutting into your principal. Your tax bracket in retirement will be a factor in deciding which course to follow.

Q. *Your column has helped us in our retirement planning. We have checks coming in every month, except that February and May are our low spots. Could you suggest any stocks which pay dividends in February, May, August, November?*

A. You'll find these generous dividend payers, among others, in the February, May, August and November division:

Boston Edison, California Water, N.Y. State Electric & Gas, Pacific Lighting, American Can, Columbia Gas, American Natural Gas, Stone & Webster.

I suggest you discuss these with your broker and get his help in making a selection.

(And while you're at it, don't overlook the issues which regularly pay dividends at the close of January, April, July, and October–or those which distribute dividends regularly on the first day of March, June, September, December. So, you see, you have considerable latitude.)

Q. *My husband plans to retire next year and begin playing the stock market. He has studied all kinds of charts and books–has in fact, charted about 50 stocks for the last year. Some have gone up. He made a little money on some airplane stock last year. He has also bought some $5 mining stocks. Would he be better sticking to just charting, and not buying? Other stocks, such as Ford and Chrysler, he has bought and sold at the wrong time. It seems to me he should just relax.*

A. Relaxation, I suppose, takes many forms: following a golf ball across a meadow or numbers across a trans-lux stock market tape; cataloguing stamps or charting stocks. Who's to say what's best?

If you will have money to lose in retirement, I see nothing morally wrong with his gambling in $5 mining stocks. It may prove a small cost for keeping him out of your hair. If he wants to make a hobby of sitting around brokerage boardrooms 5½ hours a day, I suppose you might say: "Better there than in my kitchen."

If, on the other hand, you won't have money to lose in retirement, it would be far better if you invested in–and held–such dividend-paying stocks as Ford, Chrysler and others, and restricted the stock market gambling to trading on paper.

I suppose there have been men who became wealthy speculating during retirement, but I can't think of any. And if you're not working–bringing money in–stock market losses can just about ruin retirement peace of mind.

Q. *I am 1½ years from retirement at 62. I hold mostly growth stocks. I've been thinking of making some changes now to increase income preparatory to retirement, but have noticed your reply in a similar instance in which you say such a switch can be made in a few minutes, so why not wait? It can be made in minutes, but what happens if the market is down when one finally makes the switch? If what has been worth, say, $75,000 in growth stocks a few months ago might at the moment a switch is to be made, be down to only $65,000? To be sure, income stocks might be down also, but usually not as much as the growth stocks. I'd appreciate your comments and a list of income stocks to be watched.*

A. There isn't much point to arguing about where the market might be 18, or 24 or 30 months from now. No one knows.

There is also not much point to arguing whether at the time of a switch growth stocks will be up and income stocks down–or vice versa. Many income stocks, as a matter of fact, did come down more than growth stocks in recent years. At this very moment, income stocks are cheaper–in relation to growth issues–than they have been for years.

But apart from any attempt to guess the best time to jump from one group to another, there are other, more concrete, considerations:

1. If an investor has been successfully building a growth stock portfolio during his working years, we can assume he has a capital gain. Why take this profit while he is still employed and pay a tax based on his earned income? If he waits until after he's retired, his tax bracket will be much lower. (Of course, if he has a LOSS on a growth stock, he should take it while still employed, so as to cut down his tax on earnings.)

2. If he is comfortable enough during his working years to have money left over for acquiring growth stocks, he obviously is not in need of additional income. Why switch growth to income stocks and pay an unnecessary tax on unneeded income?

Obviously, all rules are subject to bending. If you intend to retire next Jan. 1 or next July 1 and have additional money to invest now, you could make a good case for buying income stocks. Why take a chance on a growth stock and then have to pay another commission to get into income securities? But if you are already invested in growth issues, why not choose the best time, tax-wise, to make the switch?

Q. *I am now retired. Having been conservative all my life I now need your help in protecting myself against inflation. We have accumulated $75,000–all in savings accounts. We have never owned stocks or real estate. The* *interest from this money comprises about two-thirds our income.*

A. The dictionary describes a conservative as one who wants to preserve established principles, who favors stability and traditional methods.

The conservative has his arguments when it comes to politics, or morals, or international diplomacy. But when he applies the term "conservative" to his attitude toward the dollar he is in very real danger, because he is trying to apply a stable yardstick to an item which refuses to stand still.

If you've held some of these dollars for only as little as 10 years you've already lost about 20% of them in terms of buying power. So the course you thought was "conservative" was actually a gamble which went against you.

I am NOT saying that dollars should not be accumulated. Everyone needs some dollars—the amount depending upon his responsibilities.

But I AM saying that once one covers that responsibility he takes risks with the remainder, whether he does so consciously or not:

Although all investments in equities—real estate, securities, etc., etc.,—do not show a profit or even help offset inflation, I can only argue that it's a risk which most of us should consider—if only as a counterbalance to the dollars we all must hold.

Just because you have nothing but dollars now does not mean you should have nothing but common stocks by tomorrow afternoon. Talk over your program with a reputable broker, move part of your funds, slowly, into top quality utility, oil, rail and natural resources securities —common shares and convertibles. Buy quality and hold. Do NOT become a trader.

17 If You're Successful You Will Have to Plan Your Retirement Differently

For those who have high income, whether from inherited wealth, self-employment or from compensation as an employee, a sound retirement program will differ in many ways from those of individuals with smaller earned income. The reason: Income taxes.

Take the executive with a successful company. He may have substantial retirement benefits tied to his employment.

Even the successful self-employed professional—the doctor, lawyer, accountant, etc.—will have to approach retirement planning somewhat differently from the average wage earner.

Basically, he must give consideration to two problems: 1. What present savings program will best help him now set aside a sufficient amount after meeting current high taxes? 2. What investment program will help him cut taxes even after retirement when, thanks to his successful career, he may still be in a fairly high tax bracket?

Expressed another way: The successful earner must look for the investment which will subject him to a minimum tax during his period of accumulation as well as free him from as much taxation as possible in retirement.

There are two avenues open to him:

He may buy securities which provide wholly or partly tax-free income.

He may invest primarily for long-term capital gain which is taxable at reduced rates.

First, the advantage of stressing long-term gain.

Let us weigh the advantages of investment in a good dividend payer (e.g., American Telephone) as against a security which gives a low current yield but has a history of capital appreciation (e.g., IBM). If the individual is in the high surtax brackets as a result of his compensation income, he actually has no choice. Even with the exclusion granted current dividends, he must select the growth security over the high dividend payer. And the higher his earned income, the more taxes dictate such choice.

By the selection of the growth security, he forgoes a current return which may mean very little to him after taxes in return for a security which builds up capital values ultimately to be realized as a capital gain profit by sale of the security.

In seeking capital gain, which stocks hold the greatest promise? While not exclusive, the following have real potential along those lines:

1. Companies following an earnings retention policy;
2. Stock dividend companies;
3. Companies whose operations are tax protected.

EARNINGS RETENTION COMPANIES

These are the companies which plow back earnings into business operations rather than distributing the largest portion to stockholders in the form of dividends. They offer these advantages:

1. Values build up faster within this type of company than in the company which distributes a substantial portion of its earnings. And those values eventually will be reflected in market value of the stock. The investor buys with the intention of holding the security for growth in its values, then sells his holdings for a capital gain profit. He passes up current dividends which would be taxed as ordinary income in order to realize profit on sale which is a capital gain profit. Regardless of whether earnings are retained by the company or distributed to stockholders in form of dividends, Uncle Sam first takes his cut through the corporate tax.
2. Where a substantial portion of earnings is distributed to stockholders, there is tax dilution because of tax on dividends received. Earnings retained by the company produce additional earnings so that even if the same percentage of earnings is retained from year to year, yield (based on original price paid by stockholder) nevertheless increases. He might hold his stock for that increased yield which might be substantial even after taxes then or he might sell to another at a high market price reflecting that increased yield.

   Take Minnesota Mining and Manufacturing. This company follows an earnings retention policy. For some time, it has retained about 50 per cent of its earnings for business expansion, distributed only about 50 per cent to stockholders as dividends. From the mid-'30s to 1960, this stock sold at a low (adjusted) of ½ and traded over 100 at the start of the 1970s.

An investor who some years back bought at close to the low, and sold out recently, would have reaped a profit of more than 2,500 per cent after taxes. Or, if he retained his shares, he would currently be receiving a yield of 100 per cent annually based on original investment cost.

STOCK DIVIDEND COMPANIES

There are many growth companies which pay part or all of their annual distribution in the form of additional shares of stock in order to preserve cash for expanding the business. Such a distribution is exempt from the regular income taxes which are levied on cash dividends. Instead, the average cost of your original investment is reduced by the amount of the stock dividend. When, and only if, you ever sell your shares, your dividend distribution is thus converted into a long-term capital gain and therefore taxable at only one-half your regular income tax rate.

If you hold 100 shares of a young, growing company, the directors may decide that rather than pay you a dividend of 25 cents a share in cash, which would deplete the firm's working capital, they will vote a 10 per cent dividend in company stock. This means you will receive a certificate for 10 shares of stock (10 per cent of 100 shares). You now have 110 shares instead of 100, and although this practice merely means the cutting up of the corporate pie into smaller pieces, a stock dividend is always a welcome payment, because in addition to making you feel richer—110 shares instead of 100—it also gives you a tax choice.

You may retain the stock dividend. In which case you owe no current income tax.

Or you may wish to sell the additional 10 shares, pocket the proceeds and pay income tax. To the extent the proceeds of this sale exceed the pro rata cost of the original stock you have a capital gain. That is taxable at only one-half your regular income tax rate.

Here are some companies which have paid dividends in stock regularly for 5 years:

Acme Markets
Aerosol Techniques
Air Products & Chemicals
Apco Oil
ASPRO, Inc.
Avondale Mills
Barber Oil
Barry (R.G.)
Barton Brands
Beech Aircraft
Brown-Forman Distillers
Buell Industries
Caldor, Inc.
Clopay Corp.
Citizens Utilities
Coleco Industries
Columbia Broadcasting
Cramer Electronics
Crowell-Collier
Dart Industries
Diebold, Inc.
Disney (Walt) Productions
Duro-Test
Eastern Gas & Fuel
Evans Products
Fabien Corp.
Fed-Mart
First Charter Financial
Fishman (M.H.)
Fluor Corp.
Forest Laboratories
General American Oil
General Instrument
Georgia-Pacific
Intl. Flavors & Fragrances
Ketchum & Co.
Kidde (Walter)
Leslie Fay
Litton Industries
Lucky Stores
Manhattan Industries
Marriott Corp.
Millmaster Onyx
Missouri Public Service
Occidental Petroleum
Omark Industries
Pittston Co.
Poloron Products
Polychrome Corp.
Publicker Industries
Rochester Gas & Electric
Rohm & Haas
Ronson Corp.
San Juan Racing
Seagrave Corp.
Servomation Corp.
SGL Industries
Speed-O-Print Bus. Mach.
Sun Oil
Synalloy Corp.
Tasty Baking
Texas Industries
Tootsie Roll Industries
Union Financial
Wesco Financial
Wieboldt Stores
Wood Industries

The majority of the companies in the preceding list are traded on the New York Stock Exchange. A few are traded on the American Stock Exchange and over-the-counter.

COMPANIES WHOSE OPERATIONS ARE TAX PROTECTED

Some companies are given special tax protection because of:

1. The nature of the industry within which they operate, or
2. The method of operations regardless of industry.

A good example of a company falling within the first category is an oil company.

It benefits from percentage depletion which allows tax offsets against income regardless of the cost of the property producing the income. While cash earnings are not reduced, tax earnings are—which means that the tax take going to the collector is reduced. In turn, that means more profits after taxes for distribution to stockholders or for further expansion of business activities.

An industrial study covering the year 1953 made a comparison between five producing oil companies and five leading industrial companies. That study showed that the oil-producing companies kept 90 per cent of their total cash earnings after taxes against less than 53 per cent for the industrials.

On further analysis of the tax protection given the oil companies, Amerada Petroleum (now Amerada Hess), the United States' largest crude producer was a striking example. Over a period of seventeen years, Uncle Sam took only about 4 per cent of its total income in taxes. For years, the average industrial company, once its income exceeded $25,000, paid taxes at a rate of around 50%.

In the second group are companies whose business operations might have a salubrious effect on the nation's economy. The company which engages heavily in research hopes to develop new products and new markets. If it is successful, that has the effect of creating new employment opportunities—a direct benefit to the economy. Lionel Edie, in a survey on growth of the economy, reveals that the average American company grows at a rate of 3 per cent a year but that the research-minded company might show a growth factor of 10 per cent a year.

Our tax law gives an incentive to companies in encouraging research projects. Many of the research costs which formerly had to be capitalized (and didn't give a current tax deduction) now may be taken as an expense with the effect of reducing taxable income and corporate tax due. In effect, tax money underwrites a company's current research program. Of course, tax money doesn't underwrite a research program in its entirety so heavy research expenses mean a drop in current income, leaving less available for distribution to stockholders currently. But if the research program results in success, a stockholder has forgone a current return for a buildup in values of the stock he holds. There is a capital appreciation of his stock holdings which he can eventually realize by sale—and the realized profit is a capital gain profit which is given tax protection.

TAX-EXEMPT BONDS

There is an important class of security which yields a regular, non-taxable income. These are the tax-exempt bonds.

Such bonds are issued by state and municipal governments or their authorities. In investment circles they are all called "municipals," although they include obligations of counties, special tax districts, or school, port, sanitation, airport, highway, tunnel, toll bridge, turnpike or public housing authorities. Or, for that matter, obligations issued by the states and territories themselves.

These all fall into four principal types—direct and general obligations, revenue bonds, special assessment bonds, tax anticipation warrants.

The first are those for which the full credit of the issuer is pledged, including all taxable property. Such bonds are usually issued for schools, municipal improvements and buildings. Obviously, because of the credit behind them, these are the safest.

Revenue bonds are sold to raise funds for a specific purpose—construction of waterworks, a sewer system, toll bridges, tunnels, turnpikes. These generally are a direct lien on the earnings of property for which the money is being raised.

Special assessment bonds ordinarily are paid from assessments levied upon property benefiting from the particular improvement for which the money was raised—as in the case of new streets. In some cases, however, the state or city stands back of the guarantee, so that such a bond is as safe as the direct and general obligation bond.

Tax anticipation notes are generally issued for a short space of time, in anticipation of taxes in process of collection. Ordinarily, they provide a short-term investment and would not be a normal source of retirement income.

Because the income from them is exempt from Federal (and, in many cases, state) income taxes, these municipals normally yield considerably less than common stocks, or ordinary corporate bonds. But their value to the individual investor may nevertheless be considerable, depending on his tax liability.

Obviously, until a considerable tax liability is reached, there is no reason to accept lower income on your investments merely for the sake of tax exemption.

However, above such a dividing line, freedom from taxes becomes important. For instance, during recent years when money conditions were very tight, yields from quality tax-exempt bonds in the neighborhood of 7 per cent were available. At the same time, yields of about 9 per cent from quality industrial but taxable bonds were available. Subsequently, when credit conditions eased, yields from both tax-exempt and taxable bonds dropped. Even after such drop, yields close to 6 per cent could be secured from highest-quality tax-exempts; yields from industrial bonds, somewhat in excess of 7 per cent. As a result, it was possible to invest in quality tax-exempts to get a return equal to or higher than that from a taxable bond, net after taxes.

To illustrate: Investment of $1,000 in a tax-exempt bond yielding 5.5 per cent means a return of $55 a year. A tax-free return of $55 exceeds $86 from a fully taxable investment for a single individual with taxable income under $20,000 a year. To get more than $86 from $1,000 invested in a taxable bond, such an investor would have to invest in one yielding more than 8.6 per cent. On investment in a taxable bond to get the same return, net after taxes, as that offered by a quality tax-exempt bond, he would have to accept reduced safety on investment.

As the taxable-income figure rises, the exemption feature of the municipal bond becomes increasingly valuable. The municipal bond yielding 5.5 per cent could equal a return of 10 per cent from a taxable investment for a person with taxable income of $30,000, and, of course, the municipal bond would be considerably safer.

The following table shows yield which must be secured from a fully taxable investment, such as a bank savings account, a corporate bond, etc., to equal that available from a quality tax-exempt bond, yielding 5.5 per cent.

Taxable Income	*Taxable Equivalents For 5.5% Tax-Exempt Bond*	
$16,000	8.3%*	7.6%†
20,000	8.8	8.1
26,000	10.0	8.6
35,000	11.0	9.4
40,000	12.2	10.5
45,000	13.7	11.0
60,000	15.2	11.7

*Separate return
†Joint return

The tax-exempt bond remains, however, a highly specialized field of investment. While a stock exchange brokerage house can put through an order for fifty shares of General Motors with very little variation in ultimate cost to you, the purchase of municipal bonds should be made only with the advice of and, preferably, through a firm specializing in this field or having a department devoted to trading municipals.

Tax-exempts are traded over-the-counter. Activity may vary widely, since some issues run into the hundreds of millions of dollars while others may represent a $250,000 financing for a rural school district. That would mean that, in all, there are only 250 bonds in the market with the floating supply available for trading practically negligible.

Tax-exempts, as a rule, rank very high indeed on the safety parade. The number of defaults in this field in the past quarter century has been negligible. Yet the same rules of safety which govern the yield on stocks and bonds also pertain to the pricing of tax-exempts.

In general, long-term tax-exempt bonds of the highest quality currently yield about 5 per cent. If a tax-exempt bond yielding 7 per cent is brought to your attention, you must be prepared to accept a lower safety factor. That high yield *does not mean that the laws of safety and value have been repealed.* There are reasons.

The reasons which go into determining tax-exempt bond yields vary. In the first place, the question of the guaranty behind the principal and interest are of utmost importance. If a strong, economically sound state stands 100 per cent behind the bond, you have a security which will likely sell at a price to yield somewhere about 5 per cent. If the bond is guaranteed solely by a land reclamation project with no support in meeting principal or interest from the state, you must look into the possibilities of the land project itself before you invest since the value of your holding will depend solely on how this project succeeds.

Length of maturity is another factor, as is the amount of bonds outstanding. In fact, some small, high-grade issues are labeled "collector items," meaning that various investment institutions want them in their portfolios because they are rare, and because they give them diversification.

We repeat, tax-exempt bonds may or may not have a place in your present or future investment program. If your tax problem is such that they are desirable, be sure you discuss the matter fully with an expert before you jump. Below, we list—entirely for illustration purposes and by no means as a recommendation to buy—a few examples of tax-exempt bonds. The list includes issues of many states and their subdivisions. By all means check on the state tax exemption, too, before you buy.

There are literally thousands of municipal bond issues outstanding. But examples of yields obtainable in the spring of 1972 follow:

	Coupon	*Maturity*	*Yield to Maturity*
CALIFORNIA			
California, State of	3.50%	4/1/74	4.50%
L.A. Dept Wtr & Pwr Rev.	2.25%	9/1/75	4.75%
Los Angeles Chsd	4.00%	9/1/75	3.75%
California, State of	1.75%	11/1/77	5.50%
Sacramento P.H.A.	2⅛%	12/1/78	4.90%
L.A. Co. Flood Cont. Dist	2.75%	5/1/79	5.40%
Los Angeles USD	3.25%	8/1/79	5.20%
Met. Wtr Dist of So. Calif.	3.50%	2/1/80	5.35%
Los Angeles	2.50%	11/1/80	5.65%
L.A. Dept Wtr & Pwr Rev.	2.50%	5/1/81	5.80%
Los Angeles Co. FCD	2.75%	5/1/81	5.70%
L.A. Dept Wtr & Pwr Rev.	2.90%	5/1/81	5.70%
Los Angeles	3.25%	2/1/82	5.60%
Santa Clara County	3.10%	5/1/83	5.70%
L.A. Dept Wtr & Pwr Rev.	3.10%	3/1/84	5.80%
L.A. Dept Wtr & Pwr Rev.	2.90%	5/1/84	5.90%
L.A. Dept Wtr & Pwr Rev.	3.50%	1/1/85	5.75%
L.A. Dept Wtr & Pwr Rev.	4.10%	10/1/85	4.50%
L.A. Flood Cont. Dist	4.00%	3/1/87	5.40%
Los Angeles P.H.A.	2⅜%	11/1/90	6.00%
East Bay Mud	3.40%	9/1/91	5.90%
CONNECTICUT			
Conn. Expway 5th Ser. Rev.	3.90%	1/1/78	4.25%
Conn. Expway 5th Ser. Rec.	3.90%	1/1/81	4.60%
Conn. Expway 5th Ser. Rev.	3.90%	1/1/83	4.75%
Bridgeport	4.25%	1/1/84	4.50%
New Haven	4.25%	2/1/84	4.60%
Fairfield	6.25%	1/1/89	5.00%

MARYLAND

Maryland St. Road Comm. Rev.	3.10%	7/1/73	3.50%
Maryland St. Road Comm. Rev.	3.00%	8/1/73	3.50%
Baltimore	2.75%	8/15/81	5.80%
Baltimore	3.00%	9/15/81	5.70%
Baltimore	3.25%	8/1/85	6.00%

MASSACHUSETTS

Massachusetts	3½%	2/1/73	2.75%
Taunton	2%	1/1/77	5.50%
Boston Ser. "A" Housing	2%	8/1/83	5.75%
Boston Met. Dist	2.40%	12/1/83	5.50%
Holyoke (When Issued)	4.90%	2/1/85	4.80%
Massachusetts	3.00%	2/1/88	5.70%
Boston Rapid Transit	3.00%	6/1/94	5.85%

NEW YORK

Brookhaven CSD#11 (Suffolk)	4.00%	5/1/74	4.00%
N.Y.S. Power Auth., Rev.	2.75%	1/1/75	4.50%
Webster (Monroe)	3.75%	3/1/75	4.50%
New York City	6.25%	4/15/75	4.90%
Islip UFSD#7 (Suffolk)	3.90%	2/15/76	5.00%
New York City	4.25%	2/15/76	5.50%
Winfield CSD#1 (Herkimer)	3.25%	5/1/76	5.00%
Islip UFSD#3 (Suffolk)	3.10%	6/1/76	5.10%
Callicoon, Etc. CSD#1 (Sullivan)	3.40%	6/1/76	4.80%
Colonie (Albany)	3.50%	3/1/77	5.20%
Nassau County	2.50%	10/1/77	5.25%
New York City	2.80%	11/1/77	6.25%
Amherst, Etc. CSD#3 (Erie)	3.90%	12/1/77	5.00%
Chester, Village of (Orange)	5.75%	3/1/78	4.40%
DTD 12/1/72–1ST CPN 3/1/72		3/1/82	5.10%
Babylon UFSD#5 (Suffolk)	4.00%	6/1/78	4.75%
Nassau County	3.60%	6/15/78	4.90%
New York City	3.25%	9/1/78	6.50%
Baldwinsville, Village of	5.10%	8/1/79	4.70%
DTD 11/1/71–1ST CPN 8/1/72		8/1/86	5.40%
Wheatland, Etc. CSD#1 (Monroe)	3.40%	11/1/78	5.15%
Lysander, CSD#1 (Onondaga)	3.50%	12/1/78	5.30%
Glen Cove (Nassau)	2.75%	1/1/79	5.60%
Brookhaven CSD#4 (Suffolk)	5.70%	3/1/79	4.70%
5M-Denominations (When Issued)		3/1/85	5.60%
Long Beach (Nassau)	6.40%	6/1/79	4.85%
New York City	3.90%	7/1/79	6.30%
Valley Stream (Nassau)	5.75%	7/1/79	4.70%
Nassau County	2.10%	8/15/79	5.80%
Orangetown & Clarkstown CSD#1	3.40%	11/1/79	5.35%
Amherst, Etc. CSD#3 (Erie)	3.90%	12/1/79	5.10%
Glen Cove (Nassau)	2.75%	1/1/80	5.80%
Riverhead, Town of (Suffolk)	4.75%	1/15/80	4.75%
Dewitt, Town of (Onondaga)	3.50%	3/1/80	5.50%
Fallsburgh (Sullivan)	3.00%	4/1/80	5.90%
Gloversville (Fulton)	3.80%	5/1/80	5.50%
Suffolk Co. Wtr Auth., Rev.	2.75%	6/1/80	5.90%
Westmoreland, CSD#1 (Oneida)	2.70%	7/15/80	5.85%

ROAD, BRIDGE REVENUE BONDS

			Yield to Maturity
Florida Turnpike Authority	4¾	11/ 1/2001	5.28
Florida Turnpike Authority Revenue	7.10	11/ 1/2010	6.12
Illinois Toll Highway Revenue	3¾	1/ 1/1995	5.32
Illinois Toll Highway Revenue	4¾	1/ 1/1998	5.11
Illinois Toll Highway Revenue	6¾	1/ 1/2010	5.95
Indiana Toll Road Commission Revenue	3½	1/ 1/1994	5.22
Jacksonville Expressway Authority Rev.	4	10/ 1/1992	5.56
Jacksonville Expressway Authority Rev.	4.10	10/ 1/2003	5.51
Kansas Turnpike Authority Revenue	3⅜	10/ 1/1994	4.90
Kentucky Turnpike Authority Revenue	4¾	7/ 1/2006	5.85
Kentucky Turnpike Authority Revenue	6.20	7/ 1/2011	6.00
Maine Turnpike Authority Revenue	4	1/ 1/1989	4.57
Maryland Bridge & Tunnel Auth.	5.20	10/ 1/2008	5.20
Massachusetts Turnpike Auth. Rev.	3.30	5/ 1/1994	4.51
New Jersey Turnpike Authority Rev.	3¼	1/ 1/1985	3.25
New Jersey Turnpike Authority Rev.	4¾	1/ 1/2006	5.44
New Jersey Turnpike Authority Rev.	5⅛	1/ 1/2008	5.32
New Jersey Turnpike Authority Rev.	5.20	1/ 1/2008	5.36
New Jersey Turnpike Authority Rev.	7	1/ 1/2009	6.08
New York State Thruway Authority Rev.	3.10	7/ 1/1994	5.89
Ohio Turnpike Authority Revenue	3¼	6/ 1/1992	3.82
Oklahoma Turnpike Authority Revenue	4.70	1/ 1/2006	5.67
Oklahoma Turnpike Authority Revenue	6¼	1/ 1/2004	6.19

PUBLIC AUTHORITY, ELECTRIC & OTHER REVENUE BONDS

Chelan County, Wash., P.U.D.#1	5	7/ 1/2013	5.39
Chicago O'Hare Airport Revenue	4¾	1/ 1/1999	5.40
Columbia Storage Power Ex.	3⅞	4/ 1/2003	5.81
Consumers P.P.D. Electric	5.10	1/ 1/2003	5.56
Consumers P.P.D. Nuclear	5.10	1/ 1/2003	5.56
Dallas Fort Worth Airport Revenue	6¾	11/ 1/2001	6.12
Delaware River Port Authority Rev.	5⅝	1/15/2009	5.69
Douglas County, Wash., P.U.D.#1 Revenue	4	9/ 1/2018	5.76
Grant County, Wash., P.U.D.#2 Revenue	3.80	4/ 1/1998	5.97

Grant County, Wash., P.U.D.#2 Revenue	3⁷/₈	11/ 1/2005	5.90
Grant County, Wash., P.U.D.#2 Revenue	3.85	4/ 1/2009	5.73
Massachusetts Port Authority Revenue	3.80	7/ 1/2004	4.95
Massachusetts Port Authority Rev.	6	7/ 1/2011	5.80
Nebraska P.P.D. Electric	6.60	1/ 1/2004	6.06
Nebraska P.P.D. Nuclear	6.60	1/ 1/2004	6.06
New York State Power Authority Revenue	3.20	1/ 1/1995	4.19
New York State Power Authority Revenue	3³/₄	1/ 1/2006	4.44
New York State Power Authority Revenue	4¹/₈	1/ 1/2006	4.45
New York State Power Authority Revenue	4.20	1/ 1/2006	4.48
New York State Power Authority Revenue	4³/₈	1/ 1/2006	4.55
New York State Power Authority Revenue	5¹/₂	1/ 1/2010	5.48
New York State Power Authority Revenue	5⁵/₈	1/ 1/2010	5.55
New York State Power Authority Revenue	5⁷/₈	1/ 1/2010	5.64
New York State Power Authority Revenue	6⁷/₈	1/ 1/2010	5.97
New York State U.D.C.	6.60	1/ 1/2011	6.09
Omaha P.P.D.	5³/₈	2/ 1/2006	5.57
Port of New York Authority	4	3/ 1/2002	5.70
Port of New York Authority	4³/₄	7/15/2003	5.76
Port of New York Authority	5	2/ 1/2003	5.76
Port of New York Authority	5³/₈	11/ 1/2006	5.92
Port of New York Authority	5¹/₂	12/ 1/2003	5.80
Port of New York Authority (W.I.)	5.80	2/ 1/2007	5.99
Port of New York Authority	6	2/ 1/2006	5.91
Port of New York Authority	6.40	11/ 1/2005	6.01
Port of New York Authority	6⁵/₈	8/ 1/2005	6.12
Yuba County, Calif., Water Agency	4	3/ 1/2016	5.69

Tax-exempts are a worthwhile investment for the person with an income tax problem. But he should bear two important factors in mind:

1. There is no point going into tax-exempts to provide for the first $2,000 to $3,500 or so of annual income, since this amount is normally exempt from income tax or subject to a very small tax for a retired couple over sixty-five.
2. Tax-exempts are practically always a form of debt. This means their yield is fixed and therefore of no value in fighting inflation. Furthermore, the price of a municipal bond is inversely tied to money rates. When money rates go up, the municipal bond tends to go down, since its fixed yield is worth less.

Thus it becomes clear that while tax-exempt municipals should be part of every large retirement portfolio, they are not the complete answer.

Their value to you varies directly as your income. They can be helpful in cutting down taxes where taxes take a considerable part of your income. But it's safe to say that in no case should municipals constitute the entire portfolio.

Blinding oneself to the possibility of inflation merely to beat the tax man might prove, in the long run, to be too much like cutting off your nose to spite your face.

SOME QUESTIONS AND ANSWERS

Q. *I am single, 36, earning $10,000 to $14,000 a year with about $7,500 in E bonds and insured savings accounts. I am interested in investing $100 a month in a growth type stock, but would like an issue which defers dividend payments, since I already have an income tax problem. Is there any such investment?*

A. There are several forms of investment suited to those with an income tax problem.

Two—E bonds (which you already own) and tax-exempt "municipal" bonds—offer tax help, but at the cost of giving up capital growth. That is a high cost for a young man and, it seems to me, therefore rules out their use except for a small portion of investable funds.

You should consider any young growth company which pays no dividends, preferring to plow back all its earnings. This may present a higher factor of speculation than you wish to assume, since there's no way of telling whether many of these young companies will live, let alone prosper. The mortality rate is high.

Finally, there are companies which regularly make all or a substantial portion of their annual distribution to shareholders in the form of additional shares of stock—the so-called "stock dividend" payers. (See list in this chapter.) Many of these are well-established corporations which, not unlike the young, struggling corporations, still prefer to plow back most of their earnings and distribute shares instead of cash dividends.

You should realize, of course, that a stock dividend means very little.

If the corporation pays a 5% stock dividend, a holder of 100 shares becomes the owner of 105 shares, but does not increase his stake in the company because his increased holdings represent exactly the same percentage of the entire pie that his 100 shares did before the stock dividend.

But you feel better with 105 shares than you did with 100. And it isn't subject to income tax.

Q. *Would it be to one's advantage to invest in tax-exempt securities if he is in the 30% tax bracket?*

A. That's just about on the borderline. If you buy a common stock yielding 5%, income taxes–in your bracket–will take 1½%, leaving you 3½%, net. If you buy a 5% tax-exempt municipal bond, you keep the entire 5%.

Your problem: Are you content to give up any chance of capital gain (in the common stock) for the sake of the additional 1½% current return? If you are, tax-exempts are for you.

18 Joint Ownership—Is It for You?

Co-ownership of property with right of survivorship is an ancient form of ownership. It has not lost its popularity with family units. Thus, it probably is usual rather than unusual for a husband to maintain at least one bank account–checking or savings–with his wife. Existence of such a bank account has practical advantages in that it enables either the husband or the wife to make withdrawals for household costs or expenses incurred for the family. However, co-ownership is not limited to bank accounts. Many family residences are held in the joint names of husband and wife. So are U.S. savings bonds, stocks and securities. Moreover, co-ownership isn't limited to a husband and wife. For instance, a joint bank account may be maintained by a parent and adult child.

Regardless of its popularity, lawyers caution against the creation of joint ownership of property until all possible advantages and disadvantages are carefully weighed. True, joint ownership with right of survivorship may have definite advantages to a particular family. However, such form of ownership also may have some serious drawbacks. While it may be easy to create co-ownership with right of survivorship, it may be difficult to dissolve such ownership at a later date–if drawbacks should exceed advantages. Before creation of joint ownership, it is essential to consider state and Federal law consequences in light of your particular family situation and only after taking into account the particular type of property which will be held jointly.

Joint ownership may or may not be right for you. While this form of ownership often is useful, it frequently can carry unrealized risks and adverse consequences. Regardless of a popular misconception, it is not a valid substitute for a will.

WHAT BENEFITS MIGHT BE GAINED FROM JOINT OWNERSHIP?

Joint ownership may have advantages without any real drawbacks in your particular situation–but check first. There are pros and cons to such form of ownership. Even where there are benefits, the benefits may be more easily secured through some other legal arrangement, e.g., family trust. Moreover, depending upon the particular type of asset or property, joint ownership may offer no advantages. It may be a cumbersome and disadvantageous form in which to hold property.

On a creation of joint ownership, what benefits might be secured? The following advantages usually are cited.

Probate costs on the death of one joint owner are avoided. On such death, the survivor becomes sole owner of the property.

There is a privacy to joint ownership. Because jointly-owned property with right of survivorship is not part of a deceased owner's probate estate, sole ownership secured by survivor is not publicized. A probate record, available to the public, does not include such jointly-held property.

There may be convenience and practical advantages to joint ownership. For instance, in the case of a bank account, funds are available to either husband or wife to pay household expenses.

Estate proceedings of probate can be avoided–and such proceedings can be lengthy. For instance, in the case of a joint bank account, the survivor may secure balance in such account immediately after presentation of certain required papers, e.g., proof of death and tax waivers.

Joint ownership promises an intangible benefit. It tends to strengthen and confirm unity in the family. Joint ownership is an expression of mutual trust.

Jointly-held property, such as a residence, may be freed from creditors' claims in some states on the death of a joint owner.

Joint ownership of income-producing property may yield tax savings. In the case of a husband and wife filing a joint return, that may not be so for purposes of Federal income tax. Each joint owner's share of income will be taxed on the couple's joint return. However, not all states with income tax laws permit a husband and wife to secure tax reduction by filing a joint state return. Division of income from jointly-held property between husband and wife thus might yield state income tax savings on separate state returns. Moreover, division of income produced by jointly-owned property may offer Federal and state tax reduction where the joint owners are other than husband and wife, e.g., parent and child.

The foregoing may appear to be an impressive list of advantages favoring joint ownership. Unfortunately, the listing shows only *possible* benefits which *might* be secured through joint ownership. There is no guaranty that a particular benefit sought will be secured.

WHAT ARE THE POSSIBLE DISADVANTAGES?

In a leaflet warning of the dangers in joint ownership, a bar association stated that it "looks simple, but it is not. It has rigid legal limitations. The effects of these limitations are important." Joint ownership can have serious drawbacks.

Putting your property in joint ownership is no substitute for a will. It is practically impossible to get everything an individual owns into joint ownership. Some property items presently owned may be overlooked; additional property items with substantial value may be acquired at a later date. Without a will, those items would be disposed on the owner's death under state law of intestacy, perhaps to unintended beneficiaries, in intestacy proceedings more costly than probate.

If both co-owners died in a common accident so that the order of deaths cannot be established, lack of wills again could mean intestacy.

Where joint ownership includes a right of survivorship, jointly-owned property always goes outright to the survivor. Obviously, in many instances, that might not be desirable. A surviving co-owner without experience in financial matters, such as a widow, might be suddenly faced with the unwanted responsibility of management and conservation of valuable property.

Joint ownership may be a cumbersome way to hold property. In fact, it may "tie up" property and prevent its disposal. For instance, there may be tax obstacles which would make it costly to terminate joint ownership after it has been created. It might be advisable to dispose of the jointly-held property at a subsequent date, but one of the co-owners might be legally incompetent at such time.

While joint ownership may save probate expenses on death of a co-owner because the property is not part of his probate estate, jointly-held property is not necessarily excluded from the deceased's owner's *taxable* estate. Joint ownership may result in estate tax problems without any estate tax savings.

Creation of joint ownership may carry an unexpected cost in the form of gift tax liability. Valuable property placed in joint ownership can result in a completed gift on which gift tax currently is payable.

Joint ownership will not always yield probate savings. State law—and the laws of different states vary—must be carefully checked. For instance, until recently, in New York, there was a *conclusive* presumption that funds in a joint bank account automatically belonged to the survivor. However, conclusiveness of that presumption was eliminated by a law change.

Property may pass to unintended beneficiaries on the death of co-owners. For instance, a childless couple holds property jointly. Brothers and sisters of the husband are close to the couple. Husband dies first. Wife dies shortly thereafter, survived by distant relatives. Jointly held property passes to the wife's distant relatives, rather than to her husband's brothers and sisters.

SHOULD YOU HOLD PROPERTY IN JOINT OWNERSHIP?

A categorical answer cannot be given. A number of different factors must be considered before property is placed in joint ownership with another—and they must be considered carefully.

Generally there are three different forms of co-ownership: (1) Joint tenancy. (2) Tenancy by the entirety. (3) Tenancy in common. The legal consequences flowing from these different forms of co-ownership vary. Moreover, state law covering these forms of ownership may differ in minor or major degree from state to state.

The type of property which may be placed in co-ownership is another important factor. A joint bank account maintained by a husband and wife might not only offer convenience, but have advantages without any drawbacks. On the other hand, the husband who decides to place all of his investments in joint ownership with his wife might be taking a step which subsequently could have serious and adverse results.

JOINT TENANCY—ONE FORM OF CO-OWNERSHIP

There is no question that many couples hold some of their properties in the form of joint tenancy. Joint tenants collectively form a fictitious entity. The outstanding characteristic of a joint tenancy is the right of survivorship. Thus, on the death of one joint owner, he leaves no property interest which his heirs can inherit. Surviving co-owner acquires outright ownership of the jointly-held property.

Under the joint tenancy form of ownership, there usually are only two co-owners. However, a joint tenancy can exist when there are three or more co-owners.

Joint tenancy, although common between husband and wife, is not limited to a husband and wife. A parent and child could own property as joint tenants. In fact, joint tenancy can exist even though the joint tenants are not related by blood.

A joint tenant has the unilateral right to transfer his interest in the property to another. In other words, a joint tenancy can be destroyed where one co-owner transfers his interest to a third party or takes legal steps to partition the property. While this unilateral right exists in theory, it is important to remember that it may be difficult for a joint tenant to transfer his interest to a third party in practice. For instance, a father and his adult son who hold property as joint tenants might join in transferring such property to a third party without a court proceeding. On the other hand, transfer of jointly-held property by a grandfather and his minor grandson might require court proceedings, approving such transfer, at least as regards the minor grandson's interest. True, even without court proceedings, the grandfather might transfer his interest in the property to a third party with such third party becoming a tenant in common with the grandson. However, in many instances, such a transfer by the grandfather alone might not be practical.

Under joint tenancy, each joint tenant has the same rights of enjoyment in the same property.

TENANCY BY THE ENTIRETY–HUSBAND AND WIFE OWNERSHIP

The tenancy by the entirety includes a survivorship right exactly like that of a joint tenancy. However, there are some major differences between the two co-ownerships.

The tenancy by the entirety can exist only between husband and wife. Thus, there are only two co-owners, who are married. Unlike the joint tenancy, the tenancy by the entirety cannot be dissolved or severed by the unilateral act of one tenant.

The tenancy by the entirety is not recognized by all states. Moreover, even where such co-ownership is recognized, the legal rules covering it may vary from state to state.

Under a joint tenancy, the tenants have equal rights of enjoyment, even where such tenants are husband and wife. Under tenancy by the entirety, the rights of the wife may be subordinate to those of the husband in some states while the husband lives.

In many states, a conveyance of property to husband and wife will create a tenancy by the entirety. Obviously, this can create problems because legal rights under entirety ownership differ from those under joint tenancy. State law therefore must be checked carefully. For instance, the parties may want to preserve unilateral right to sever co-ownership possible under joint tenancy but not under tenancy by the entirety. Also, parties may not want the rights of a co-owner wife to be subordinate to those of the husband, a condition which may exist under entirety ownership.

TENANCY IN COMMON–NO SURVIVORSHIP RIGHT

Under this form of co-ownership, the tenants hold the same property together without division into individual parts. They share in respect to title, use and enjoyment of the property. However, that does not mean that they share equally. Unlike the joint tenancy and tenancy by the entirety, tenants in common may have unequal ownership, e.g., one tenant owning a 60% interest; the other, 40%.

This form of co-ownership differs from the others in that there is no right of survivorship. During life, a tenant in common can sell or give away his holding. At time of his death, he can leave his share as he wishes by his will or allow his rights to pass to his heirs at law.

A husband and wife may own properties as tenants in common. However, unlike the tenancy by the entirety, tenants in common are not limited to husband and wife. Thus, property might be held by tenants in common who were brothers, sisters, parents and children, etc. This form of co-ownership also can include more than two co-owners.

GET LEGAL ADVICE BEFORE YOU ACT

An individual may see advantages to be gained by holding property in joint ownership with right of survivorship with another family member. For instance, a husband may wish certain property to go to his wife on his death outside of probate and probate expenses. However, co-ownership of property does not automatically carry with it right of survivorship. For instance, where property is held by tenants in common, surviving tenant doesn't secure outright ownership of the entire property on death of the other co-tenant.

Formerly, where there was a question as to whether a particular co-ownership included the right of survivorship, there was a tendency to presume that such survivorship right existed, e.g., joint tenancy or tenancy by the entirety. However, today the tenancy in common is the more favored presumption. Thus, even though the co-tenants were husband and wife, doubts as to whether their co-ownership was a joint tenancy, tenancy by the entirety, or tenancy in common now might be resolved by holding that they were tenants in common. In such case, the wife would not have survivorship rights. Where survivorship right in wife is desired, the husband's attorney will take careful steps to make certain that it is secured. On the other hand, if the husband adopts a "do-it-yourself" approach, he may create co-ownership with his wife without survivorship right.

Even where co-ownership of property by a husband and wife includes survivorship right, it is still advisable for both parties to have wills. For instance, in the event of simultaneous deaths, the survivorship right of the co-tenancy would not be operative. An amount representing each spouse's contribution toward the acquisition of the jointly-held property would pass to his or her estate. In such case, this would mean a property distribution under the laws of intestacy in the absence of wills.

JOINT BANK ACCOUNT

Opening a bank account in the names of "A and B or the survivor" usually is sufficient to show an intent to have the survivor take any funds in the account on the death of the other joint owner–but not always. For instance, until quite recently in New York, such designation would have created a *conclusive* presumption that the right of survivorship existed. Balance in the account automatically belonged to the survivor. While a presumption of survivorship right still exists, it is no longer a conclusive presumption. It can be rebutted. State courts will look to intention when the bank account was open and also control over the account exercised thereafter by both joint owners.

Where the joint bank account is in the name of husband and wife, it will be easier to prove a true joint estate with right of survivorship. However, where the relationship is more remote, right of the survivor to all the funds in the bank account may be subject to successful attack. That possibility does exist where balance remaining in the account is a sizable sum and the account might have been created in an attempt to defraud creditors or might have resulted from undue influence by the survivor over the deceased who opened the account.

Where an individual opens a bank account in joint names but retains control over the account, all interest earned on funds in the account still is taxed to him. Thus, if an individual opens a joint savings account in his name and the name of another but keeps control of the passbook, savings interest will be taxed to him. No portion of this interest will be taxed to the other joint owner.

Opening of a joint bank account will not necessarily result in a completed gift. That would be true when an individual opens a joint savings account but retains the passbook. Even though a substantial sum is deposited in the joint savings account, the individual opening the account would not have to be concerned at such time with possible gift tax liability.

The Internal Revenue Service says that if an individual creates a joint bank account for himself and another, but has such control over it that he can recover the entire fund without the consent of the other, there is no gift at the time the joint account is opened. Any gift is delayed until the other joint owner draws upon the account for his or her benefit. Value of the gift then is measured by the amount withdrawn. Where a joint bank account is opened for family convenience, the amount involved usually is relatively small. Thus, even if there should be a completed gift from one joint owner to the other (e.g., on withdrawals), the amount of such gift probably would be below that on which gift tax is levied. However, creation of substantial joint bank account over which other joint owner also has control could result in a completed gift in an amount on which gift tax would be incurred.

SAFE DEPOSIT BOX IN JOINT NAMES

A safe deposit box rented in the joint names of two family members often makes good sense, e.g., husband and wife, father and adult son, etc. Each of the joint tenants will have access rights to the box if necessary for family purposes. Moreover, each may have stocks, securities, valuable papers, etc. which easily can be stored for safekeeping in a single safe deposit box.

In a few states, rental in joint names may indicate an intent to have the box contents pass by survivorship. However, any such presumption can be rebutted by showing contrary intention. In most states, a safe deposit box leased in joint names does not confer survivorship rights to the contents of the box. Joint lease of a safe deposit box is not a valid substitute for a will.

Where a safe deposit box is leased in joint names, an ownership record covering contents should be maintained. Moreover, each item in the box should be labelled, showing property interests, etc. A leading trust institution warns that otherwise disputes over ownership can arise on death of one of the joint lessees.

A wife gave $40,000 received from her parents to her husband to invest for her. He bought bearer municipal bonds on which the owner's name does not appear and placed the bonds with his own securities in a safe deposit box which he rented in joint names. On his subsequent death, there was nothing to show that the bonds belonged to the wife. In increasing his taxable estate, tax authorities listed the bonds as property owned by the husband. The wife, as sole beneficiary of his estate, ultimately recovered ownership of her bonds but only after an estate tax was paid on them.

U.S. GOVERNMENT BONDS

Co-ownership of such bonds is covered by Federal regulations. A tenancy in common is created if the bonds are registered in the name of "A and B." Under such registration, there is no right of survivorship. On the death of a co-owner, his interest in the bonds will pass by will or by intestacy if he dies without a will.

If it is desired to create right of survivorship in a co-owner of U.S. bonds, the registration should be in the name of "A or B." On the death of one co-owner, the survivor then becomes sole owner and can have the bonds reissued in his name or surrender the bonds for redemption proceeds. Actually, while this registration creates a survivorship right similar to a joint tenancy, the co-owners, strictly speaking, are not "joint tenants." Unlike a joint tenant, either co-owner of the bond may present it for redemption at any time and secure all the proceeds. In the case of a true joint tenancy, a joint tenant could get only his equal share on severance of the joint tenancy.

Since World War II, U.S. savings bonds frequently are purchased in co-ownership with the right of survivorship. For instance, on such bond purchase, bonds might be registered in name of husband or wife, father or son, etc. Where that is done, certain gift and income-tax rules should be kept in mind.

A father purchases savings bonds registered in his name and that of his son with right of survivorship. At the time of such purchase, the father has not made a completed gift. There is no completed gift unless and until the father permits the son to redeem the bonds and retain all proceeds as the son's separate property. At such time, the father may have made a taxable gift to the son depending upon the value of the bonds at the time they are redeemed. Where savings bonds are purchased in co-ownership with right of survivorship, the purchaser should be aware that a gift tax may be due at a later date–if the other co-owner redeems the bonds.

There can be delayed income-tax consequences on such co-ownership purchase. For instance, in the foregoing example where the father's funds were used to purchase bonds in co-ownership with the son, interest that accrued but which was not taxed during the co-ownership period would be taxed to the father when the son cashed in the bonds. On substantial bond purchases, co-ownership might result in a double tax in a subsequent year. Where the co-owner (i.e., son) who didn't contribute to the purchase of the bonds, surrendered them, the other co-owner (i.e., father) would owe income tax on all income due to past accrued interest. The father also might owe a gift tax if a substantial sum was realized by the son when the latter cashed in the bonds.

JOINTLY-HELD SECURITIES

The New York Stock Exchange reports that about $50 billion in stocks are held in joint names. In the majority of cases, the joint owners are husband and wife with the husband generally purchasing the stocks with his funds in his and his wife's name. However, in some instances, the wife may be the purchaser or at least contribute to purchase cost.

In most instances, the co-owners wish to create a joint tenancy under which the survivor will become sole owner on death of the other co-owner. The modern legal trend, however, is to presume that corporate stock registered in plural names is held in a tenancy in common. Such tenancy does not give the right of survivorship. Thus, where the purchaser in co-ownership wishes to create a survivorship right, care should be taken in registering ownership. Where the securities purchased are those traded on an exchange, legal doubts over whether the purchaser intended to create co-ownership in the form of a joint tenancy or tenancy in common now may be avoided. If the right of survivorship is desired, this registration should be used–A and B as joint tenants with right of survivorship and not as tenants in common. On the other hand, if the co-owner purchasing the stock does not want to include right of survivorship, the stock should be registered under the names of A and B as tenants in common.

Where an individual purchases stocks and has them registered in his and another's name in co-ownership, he has made a completed gift. On substantial purchases which might occur where a husband buys stocks in joint tenancy with his wife, a husband may have made a taxable gift. However, in reducing or eliminating any gift tax, the gift tax law allows certain reductions, i.e., the annual exclusion, lifetime exemption, split-gift benefit and a marital deduction. The marital deduction can be secured where one spouse makes a completed gift to another, the general effect of which is to reduce the gift subject to tax by 50%. In the case of a joint tenancy in securities created by a husband with his wife, the gift-tax marital deduction will be available. In addition, the husband in reducing taxable gifts is entitled to a lifetime exemption. As a result, a husband can purchase a substantial amount of securities in joint tenancy with his wife without incurring any gift tax. For instance, such stock purchases up to $60,000 might be exempt from gift tax.

The purchase of securities in co-ownership also can yield income tax advantages. That is so even where securities are registered in names of husband and wife and they will file a joint Federal tax return. On such stock purchases, each co-owner will be taxed with his or her share of dividend income. Each could benefit from a separate dividend exclusion (up to $100 maximum each year) in exempting their dividends from income tax. Moreover, tax reduction of a joint return may not be available to a husband and wife under state income tax law. Division of income from jointly owned securities between husband and wife might permit them to save state income taxes on separate state tax returns. Even greater tax savings might be available where the co-owners are other than husband and wife. There could be both Federal and state income tax savings. Such co-owners must file separate Federal and state tax returns, reporting their separate incomes. Where income from jointly-owned securities is divided between two taxpayers on separate returns, such income might be taxed in lower tax brackets.

CO-OWNERSHIP OF REAL ESTATE

A recent survey showed that about 50% of all homes are bought in joint ownership, usually by a husband who takes title to the family residence in joint tenancy with his wife. Moreover, purchase of income-producing real estate in co-ownership form is common. In the latter case, co-tenancy is not limited to husband and wife, e.g., it may be in the names of brothers, father and son, etc. Such acquisition may be in the form of a joint tenancy, but title to productive real estate frequently is taken as tenants in common.

Where title to real estate–a residence or income-producing property–is acquired as tenants in common, these general legal rules apply: Surviving co-tenant does not acquire ownership of the entire property on death of a co-tenant. Interest of deceased will be distributed as he directs in his will or, in the absence of a will, under the laws of intestacy. Where one individual purchases real estate in his and another's name as tenants in common, the purchaser has made a completed gift of an interest in the property to the other at the time of acquisition. Since real estate purchase may involve payment of a substantial price, the purchaser may have made a taxable gift. However, any gift tax on such gift can be reduced by available gift tax exclusions, lifetime exemption, split-gift benefit, and marital deduction.

Where the tenants in common are other than husband and wife, there can be favorable, recurring income-tax benefits. Tenants in common, other than a husband and wife, will file separate income-tax returns. On his separate return, each tenant will report his share of income from productive real estate. If one co-tenant is in a low tax bracket, his share of the income will be taxed at low rate. Division of income from the property between the co-tenants—one in a high tax bracket, the other in a low bracket—thus can yield tax savings.

REAL ESTATE HELD IN JOINT TENANCY

Under a joint tenancy, there is a survivorship right. At death, a joint tenant cannot distribute his interest in real estate to others under his will. The surviving joint tenant secures ownership of the entire property. However, other legal consequences to joint tenants will vary depending upon whether the joint tenants are husband and wife.

(1) Where the joint tenants are other than husband and wife, the purchaser of the real estate will have made a gift of an interest to the other joint tenant at the time he purchases the property. Depending upon the value of that gift, gift tax may be incurred. However, any gift tax liability can be reduced by allowable reductions, e.g., exclusions, lifetime exemption, etc.

Moreover, expenses for mortgage interest, real estate taxes, etc.—on productive property or even a home—can be deducted by the joint tenant who pays them. Thus, the after-tax cost of these deductible expenses can be reduced where a joint tenant in a high tax bracket pays all of these expenses.

(2) Where the joint tenants are husband and wife, there may be no significant income-tax benefits from such ownership in many cases. Joint tenants who are husband and wife usually will file a joint Federal tax return. Thus, the income from productive property not only will be reported on a single return but deductible expenses, even though one spouse pays all of them, also will be deducted on the joint return filed by the husband and wife.

Creation of joint tenancy in real estate by one spouse with the other doesn't result in a gift at the time the property is acquired. For instance, if a husband purchases real estate in joint tenancy with his wife, there will be a completed gift to the wife only if the husband shows intention by an election on a gift tax return he files for the year in which the joint tenancy is created. If he doesn't show such election by filing a gift tax return, completed gift is delayed until termination of the joint tenancy other than termination by his death.

Assume that the husband doesn't elect to have his real estate purchase treated as a completed gift to his wife at the time he takes title in joint tenancy names. Husband buys property in joint tenancy with his wife, paying the entire $30,000 purchase price. Years later, the property is sold for $80,000 with the wife receiving $40,000 (50% of $80,000). At the time of sale, the husband is considered to have made a completed gift of $40,000 to his wife. Where the husband expects property to appreciate in value, he might elect to treat creation of joint tenancy as a completed gift to wife. In the example, amount of his gift to his wife and any gift tax due would be based on her interest in property with a lower value at time of purchase ($30,000) rather than her interest in more valuable property ($80,000) at time of sale.

DON'T FORGET ESTATE TAXES

Both the tenancy by entirety and joint tenancy include right of survivorship. When you buy property or acquire an asset in co-ownership with another *with right of survivorship,* you can remove that property or asset from your probate estate on your death. Probate expenses will be reduced. But purchase of property or acquisition of an asset in co-ownership *with right of survivorship* will not reduce Federal estate tax due on your death.

Under the Federal law, property held as joint tenants or in tenancy by entirety is included in a co-owner's taxable estate to the extent that he contributed toward such property's purchase. Moreover, in the absence of proof as to the amount contributed toward purchase of such property, the Revenue Service will include all of the property in the taxable estate of the first joint owner to die, even though he in fact contributed nothing.

An individual buys stocks and has them registered in his own and another's name as joint tenants. He predeceases his joint tenant. Even though all of the stocks then become the outright property of the survivor, such stocks will be included in the purchaser's taxable estate. If the purchaser survives his joint tenant, he still will have to prove that he contributed all of the funds toward the purchase of the stocks. In the absence of such proof, the Revenue Service will include such stocks in the taxable estate of the deceased joint owner, even though only funds of the survivor had been used to purchase the jointly-held property.

Holding property in joint tenancy does have advantages. There can be probate savings on the death of the joint owner. However, before taking any action, get legal advice. That's necessary to make certain that right of survivorship under particular form of co-ownership will be recognized under state law so as to exclude such property from your probate estate on your subsequent death. And even before co-ownership in property is created, first consider possible drawbacks and perhaps more attractive alternatives. For instance, a husband-father might consider purchase of property in the name of his wife or a child alone rather than in his own name and that of a family member as joint tenants. On an outright gift to a spouse or to a child, both probate and estate tax savings could be secured on the father's subsequent death.

19 A House Is a Home Is a Mortgage

Home ownership is without question the biggest single investment 95 per cent of us make in our lifetime. It not only involves the largest sum of money spent on any one item, but it involves us for a longer period of time than anything else we buy. That last is important.

A woman who is momentarily carried away and spends $40 for a hat instead of her usual $7.50 will merely throw her shopping budget out of whack for a few weeks. In fact, the family's pique at seeing spaghetti more often and steak not at all for a month may be lost in their admiration of how chic Mother looks. A man who falls for a $4,500 car instead of the $3,000 model his budget warrants will be pinched by the increased payments for a couple of years.

But a young family buying a $55,000 home when its budget cries aloud for a $30,000 limit may regret it for the next twenty to thirty years, or until it can't stand the struggle any more and is forced either to sell out for what it can get, or to give the house back to the bank.

Unfortunately, buying a home is so inextricably bound up with emotions that financial rules are often overlooked. And perhaps they should be bent a little. But you ought to understand them before you begin bending them—because if you bend them until they break—you're bound to get hurt.

Emotional factors often lead us into home ownership. What are they?

First and foremost, of course, is the sense of stability home ownership gives parents and, especially, children. Within the home, ownership also is expressed in countless comforts which can be built in to suit your convenience, since you are building for keeps. Outside the home, ownership provides both children and parents a chance to build lasting friendships, for identification with the community.

What are the minus factors?

Stability, of course, is desirable only to a point. The barfly who insisted that the more he drank the steadier he felt finally got so "steady" he couldn't move.

To a young man ambitious to further his career no matter where it may lead him, home ownership may be a serious deterrent. Rather than tear up roots, sell a desirable house, pack all the objects home ownership makes us heir to, he may decide to pass up another job offer because he is too comfortable where he is.

But these factors are all extremely personal in their application. They cannot be solved by slide rule or tax table. What of the dollars and cents considerations of housing? These can be solved by 2 plus 2 arithmetic. And they are important, too.

HOME OWNERSHIP VERSUS RENTING

Over an extended period in the past, it was cheaper to buy a house than to rent an equivalent house or apartment. That assumed that the buyer didn't buy in the time of high prices and was not forced by financial or employment circumstances to sell when prices were low. However, even in the event of the latter contingencies, it wasn't likely that the monthly amounts paid by the homeowner totaled more than rental of an equivalent home over the same period of time. For illustration purposes, consider this example of home purchase some years ago when prices for houses and mortgage interest rates were lower.

Mr. A with a couple of children decided to buy a $20,000 home. He paid $5,000 as a down payment and to cover settlement costs. He financed the remaining balance with a twenty-five-year 5¾% mortgage of $15,000.

His monthly cost as a homeowner ran something like this:

Loss of investment return on $5,000	$ 20
Payment on 25-year mortgage	94
Local real estate and school taxes	40
Insurance	8
Water, repairs	35
	$197

Those figures, of course, are only illustrations. Even in those days when interest rates were much lower, he might have been forced to pay more than 5¾% interest for his mortgage. If he had to pay 6% on his mortgage, his monthly amortization payment ran about $3 higher.

Moreover, real estate and school taxes, then as now, vary in different communities. In a rural community, his total tax might have been half or three-quarters of the amount listed. In a new suburban development busily erecting new schools for an expanding juvenile population, the figure might have been twice the amount shown.

Water rates also vary widely. If Mr. A had purchased his home in a town serviced by a private company, charging higher rates, his water bill would have been higher.

Even in the past when costs of home purchase were lower, only the wild optimist could have hoped to support a home in the $15,000 to the $30,000 price range for much less than an annual cost of 10% of his purchase price.

Of course, all this reckoning was *before* income taxes —an important consideration to the house owner.

In the first place, if he had retained the $5,000 invested and received $20 a month on it, we could assume that about 25 per cent of that income, or $5 went to Uncle Sam in income taxes. That's plus $5 for the homeowner over the renter.

Both the mortgage interest and the real estate and school taxes were and still are fully deductible from taxable income. The mortgage interest portion of his monthly $94 payment started at about $71 the first month and declined as the mortgage debt and interest due thereon was reduced.

Before making out his income tax return he fortified himself with a statement from the mortgagee listing exactly what part of the year's $1,128 in amortization payments represented interest and what part repayment of principal.

But in the first month—in any event—the $71 in interest and the $40 in taxes, a total of $111, were deductible from his income taxes. Still assuming the 25 per cent tax bracket, our new house owner had actual tax savings of about $28 to add to the $5 in taxes he was saving on that erstwhile $5,000 investment.

So he was a total of $33 better off in comparison with a man paying $197 rent. If we deduct that $28—which, after all, was an actual, in pocket, saving—we can figure that the homeowner was getting his quarters for $169 a month.

In addition, an increasing portion of that $94 monthly payment (in the first month it is $23—but rising slowly but steadily) was actually being used to reduce his debt, or increase his equity in the house. It was really a *form* of forced saving.

It is almost impossible to say how much of that $23 was *actual* savings. It is true that when he pays off the mortgage, the home is free and clear. But the elements of depreciation—the actual value of the house twenty or thirty years later when his mortgage is extinguished and the problem of how much his monthly maintenance will rise over the years in order to keep the house in shape—are almost impossible to put down in cold figures.

The comparable costs of a renter, Mr. B, are difficult to approximate. But it seems a fair estimate that to rent a similar house he would have paid at least $200 to $225, since the owner of such a home would have pretty much the same expenses as the man who bought the house for his own use. And those who rent out houses—unless it is a distress situation—are not likely to be altruists.

Our renter, Mr. B, did not lose the use of his $5,000 (as Mr. A did by putting it down as deposit). So he was ahead $20 or so a month. But he had to pay taxes on it. Furthermore, he got no benefit from any tax deduction for mortgage interest and real estate taxes. And, of course, no part of his monthly rental went toward acquiring an equity in the house.

That was the favorable side of home ownership. In the period starting with the late '30s home property values have not only been maintained generally throughout the nation but have been actually enhanced.

INCREASED COSTS ON HOME PURCHASE

Over an extended period of time, home ownership has meant acquisition of housing accommodations at a lower cost than that for rented quarters. While that generally had been the case, it is subject to exceptions. Even in the past, home purchase could have meant more expensive housing accommodations if you bought at an inflated price.

Construction costs have been rising steadily and that has been reflected in higher prices on home purchase. Moreover, a severe shortage of housing accommodations in some areas of the United States has been reflected in exceptional rapid price increases, particularly in the Northeastern area. Starting in 1966, prices in areas within commuting distance of New York City greatly outstripped the upward trend in other sections of the country. For instance, a house in New Canaan, Conn., on a half acre plot which cost $35,000 in 1966 carried a sales price of around $65,000 by 1969 and close to $100,000 in 1972.

Moreover, in recent years, money conditions have tightened. That has been reflected in a marked increase in interest rates. A few years ago, an individual buying a home could secure mortgage financing at an interest rate of less than 6%. However, mortgage rates thereafter climbed over 6%, then exceeded 7%, and in 1970 carried a cost as high as 8%. Also, in obtaining mortgage financing even at these higher interest rates, lenders were demanding larger down payments.

Rental costs also were increasing at the same time that home purchase costs were rising. However, increase in rents in many areas was not as rapid as the rise in home purchase costs. In those areas, at least temporarily, rental quarters carried a lower housing cost than home purchase.

That was not true in all sectors of the country. Home ownership still provided housing accommodations at a reduced cost compared to rental quarters in some areas. Those were the areas where home prices had risen but at a comparatively low rate, e.g., 5% or less. While an individual purchasing a home in such favored areas would pay higher mortgage interest of 8% or more, such increase in cost was reduced by tax deduction allowed for interest. True, this would be a continuing increase in cost, even after taxes, if prevailing interest rates subsequently should drop. However, the home buyer might seek to protect himself against higher interest costs over an extended period by seeking a refinance-and-pay-off clause in his mortgage. Such clause would let him refinance his mortgage without new closing costs or penalties if the interest rate did drop. Thus, continued payment of higher than prevailing rates on long-term mortgage could be avoided if credit conditions eased in the future.

To summarize: in 1971, home purchase could be an expensive proposition if the buyer bought in a high-cost area, particularly if he paid for a favored neighborhood, i.e., a suburban neighborhood carrying a "status symbol." On the other hand, in many areas within the United States, home ownership still meant savings over rented quarters, provided the purchaser shopped for value and got protective features in his mortgage.

This is a comforting thought–and no more. It should *not* be stretched into an argument favoring purchase of a single home merely as a means of making a profitable investment.

All these comments, of course, are directed at ownership of a house intended as a home for one's own use. To buy a one-family house with the idea of renting it out for profit generally means you are courting financial loss plus a management headache.

In the first place, ownership of a single family house–as your home or for renting–does not possess the flexibility required of a high-grade investment.

Unlike a listed bond or common stock, it cannot be sold on a moment's notice. Your house is a particular piece of property and you have to find a buyer who likes it as much as you did. Secondly, there is the fact you cannot profit by timing. Even if you were willing to sacrifice your home in a time of high prices, you might make a profit, but you would either have to pay a comparably high price for another house or for rented quarters.

Let's leave it that for most of us a home can be a comfortable possession–if it is properly bought.

Generalizing, home ownership offers these advantages:

1. There will be a saving over cost of renting equivalent living quarters. The amount will vary, but it will almost always exist. This saving can be put into other investments to give benefit at time of retirement.
2. Home ownership involves a form of forced savings. The homeowner is required to meet principal payments on his mortgage if he wants to retain possession of his home. These are regular payments. And basic to any soundly planned retirement program is the need to set aside funds with some degree of regularity.
3. There are real investment values in home ownership. As a homeowner pays off his mortgage, he builds up equity in his home. In recent years, comparatively few individuals have suffered capital loss when they sold their homes–most individuals were able to realize full equity value–and a rather substantial number of homeowners were actually able to profit from their home ownership when they ultimately sold their homes.

KEEP RECORDS OF HOME OWNERSHIP

You've lived in your home for a number of years. Now you're going to sell it. The first thing the potential buyer is going to check is your ownership in that home. When he buys from you, he wants to know that he will be able to take clear title. Usually, when you purchase your home, transfer of title to you is recorded at time of closing in the appropriate county clerk's office. But you've been paying on your mortgage. Suppose you have paid off the mortgage in full. Do you have a satisfaction of the mortgage and has it been recorded? If it hasn't, the record will show an outstanding lien against your property.

And your home is a tax item. If you sell for an amount in excess of cost to you plus any capital expenditures made to the home, you have a taxable capital gain unless proceeds are reinvested in another home within a comparatively short time. If you sell at a loss, you are not allowed to take tax deduction for such loss. And those tax rules come back to plague you if you have been careless in keeping records of your costs.

Say that your home cost you $20,000 (that's the down payment you made on purchase plus principal payments over the years on your mortgage). During the time you also made additions to your home at a cost of $2,000. You have no available records or receipts for these additions or basic improvements. You sell your home for $21,000. For tax purposes, you know that you have had a $1,000 loss which is nondeductible. But the tax collector might say that since you have records covering a tax cost of only $20,000, that is your tax cost–and you have to pay a tax on profit of $1,000 even though you've lost on the sale of your home.

That's one way that you can be hit by failure to keep records. Now take the situation which has been more common in recent years. You sell your home for $25,000. For tax purposes you have a $3,000 profit which is subject to tax ($25,000 sales proceeds less $20,000 cost and $2,000 improvements). But you can produce records showing only the cost of $20,000. So the tax collector says that you have a $5,000 profit. You are forced to pay a tax on a $2,000 greater profit than you actually realized.

HOW DOES HOME OWNERSHIP FIT INTO PLANNING FOR RETIREMENT?

Age changes our attitude toward many things. The elderly gent whose afternoon nap was disturbed by the celebration next door finally asked his daughter why he couldn't have any peace and quiet. She said: "Why, Dad, didn't you know, our neighbor's daughter is being married?"

"Of all the damn fool notions," growled the old man as he pulled the coverlet over his ears.

A 4-bedroom 2½-bath house may be a wonderful idea and worth every penny it costs when a young family is growing up and every nook and cranny is piled high with toys, schoolbooks and playpens in various states of disrepair.

But in retirement it becomes something else again.

Retirement is a time of readjustment to new habits,

new duties and new finances. For those fortunate enough to have amassed a stake large enough to maintain income at nearly the same level as that enjoyed during the working years, there is, of course, no financial change. But this is the exception. Most retired couples must conform to a smaller budget.

The question of home ownership for the couple preparing for, or going into retirement is entirely different from that faced by a young couple just starting out. Here is an example:

The older Quinns bought a home cheaply late in the 1930s at a bargain price—$8,500. Today that house, owned free and clear, would bring $35,000 easily. The Quinns want the house as a gathering place on Thanksgiving, Christmas, birthdays. A beautiful sentiment, but a costly one. For consider the Quinns' expenses in keeping the home:

> $35,000 at 7½ per cent (if the money were invested in conservative utility bonds) would bring $2,625 a year; heat, repairs, real estate and school taxes (net after income tax credits) come to $1,500.

Thus, it will cost the retired Quinns at least $4,125 rental for a home which is steadily depreciating, or more than $325 a month. Of course, if they were to rent such a place, they would easily have to pay $300 or $400, if not more. But the point is they no longer have to. Even in today's high rental market, they might get a cozy 2-room modern apartment for $175, and save $150 a month.

And that doesn't take into consideration the fact that home ownership imposes burdens which an elderly man or woman should not undertake and ties them to a city or climate which they might otherwise forsake in favor of more congenial regions.

Of course, here again, the emotional attributes of home ownership may outweigh the financial. But retirement is often a time of counting pennies and the simple arithmetic of what home ownership means should be set forth in black and white before retirement planners decide to keep a large house, or even, in some instances, decide to buy one.

PLANNING RETIREMENT HOUSING

It has become popular in this country in recent years to begin planning for retirement housing years before retirement occurs. This has been helped along to a great extent by the aggressive selling practices of companies developing retirement home communities in southern sections of the country. Some of these practices have come under sharp governmental criticism.

Obviously, anyone buying a retirement home either 10 years or 10 days before he retires should use the same common sense expected of anyone who is parting with his money for any commodity.

But since the commodity in question is something which may not be needed for years, there are additional financial questions which arise.

It sounds all very simple to put down a deposit of $100, or $500 or $1,000 and then make "easy" payments of $10 a month for the next 10 or 20 years in the hopes of winding up with a rose-covered retirement cottage. But the fact remains that for the next 10 or 20 years you will be putting down dollars, in effect accumulating dollars by reducing a mortgage.

Of course, if the value of the property should double, there would be your capital gain. But mitigating against this is the fact that the development company will be continuing to sell additional property all during the years—so it is not too likely that any scarcity value will attach to your parcel.

While it is logical to assume that housing costs will rise over the years, it is just as logical to assume that money put into good stocks will also rise in market value. And there can be no question that the securities will be far more liquid than a 50 X 100 lot in Section A, Subdivision 24 of a development which may not come to fruition for 10 more years.

There is no denying the comforting thought that beginning with the day you sign you can be assured a retirement home in some sunny climate 10 years hence. But it seems only fair to ask: What about the investment opportunities you are missing in the meantime? What about the changes in your own personal needs over the next ten years? What about changes in the character of the development area itself?

Before you go into such a deal, you must convince yourself that the money you are committing today, plus the money you will be putting into the property over the years to retirement will do more for you in that particular retirement home than it would in building an investment portfolio over the years.

To sum up:

1. Home ownership is not cheap.
2. It is not a way to invest your money for profit.
3. It is not flexible.

But it can give you a wonderful feeling, provided you buy carefully enough so that you can enjoy it.

TAX ON PROFITABLE HOME SALES CAN BE AVOIDED

If you sell your home at a gain, that gain normally is subject to current capital gain tax. You can avoid current tax, though, by reinvesting sales proceeds in another home. However, an older homeowner who is retiring and moving into an apartment will not be reinvesting sales proceeds in a new home.

Until recently, such homeowner therefore was penalized on profitable sale of his home. Now, under a special tax rule an individual sixty-five years or older selling his home may avoid tax on profit even though sales proceeds are not reinvested in a new home.

Under this new tax provision, such individual may avoid tax on any gain attributable to the first $20,000 of price received on sale of his home. If he sells his home for more than $20,000, he still may exclude part of his gain from taxable income. That portion of the gain which bears the same ratio to the total gain as his home's tax cost bears to sales price is excluded from income. In the past, current tax which would be due on profitable sale of home sometimes served as a deterrent to sale. That tax deterrent now has been removed.

SOME QUESTIONS AND ANSWERS

Q. *In a recent article you discussed a couple who owed a large balance on their home but had enough cash to pay it up. If a couple at retirement age had their home fully paid for but had no cash and needed additional income, would you suggest they finance their home and use the borrowed capital to buy income investments? It would seem that this would necessarily follow.*

A. Not to me, it doesn't. I have often remarked that a *retired* couple owing money on their home might as well pay off that mortgage (assuming it doesn't take their last dollar of emergency funds and assuming they plan to continue living there) since it is not likely that their money in other investments can provide as much income and safety as the same money invested in their own home.

It seems to me, then, that it follows naturally that if a retired couple own their home "down to the ground," there would be no point to creating a mortgage to borrow money with which to invest, since it is likely they will be paying more for the mortgage loan than they can get from the money invested in other securities.

If you are talking of a *young* couple, still in the capital-building years, then the question of mortgage *vs.* investments is entirely different, since earning power, hope for capital gain, inflation, taxes, etc., all enter into the picture.

Q. *We now have $1,000 in savings and are planning to buy a home in about 5 years. What would be the best place to invest this money and future savings?*

A. You give no data on your earnings or responsibilities. Even so, I'd say the best place for this $1,000 and a couple more thousand to come would be in insured savings accounts.

When you reach a sum which totals a quarter to a half year's salary, plus some money for a down payment, you might then consider investment in stock.

Q. *I borrowed $21,000 at 7 per cent to buy a home. I put up as collateral some American Standard, A.T.&T., Burlington Northern Ry., Gulf, Mobile & Ohio, High Voltage . . . Eastman Kodak. Should I sell enough to pay off the loan? I am retired and will soon receive a pension.*

A. This is a decision you'll have to make for yourself. But I can help you with the arithmetic.

You are paying 7 per cent for your mortgage money. Your stocks pay you far less.

A retired person "living close to the vest" on income from his capital can't afford to hold securities yielding 0 to 5 per cent while he is paying 7 per cent for his mortgage money.

However, if you *can* afford to pay out a few per cent more than you receive on this $21,000 in return for the advantage of holding a growth stock such as Kodak, for example, then you were right in borrowing the money and continuing to hold the securities.

Only you can decide how much current income you want to give up in hope of future capital gain.

Q. *I always made good money, but made mistakes, too. Now I have retired and must get by on my social security. It isn't easy. I own my home, worth about $22,000, and have $2,700 in the bank. There is no mortgage on the house, but you can't eat it and it won't do to borrow any money on it because I couldn't get enough income to repay the loan. Do I sit tight and just try to make a go of it, or should I try something?*

A. Rich or poor, it's nice to have a lot of money. If you haven't, you must make do with what you have: Social Security, the $22,000 invested in your home, and the $2,700 in the bank.

The Social Security you can't do anything about. The $2,700 in savings–assuming it is insured by a federal agency and earning somewhere around the 5 per cent rate now being paid for savings–is also doing just about all it can for you, considering that you should keep some liquid savings. That leaves the $22,000 invested in the house.

In today's money market, that much invested in Treasury bonds would bring you $100 a month in spendable income.

To allow the $22,000 to remain invested in the house means your "rent" presently costs you that $100, plus whatever you spend for real-estate taxes, heat, water, insurance and repairs. These could easily come to another $100 a month. So–if you could rent comfortable quarters for yourself for less than $200 a month, you would do better by selling out.

That's about the only area I see in which you can maneuver.

Q. *Do you think it wise to invest in real estate on the U.S.–Canadian border as advertised in various publications? Do you have any information on it?*

A. I don't have any information on it, and, without intending any sarcasm, would paraphrase the Morgan advice about yachts: "If you have to ask about it, you can't afford to buy it."

Real estate, I admit, is the basis for more fortunes in this world than any other investment medium. But, it is also true, every piece of real estate is a different investment and must be judged on its own merits–by an expert in the particular field involved–as an apartment house, farm, suburban property. And, what is more, managed by an expert.

To live in a southern state, as you do, and to buy some unknown acreage, 1,500 miles away is, it seems to me, as foolhardy as buying a pig in a poke. The seller knows exactly what he's doing. You haven't the slightest idea of what you're getting.

Q. *We are thinking of selling our home for $16,000.*

Should we ask for a down payment of only $2,000 or $3,000 and take a 7 per cent mortgage for the balance? Would this be too risky?

A. There's no way to evaluate the credit rating of a buyer yet unknown. A 20 per cent down payment (in this case, $3,200) would be fair, though a bit on the low side.

What you must try to evaluate is the dependability of the buyer (can he afford the house, is he a stable character, or is he likely to live there a year or two, allow everything to run down and then walk out?). You must also try to estimate your chances of reselling the house in case you have to take it back.

I don't understand your desire to limit the amount of the down payment. A 7 per cent mortgage today would be no great bargain to you, the lender, when blue-chip corporations pay more than that on current borrowings.

Q. *I earn $9,000 a year at an electronics company. We live in a furnished apartment. A home does not seem desirable at this point because I will be going back to school next year. I am buying stock under the IBM purchase plan. I've been approached to buy a lot in Florida as an investment. Would this be a good investment for eventual retirement purposes?*

A. Here you are, shying away from home ownership (and with good reason) but considering retirement property which you probably won't use for another 35 years.

I realize that many people like to schedule their lives down to the last detail. I have no quarrel with detailed planning, but letters to this column do disclose that readers have bought retirement homes or lots years before they intended to use them, only to find, now that they are nearing retirement, that family and health conditions have changed so much that they can't use them.

Of course, if you bought the right house or acreage you could easily sell it, and even make a profit on it. But if you didn't—and this is often true in long-distance deals—you might have a headache.

I don't consider a single retirement lot as an ideal investment. Too many expenses can pile up over the long years to retirement; too many conditions can change.

If you want to go into the business of retirement real estate, that's something entirely different. But that should be a full-time pursuit.

Q. *Due to ill health, we are forced to sell our house and move into an apartment. I feel we are throwing $150 a month rent down the drain. Furthermore, we get no tax credit on mortgage interest and real-estate taxes, while the proceeds of the sale, in the bank, are drawing taxable interest. We fear the stock market. So our only thought is to place the cash in E bonds and leave it there for 20 years until retirement, and then cash the bonds as needed.*

A. You're right, of course, about the loss of tax credits when you give up home ownership. However, if you had no choice, there's no sense crying over spilt milk.

If you are 20 years from retirement, you should consider doing something more aggressive with your funds than merely hiding them from the tax collector. E bonds rate as a sensible medium for some of your funds. Some money should be invested in common stocks so as to keep you abreast of inflation over the next 20 years.

You fear the stock market. So do I. But I also fear what has been happening to the purchasing power of the dollar over the years. And so should you. There's no hiding place.

Q. *We are 25, have $6,000 in savings, own some chemical shares. Our combined income is $11,000—and we can save $6,000 a year, since our rent and utilities come to only $75 a month. Would it be wise to save for 3 years, pay cash for a $20,000 home and then resume securities investing? Or should we invest in shares or a mutual fund and buy a home with a minimum down payment?*

A. Any young couple who can save $6,000 out of $11,000 annual income can do pretty much as it pleases.

Generally, I feel that the less mortgage the better—and no mortgage is better than any at all.

But at 25, with years of earning—and inflation—ahead of you, I can't make too strong a case against piling up only dollars just to pay 100 per cent cash for a house, especially since you are aiming at a very modest house.

There's no law against continuing to build up your house-shopping fund. Sometimes more cash helps make a better deal. But I'd vote to continue your securities investing, too.

Q. *We have 2 boys, 13 and 11. My husband is 40, earns $20,000 a year. We are buying a $50,000 home, which will require a down payment of $10,000. Our savings account is $5,500. We also hold 11 IBM, 34 General Electric and $1,000 in savings bonds. How can we raise the remainder of the down payment: cash in stock, borrow on insurance, second mortgage?*

A. First-mortgage money is going to be high enough, these days; second-mortgage loans could be prohibitive. I'd rule that out.

I'd say it's a toss-up between borrowing on the insurance or selling the stock. I don't like to borrow against insurance, but a young man should have growth equities and the quality of your shares is high.

I don't want to be a spoilsport (and nobody's asking me, anyway), but I'd suggest you start learning some economy menus. A $50,000 house on a $20,000 income with 2 youngsters to raise and educate looks like a pretty tight squeeze to me.

Q. *We are looking ahead to retirement in 5 years. How can we best manage our income over the next 5 years to provide for our retirement? We have no children and therefore do not have to leave an estate. We have $30,000 in savings and odd lots of Standard Oil of N.J. and Royal Crown Cola; owe $72,000 balance on an apartment building. Income from the building does not quite cover all expenses. Would it be best to pay the mortgage down to $50,000, so as to cut monthly charges?*

A. I'm a firm believer in the policy that property held for income should pay its own way. I can't see sinking $22,000 more of your cash assets into the building if it doesn't pay its way now—at a time of high real-estate rentals. After all, your $22,000 is worth as much to you as it is to the mortgage holder.

If you figure the income this $22,000 brings in now, how can you make any progress giving up that income in return for smaller mortgage payments? Any difference of a percentage point or less between what the money earns now and what the mortgage costs certainly is not significant enough to make that apartment building worthwhile. It seems to me you ought to go over those real-estate figures again and see whether this building is a boon or a bust.

The stocks you hold are O.K.

Q. *Recently you told a young couple with joint income of $18,000 that they could buy a $40,000-$45,000 home. I'm appalled at your advice. That formula which says one can own a home worth 2½ times annual income is an old clinker of pre-high-income-tax days and should be revised. I earn $1,550 a month and we live in a modest $22,000 house. I think your young couple would find themselves paying out about 42 per cent of disposable income for housing.*

A. I don't doubt that many young people are paying up to 40 per cent of their income for housing. I think it's too much. It would be much, much better if that figure were only 25 per cent. But in many areas, young readers tell me, they can't buy for less—unless they go out into suburbia or even exurbia where the savings in purchase price and mortgage costs are often swallowed up by the expense of commuting and the cost of building new schools and other facilities.

I don't have any answers. (Why don't you go after the home builders and ask them for the answer to: "Are people supposed to live in their own homes"?)

All I can say is that if young people want a home enough to lay out nearly 40 per cent of their income to enjoy it (giving up other luxuries for the sake of home ownership) this may be their only course.

Home ownership for young couples in many areas is similar to the story of the bee: It isn't supposed to be able to fly, but no one told it that it couldn't.

It seems American industry can put some sort of car in practically every garage, but can't give everyone his own garage.

Q. *You recently noted that people living in a mortgage-free home often neglect to figure their rental costs correctly. How do you figure it? Our home is in the $20,000 class—mortgage free. Our total retirement income, including social security, is $280 a month. Would we be better off renting?*

A. I find that too often persons living on a limited budget forget to figure in the value of the money they have invested in their home. This is understandable. A home is a personal matter and many people are reluctant to put a dollars-and-cents evaluation on it. Nor do I insist on it.

If a couple prefers to spend more on their living quarters and less, say, on travel or entertainment no one is justified in making an issue of it.

But that does mean that anyone wanting to make such a choice should at least know the arithmetic involved in making it.

In your case—assuming you could sell your home for $20,000—you must reckon that ownership of the house is costing you $1,400 or more a year in lost income from this amount of money. One can buy good grade bonds today yielding over 7%.

If you add that $1,400 to your expenditures for taxes, heat, repairs, water, insurance (which you would not have to make in rented quarters) you get the total cost of maintaining your home. Let's say it comes to $2,200—which is on the low side. Your rent, then comes to $183 a month. It's up to you now to decide whether, if you sold your home, you could live as comfortably and more cheaply in rented quarters.

(I've omitted in this discussion the income taxes one would pay on income from this $20,000, if invested. In your case, it would not be a factor. Those who are in, say, a 25% tax bracket would realistically have to reduce such investment income by the amount of taxes due.)

Q. *As a realtor, I think you are unfair in warning people against real estate investments unless they are experts. You can invest successfully in real estate just as you can in stock.*

A. I have no quarrel with real estate investments. Fortunes have been made in it. But I'm at a loss to discuss a $5,000 investment in a two-family house 3,000 miles from here when I have no knowledge of the specific property or of the investor's ability to judge the property.

If a person buys $5,000 worth of XYZ Corp. stock he gets the management with the equity and, what's more, he gets exactly the same share of stock that is held by investors in New York, Chicago and Los Angeles and is judged by exactly the same set of statistics.

If he buys $5,000 worth of real estate he, most likely, must do the managing of a unique property himself.

Since you are a realtor, I'm sure you'll agree real estate analysis and property management is just as sophisticated a business as any other, and more sophisticated than most.

The fact we all live in houses doesn't make us real estate experts any more than the fact many of us drive cars makes us experts on ignition systems.

Q. *My grandfather owes $10,000 on his home, valued at over $50,000. The house needs repairs, but he is afraid of additional debt. I would like to put a new mortgage on the house for about $40,000 using $5,000 for repairs, putting $10,000 into the bank for his immediate needs and investing $25,000 for income to meet the new expenses. Is there some investment I could make with the $25,000 which would meet the obligations on the $40,000 mortgage?*

A. You're heading for trouble, sure as shootin'.

(Not that I think you'll get there. You're not going to find many banks willing to lend 80% on an old house, in need of repairs, owned by an elderly man—who is presumably without sufficient income to maintain it.)

In the first place, if he fears additional debt, just what do you think you're doing to him by increasing the mortgage from $10,000 to $40,000?

Second: Even if you were able to raise $40,000 on a mortgage, how can you figure on having $40,000 to divide among your various schemes. Right off the bat, $10,000 of that would have to go to wipe out the $10,000 mortgage already on the house. You don't think for one moment that anyone is going to lend you $40,000 on a $50,000 home which already has $10,000 outstanding against it?

Third: If he can't keep the place in repair now after making payments on a $10,000 mortgage, how will he fare after he has to pay interest and amortization on a mortgage 4 times larger—and at prevailing interest rate much higher than he is paying now.

And there's no way you can safely invest whatever is left on that new mortgage money and earn enough to cover the increased interest and amortization.

This hope of making a profit on borrowed money springs eternal. But I assure you it is an illusion except in the rare case where some lucky gambler makes a killing out of all proportion to the cost of the loan.

While I have no basis for judging how your grandfather should live, the obvious thought comes to mind that perhaps an elderly gentleman, alone, with insufficient funds, should not be occupying $50,000 worth of real estate for his sole use. If you are concerned about him, you should give some thought to reducing his real estate load, getting some value for him out of this large equity, instead of loading on additional debt.

Q. *Recently, in discussing the mortgage on a $40,000 house, you said the monthly payment of around $150 "might be one-half your weekly salary." Are all your readers earning $300 a week?*

A. Not by a long sight. But that young man planning to raise a family in a $40,000 house had better be.

Q. *I live alone, paying $90 for my apartment. I've been considering an $18,000 home. Would I be better off owning?*

A. Home ownership might offer many satisfactions you don't enjoy now. But financially, I can't see it.

An $18,000 home—even if paid for 100% with your own funds—will cost more than $90 a month to support. The $18,000 alone, invested in good quality utility bonds, is worth more than $100 a month income. Then you would have to add realty taxes, insurance, water, repairs, heat.

20 Insurance and Annuities in Your Future Planning

For the person looking ahead life insurance and annuities are unique.

They represent the only devices by which you can create an estate for your family or a lifetime income for yourself with a single payment.

Nothing else you can buy, or invest in, can promise you that with the payment of the first premium running to, say, a hundred dollars or so, your family is immediately assured protection of $5,000 or $10,000 upon your death.

Nothing but an annuity can assure you that with the payment of X thousand dollars you and your wife are assured a monthly check of, say, $100, no matter how long either of you might live.

If you were born heir to a fortune, such contracts wouldn't mean much.

But for most of us "another day, another dollar" folk, they represent all the difference between worry and peace of mind. And avoiding worry, securing peace of mind is what this book is all about.

Life insurance is, of course, the most direct of these policies. Your payment of X dollars a year is lumped with the payments of millions of others, thus spreading the financial risk of death. In its simplest form, life insurance isn't much different from fire insurance on your home. Everyone in the community puts a little into the pot so that no one will be too badly hurt in case of fire.

It is obvious, therefore, that life insurance coverage should be a part of every person's financial planning, and his retirement planning as well. For what many individuals fail to realize is that insurance offers investment values toward retirement even when the insured lives out his normal life expectancy or beyond. There is a saving aspect—an investment aspect—involved in insurance which goes beyond the insurance feature.

When an individual takes out insurance, he is not only making certain that his family will receive a capital amount for their continuing living needs if he should die prematurely, but as he continues to pay premiums he is building capital values for himself which are a valuable adjunct to other investments he is making towards his retirement.

WHAT KIND OF INSURANCE?

Insurance needs vary according to your age, family situation and capital.

The young man with small children needs protection first and foremost. And because he probably is earning less than an older person, and because—with a growing family—a large percentage of that income must be applied to current living costs, he must try for maximum coverage at minimum cost.

An older man who has higher income and grown children may give more emphasis to the investment feature in insurance—to how it can implement other savings in providing retirement income for his wife and himself.

The insurance which is right for the younger man may be wrong for the older man—or vice versa. At any one period in your lifetime there may be a right and a wrong way to buy insurance. So it is necessary to consider what types of insurance policies are available.

In general, there are three types, but with numerous variations:

1. Term insurance is the cheapest insurance. It provides the largest amount of insurance for a given premium. But it pays off to the insured's beneficiaries only if he dies during the period of the contract, which may run only five years, and then must be renewed. And after age 65, most companies won't sell it to you. Bluntly put, the insured must die to win. If he outlives the policy, even by an hour, his beneficiaries collect nothing. If he outlives the policy and wants to continue this protection, he must sign up again at a higher rate. Unlike other types of policies, it has no investment feature.
2. Ordinary life insurance includes both insurance coverage and investment features. Under this type of insurance, premium payments remain constant, cost does not increase as you get older. Also, cash values are built up within the policy against which you can borrow in times of emergency. These values also provide a cushion to safeguard against lapse of insurance if you fail to pay premiums for a

time. And if you discontinue the insurance, you can recover part of the premiums that you've paid in, depending upon how long the policy has been in effect. Unlike term which gives insurance coverage only for a stated period–five, or ten, or twenty years–ordinary life pays your beneficiary regardless of when you die. Because of this and the investment feature in continuing insurance coverage, premiums are higher than on term insurance.

3. Limited payment life is the most expensive of the three general types of insurance because of its premium arrangement. A fixed, unchanging premium is paid, but only for a set number of years. Thus, an individual purchasing ten-payment life would fully pay up on his insurance policy after ten years. It has the greatest investment feature with cash values building up rapidly.

The insurance buyer should review the "whole picture" before making a decision. If he needs maximum coverage for a young and growing family NOW for a minimum outlay, his choice should be term insurance–at least for the number of years his children will be minors.

If he can handle a more expensive lifetime program, he should do some arithmetic first and see whether the added expense now will not work out to a plus later on. Term insurance, as noted above, builds no cash values. Other forms–such as straight life–do.

Here is a table showing how–if a young man can manage it–a straight life policy might prove less expensive than term insurance. Compared are typical premium costs for three $10,000 non-participating (no dividends payable) policies issued at age 30 and kept in force through age 65–including a level term policy to age 65, a five-year renewable and convertible term policy and a straight life policy:

	Term to 65	*5-Year Term*	*Straight Life*
Yearly Premiums:			
First 5 years	$ 100	$ 54	$ 160
Next 5 years	100	60	160
Next 5 years	100	76	160
Next 5 years	100	100	160
Next 5 years	100	144	160
Next 5 years	100	210	160
Next 5 years	100	330	160
Total Premiums to Age 65	$3,500	$4,880	$5,600
Cash Value at Age 65	NONE	NONE	$5,510

USING LIFE INSURANCE WHILE PLANNING RETIREMENT

Except for term insurance, all life insurance involves savings–compulsory savings. In other financial plans, you can say you'll start when you can, or when it's necessary. But in life insurance, you can't safely make that statement. If you wait too long, your physical condition may so change that you may fall below standards for acceptance. Delay in such case means that you may not be able to get insurance coverage without the payment of an extra premium, and perhaps be unable to secure coverage in any case.

And even with continued good health, rates climb sharply with the years.

So unless you're willing to gamble on your insurance coverage, you may want to buy insurance before you think you actually need it. And that's all to the good, for the earlier insurance is purchased, the lower is the annual premium cost. And you will always find that something can be worked out.

Let's take a father, with a $10,000 insurance policy, a family and a home to support on a medium salary. He needs additional protection, for, in addition to his wife and children, there is that ever-present mortgage.

Money is tight, but insurance is so adaptable he can always manage.

In the first place, he might cover his mortgage with life insurance offered through the bank. That is by far the cheapest method, since the savings in putting both contracts into one are passed on to him. Thus, if he should die, the mortgage would be paid off and all the payments he made on it returned to his widow.

Or he could buy separate declining-balance term insurance, which goes down in coverage as his mortgage is paid off.

Or he might take out straight term insurance not related to the mortgage, but with an option which allows him to convert it to ordinary life within a certain period, even if his health changes. Additional cost of such an option is moderate. He thus secures additional life insurance coverage while his income is lower. Later, when his income increases, he can convert to an ordinary life policy. He still continues full insurance coverage for his family after conversion, but now he is building permanent values for himself as well.

Or go to the other extreme. Consider the individual who has high income now, who can well afford to take out the most expensive type insurance policy, but whose income will drop from a peak to a rather modest amount sometime in the future. He might be a professional athlete, a theatrical performer, anyone in a field where maximum earning period is compressed into a comparatively short time.

Such an individual might take out a ten-payment life. If he dies shortly after taking out the policy, his beneficiary would receive the full amount of the policy. And if he lived for the full ten years, he would have paid-up insurance for life, plus a growing investment. His insurance program would be a form of forced savings. Thereafter, values would continue to increase. Ultimately he could cash in the policy for an amount in excess of what he had paid in premiums.

When you purchase insurance which builds permanent values, you are getting insurance protection and savings at the same time. If you die prematurely, your family is protected. If you live to reach retirement, the savings factor becomes important. You could then surrender your policy for its cash value, which might approach or even exceed your premium payments. This cash then could be put into other investments to produce retirement return. Or you could convert to an annuity that would pay you and your wife an income for a period of years or for life.

ENDOWMENTS OR ANNUITIES

In any form, the primary aim of life insurance is protection. But when you invest in an endowment or an annuity, you begin saving for retirement from the moment you pay your first premium.

What is an endowment policy? It is a policy primarily aimed at saving money. But it also includes a guarantee that if you do not live long enough to complete your savings plan, the insurer will complete it for you. It will pay face amount of the policy (the total amount you intended to save) to your beneficiary. Thus, it includes a life insurance feature under a savings plan directed at retirement.

On the other hand, an annuity is fundamentally a savings program. You buy a contract by paying premiums (either over a period of years or in a single payment) which provides that when you reach a certain age, installment payments will be made to you. In the usual situation, the annuity payments will continue for your life regardless of how long you live, but you could contract to have payments made for a fixed number of years, even beyond your lifetime.

You purchase an annuity which provides that payments will start when you reach age sixty-five. You might contract to have payments made to you for five years after sixty-five–or until you are seventy. Or the contract might provide that you are to receive smaller installment payments but such installment payments are to continue for as long as you live. And you might even contract under a joint and survivorship annuity to provide that payments are to continue to you for life and thereafter to your widow for her lifetime.

An endowment might be converted to an annuity at time of maturity of the policy. In fact, it frequently is. You complete the savings program under the endowment at age sixty-five. Instead of taking a lump-sum payment, you elect to take payments in installments in the form of an annuity. The same may be done with any insurance plan which builds up a cash value.

USING THE ANNUITY IN YOUR RETIREMENT

Unlike any other form of savings, there is a guarantee behind annuity return backed by the resources of the insurance company which issues the policy. It has certainty. And because of the variety of annuity policies available, it permits considerable flexibility in planning your retirement.

The annuity, of course, has a drawback. The guaranteed return is payable in fixed dollars–and the dollar may buy less in the future due to continued inflation. Even so, investment in an annuity can be an integral part of one's retirement planning. In 1965, a record total of 548 million dollars was invested in retirement annuities. This was an increase of more than 100 million dollars over similar investments in 1964. To a large degree, this reflected investment by older persons who sought the peace of mind provided by a guaranteed return for life. No matter how long an annuitant lives, he has a contract calling for continued payments.

NEW ANNUITIES BECOME AVAILABLE

Although the usual annuity offers certainty, it has the drawback that the guaranteed return is payable in fixed dollars. With continued inflation, a fixed-dollar return will lose purchasing power over a period of years. To eliminate the inflation drawback of the usual annuity, insurance companies now are starting to offer annuity contracts which provide a varying return.

A cost-of-living annuity is now available in the U.S. and Canada. At an extra premium cost, this annuity provides a return which will rise with the cost-of-living index. If the cost of living goes up, the return under this annuity also increases; a higher return offsets the loss in purchasing power of the dollar.

Insurance companies have also developed the variable annuity. Without considering the details of financial and funding aspects of this new type of annuity, it offers a return backed by investment values–property such as stocks which fluctuate. The annuitant is not promised a fixed and unvarying return in a designated number of dollars. Over an extended period, studies have revealed that property values such as stocks do tend to increase with the loss of purchasing power in the dollar. If past history is repeated, the variable annuity promises an increased return to the annuitant if the cost of living continues to increase and the dollar continues to lose purchasing power.

The cost-of-living annuity and the variable annuity are directed at elimination of the economic drawback of the usual annuity, giving a return in fixed dollars which, up until recently, has been the only one available from insurance companies. More insurance companies are offering these forms of annuity contracts to the individual who wants some retirement income to include the safe return promised by insurance company payment but which also is protected against inflation.

CONSIDER THESE USES WITH SOCIAL SECURITY

You have reached sixty-five, the age at which you intended to retire. (Or you could have retired at sixty-two with reduced benefits.) You are now drawing Social Security benefits. You are also drawing pension benefits from your prior employment. The latter, like Social Security, will continue for your lifetime. However, these combined payments are not sufficient to maintain you in the standard of living to which you are accustomed. The savings that you have accumulated for retirement also yield income but still not in amount sufficient to maintain your living standard. So from time to time it will be necessary for you to invade your savings capital for living needs.

If you live out your normal life expectancy, your savings capital will be sufficient to guarantee comfortable retirement. But there is one drawback about that guarantee. You have no way of knowing how long you will live. If you were to live beyond your life expectancy, you'd consume your entire savings capital. So at an advanced age, you might find yourself forced to get by on Social Security and pension payments—on reduced rations.

That's where the annuity comes to your aid. At age sixty-five you might take a portion of your savings capital and invest it in a paid-up annuity to become effective at once.

Those annuity payments contain a guarantee. So, as long as you live, you are sure of receiving Social Security benefits, pension payments and installment amounts from your annuity. The combination of these three payments is sufficient for you to live in comfort during your retirement years. And you have the guarantee that such payments will continue for as long as you live.

Of course, it is not necessary to wait until you reach retirement age to invest savings capital in an annuity.

Long before retirement, you might take out life insurance coverage to protect your family in case of your premature death but with the intention of converting permanent values building up within the policy to an annuity if you reach retirement.

If you had invested in an endowment during your working years, probably that was your intention from the very start. And you might even invest some of your savings in an annuity during your working period to pay off at retirement age. Instead of putting such savings in stocks or bonds or other types of investment, you might use those savings to pay premiums on an annuity policy. At time of retirement, the annuity matures and your savings plus interest is returned to you through installment payments.

You can use the annuity in conjunction with the so-called lag periods in Social Security. Your wife is younger than you. Assume that you will retire in 1985 when you are sixty-five years of age and will draw full Social Security benefits based on prior employment. On such retirement, you will be entitled to some $344 a month until your wife reaches 62. At that time, total amounts payable to you and your wife will jump to $516.

Until you start drawing benefits for self and wife, you would draw Social Security payments which are about $170 a month less than that which you will draw when you both begin to receive Social Security. To provide for a level and certain retirement income from the moment you retire at sixty-five, you might purchase an annuity with guaranteed payments of $170 a month until your wife becomes eligible for payment.

TAXES ADD TO INVESTMENT FACTOR OF INSURANCE

Ten years ago you started to put your savings in stock as part of your retirement program. Over the years, your choice of investments has been proven sound. Your stocks have gone up in value. But now that you've reached retirement age, you wish to switch investments, perhaps to other stocks which, while providing less growth, offer greater security. For instance, you wish to switch to good-paying utility stock.

On your conversion of investment, you are going to incur a capital gains tax. When you sell your present holdings to reinvest, the profit realized on sale will be subject to a current tax.

To the extent of that tax, you will have less cash proceeds to reinvest in your new investment. In other words, capital gains tax consumes some of your capital, leaves less to reinvest and that means a reduced return.

Suppose instead of investing in stocks, you had used some of your savings to pay insurance premiums. Instead of surrendering your policy for cash, you now convert to an annuity.

While there has been a change in the type of investment somewhat similar to a switch from one stock to another, there is no capital gains tax due on the switch from insurance to annuity contract. In other words, savings capital is preserved intact without any dilution due to capital gains tax which means bigger annuity payments for you.

Thus, in effect, when you purchase insurance, you purchase family protection with ultimate retirement benefits for yourself if you live long enough—retirement benefits which will not be reduced by taxes.

You are now allowed to convert tax-free one life insurance contract for another, for an annuity, or for an endowment. Also you can exchange an endowment contract for another endowment or an annuity contract, and an annuity for another contract—all tax free.

In seeking to guarantee themselves increased lifetime, retirement income, more insureds are converting life policies to annuities. At the end of 1970, some 540,000 of these insurance-to-annuity conversions were producing 705 million dollars a year in guaranteed incomes. Merely because another insured person has seen fit to convert his insurance into a retirement annuity should not dictate similar action on your part. Perhaps, due to your personal and family situation, such conversion is not advisable. On the other hand, your need for continued life insurance may be greatly reduced at the time of your retirement. In such case, you might consider conversion of a life policy to an annuity to increase your retirement income.

And annuity payments themselves are given favorable tax treatment. Under the tax law, you divide the tax cost of your annuity policy by your life expectancy (based on Treasury tables) to get an annual exclusion. Only payments in excess of that exclusion are taxable. For example, say your annuity policy pays you $100 a month —$1,200 a year. And, based on Treasury tables, your annual exclusion is $1,000. Only $200 of the $1,200 received annually would constitute taxable income. The exclusion continues as long as you live. Thus, you might recover the entire amount you paid for the annuity policy in the form of a tax-free recovery and still be entitled to a continuing exclusion in the same amount as before, for as long as you lived.

Some annuities, rather than being based on life expectancy, guarantee payment for a fixed period. For instance, the annuity contract might provide for installment payments over a 10-year period, then to terminate. In such case, the exclusion allowed on annuity payments is computed by dividing ten years into the tax cost of the annuity. And on annuity payments, only amounts in excess of that exclusion are treated as taxable income.

To sum up:

> Life insurance protection is a must for everyone who has or in future will have someone dependent upon him. Furthermore, when converted to an annuity, it is the only investment you can make which will provide you a fixed income for as long as you live.

There is, of course, one serious drawback to the usual annuity which prevents its use as the perfect, all-inclusive retirement "food." Such annuity is payable in a fixed number of dollars, and a dollar, to paraphrase the popular song, is a sometime thing.

If thirty years ago you had contracted for an annuity to begin paying you the then munificent sum of $100 a month, starting next January 1, you would be a worried man today. Even if you plunk down thousands of dollars in a lump-sum purchase of an annuity to begin paying you $300 a month now for life, you may be an unhappy person ten years from now if modest bungalows rent for $200 a month.

In other words, all forms of insurance payments are safe —but, up until recently, were limited to fixed dollar amounts. Recognizing this, several insurers now offer a cost-of-living life policy, and some now issue a cost-of-living annuity as well as variable annuities, which hopefully will be geared to inflation.

SOME QUESTIONS AND ANSWERS

Q. *You mention a joint annuity. What is this, and how does it compare with a savings bank account?*

A. There is very little comparison.

A savings deposit remains constant so long as you withdraw only the interest it earns. Your income depends merely upon how much money you have on deposit, and the rate of interest the bank is paying.

An annuity is a *contract* you buy from an insurance company or charitable or religious institution. The contract is offered essentially in one of two forms—lifetime or refund. A lifetime contract says the company will pay you so much every month, or quarter, or year for the rest of your life—period. After your death, there is no estate. Finished.

A "refund" type of contract calls for paying you this income for your lifetime, *and*, if you do not live long enough to collect all you paid in, it will pay the balance to your estate. Naturally, this form yields a bit less than the lifetime contract.

A joint annuity merely changes these terms to cover the lives of two people, even after one dies.

An annuity's payout depends upon the amount of money paid in, the age and sex of the persons who are to receive the payments. Women statistically live longer than men; therefore, they receive less income.

Q. *Would a $10,000 lifetime annuity be wise for a widow of 73? It would leave me with about $23,800 in savings and stock—Kodak, General Electric, Mobil and bonds of about $6,000.*

A. An annuity can provide more income for you and with far greater safety than you can obtain elsewhere—*if* you are not interested in leaving an estate.

If you are ready to cut into your estate by $10,000, via an annuity, you would be justified in continuing to hold lower-yield growth stocks such as Kodak and General Electric (Mobil yields close to 4 per cent).

Another approach would be to put the entire $33,000 into high-grade bonds yielding about 7 per cent and keep the estate intact.

You are not clear about that $6,000 in bonds. If these are E bonds, the money should be put to work bringing in current income—either in H's or in corporate securities.

Q. *My mother was left a widow at 52, with about $19,000 to invest. Would an annuity be a good idea? There are younger children.*

A. I can't see an annuity for 2 important reasons:

1. At 52, a woman can't get enough income from an annuity to justify her exhausting capital;
2. If there are young children, an annuity would leave little protection and might well leave them out in the cold.

It seems to me that part of this money should be in insured savings accounts and part in high-grade commons yielding about 5 per cent.

Q. *I am a widow of 78, offered $137 a month income from a $15,000 annuity, with any unused portion going to my heirs. But what about inflation?*

A. The inflationary trend is a problem.

But—an income of about $1,650 a year from $15,000 paid in is about twice what you could get from an investment which is not tied to dollars. So, it seems to me, you could feel safe with the annuity.

Q. *I am 65, would like to invest $15,000 in an annuity, leaving no estate. Where do I buy it? Will they send the money to Italy if I retire there?*

A. Annuities are bought from life-insurance companies or religious and charitable institutions.

Buy it from a reputable company or organization licensed to do business in your state. There should be no problem about sending the monthly check to Italy.

Q. *I am retired at 64, with about $12,000 in life insurance and $12,000 in E bonds. My insurance agent is urging me to convert the $24,000 into a joint annuity* *which will pay my wife and me $130 a month for as long as either lives.*

A. I've frequently written of annuities and the generous worry-free income they can provide for retirees. *But–*

Annuity payments are based on sex and age. Women, for example, get less monthly income than men because they live longer. A person starting to collect payments at 64 will get less than one beginning to collect at age 68 or 72.

My guess is that your wife is much younger than you, which means an annuity covering both of you is not likely to be too generous at your ages–as the figures you quoted indicate.

$24,000 invested today in high-grade bonds will yield about $165 a month "forever"; in other words, with no exhaustion of principal.

Q. *We are in our mid-50s, plan to retire next year. We own 1,328 A.T. &T. and would like to buy an annuity for $100,000. We paid $41,373 for the stock. How would I figure the cost since the shares have been split? Which would you sell first, the newer shares or those acquired first? Would a life-insurance company accept stock in payment for an annuity?*

A. If you sold the entire 1,328 shares at one time, your capital gain would be the difference between what you received for them and the total of all money paid to acquire the shares–in your case, $41,373.

If you bought shares at different times, the prices you paid for those individual blocks are your cost for the number of shares each block has grown to today as a result of splits.

In other words, if you bought 100 shares in the early 1950s, you would have 600 shares today in that particular block, and the cost of the 100 shares would be the tax-cost basis for the 600 shares.

If you bought 100 shares after the 3-for-1 split in 1959, but before the 2-for-1 split in 1964, you would have 200 shares today as a result of that investment and the amount you paid for the 100 shares would be your tax cost for that particular 200 shares.

If you aren't going to sell all the shares, sell the block which cost you most, so as to keep your gains tax down. (As a matter of fact, I don't see why you should sell anything until after you retire. Why pay capital-gains taxes in a tax bracket set by your earnings, when next year's retirement tax bracket will be much lower?)

As to the uses of this, roughly, $73,000 (before taxes):

I don't think you will find an annuity too generous. At 55, a joint annuity wouldn't yield too much above $5 per month per $1,000. Frankly, I don't see that it is worth fixing your income for life at the young age of 55, with years of inflation ahead of you, in return for an income only slightly (if at all) above what you could get from an inflation-hedge investment in common shares. Time enough for an annuity when you get much older, when annuity payment rates are higher, and years ahead in which to worry about inflation are less.

I don't know of any insurance company which would accept your shares in payment for an annuity. A religious or charitable organization, however, will accept securities in payment for an annuity. Their payments are generally a bit below those paid by life insurance companies.

Only arithmetic will tell you whether a sale of stock, payment of taxes, and purchase of a life insurance company annuity will yield more than turning over the shares to a religious or charitable organization for their annuity.

Or you could depend upon the A.T. & T. dividends, plus, let's say, another $2,500 obtained by selling that much in shares annually, on the premise that A.T. &T. would appreciate enough in market price over a long period of time to keep your assets up to their present mark.

Frankly, I don't think one can be too comfortable cutting into capital on such a basis, even with as sound an investment as A.T. &T.–but you do have an unusually large block of stock.

Otherwise, you must liquidate it over a number of years, so as to keep your tax bite down, and gradually shift your funds into securities yielding closer to 5 and 6%.

Since you do not need to leave an estate, you might consider an annuity in about 10 years.

Q. *I plan to retire in two years, when I will be 65. We own no stocks, but have $20,000 in savings and an annuity with a cash value of $16,000, which I intend to cash after I retire, using that amount to earn additional income, rather than dissipate it via the annuity's monthly payments. I've been considering a no-load mutual but I think the market is too high and should drop in the next 2 years. Or should I buy at today's prices? Or buy closed-end investment-fund shares?*

A. If you feel you must leave an estate–that is, live only on income from your money and not cut into capital–then obviously you would have to cash the annuity. But if that's true, why did you buy an annuity in the first place? Certainly it is not the best way to appreciate capital over a long period of years.

But before you cash in the annuity, do a little investigating and see whether that contract won't do more for you than the same money in some other medium.

I agree you should have some money in equities rather than in dollars and in dollar-fixed annuity payments. But why can't that equity portion of your portfolio be purchased with some of the dollars now in savings?

In other words, I think an annuity plus common shares (either in a mutual fund or a closed-end fund investment) makes a good retirement combination.

As to timing lump-sum purchases of a mutual fund (or any equity investment)–I won't even try to guess. But why not play it cozy and space your buying over the next year and a half rather than try to find the bottom?

Q. *We are in our early 50s, both employed and earning a total of about $16,000 a year. We have about $15,000 in savings, including bonds, credit union and retirement fund. We save $100 a week, which we put into savings bonds. We've been approached to buy an annuity by paying $116 a month for 12 years. It will return us about $125 a month in retirement. What would you do?*

A. Annuities can play an important role in retirement planning. This one will cost you $16,700 over the next

12 years. I have no way of knowing what you could accomplish with that money in other investment media over the next 12 years. You might build that $116 a month, invested in stocks, into a $50,000 stake–or you could lose most of it.

The only point I want to raise is that everything you are doing in the way of retirement planning is in the way of fixed dollars–savings, credit union, retirement fund, savings bonds.

Your pre-retirement years (saving period) and post-retirement years (consuming period) will total more than 25 years. Under the circumstances, it seems to me that you should do something about inflation. The next 25 years might see a lot of it.

By switching from savings bonds to an annuity program you are doing nothing about inflation–merely switching from one form of dollar-fixed investment to another. Somewhere in your program there ought to be some equities such as common shares which, you could hope, would keep you in step with living costs in 1979 and thereafter.

Q. *We are in our mid-50s and it may be a little late to start an annuity. But I feel we should have something more than bank savings and bonds. In the event of inflation would an annuity protect us better than investment in a business or real estate?*

A. It is never too late to buy an annuity. You may do so right up to the year you retire and want to begin receiving income. You can get any argument you want on when one should begin to buy his annuity. It can be bought with quarterly premiums, beginning with your first pay check. Or you can convert other forms of life insurance. Or–as mentioned above–you can put cash down when you want to begin receiving income.

Many people like to feel assured, starting at age 25, that they will have income of $100 a month at age 65, and therefore take steps at 25 to begin buying an annuity. I like guarantees, too, but am inclined to be a bit leery about "buying" $100 a month 40 years off if I have no way of knowing what that $100 will buy.

The argument made by those who favor an early start on buying an annuity is that as the years pass you are buying the contract with dollars constantly declining in value. That's true. But I still don't see how anyone can hope that his payment dollars will be cheaper, or even as cheap, as those he begins to receive upon retirement.

An equity investment, one in which you take on the risks of ownership–whether it's owning a stock, or a gas station or an apartment house–could be expected to keep you in step with inflation, since you, too, would then own things which would tend to rise with the general price level. These things could be liquidated upon retirement in order to buy an annuity.

It seems to me that if one has to give up inflation protection, it's far better to do so between the ages of 65 and 100 than between the ages of 25 and 100. Moreover, this investment program could offer another advantage. By the time you reach 65, either a cost of living annuity or variable annuity might be worth considering. At that time, you could use savings in equity investments to buy one of these annuities which could offer protection against continuing inflation. That is, you can do that if you still insist on investment of all of your funds in an annuity contract.

Q. *You continue to say that annuities leave no estate. Aren't you familiar with refund annuities? They do leave a balance for the estate.*

A. It "ain't necessarily so."

There are various forms of annuities. They may call for benefits to be received monthly, quarterly, semi-annually, or annually; for the lifetime of the annuitant, for 5 years certain, 10 years certain, 20 years certain, as well as refund annuities.

The first (lifetime) ends with the life of the annuitant. After his death there are no further benefits–the contract is canceled. The 5-year certain plan calls for payments for the lifetime of the annuitant (and at least for five years, if he does not live that long). The 10-year and 20-year contracts carry, respectively, the same provisions. The refund annuity covers the lifetime of the annuitant and at least until total benefits paid out equal the price he originally paid in to the insurance company. The balance, if any, can be paid his heirs either in a lump sum, or via continuation of the regular monthly or quarterly payments, just as though the annuitant were still alive.

Now–there are two important points you've overlooked.

1. You don't get these extra clauses for nothing. For example (quoting the rate book of one of the large life insurance companies) a woman in her sixties can get $6.31 a month for life from a $1,000 annuity. If she wants the 5-year certain plan, her monthly benefits drop to $6.22; for 10-year certain they drop to $6.03; for 20-year certain, to $5.27. If she wants a plan which will pay her heirs a cash refund, she must accept a $5.61 monthly payment; if she wants any refund paid to her heirs via a continuation of her monthly benefits, she can get $5.72. These amounts will vary from company to company. All I am trying to show here is that life insurance companies employ skilled actuaries and, as a result, you can be sure that you will pay for what you get.
2. None of these programs guarantees that there will be any money left over for the estate. Even if she buys the 20-year certain plan she may live 20 or more years. So there would be no balance as an inheritance.

And if she buys one of the refund form annuities and lives long enough to collect payments totaling the price originally paid in, there will also be no balance for the estate.

So–to repeat–no form of annuity guarantees that money will be left for your heirs.

Q. *I will soon have an annuity policy coming due. I can take $12,970 in cash or $80 a month for the rest of our lives (we're in our sixties). We have rental real estate, our home, worth about $60,000, savings and sizable blocks of sound common stocks, including a bank stock which pays*

%, but has shown remarkable growth. What you suggest?

A. Considering your overall picture—which indicates a comfortable retirement income, enhanced by the additional funds which could be raised by sale of your home, if necessary—I would vote for taking the $80 a month.

I'm just as conscious of the inroads of inflation as the next man, but $960 a year from roughly $13,000 is more than could be obtained from an inflation-hedge stock yielding 5%. And that margin can take care of a lot of inflation during your lifetime.

Furthermore, you do have substantial investment already in inflation-hedge stocks and real estate.

Q. *As an insurance underwriter, I must disagree with a recent column in which you took a dim view of insuring young children. There are various reasons for insuring children: The insurance is provided at a bargain rate; it protects against hazards of later uninsurability; it offers various policy options, including additional insurance; it gives the child's savings plan an early start; it provides educational funds.*

A. I'll grant you right at the start that my judgment is warped by sentiment. I feel queasy about life insurance on children.

I'll also concede right off the benefits of protection against later uninsurability and the obtaining of various policy options. They may or may not prove to be of value.

I'm not so prepared to accept the other benefits. The rates may be a "bargain," but they are paid for a helluva long time. A $5,000 policy on a youngster of 5 would cost only $44.55 a year, whereas at age 25 it jumps to $71.35. But if we're talking of carrying this policy out to age 70 we find the youngster's policy from age 5 costing a total of $2,996 whereas the man who began his own plan at age 25 pays only $216 more, and in cheaper dollars, too.

I would also question the savings factor and the educational fund points. A savings program is important, but not the sole answer to every financial problem. And tuition fees are not going to sit still for the next 13 years.

I'll say this to any life insurance underwriter: If you're out to sell more life insurance, why not sell more of it to Dad? That's where it is needed most.

Q. *I'm 26, married. A friend who sells mutual funds is advising me to cancel my insurance and put the money into a fund where I would be covered by $15,000 term insurance.*

A. I'd hesitate, for several reasons: 1) The insurance on the mutual fund is not a $15,000, 15-year policy, but a declining-balance term policy. In the last year, for example, your insurance protection would be only $1,000. 2) A young man can get lifetime insurance options which often are denied older men. And you shouldn't plan on going through life, after age 41, with no life insurance. 3) I don't have enough facts to check your figures, but I seriously doubt that diverting your insurance premiums to a mutual fund would buy you a $15,000 plan.

Q. *I'm 27, just married and interested in buying mutual fund shares. But my insurance man says I'd do better by first starting a life insurance program.*

A. I'd be inclined to agree. At 27 you can nail down some lifelong insurance protection at rather low rates. I'd sign up for some lifetime protection now. After that's out of the way you can consider mutual funds with—if you still need it—additional term protection in the form of declining balance insurance.

21 What You'll Get from Social Security

The government is aiding you in providing for your retirement. Under the liberalized Social Security law, just about every individual working for a living—and that might mean working for yourself, or for someone else—will draw a pension from the government. Doctors are now included under the Social Security program along with other professions and self-employed individuals.

The amended Social Security law now includes an earlier retirement provision for men similar to that enacted for women a few years back. Regardless of your sex, it is now possible for you to start drawing Social Security benefits as early as age sixty-two. As is the case with a woman retiring early, the man retiring at age sixty-two will draw proportionately smaller Social Security benefits. If he waits until sixty-four, he will receive a still larger amount, and of course, if he delays retirement until sixty-five he will get the maximum benefits to which he is entitled.

The number of us coming within the Social Security program not only has been extended, but the monthly payments have been increased. What you can expect to get in form of monthly benefits will vary with your earned income during your working period. The amount of Social Security benefits is determined under a formula based on your average monthly compensation while you are working.

SOCIAL SECURITY PAYMENTS HAVE BEEN INCREASED

As of spring, 1965, maximum Social Security benefits were secured when average monthly wage upon which benefits were based reached $400—that's earned income of $4,800 a year. So the individual who had earnings of $4,800 or more for a sufficient number of years got maximum Social Security benefits.

Under successive changes in the Social Security law, however, the earnings base on which Social Security benefits are computed has been increased most recently from earned income of $9,000 a year in 1972 to $10,800 in 1973 and then to $12,000 in 1974. Moreover, withholding tax rate from pay of employee and also tax rate for required employer contribution have been increased. For instance, in 1970, both employer and the employee contributed at a 4.2 per cent rate for Social Security exclusive of additional contribution for hospital insurance. Starting in 1971, each has contributed at a 4.6 per cent rate for Social Security alone. Based on a higher earnings amount and a higher tax rate, the maximum Social Security benefits also are increased. These tax-free benefits will provide a welcome addition to other income needed for comfortable living in retirement. For instance, consider a middle manager in industry who now has reached his late forties. He will retire in 1989 on reaching 65. At such time he might secure Social Security benefits for himself of about $350 a month. Assume further that his wife also reaches 65 then, so that maximum benefits for a couple based on his earnings are available. The full monthly benefit for an employee's wife generally is equal to one-half of the husband's primary Social Security benefit. Thus, she might secure an additional payment of about $175 to further increase the couple's retirement income. In this example, the couple might benefit from total Social Security benefits in excess of $520 a month. While tax-free income of $520 a month will be important to this couple in retirement, its value will depend upon purchasing power of the dollar, almost two decades in the future. That is a factor you must consider in attempting to place a value on Social Security you will receive upon retirement.

However, changed Social Security law now includes a cost-of-living adjustment. This adjustment will increase benefits in the future in seeking to preserve the value of Social Security in terms of current purchasing power of the dollar. Beginning in 1975, Social Security benefits can be increased if there has been a significant increase—at least 3 per cent—in the cost of living as determined by the Consumer Price Index. This increase becomes effective automatically unless Congress acts to increase benefits, e.g., increase benefits by more than the automatic increase.

Note that in the past, Congress has acted to increase Social Security benefits. For instance, assume that an employee will retire in the near future. He will reach 65 in 1975. His wife will also reach 65 in the same year and will be entitled to a wife's benefit due to his earnings. Due to the latest increase in Social Security benefits, benefits for this couple have been increased by some $80 a month or $960 a year. Moreover, that is a tax-free increase.

On retirement in the near future, this couple formerly would have secured a total monthly benefit of about $345.

Now, upon retirement in 1975, this couple will be entitled to monthly benefits of approximately $425. For others who will not attain 65 for ten or fifteen years, maximum Social Security benefits will be more. For the young employee with many, many years before retirement, benefits will be still higher. For instance, even without any cost-of-living adjustments which would mean a further increase in benefits in the future, a young man could expect Social Security benefits for himself and spouse upon retirement of more than $605 a month.

What does this mean? It means that in order to plan your retirement investing soundly, you should continually recheck how much you will be entitled to upon retirement. If that sum comes near meeting your estimated living costs, for example, you can take more chances with your investments than you should take if it were to fall far short. In the latter case, you would have to invest with more emphasis on safety, and less on high and risky yields.

SOCIAL SECURITY IS A FOURFOLD PROGRAM

Benefits under Social Security are not limited to retirement payments. Social Security provides four different benefits—all of which are important in retirement planning. Three of these have direct bearing on post-retirement; one has importance in pre-retirement. Under Social Security, a covered individual can benefit as follows:

1. Retirement payments for self and spouse at sixty-five years of age and reduced benefits as early as sixty-two.
2. Survivorship payments to certain survivors after death, e.g., surviving spouse.
3. Medicare benefits to meet hospital expenses after sixty-five and also doctor bills if he joins the voluntary portion of this new government-sponsored health insurance.
4. Disability payments if he becomes disabled before reaching sixty-five.

COORDINATING YOUR RETIREMENT PROGRAM WITH SOCIAL SECURITY

When an individual plans his retirement program, he mentally will set a target date—most often his sixty-fifth birthday. And in planning a retirement program he thinks not only of himself but also of his wife. But an individual may not be able to continue to work to the target retirement age—his health may force him to retire earlier than anticipated. Or even if he reaches the retirement age, he might die shortly thereafter and since most wives are younger than their husbands and women live longer than men, his wife may survive him by many years. So he has to take into account how she will live after his retirement or death.

In all the above situations, Social Security benefits may give financial aid. But the extent of benefits will vary with the circumstances, so it's necessary to consider some basic provisions contained in the Social Security law.

IS YOUR WIFE YOUNGER THAN YOU?

Let's say that your retirement planning has been geared to age sixty-five. Your employer has a compulsory retirement provision at that age and you will start to draw employment pension benefits then. Also, when you reach sixty-five, maximum Social Security benefits for yourself are available. If your wife is older than you or the same age, you can draw Social Security benefits for yourself and for her. If she's younger than you, but the age spread is only three years (when you're sixty-five, she is sixty-two) you can secure full Social Security benefits for yourself and reduced benefits for her.

But suppose she is considerably younger than you—ten years younger. When you retire at sixty-five, you can draw benefits only for yourself. Consider what that means if it is assumed that you will get maximum benefit rates under Social Security law at time of retirement shortly after 1985. You draw $344 monthly. Seven years after your retirement, you could elect to take benefits for yourself and your wife—maximum amount payable $473 monthly. And if you decide to wait until she reaches sixty-five—that's ten years after you've retired—Social Security benefits for both of you will be $516.

There is a spread between Social Security benefits to which you're entitled at age sixty-five and additional payments when your wife reaches sixty-five of $172 a month. Over a year, that's a difference of about $2,064. And in your case, over a period of ten years there would be a total difference of some $20,640.

That's the difference in tax-free money. If you were in the lowest tax bracket after retirement, $20,640 tax-free income is the equivalent of more than $17,840 taxable. For the executive retiring with substantial investment income taxed at 50 per cent, that spread of $20,640 is the equivalent of $41,280 in taxable income which is lost until his wife reaches sixty-five.

That spread between Social Security payments payable to a husband at the time he reaches sixty-five and additional Social Security payments which become payable when his wife reaches either sixty-two or sixty-five is commonly referred to as the "spread due to the lag period."

By planning your own retirement program, you can arrange so that income from the time you retire doesn't fluctuate due to the lag period in Social Security. For instance, in a situation where a husband is ten years older than his wife, he might take out an annuity providing for payment for ten years in an amount sufficient to match loss of Social Security benefits until his wife reaches sixty-five. When his wife reaches sixty-five, the annuity would terminate. But additional Social Security payments then due would make up for loss of annuity payments. Or if the intention was to secure coverage for the wife at age sixty-two, he might take out an annuity providing for payments over a seven-year period.

U.S. Savings Bonds might be utilized to give the same result. For instance, at age fifty-five, the husband might buy such bonds in an amount so that if he held them for ten years they would yield him $2,064 after tax on surrender then. Over ten years to retirement, he makes a similar investment each year. Then, by cashing the bonds in at the same rate, he could approximate the difference in Social Security benefits until his wife is entitled to benefits. When his wife reached sixty-five, the capital invested in U.S. Savings Bonds would have been consumed, but Social Security payments would then be increased.

If Social Security benefits again are increased, as they have been in the past, your monthly retirement amount would be lifted. However, since a wife's benefit is 50 per cent of her husband's, the spread between benefits for a husband and full benefits for a couple would be even greater than the preceding example indicates.

WILL YOU RETIRE BEFORE 65?

An individual may choose to retire at any age between sixty-two and sixty-five and still get Social Security benefits. However, on retirement before sixty-five, Social Security benefits are reduced. For instance, an individual retiring in 1975 might qualify for maximum benefits for self alone of $283 a month on retirement at age sixty-five. On the other hand, if retirement took place at age sixty-two, maximum benefits would not exceed $220.

Millions of employees can expect to draw pensions from pension plans established by their employers. Up until recently, most of these plans used a retirement age of sixty-five. However, many have been revised to permit earlier retirement, for instance, at age sixty-two. An employee retiring at sixty-two will draw a pension at a reduced amount compared to what he would have secured had he delayed retirement until sixty-five. Thus, pension from employment not only will be reduced but so will Social Security payments on pre-sixty-five retirement.

For many individuals, retirement at sixty-two, though, has strong appeal. If you are considering retirement at such age, you will have to consider the effect on the total amounts you will receive in the form of employment pension and Social Security. The total will be reduced as a result of early retirement. You will have to save more in retirement funds if you are to live as comfortably as the individual who delays retirement until sixty-five.

Social Security payments to retirees are dependent on average earnings during the previous working career. Up to 1966, the top average earnings taken into account were limited to $4,800 a year. For the year 1966 and 1967, top earnings up to $6,600 were included. Through the 1968–1971 period, average earnings included rose to $7,800 and in 1972 to $9,000. In 1973, average earnings taken into account rise to $10,800 and then to $12,000 in 1974. However, for many years, individuals retiring at 65 will have Social Security benefits based in part on top earnings of less than $12,000 a year, i.e., in part on earnings up to $7,800 a year; in part on earnings up to $6,600 a year, etc. Thus, even though an individual had very high earnings throughout his working career, he will get less than the new maximum Social Security benefit.

Prior to 1975, the cost-of-living adjustment now contained in the Social Security law will not be in effect. Thus, it is possible to calculate maximum benefits for an individual alone and for an individual and spouse where he and spouse reach 65 between now and 1975. However, the individual who will reach 65 after 1975 could benefit from Social Security increases due to cost-of-living adjustments. Thus, only estimates of future Social Security benefits can be made for such individuals. The following table therefore includes only projections of maximum monthly Social Security benefits to which an individual will be entitled, for self alone and self and spouse depending upon when he retires at age 65.

Year of Retirement	*Monthly Social Security (self)*	*Monthly Social Security (wife also 65)*
1972	$259	$389
1973	266	399
1974	274	411
1975	283	424
1976	298	447
1977	307	460
1978	314	471
1979	322	483
1980	328	492
1985	344	516
1990	355	532

WILL YOU SLIDE INTO RETIREMENT?

Many individuals go into retirement on a gradual basis. That's particularly true of self-employed people, e.g., the attorney or accountant. At age sixty-five, the individual works only part time—for instance, the accountant might come in to help out during the busy period, not work at all during slack periods. Such an individual still will have earned income but greatly reduced in amount.

For a retired couple age sixty-five, Social Security benefits could mean as much as a tax-free income from a $100,000 investment. So loss of Social Security is not an insignificant one.

An individual who has reached seventy-two may earn any amount of income without losing any of his Social Security benefits in whole or part as a result of earnings. These are the rules on such earnings and possible loss of benefits.

An individual under seventy-two can earn up to $1,680 a year in employment without loss of Social Security benefits. However, $1 in benefits is lost for every $2 in earnings between $1,680 and $2,880. Thereafter $1 in benefits is lost for every $1 in earnings over $2,880. However, there will not be any loss of benefits for any month in which an individual earns $140 a month or less and does not render "substantial services" in self-employment.

Where an individual continues to work part time after he starts to draw Social Security benefits, he might lose little in the way of benefits even though he earns more than $1,680 if part-time work is crowded into a short period. However, if part-time work extends over the year, he should weigh the value of such earned income against the loss of Social Security benefits.

This earnings penalty must be considered by the individual who would prefer to continue to work on a reduced scale after sixty-five. For instance, a couple, both age sixty-five in 1973 and entitled to maximum benefits due to the husband's prior employment, can receive Social Security payments worth about $5,500 in taxable income —if their income is taxed in the lowest tax bracket. The value of the tax-free treatment given Social Security benefits increases with the amount of other income subject to tax. For that reason, the individual upon retirement should weigh the value of any earned income against the loss of Social Security benefits. The individual who thinks of supplementing his retirement income by working part-time after sixty-five may actually be losing while continuing to work.

WHAT IF DISABILITY FORCES EARLIER RETIREMENT?

You are fifty-five now. Your children are grown and self-supporting. Your retirement program has been geared to retirement at sixty-five. A pension through employment becomes effective at that age. You have insurance contracts which also will start to pay off in form of annuities then. You are making other investments with your savings, including U.S. Savings Bonds which you will start to cash in ten years hence. All in all you have a soundly planned program for retirement at age sixty-five. But suppose five years hence, at age sixty, arthritis cripples you so that you're forced into earlier retirement.

Social Security will give you some financial aid. The Social Security law now includes a disability provision. Long before early retirement at sixty-two or normal retirement at sixty-five, an individual who comes under the Social Security program can draw benefits if he becomes disabled to such an extent that he cannot engage in any substantial gainful activity. Formerly, an individual had to be fifty or over to draw early benefits from disability. There is no such age requirement now. However, while disability benefits include family payments for the wife and minor children of a younger man, in your situation, at age sixty, disability payments will cover only you. Your children are grown. Your wife is still in her fifties. That means you will get only retirement benefits that a single individual, age sixty-five, draws currently. Additional benefits can be secured for your wife but only when she reaches sixty-two.

To guard against illness which might force premature retirement, you might take out loss-of-income insurance or an insurance contract which provides for a full annuity at age sixty-five but also permits you to elect a reduced annuity before that age. And if you already have an annuity contract, you might check elections allowing you to take reduced earlier annuity. Such annuity payments might carry you over a "short ration" disability period until Social Security benefits include payments both for yourself and your wife.

IF YOU BECOME ILL AFTER 65

The introduction of Medicare was the most important change made in the Social Security law in 1965. What is Medicare? It is a broad system of health insurance which is now available to almost all individuals sixty-five and older. It covers everyone over sixty-five who is entitled to Social Security benefits. Even though an individual intends to continue to work after sixty-five, and because of earnings will not be able to secure Social Security payments, he should file application. In the event of illness, such individual could qualify for Medicare benefits.

The Medicare program is divided into two parts. *Hospital insurance* which became effective July 1, 1966, provides coverage for hospital expenses. Starting January 1, 1967, it also aids in meeting expenses of care in a nursing home. The cost of this insurance is borne by the government. The second part provides coverage for *medical and doctor bills* as distinguished from hospital expenses. An individual qualifying for Medicare benefits must sign up if he wants medical coverage. Moreover, there is a cost:

Starting in mid-1971, this cost was increased to $5.60 a month per individual for voluntary medical coverage, from a premium of $5.30 which prevailed earlier. The Government makes a matching contribution for each individual. In the future, this cost will be varied as determined by the Social Security Administration. It could be increased as it was in the past.

MEDICARE IS A BARGAIN

As we get older, we are more prone to illness. Expenses relating to health tend to climb. In the case of a retired individual, expenses of an illness might have minor or serious effects on his budget depending upon the illness and its duration. With insurance—and it is now available through Medicare—the older individual can take steps to avoid serious drain on his retirement income and capital in the event he becomes sick.

Under hospital insurance, Medicare pays certain covered services for the first sixty days of hospitalization after initial expenses of $68. Thereafter, the patient pays $17 a day and Medicare meets the remainder of covered costs for an additional thirty days. In addition, if "spell of illness" requiring hospitalization continues beyond 90-day benefit period, you can benefit from a lifetime reserve of 60 days for continued hospital care. However, you pay a charge of $34 a day (not $17) for each of these 60 days used.

Hospital insurance also covers post-hospital care costs (after at least 3 consecutive days of hospitalization) in a qualified "extended care facility" such as a nursing home. This post-hospital benefit in a nursing home can continue up to a hundred days. Medicare meets all covered costs for the first 20 days. The patient pays thereafter $8.50 a day of such costs. To qualify for extended care benefits, though, you generally must be admitted to the qualified facility for treatment of the condition which caused hospitalization—and within 14 days after hospital discharge.

This hospital benefit (90 days) and post-hospital extended care (100 days) are recurring and are allowed for each "spell of illness" or "benefit period." Generally, each benefit period begins with the first day you are furnished inpatient hospital or extended care services and ends when you have been out of the hospital or extended care facility for 60 days. For instance, an illness hospitalizes you for several weeks. You are then discharged and 60 days pass. Subsequently, you again become ill and require hospitalization. Hospital insurance benefits in this situation would cover each separate period of hospitalization.

Under medical insurance—the voluntary part of Medicare—the patient must pay the first $50 in doctor bills and other covered cost each year; thereafter, he pays 20% of additional costs and Medicare the remaining 80%. There is an exception made for reasonable charges of a radiologist or pathologist for services provided that the patient is hospitalized; all of such charges (100%) are paid by Medicare.

HEALTH INSURANCE TO SUPPLEMENT MEDICARE

Medicare will not cover all the expenses of an illness. For instance, the hospital insurance ends at the end of ninety days. Moreover, even if the hospital stay is for less than ninety days, the patient will have to bear part of such expenses. While covered expenses include room and board, that coverage usually is for a semi-private room. If an individual wants a private room, generally he must pay for such extra expense out of his own pocket.

There are also gaps in the medical insurance part of Medicare. A covered individual must pay for part of doctor bills incurred.

Nursing home care, as distinguished from hospitalization, became available starting in 1967. Again though, not all nursing home care expenses are met by Medicare. All covered expenses are met for the first twenty days in a nursing home by Medicare. The patient pays $8.50 a day thereafter for the next eighty days. Nursing home coverage for any one illness ends after one hundred days.

In the case of a retired couple, the husband may be covered by Medicare because he has reached sixty-five. However, his wife may not be covered because she still has not attained sixty-five. To safeguard against expenses in the event she became ill, private insurance coverage for her still is important in retirement planning.

Even for a single individual covered by Medicare or for a husband and wife, both of whom are sixty-five, supplementary private insurance should be considered in retirement planning. Actuaries estimated that about 30 per cent of the expenses incurred by senior citizens will not be covered by Medicare. There are new health insurance policies available to supplement Medicare benefits—and depending upon the extra coverage desired, they may be secured at comparatively modest cost.

In general, these private insurance policies fall into two categories: One is the cash indemnity approach. For instance, if the insured is hospitalized, this type of policy provides a cash benefit, e.g., $100 a week for fifty-two weeks. The other type of policy is a direct supplement. For instance, this policy might pay the first $68 of hospital costs which are not covered by Medicare and also meet the $17 a day co-insurance expense from the sixty-first to the ninetieth day. Moreover, these policies continue coverage after Medicare lapses, e.g., coverage of all expenses for an additional thirty days of hospitalization after the ninety-first day.

For income tax purposes, the Internal Revenue Service treats the two categories of private insurance differently. According to the Revenue Service, the premium for the cash indemnity or disability income policy cannot be deducted as part of the insured's medical expenses. However, recovery under such a policy is tax-free. On the other hand, premium for hospital reimbursement policy can be taken as a medical expense. Moreover, a favorable tax rule applies in deducting such health insurance premiums. A deduction up to $150 for health insurance premiums can be secured outside of the 3%-of-income limitation in deducting medical expenses.

WILL YOUR WIFE QUALIFY FOR SOCIAL SECURITY IN HER OWN RIGHT?

"The rapid increase in labor force participation of married women is the most significant employment trend in the century today." The United States Dept. of Labor reports that they represent 50 per cent of the total growth in the labor force during the 1951-'60 period. Married women in the working force now outnumber single women. In fact, one out of every three wives now is working, with an additional 40 per cent of the married women between ages of thirty-five and fifty-four, not presently employed, considering employment.

Not only are more wives working today, but the type of married woman who is employed or who is seeking employment has changed. Mature women between the ages of forty-five and sixty-four account for more than fifty percent of the 1950-'65 increase in working wives. At the start of 1964, the average woman worker was married and forty-one years of age. In 1920 she was single and twenty-eight years old. Moreover, better-educated women are working in greater numbers than ever before. It is estimated that more than half the wives with a college degree are in the labor force against less than 25 per cent for those who only finished primary school. In recent years, the percentage of married women with higher educational attainments taking jobs has steadily increased while the proportion of married women with fewer years of schooling in the labor force has remained relatively constant.

Moreover, the working wife is earning more money through her employment. The full-time working wife now contributes about 38 per cent of the family's income on the average. In other words, her earnings will average about 60 per cent of her husband's compensation.

BENEFITS THROUGH HUSBAND'S EMPLOYMENT vs. WIFE'S OWN EMPLOYMENT

Even though a wife never was employed, she can secure Social Security benefits through her husband's employment. For instance, assume that the husband retires and qualifies for maximum possible Social Security benefits in 1972. Monthly payments to him would equal $259.40. At sixty-five, his wife would qualify for Social Security equal to 50 per cent of her husband's benefit (or a reduced amount as early as age sixty-two). If she takes benefits at sixty-five through her husband's employment, the couple could secure an additional $129 a month, i.e., 50 per cent of $259. A working wife, though, may have completed a sufficient number of covered quarters to qualify for Social Security through her own employment. Such benefits, moreover, may exceed those to which she would be entitled through her husband's employment. For instance, on husband's retirement in 1972, maximum benefits for a wife through husband's employment would run $129 a month. However, if the wife qualified for Social Security through her own employment, and benefits to her were based on an average monthly wage of around $150 a month, she might secure greater benefits than those available through her husband's employment. In fact, if she had good but not exceptionally high earnings (under $10,000 a year) during her working career, benefits to her through her own employment could significantly increase the couple's retirement income. For instance, assume that she, slightly younger than her husband, retired in 1973 upon reaching 65 and was entitled to maximum benefits through her own employment. She would receive maximum benefits of more than $275 a month against slightly more than $129 a month through her husband's employment.

22 Don't Forget Your Pension

At one time the term "pensioner" carried an ugly connotation. He was the individual who had grown too old to work, was turned out to pasture, and sometimes, depending upon the whim of his employer, drew an allowance often just sufficient to subsist on. Today, the word carries an entirely different meaning. Both large and small firms have adopted formal retirement plans for employees which will provide pensions for them upon retirement.

While the amounts payable will vary from pension plan to pension plan and even from employee to employee, even the modest pension will be an important addition to an individual's income at retirement. In some instances, retirement benefits from prior employment will be substantial.

In investing on your own for your retirement, you should give primary consideration to the *amount* you may receive as an employment pension from your employer, Social Security, or public school or religious or governmental organization. And *when* you can begin receving it.

The earlier you can determine this income, the better you can merge it into the overall program you hope to set up. If the amount is substantial, you may be justified in reaching out for high income with your private investments. The increased risk would be justifiable since you have a solid and substantial base pension income.

If you have a choice of taking your pension at fifty-five or sixty instead of having to wait until sixty-five, that will make a difference in your investments. It will mean, if you hope to retire at fifty-five, for example, that you should shift the emphasis on your investing to nearby income, rather than to long-term growth. Time and amount of pension are important.

You might be entitled to only a modest pension of say \$50 or \$60 a month. Or you might find yourself in the happy situation which employees of Sears, Roebuck, the mail order house, find themselves. Many of those employees will find that retirement benefits run close to, may even exceed, salary they currently receive for working full time. The mail order house has followed the practice of investing a substantial portion of its contributions to its employees' pension trust in Sears stock. Over a period, that stock has shown tremendous appreciation, with the result that employees now have very substantial capital interest in their pension plan.

At least one Sears employee is considerably better off after retirement than he was working full time. He earned \$80 a week. Over a period of years his accumulated benefits in the pension plan achieved a value of \$121,000. On retirement it was estimated that he had to pay a tax of some \$15,000. (Employee pension benefits are given tax-favored treatment under the tax law.) After payment of tax, the Sears employee had \$106,000 in stock and cash. If he invested for only a 5 per cent return on that capital, he nets \$5,300 a year. And with increased Social Security benefits he receives over \$1,200 a year more. So on retirement he is getting about \$125 a week against the \$80 he formerly earned.

The Sears retirement plan is the classic, used to illustrate the possible benefits from an employment retirement program. However, there are few plans which will give such a tremendous return to employees. The Sears retirement plan has called for heavy investment in Sears stock and the extraordinary benefits which will become payable to retiring employees are largely due to the tremendous increase in the value of that stock over a period of years. Still, any employee will secure additional income on retirement if his employer has a retirement plan in effect, and, as has been pointed out, income may be substantial.

EMPLOYEE RETIREMENT PLANS DIFFER

As an employee, how much will you be entitled to in the way of pension after retirement? There are many factors which will decide that. Best source of information is your employer. That might be the personnel director or treasurer in your company. It will vary with the company, but there is always some responsible official who can advise on pension benefits. Some companies follow the positive practice of constantly keeping employees informed of what they can expect in the way of retirement benefits, though companies can't always tell a particular employee the exact amount he can expect at retirement.

A typical pension may call for employer contributions to a pension fund with those funds invested through an insurance company. On retirement, the insurance company pays the employee an annuity. Other plans may call for investment through a financial institution, like a trust company, which in turn puts the fund into stocks, bonds, and other investments.

The pension plan may call for annual contributions by the employer only—or it may also permit an employee to contribute toward his own retirement. Ultimate payoff to the employee may also vary, based on length of employment, salary paid over the entire working period or over a comparatively short period (say, over the last five years of employment), etc.

Not all employee retirement plans are the so-called pension plans. An employer, instead, may adopt a profit-sharing plan for his employees' benefit.

Under the latter, contributions to the plan will bear a direct relationship to the success of the business. If the business operates unprofitably in a particular year, the employer might make no contribution in that year.

The investment policy governing a pension plan may be an important factor for an employee to consider in determining the program he embarks upon for his own retirement. For instance, the pension plan covering Charlie Jones may provide for a fixed annuity payable by an insurance company. But the retirement payments to Joe Smith may depend to a large extent upon how successful the investments were in stocks or bonds. Charlie Jones, whose employment coverage provides for an insurance company annuity upon retirement, may wish to invest his own savings toward retirement in sound, common stocks. On the other hand, Joe Smith who has a company pension plan already based on stocks and bonds may wish to invest all or part of his own savings in an insurance company annuity.

PENSION PLANS ARE BEING LIBERALIZED

On any revision in a pension plan established by employer for employees, you should check to see how the changes affect your retirement planning. Pension plans are being revised not only to provide greater payments to employees at normal retirement age but also to provide other benefits.

One recent survey of pension plans revealed that more than half now provide benefits in the event that disability forces early retirement of an employee. Increasingly, there is no minimum age requirement, provided that an employee meets certain length of service tests, e.g., ten to fifteen years of employment rather than twenty or twenty-five. Thus, while younger, short-service employees still will not get disability benefits through a pension plan, more employees in the middle-age group, in addition to older employees, will qualify for such benefits.

If a serious disability forced you into early retirement, some income from prior employment still might continue in the form of disability pension. Moreover, disability benefits under Social Security now will be available under more favorable tests to many employees who formerly were barred from such benefits.

Pension plans are also being amended to permit earlier retirement. In fact, such amendment no longer may involve a single employer but an industry, e.g., auto, steel, etc. But should your personal planning be directed toward earlier retirement? True, an employee retiring before normal retirement age under one of these revised pension plans will get a higher pension than formerly, but still less than if retirement were delayed until normal retirement age. One insurance company has pointed out that an employee entitled to a pension of $400 a month might increase that amount to about $600 a month if retirement is delayed for five years.

In his retirement planning, a married employee will consider both himself and his wife. If he should die prematurely, his insurance and savings toward retirement will be used to meet his widow's living needs during the period she survives him. Although a pension plan's primary purpose must be directed toward retirement income for an employee, within certain limitations, survivorship benefits can be offered, and such benefits are being increased. The combination of insurance and pension survivorship benefits might allow an employee to take a somewhat more aggressive position on investment in securities in seeking greater retirement capital. His premature death would not necessarily require his widow to sell the husband's securities at an inopportune time to get cash for living needs.

SHOULD AN EMPLOYEE CONTRIBUTE WITH AN EMPLOYER?

Some retirement plans set up by the employer for the benefit of employees do not permit employees to contribute to the plan. However, a number, by no means insignificant, permit an employee to contribute and as a result increase the benefits which will be payable to him upon retirement. Is it advisable for an employee to make such contributions? A large number of employees who could make such contributions have never even stopped to consider the advisability.

One factor to be considered is the investment policy and practice of those supervising the pension fund. If these policies and practices closely coincide with those of the employee, distinct advantages may be secured by investing in the plan set up by employer.

Under the tax law, investment return secured from contributions made to a "qualified" retirement plan—and that includes both employer and employee contributions—is tax free. If $100 is invested in a qualified plan and that $100 yields $4 as investment return, the second year after contribution the employee has $104 set aside for his retirement. If he invested the $100 directly in a sound security, the $4 it produced would be subject to current tax. Depending upon the employee's income tax bracket, that current return might be subject to a light or a very heavy tax.

A highly paid executive has income which places him in about the 70% tax bracket. He invests $100 in a security yielding 4%. At the end of a year when he has paid a tax of around $2.80 on the $4 return, he keeps only $1.20 after taxes. Thus, he has total amount of $101.20 in capital and after-tax return being held for retirement. Over a 10-year period, the compounded after-tax return would have increased his initial $100 capital investment to about $114. If he had made the same investment in his employer's pension plan giving a return of 4%, tax-free compounding within that plan would have increased his $100 original investment to about $150 at the end of 10 years.

23 Taxes and Your Investment Program

In the selection of any investment, its value must be measured against the investment objective sought. With a graduated income tax, that measurement must be made in "after tax" terms. Depending upon an individual's income, earned from investments, tax impact will vary. This means that no individual planning an investment program can safely ignore the effect of taxes. What may be an ideal investment in one individual's program may be a very poor one for another individual of the same age, same family unit, same retirement age goal—because the second individual's income is considerably higher or lower than the first's.

Consider this situation. An individual plans to reinvest income he receives from a particular investment. He is attracted to a common stock yielding 5 per cent which has a considerable degree of stability and offers safety as to capital investment. If the individual is married and has taxable income of $7,000 a year, the 5 per cent return from the stock shrinks to about 4 per cent after Uncle Sam takes his tax cut from investment return. If our planner invested a 4 per cent return consistently each year, he would double his original capital investment in a period of about 17 years.

Now take another individual with the same reinvestment objective in mind, but with taxable income of around $50,000. If he invests in the common stock yielding 5 per cent, that return shrinks to about 2.5 per cent after the tax collector has taken his share. In order to double the amount of original capital invested, the second individual must reinvest current return for a period of twenty-eight years. While both individuals consistently reinvest full return from the investment, the first individual doubles his original capital investment in eleven years less time than is needed by the second investor.

Continue the comparison one step further. Assume both investors are in their late forties, are making investment with retirement in view, and hope that by age sixty-five, when they retire, capital will have compounded to double the amount originally invested. In the case of the first individual investing in the stock yielding 5 per cent, that investment goal will have been achieved by time of retirement. At age sixty-five, the amount of capital he originally invested will have doubled in amount. But in the case of the second individual, reinvestment policy would have to be continued until the individual reaches seventy-six. In the first instance, retirement objective has been achieved. In the second instance, retirement planning has resulted in failure. Yet both individuals invested in the same security.

REINVESTMENT OF INVESTMENT RETURN

In a life-long investment program, the planner will intend to reinvest investment return right up to his retirement, and the amount reinvested will in turn produce an investment return with a compounding effect. Importance of the compounding of invested return can best be shown by illustration.

An individual invests $100 in a security which after taxes yields him 4 per cent. If he reinvests that 4 per cent return each year, in the seventeenth year his $100 would have grown to $200. So over seventeen years reinvestment produced an extra $100 for his retirement. But if he continues to reinvest the investment return, it will take only eleven more years to produce an additional $100 for his retirement period. And if he continues to reinvest, his original capital plus reinvested capital will produce another $100 in seven years. In a period of less than thirty-six years $100 invested to give an after-tax return of 4 per cent grew to $400. If our investor started planning for his retirement at age thirty, retirement capital would have grown fourfold at age sixty-five.

But take an individual who has an after-tax return of only 2 per cent because of the amount taken by Uncle Sam. It would take him seventy-one years before his investment capital of $100 would grow to $400. If this individual started a retirement program at a very young age and outlived his contemporaries, he would die before he attained his retirement objective. Ridiculous, but it serves to illustrate how taxes can affect a lifelong investment program.

As income increases, the tax on it increases and the net return from a fully taxable investment shrinks. In the case of an individual subject to the highest tax rates, shrinkage is so extensive that he gets comparatively little in the form of current return from a taxable investment. For instance, in 1972 an investor in the top bracket would net in the form of current return from investment only 1.2 per cent after taxes, even though such investment yields 4 per cent in a before-tax return.

The income tax is a graduated tax with rates increasing with increases in income. True, tax rates now in effect are lower than those of the 1960s, but such rates are still high. In the upper brackets, they rise to 70 per cent. As income increases, return from investment is decreased by higher tax on it. The following table shows how current investment return shrinks as income increases. The amounts shown at the top of the table—5 per cent, 6 per cent and 7 per cent—are current return given by investment before Uncle Sam takes his cut. The amounts shown under such before-tax yields reflect what an investor keeps after taxes on that yield, depending upon his tax bracket.

Income Tax Bracket	*5%*	*6%*	*7%*
2,000– 4,000	4.05	4.86	5.67
4,000– 6,000	3.95	4.74	5.53
6,000– 8,000	3.80	4.56	5.32
8,000– 10,000	3.75	4.50	5.25
10,000– 12,000	3.65	4.38	5.11
12,000– 14,000	3.55	4.26	4.97
14,000– 16,000	3.45	4.14	4.83
16,000– 18,000	3.30	3.96	4.62
18,000– 20,000	3.20	3.84	4.48
20,000– 22,000	3.10	3.72	4.34
22,000– 26,000	3.00	3.60	4.20
26,000– 32,000	2.75	3.30	3.85
32,000– 38,000	2.50	3.00	3.50
38,000– 44,000	2.25	2.70	3.15
44,000– 50,000	2.00	2.40	2.80
50,000– 60,000	1.90	2.28	2.66
60,000– 70,000	1.80	2.16	2.52
70,000– 80,000	1.70	2.04	2.38
80,000– 90,000	1.60	1.92	2.24
90,000–100,000	1.55	1.86	2.17
100,000–.......	1.50	1.80	2.10

Based on separate return rates

TAXES REQUIRE A CONSTANT CHECK ON YOUR INVESTMENT PROGRAM

Even in these days when the college graduate can command a high starting salary, he will probably not earn $10,000 a year to start. It will take him some years before he can reach that income mark. And since he will earn under $10,000 a year in his early working period, to reach even the average annual income figure over his lifetime he will have to earn more than that amount during some period prior to retirement.

And, of course, for the exceptional individual, outstanding either because of ability or energy or both, the spread between earned income received in his lowest and top earning year will be substantial. An investment by the latter individual in his early working years in a common stock promising considerable safety, modest appreciation and good yield might be one way to start his investment program directed at retirement. But to continue this investment as his income climbs would definitely be unwise. While his income is still low, much of the current yield from investment is carried over to a good current yield after taxes. But as his income becomes subject to increasingly heavy taxes, that good yield is considerably depleted after the tax collector takes his share of it. On additional investments, such an individual would be able to put aside much more capital for his retirement if he shifted his investments in whole or in part to a security which gave less in current return but promised greater capital appreciation over the years.

Elsewhere in this book discussion is directed at type of investment the successful man must look to if he wants to plan soundly. Generally, he will avoid securities which are attractive chiefly because of high current yield. After taxes, in his case, that yield is sharply reduced. That means that even if he reinvests the entire net yield, he is able to reinvest only a comparatively small amount.

He should, instead, look to those investments which furnish tax shelter—the earnings-retention companies, the stock-dividend companies, and the companies which are granted tax protection under the tax law.

LAW GIVES TAX PROTECTION AFTER RETIREMENT

It will be the unusual situation in which the retired individual does not suffer some drop in income after retirement. While he may still draw some compensation benefits (e.g., employment pension), he will no longer be working full time and drawing full-time pay. His earned income will drop substantially. And since our income tax structure is graduated, he will be paying a reduced tax.

But aside from this, the law does give tax relief to individuals when they reach retirement age. For instance, the retired individual presumably will be drawing Social Security benefits. *These benefits are tax free.* Thus, from an accounting point of view, he receives income from Social Security. For income tax purposes, he ignores it. Also, retirement payments made to a retired employee by his former employer are subject to special tax rules which may have the effect of subjecting them to a greatly reduced tax.

Tax relief is not limited, however, to income received by an individual after retirement. The tax law covering those who have reached age sixty-five contains special provisions which give additional tax relief.

Until age sixty-five, a husband and wife are allowed two personal exemptions—$750 each. When an individual reaches sixty-five, he is granted an additional $750 personal exemption due to his age. That means a married couple, both of whom have attained sixty-five, are entitled to double exemptions—total for both, $3,000.

In fact, while they would have to file an income tax return, income over and above Social Security payments would have to exceed $4,300 before they would be liable for any tax. In addition to double exemptions for each on a joint return, they benefit from a low income allowance or a standard deduction in a further reduction of income subject to tax.

TAXES REQUIRE REVALUATION AFTER RETIREMENT

The fact that certain types of income received after retirement may be completely tax free (e.g., Social Security payments), or tax protected (e.g., annuities, employment pensions), may often require a switch in investments after retirement. A fully taxable return of 4 per cent yields 3 per cent to one earning about $10,000. The fact that 20 to 25 per cent of current investment return goes to Uncle Sam during one's working years may dictate selection of an investment which gives less of a current return but offers greater capital appreciation. But after retirement, switch to an investment which gives a higher current return may be advantageous before and after taxes.

Unlike what took place during the working years, additional income from a switch in investments is no longer subject to a comparatively high tax. Social Security payments received are real income but for tax purposes they are ignored. On remaining income, added personal exemptions and deductions reduce taxable income even further. A 6 per cent fully taxable investment formerly giving less than 5 per cent might in retirement yield more than 5 per cent after taxes. Switching investments after retirement to those giving a higher yield might increase income both before and after taxes. And it's the after-tax income which is available for spending on living needs.

So we come up with these general rules. During the capital building period prior to retirement, the individual must give serious consideration to the impact of taxes on investment unless he is in the very lowest tax bracket. Loss of 1 per cent of return due to taxes may have comparatively slight consequences over the short term, but the compounding effect over a long period—as is involved in many investment programs—can have serious consequences. After sixty-five, the tax-protected investment may become less important. The changed tax status of the retired individual gives him some protection from taxes which he did not possess before.

SOME QUESTIONS AND ANSWERS

Q. *I have only myself as a dependent. How can I cut down taxes on $27,000 in savings, and on some shares of Rochester Gas & Electric, Eastman Kodak, Monsanto and General Motors.*

A. The blocks of stocks, it seems to me, are too small to create much of a tax burden.

If you want to do something about the bank interest you might switch this money into tax-exempt municipal bonds sold by cities, states and their various departments. Income from these is exempt from federal income taxes.

Q. *Is it possible to take a tax loss any time of the year, or just at the end of the year? Some time ago, I bought 200 American Investment at 16. Even earlier I had bought, in my wife's name, 200 shares at 17. How long must I wait to buy back the 400 shares, if I sell them now? If I wait until the end of the year, the stock may be higher.*

A. You establish a tax loss any time you sell securities for less than you paid. As of the moment you have about a 4-point loss on your 200 and 5 points on your wife's holdings.

If you feel the stock will rise by the end of the year, why do anything now? You can take a loss for purposes of reducing your income-tax payments right up to the last trading day of the year.

In any event, stock sold to establish a tax loss may be bought back after waiting only 31 days.

Q. *I am a teacher who will retire in 2 years. Since my earning days are nearing an end, I would naturally, at this point, like to supplement my retirement income. Over the years I've bought common stocks and E bonds and built savings accounts. Now, and seemingly at a bad time, I'm faced with a decision as to what to do with my investments. I hold $15,000 in E bonds, the same amount in savings, $10,000 in mutual funds and odd lots of A.T.&T., Northern Illinois Gas, Douglas, Magnavox, Parke Davis, etc.*

A. I think you're borrowing trouble.

You may intend to quit in 2 years, but that's no reason to do anything now. You certainly don't want to add any income now to what most likely is the highest tax bracket of your career. So, at this point, I don't think you want to supplement your retirement income. Time enough for that when you retire.

Secondly, if you have held these for any length of time, you have taxable gains (you certainly have a taxable gain in the E bonds). Why sell out and take those gains now when your tax bracket is much higher than it will be after you retire?

In short, I don't think you have anything to worry about in the investments you hold and you certainly don't have to make any decisions now. The first year in which you have no taxable income will be the time for taking profits, paying capital-gains taxes, and switching to a high-income portfolio.

Q. *I began buying utility shares in 1948 and now—following splits—have 301 shares in 6 different companies. If I sold now, must I have evidence of these transactions for income-tax purposes? It seems all utilities rise and fall in unison, regardless of location. Why?*

A. If you sell any stock, you must have a record of what you paid for the original shares. You needn't have retained any notices of splits, since these are matters of public record. But you will need the brokerage confirmation slip showing what you paid. How else can you compute your eventual gain?

All utilities are government regulated, so that profit ratios are controlled. However, I think you will find that utilities in some faster-growing cities and areas of the country have moved up in price more than others.

Q. *Filing my income-tax return this year brings up the old, irritating problem: my company doesn't withhold a sufficient amount and the interest on my bank savings just about "murders" me. We have some shares of A.T.&T. on which we escape taxation since the total dividends are less than the dividend credit granted me and my wife. The savings account is about $15,000—my life's savings—and I have to pay a tax on the interest from the entire amount. Therein lies the rub. I plan to retire in about 2 years. Where could I invest $10,000 in savings so as to get a rea-*

sonable return for the next 2 years? I may need the money, without suffering a loss, when I reach 65.

A. You can always increase the amount withheld by dropping one of the personal exemptions from your employer's records. This would withhold more money, but not change your ultimate tax bill.

Frankly, I don't see what all the fretting is about. If your employer doesn't withhold enough, the extra money comes to you, and you have proved your ability to save it. If you put this extra money into the bank and collect interest on it, *something* is left over—no matter how high your tax bracket. So you're certainly not losing anything under the present state of affairs.

If you are in a high tax bracket, you might consider some tax-exempt municipal bonds. However, with 2 years to go, I don't think the avoidance of income taxes on $750 of annual bank interest should be your prime concern.

It seems to me that you should be gradually acquiring good securities for retirement income so that you can hope to offset inflation in the years ahead.

Q. *My husband has been engaged in his profession about 15 years. We've invested in a farm, a rental duplex, $40,000 in bonds, $33,000 taxable industrials and $7,000 in tax-exempts. Our income taxes have been high—running to about $7,000 a year. We have also been accumulating mutual funds—arriving at a total of about $46,000—and more recently individual stock issues—RCA, Pan American, Ford, Chrysler, A.T.&T., Outboard Marine, Ampex. We bought RCA at 33 and Pan Am at 10 and sold at 40 and 15, respectively, which we realize was a big mistake. Do you agree?*

A. There seems to be plenty of diversification. I assume you have time to watch over real estate in addition to tending to professional chores.

There isn't much here that is radically wrong—but a few points could be raised:

If you are in a high tax bracket, there isn't much point to $33,000 in taxable corporate bonds. Judging by your tax bill of $7,000 a year, you don't have much more than half of that interest after taxes. If you feel better with a large dollar position, that money should be in high-grade tax-exempts or tax-deferred E bonds.

Whatever money goes into common stocks should be in high-grade growth stocks to be held long-term. There was absolutely no sense to your buying RCA at 33 and then selling it at 40, even if it were a long-term gain. If you buy RCA—and it belongs in your portfolio—it should be for long-term growth, which is another way of saying until retirement, and, perhaps, even longer.

To sum up: whatever money you want in dollars, put into tax-exempt or tax-deferred investments. Whatever money you have in common stocks should be in high-quality, low-dividend, long-term issues.

24 Retirement Planning for the Self-Employed

Starting in 1963, about 8 million self-employed individuals became eligible to set up their own tax-protected retirement plans. Under a change in the Federal law, they now are able to use tax-deductible dollars in building up savings for retirement, enjoying some of the benefits which formerly were available only to employees through a tax-qualified retirement plan. However, the benefits available to the self-employed individual setting up his own retirement plan are not as liberal as those available to the executive through an employment retirement plan.

Should the self-employed individual use this type of retirement plan? There are distinct advantages. But there are also drawbacks. Before setting up his own retirement plan, a self-employed individual will have to weigh the advantages and disadvantages of such a qualified plan as they apply to him. In some instances the benefits to be gained will far outweigh any possible drawbacks. In other instances the disadvantages to a particular self-employed person will exceed the advantages. He will want to continue to save for his retirement outside of any tax-qualified plan.

WHO CAN BENEFIT?

The change in law permits self-employed individuals—sole proprietors and partners who are active in a business or a profession—to set up a qualified pension or profit-sharing plan. For tax purposes, a self-employed individual is treated as if he were an employer of himself. Thus, the doctor, dentist, lawyer, accountant, engineer, architect, and members of other professions practicing alone or in partnership will be able to set up this new type of retirement plan. The farmer, businessman, or other individual active in a trade as a sole proprietor or a partner can do the same.

WHAT BENEFITS CAN BE GAINED?

The immediate benefit is a tax deduction for the contribution which a self-employed individual makes to his retirement plan. However, there are other advantages.

Return on funds contributed to the plan compound tax-free. On an investment outside of such plan, a 4 per cent return on investment is cut to 2 per cent after tax if the investor is in the 50 per cent tax bracket. On funds contributed to a plan, the 4 per cent return would not be subject to current tax. Regardless of the individual's tax bracket, the return would compound at a 4 per cent rate.

Over a period of years, greater rate of compounding could produce a substantially greater capital amount available at time of retirement.

Upon retirement, withdrawals (except to the extent that the saver got no deduction on his contribution) will be taxed as ordinary income. Thus, it has been said that a self-employed retirement plan doesn't save taxes but only defers them. That is not necessarily so. To the extent that current tax on income is avoided to be taxed at a later date when the saver is in a lower tax bracket, there will not only be tax deferment but tax savings. At the time of retirement, loss of earned income normally will put the saver in a lower tax bracket. In addition, at age sixty-five the saver benefits from extra tax exemptions which will further reduce the amount of his income subject to tax.

Thus, by setting up a tax-qualified retirement plan, a self-employed individual stands to benefit in three ways:

1. He gets current tax deduction in the year he makes a contribution to his plan.
2. Return on contributions made to the plan compounds tax-free.
3. Income tax deferred may yield tax saving because at the time of retirement, a self-employed individual may be in a more protected tax position.

WHAT ARE THE DRAWBACKS?

There are disadvantages to the self-employed retirement plan. Before setting up such a plan, the self-employed individual must consider whether he will benefit more from setting up his own retirement plan than he would from investment saving individually outside of such a plan. What are the drawbacks?

1. If the self-employed individual has permanent employees, he will have to include them in the retirement plan he sets up for himself. That means that he will be required to contribute to his plan for the

benefit of such employees. While he will be permitted full tax deduction for such employee contribution, there will still be an after-tax cost to him. Generally, permanent employees include those who have worked full time for the self-employed individual for three or more years.

2. Unless a bank is named trustee of the retirement plan, there are substantial limitations on the type of investment which can be made. Outside this plan, a self-employed individual may have greater flexibility in selecting the type of investment for his savings.
3. Except in case of serious disability or death, the self-employed's savings within this retirement plan are not available prior to retirement for emergencies. Outside a self-employed retirement plan, an individual can readily withdraw funds from his savings to meet any increased financial obligations due to an emergency.
4. Operation of a self-employed retirement plan must meet certain technical tests. There can be tax penalties on withdrawals. Excessive contribution to the plan in an attempt to save more may also result in a penalty.

HOW DOES A SELF-EMPLOYED RETIREMENT PLAN WORK?

The self-employed individual can set up either a profit-sharing plan or a pension plan. Generally, a pension plan calls for a designated contribution each year. If a profit-sharing plan is set up, a definite formula for determining the amount of contributions must be established, including a definition of the profits to be shared. However, under a profit-sharing plan, the self-employed individual would not be forced to contribute in a year when he had reduced earned income.

Where a self-employed individual has set up a plan, generally he may contribute each year $2,500 or 10 per cent of his earned income—whichever is less—in saving for his retirement.

The permissible contribution he makes for himself is deductible from his gross income. In effect, the amount deductible is treated as a business expense.

Withdrawals and payments from contributions in the plan cannot be made until the self-employed individual reaches 59½. However, early withdrawals are permitted in case of death or serious disability. In any case, withdrawals must begin no later than 70½.

WHAT IS EARNED INCOME?

The amount which a self-employed individual can contribute to a retirement plan depends upon his earnings. Generally, that is income he receives from personal services. Where both personal services and capital are important income-producing factors in operation of a business, earned income now means entire net profits from the business.

Consider these examples of earned income for the self-employed:

1. A doctor has a net profit of $40,000 from professional services. His patients look to him as the person responsible for the services rendered. The full amount of his net profit constitutes earned income.
2. A self-employed grocer has net profit of $40,000 from his wholly owned retail grocery business. Both capital and personal services are material income-producing factors. His earned income also is $40,000.
3. A and B are partners in a stock brokerage firm. A supplies all necessary capital but performs no personal services. B has no capital, but performs all personal services required by the firm. They share profits equally. Both capital and personal services are material income-producing factors. The firm has a net profit from brokerage commissions of $50,000 and a total net profit from all sources of $70,000.

   A has no earned income from the partnership since he performed no personal services.

   B has an earned income of $35,000 (50 per cent of $70,000).

$700 A YEAR MORE FOR RETIREMENT SAVINGS

The full tax deduction on a contribution made to a self-employment plan allows one to save a greater amount each year for retirement. Consider this example:

A married individual has earnings of $25,000 a year. He may contribute $2,500 annually to his retirement plan and secure tax deduction for $2,500. However, he has high personal expenses for which he cannot take any deduction, e.g., costs of a comfortable living standard, education fees for children, premium on life policy for family protection in event of premature death, etc. In addition, he has Federal and state taxes to pay on his income. At the present time, he has only $2,000 left to save for his retirement.

If he sets up a self-employed retirement plan, a contribution of $2,500 increases his tax deductions by $2,500. In his tax bracket, that tax deduction cuts his tax liability by some $750. He has not reduced his personal expenditures or his living standard. However, the retirement plan allows him to increase his retirement investment from $2,000 a year to $2,500. He is using $500 in tax savings to save more for himself.

The value of the tax deduction is obvious here. With a plan, he has $250 more after-tax income to maintain his living standard. Moreover, with the plan, tax savings allow him to put away an additional $500 a year for retirement.

WHAT ARE THE TAX SAVINGS FOR OTHER SELF-EMPLOYEDS?

As a self-employed individual's earnings increase, benefits of a retirement plan also increase. Such an individual must have at least $25,000 earnings before he is permitted to make a maximum annual contribution of $2,500 a year to his plan. At that and higher earnings levels, he also secures the maximum deduction ($2,500) for his contribution. Thus, the individual with higher earnings can make maximum contribution and get maximum deduction. In higher tax brackets, value of the deduction increases with his income.

There is a direct relationship between a self-employed's earnings and the amount he can contribute and deduct for such contribution. The following table shows the tax savings value of deductible contributions for those with different incomes and personal status.

Earned Income	*Deductible Contribution*	*Tax Savings*
$ 10,000	$1,000	$ 220
15,000	1,500	375
20,000	2,000	560
30,000	2,500	960
40,000	2,500	1,125
50,000	2,500	1,250
100,000	2,500	1,500

The table assumes that the self-employed is married and is filing a joint return. Tax savings for a self-employed filing a separate return would be greater. Even so, tax savings finance 22% of current contribution cost for a married self-employed with $10,000 in earned income and 60% from the individual with $100,000 earnings.

WHAT IS THE CUMULATIVE VALUE OF TAX SAVINGS?

A self-employed individual with income of about $40,000 a year contributes $2,500 to a retirement plan. He gets a tax deduction of $2,500 for such contribution. In his tax bracket, that deduction has a value in the form of tax savings of $1,200. Thus, when this self-employed individual contributes $2,500 to the plan, he is actually contributing only $1,300 of his own funds. Tax money in the form of a reduced tax liability contributes $1,200. Moreover, return on the entire contribution compounds tax-free within the plan. The self-employed individual not only gets tax-free compounding on his real contribution ($1,300), but also gets a tax-free yield on tax money contributed ($1,200). Over a period of time, the value of the annual tax savings ($1,200) will be increased because return on that part of self-employed's contribution is being increased by a tax-free return.

Assume that a married self-employed individual will make maximum contribution to his plan. On his real contribution and that part of his contribution reflecting tax money, he gets a 5 per cent return. Over a twenty-year period, how much will he have saved for retirement? How much of those savings will reflect tax money contributed plus tax-free compounding on it?

The following table shows the results. It is based on the lower rates which again will be in effect when the temporary surtax lapses.

Earned Income	*20-Year Retirement Amount*	*Contributed by Tax Savings*
$ 10,000	$33,005	$ 7,275
15,000	49,600	12,400
20,000	66,130	18,515
30,000	82,600	31,740
40,000	82,600	37,200
50,000	82,600	41,330
100,000	82,600	49,600

LIMITATIONS ON INVESTMENT

When a self-employed individual sets up his own retirement plan, he loses some of the investment flexibility he would have on saving outside the plan.

Under the plan, if he wants maximum selection of investment media, he must set up a trust, naming a bank or trust company. If he does that, he can retain the power to direct investment of his contributions or disapprove a proposed investment. If he doesn't use a bank as a trustee, investment is more limited.

His contributions may be paid directly to an insurance company to buy nontransferable annuity contracts. Or he may have a trustee—and in this instance it need not be a bank—who will invest his contribution solely in insurance company contracts.

Use of a trustee is not required to invest contributions. The self-employed might use a custodial account of a bank. If that is done, investment must be solely in shares of a mutual fund, an annuity, endowment or life insurance contracts.

There are two other permissible investments available. Self-employed contributions might be invested directly in nontransferable face-amount certificates. These are certificates registered with the Securities & Exchange Commission and sold by face-amount certificate companies registered under the Investment Company Act of 1940. Contributions may also be invested directly in a new series of U.S. Government bonds similar to E bonds. These bonds are issued in the name of the self-employed, are nontransferable, and can't be cashed in until the owner is 59½ years old or becomes disabled or dies.

HOW CAN RETIREMENT FUNDS BE WITHDRAWN?

The self-employed can't draw out benefits until he is 59½ years old unless he becomes permanently disabled before that age. However, earlier benefits are payable to his beneficiaries in case of death. He also may not delay withdrawals unduly. He must start getting benefits by the time he reaches 70½.

HOW ARE RETIREMENT WITHDRAWALS TAXED?

If a self-employed individual withdraws his entire retirement savings upon retirement, such lump sum distribution is ordinary income. He doesn't have to pay a tax, however, on the amounts of distribution for which he didn't get a tax deduction at the time of contribution. In addition, he is permitted to pay tax under an averaging formula. The tax on the lump sum distribution is five times the increase in tax resulting from adding 20 per cent of the taxable portion of such distribution to his other income in the year of withdrawal.

How does this rule work? In year of retirement, married self-employed has $10,000 taxable income. His taxable portion of withdrawals from his retirement plan is $20,000. He adds $4,000 (20 per cent of $20,000 retirement distribution) to his taxable income of $10,000. The tax on $14,000 is $2,760. Tax on $10,000 ($4,000 excluded) is $1,820. Difference in tax on $14,000 and $10,000 income is $940. Multiplying that difference by 5 gives $4,700. That is the tax due on $20,000 retirement withdrawal.

If a self-employed individual has invested in an annuity, annuity payments he receives on retirement are taxed only when received. However, if he cashes in the annuity for a lump sum when he retires, he is taxed under the lump sum distribution rule previously described. If he invested in the special U.S. Government bonds, he is taxed when he cashes in such bonds.

WHO IS AN EMPLOYEE?

Where a self-employed individual has no employees, the retirement plan he sets up benefits him alone. However, if he has employees, his plan must cover them also. Employees who must be covered by his plan are all those (except part-time and seasonal workers) who have been employed by him for more than three years. While he is allowed deduction for contribution made in behalf of such employees, he will have an after-tax cost due to such contributions. That is one of the drawbacks to a self-employed retirement plan.

PENALTIES CAN BE INCURRED

There are some things which the self-employed can do and some things that he cannot do if he wants tax benefits from his retirement plan. Generally, he can't borrow from his plan or buy or sell property to it.

He can also be penalized if he seeks to save at an accelerated rate for retirement by making contributions to his plan greater than that which is permitted under this new law. He can also be penalized if he attempts to use his plan for other than retirement purposes. Thus, penalty will apply if he attempts to withdraw funds from his plan before the permissible age. Withdrawals before then (except in the case of total disability) are classified as premature distributions which carry with them tax penalties.

25 Investment Programs for Your Children

The world of finance is generally believed to be an adult world even though anyone who has raised a family is very much aware that a good part of his financial efforts and his financial planning are directly involved with "the kids."

Children are expensive to bring into the world, to rear, to educate and to send out into the world. With the educational process today not only costly, but prolonged, even parents with only two or three children to educate must figure on a grand sum of somewhere around $75,000—especially if (as is now required for entry into most professions) graduate work is required. And schooling alone is not the only expense.

A glance through the society pages today will prove to those who grew up in less affluent times that the old parental admonition: "If you want to get married, get yourself a job first" is no longer in vogue. Young people entering their 20s, with anywhere from 2 to 5, and even more years, of educational expenses ahead of them are now setting up families and the once-humorous remark about the graduation ceremony being disrupted by cries of "daddy!" from the audience is no longer news.

This being so, it behooves the prudent man planning his lifetime financial program to seek out the most efficient plan he can find to finance this prolonged and increasingly expensive educational process.

One of the sure-fire methods of cutting down this bill is to get the money involved out of the provider's tax stream.

The income tax is a graduated tax. At one time the top tax rate exceeded 90 per cent. The rates have been reduced somewhat. Now they start at 14 per cent and climb to 70 per cent. However, even under those reduced rates, some individuals can be subject to very high taxes—a tax rate up to 70 per cent.

As a result, an individual in the highest tax bracket is a junior partner with the Internal Revenue Service in sharing any return he gets from his investments. Such an individual keeps only $3,000 of an investment return of $10,000; the tax collector takes $7,000. In terms of yield, such individual keeps only 1.5 per cent after taxes of a 5 per cent return from a particular investment; 1.35 per cent of a 4.5 per cent return; 1.2 per cent of a 4 per cent return, etc.

If an individual in the highest tax bracket could shift income from some of his investments to members of his family, a good deal more of that income would be kept by the family unit. For instance, up until recently, a father could shift dividend income of about $1,800 from some of his stocks to a minor child so as to free such dividends from income tax. While a tax return had to be filed for such child, no tax was due. The dividend income of $1,800 shifted to the child was freed from tax by personal exemption allowed the child, a dividend exclusion, and a low income allowance. Before the shifting of $1,800 in dividend income, a father in the 70 per cent tax bracket would have kept only $540 after taxes. That same income paid to the child was freed from tax so that the family unit kept $1,800. In other words, the after-tax return from such $1,800 in dividends was more than tripled.

A child under 19, or if older but attending school, remains the tax dependent of a father, providing chief support. Thus, in the above example, a double personal exemption for the child was secured. On the child's tax return, the child claimed a personal exemption for himself. The child, however, still remained the tax dependent of the father so that the father also claimed a dependency exemption for the child on the father's tax return.

NEW RULE COVERS SHIFTING OF INCOME

Late in 1971, Congress changed the tax law so that tax benefits from shifting income to a dependent, such as a minor child, were reduced somewhat. However, tax savings for the family have only been reduced; they have not been eliminated. Now the tax dependent of another taxpayer is allowed a standard deduction or low-income allowance on a return filed by the dependent, only to the extent that the dependent has earned income.

Even so, shifting of investment income to a dependent family member still can yield significant tax savings within the family unit. For example, a minor child, tax dependent of the father, has no earnings during the year. The child does have taxable income, though, due to dividend income shifted to him from his father. In filing a return for the child, the child is entitled to a personal exemption of $750 and a dividend exclusion of $100. Thus, until dividends received by the child exceed $850, the child owes no income tax. On dividends received by the child in excess of that amount, the excess is taxed at a low starting rate of 14 per cent. If the father shifted $2,000 in dividend income to the child, the child would owe an income tax of about $170 after personal exemption and dividend exclusion. On the $2,000 dividend income before it was shifted to the child, the father, in the top tax bracket, would have been liable for an income tax of $1,400.

Even in the case of an individual in a lower tax bracket, this shifting of income can yield tax saving, thus increasing the investment return kept within the family unit. A father in the 50 per cent tax bracket shifting $1,000 income to a child could almost double the amount kept within the family unit.

There are several vehicles for effecting this shift of income:

USE OF A BROKERAGE ACCOUNT

In seeking to shift investment income and to reduce tax on such income for savings within the family unit, one investor did this:

He entered into an agreement with his relatives under which he opened a joint stock trading account in his and their names. He retained limited power of attorney which authorized him to buy and sell for the account. He was to bear all losses, but any gains were to be divided among his relatives and himself.

Withdrawals from the account first were applied to reimbursing him for the deposits he made in behalf of the relatives, in accordance with his agreement with them. As a result, initial profits were taxable to him because they were earned by him through a combination of his knowledge and capital. However, to the extent that subsequent profits were allowed to remain in the account and were reinvested, these gains represented additional capital belonging both to the investor and to his relatives. Subsequent profits derived from such additional capital were shared by the taxpayer and his relatives and were taxed to them according to the division of profits under the investment agreement.

Where one family member intends to shift investment income to another so that such income would be taxed in a lower bracket and, thus, more retained by the family, the Revenue Service will agree to such tax shifting only if there has been a completed gift of the property producing the income. In the case of this brokerage account, the Revenue Service, after some debate, has agreed that this arrangement is legal. It has ruled that shifting of income and tax among family members will be allowed in a similar situation. Thus, tax on investment return can be reduced with a greater amount of net income retained by the family.

OUTRIGHT GIFT OF SECURITIES

In seeking to shift income that he gets from investments to a family member taxed in a lower bracket, an individual might make an outright gift of securities. On such an outright gift, ownership of the securities is transferred to the family member and income from such securities taxed at lower rates. Where this outright gift is made to a family member who is an adult, a gift does not raise any complex legal problems. However, an outright gift of securities directly to a minor child is not advisable.

In the past, where an adult family member wished to shift investment income to a minor child through a gift of securities, creation of a trust for such child was essential. During the minority of the child, the trustee held title to the securities for the child. Thus, legal formalities of a trust were required.

USE OF A CUSTODIAN ACCOUNT FOR A MINOR CHILD

In all fifty states, it is now possible to shift investment income and tax on that income to a minor child by use of a custodian account. A direct gift of securities to a person under twenty-one is possible by registering the security in the name of a custodian. Generally, the custodian may be a parent, child's guardian, grandparents, adult brothers or sisters, uncles, aunts, etc. It is even possible for the donor of a gift of securities to a minor child to act as custodian. However, for estate tax reasons, that is not advisable.

A custodian is given the right to sell securities for the account of the child, collect proceeds and investment income and use them for the child's benefit or for reinvestment. While the custodian is given broad powers over the account during the child's minority, there are some minor limitations. For instance, the custodian acting in behalf of the minor child, is required to act with prudence in seeking reasonable income and in preservation of capital. For that reason, he can't take proceeds from sale of an investment or income from investments to buy additional securities on margin.

During the minority of the child, the custodian manages the investment property for the benefit of the child. When the child reaches age twenty-one, property in the custodian account is turned over to him. No formal accounting by the custodian to the child is required. The child, on reaching majority, may sign a simple release, freeing the custodian from any liability. However, on reaching twenty-one, the child may require a formal accounting if he has doubts as to the propriety of the custodian's actions while he acted as custodian. Because the child may demand such formal accounting and also for record-keeping purposes, a separate bank account should be opened in which proceeds from sale of investments and investment income are deposited pending reinvestment in behalf of the minor child. Such step will furnish a convenient record showing receipt of sales proceeds, investment income and reinvestment.

SAVINGS FROM THE CUSTODIAN ACCOUNT

During the child's minority, the custodian may accumulate investment income and reinvest it. However, the custodian also may use income for the benefit of the child. As long as income from the custodian account is not used to discharge a legal obligation (e.g., a parent's obligation to support the child), income realized by a custodian account is taxed to the child. However, unless the custodian account produces a substantial amount of annual income, tax on that income will be at a minimum rate, if any tax is incurred at all. The child is entitled to a personal exemption of $750. If income produced by the custodian account comes from dividends from stock investment, the child also is allowed a $100 dividend exclusion. While a tax return would have to be filed for the child if custodian income totals $750 or more a year, no tax would be incurred in this situation even though such income totaled $850.

Consider the income-tax savings which might be secured where the custodian account does produce $850 a year in dividend income. Let us assume that child's father, whose income is taxed in a high bracket, establishes this custodian account. Dividend income of $850, formerly reduced to $250 after father paid tax on it, is completely free of income tax now that it is paid to the child. This, of course, is an extreme example, involving a father in the top tax brackets. However, even for a father in a lower tax bracket, income-tax savings could be secured for the family by use of the custodian account.

There is an added income-tax advantage. Even though income being accumulated by the custodian for the child is substantial, a parent who is the chief support of the child still may claim the child as a tax dependent on the parent's tax return. For instance, that would be so where the child is under nineteen, or, regardless of age, is a full-time student. Thus, even though the child uses his $750 exemption to avoid tax on custodian account income, the parent continues to enjoy a $750 tax dependent exemption for the child. Thus, a minor may yield a total family tax exemption of as much as $1,600 instead of the $750 per child where no custodian arrangement is set up.

USE OF A TRUST

In seeking to shift investment income and tax on it to a minor, the custodian arrangement does offer advantages. However, investment generally is limited to securities. Where a gift is made through a trust, the trustee may make any investment permitted by the trust agreement. For instance, investment might be made in real estate if trustee was permitted to make it under trust agreement.

Where a gift in trust is made for the benefit of a minor, trust income generally will be accumulated in whole or in part for the child during the child's minority. Under recent changes made to the tax law, new rules cover trusts that accumulate income. The trust, as a separate taxpayer, must pay a tax on trust income accumulated during such year. Subsequently, when accumulated income is distributed to the child beneficiary, the child also must pay a tax on the distributed income. However, that does not mean that there will be a double tax on the same income—first on the trust and then on the child beneficiary in a later year.

Generally, these income-tax rules apply:

1. In the year income is accumulated by a trust, it must pay a tax on such income. However, unless the trust produces a very substantial amount of income over and above $100 income exemption of the trust, rate of tax will be quite low.
2. In subsequent years, when such accumulated income is distributed to the child beneficiary, the child will realize taxable income. However, tax on such accumulated-income distribution will be calculated as if such income actually had been distributed to the child in the previous year of accumulation. If the child had no earnings in such earlier year, no tax might be incurred on such accumulation until it exceeded $850. Even if it exceeded such amount, the excess would be taxed at a low starting rate of 14%.
3. Moreover, in figuring any tax due from the child in the year of distribution, the tax previously paid by the trust on such accumulated income will reduce the tax due from the child beneficiary. Thus, the tax previously paid by the trust on accumulated income could eliminate any tax due from the child on such income in the year distributed. In fact, the tax previously paid by the trust could exceed the tax due from the child so that the child could actually secure a tax refund. Generally a trust for a minor will accumulate income. Over the period during which income is accumulated, income records for the trust and also for the minor beneficiary therefore will have to be maintained. Such records are required in order to calculate tax liability. Thus, there is now an added record-keeping requirement, where a trust is used to shift investment income for tax savings within the family.

Note that these new tax rules covering a trust and minor beneficiary apply only where the trust accumulates income. If the trust must distribute its income currently, no tax will be due from the trust. However, similar to the custodian arrangement, trust income taxed directly to the child could be freed from tax unless it exceeded $850 a year. Even if it exceeded such amount, excess would be subject to tax at a low rate.

USE OF TAX-FAVORED TRUST

On a gift to or for the benefit of a family member, a gift tax return may be required. However, a gift tax exclusion may be available to minimize or to avoid completely any gift tax.

A gift tax exclusion is allowed a donor on a gift in trust for a minor child, if the trust agreement meets these tax tests:

1. Income may be used for the child during his minority, but it does not have to be so used. If it isn't, income is accumulated.
2. When the child reaches twenty-one, any accumulated income and trust principal is to be distributed to the child. If the child dies before he reaches

twenty-one, this distribution is to be made to his estate.

As previously noted, any accumulated income will be taxed to the trust initially. On subsequent distribution of accumulated income, the beneficiary also will realize taxable income in year of distribution. However, the tax previously paid on the accumulated income by the trust will be offset against any tax due from the beneficiary. In many instances, due to this offsetting, no tax will be due from the beneficiary on the accumulated income distribution. In fact, the beneficiary might be entitled to a refund of part of the tax paid by the trust in an earlier year.

If income is distributed currently or used for the benefit of the child, tax rules similar to those applied to the custodian arrangement apply to the gift in trust. Income distributed or used for the child currently will be taxed to the child unless such income is used to discharge a legal obligation to support the child. Thus, if the trust produced $850 in dividend income, all of which was distributed, trust would pay no tax. Nor would there be any tax on such income included on the tax return filed for the child. The child benefits from a $750 exemption and could secure a $100 dividend exclusion in this situation—a total of $850.

Similar to the custodian arrangement, use of this trust promises an extra income tax advantage and also estate tax savings. Even though the trust produces high income, a parent, chief support of the child, may claim the child as a tax dependent on the parent's tax return. Also, the creator of the trust has made a completed gift for the benefit of the child and thus future estate tax savings might be secured. For possible estate tax savings, though, it was previously pointed out that a donor on a gift to a child under the custodian arrangement should not have named himself as custodian. He should name someone else. This tax precaution also is important in the case of this trust for a child. Creator of the trust should not name himself trustee.

USE OF SHORT-TERM REVERSIONARY TRUST

By an assignment of income alone, a donor can't shift tax on such income to a family member in a lower tax bracket. While such assignment may be recognized for other legal purposes, such income still would be taxed to the donor even though it was paid to another. That generally is true regardless of whether the income is earned or derived from investments. Thus, the lawyer who earned but had not received payment of a fee might assign the fee and thus shift income to another family member. However, the lawyer still would have to pay income taxes on such fee.

However, there is an exception to this tax rule covering assignment of income where the income is from investments. It is possible for an individual receiving a return from investments to transfer such investment income without complete surrender of ownership of the property which produces it. This transfer of investment income which would also shift the tax is possible through the short-term reversionary trust.

The name "short-term reversionary trust" carries implications of a complex transfer in trust. Actually that is not so. Although carrying a formidable name, the transfer is not a complicated one. The grantor transfers investment property to a trust. The trust is to continue for a period of years. During the term of the trust, income will be distributed or accumulated for the benefit of another. At the end of the trust term, the trust terminates and the grantor gets back his investment property. Under this trust, the grantor has a *reversionary* interest. He has surrendered ownership of his property only for a specified period of time. When that period ends, he gets back his investment property—it *reverts* to him. He has given away only the income earned by the investment during the period of the trust.

And he has been excused from paying any taxes on that income.

However, to shift his income legally, and to avoid the tax liability on such income, the trust must continue for a definite period. Under the tax law, the trust generally must run for a period of at least ten years. There is an exception to this ten-year rule: The agreement may provide that the trust is to continue for at least ten years or for the life of the trust beneficiary, whichever is shorter.

The short-term reversionary trust now is being widely used. For instance, a father with a high income from earnings and investment return is taxed in a high bracket. He would be willing to shift income from some of his investments to his eleven-year-old daughter. However, to safeguard against the possibility that disability sometime in the future might result in reduction in his earned income, he does not wish to give away investment property permanently. He establishes a trust for his daughter which is to continue for ten years, until she reaches twenty-one. The trustee may distribute income to the daughter during her minority if she should need it, but the intention is to accumulate such income for her.

Let us assume the trust income is accumulated. Investment income produced by the property transferred to the trust would be taxed to the separate trust entity. It would no longer be taxed to the father. The trust, in a lower tax bracket, would keep more of the investment income after taxes than did the father before this transfer in trust. When the daughter reaches twenty-one, accumulated income, taxed at a low rate, could furnish her with a substantial capital sum. It could be used by her to continue her education, a dowry on her marriage, etc. However, when the trust terminates, the father would get back his investment property.

SAVINGS FROM SHORT-TERM REVERSIONARY TRUST

A trust cannot be used to shift tax on investment income where such income is used to discharge a legal obligation. That is to pay expenses which legally are the obligation of parent to a minor child, or son toward dependent, elderly parent. That tax rule covers all trusts, including the short-term reversionary trust. However, there may be instances where income form short-term reversionary trust will not result in use to discharge legal obligation. To illustrate this legal obligation rule, consider these two situations:

Stanley Smith establishes a reversionary trust which is to continue for ten years or for the life of his elderly mother, whichever is shorter. John Jones establishes similar trust for his mother, who is also elderly. The time test—the *short-term* factor—for a valid reversionary trust is met in both instances. Both trusts will continue for ten years or for the life of the beneficiary, whichever is shorter. Thus, even though a mother-beneficiary died before ten years had passed, the time test will have been met.

1. In the case of Stanley Smith, his mother is almost destitute. She has no income or capital of her own. In the absence of contributions from her son for her support, she would have to seek public relief. Under state law in this situation, Stanley Smith, since he has the financial resources, would be required to support his mother. When he creates the short-term trust for her benefit, trust income paid to her still would be taxed to him. He cannot use a short-term reversionary trust to shift some investment income and tax on it to his mother. He cannot secure tax savings which would allow him to continue his present support contributions at a reduced cost or to increase his contributions at no additional cost.
2. The situation of John Jones is different. His mother does have capital and she receives sufficient income to meet her living needs. However, her son makes additional contributions to her so that she can afford extras which make for more comfortable living. In this situation, the mother is not a dependent under state law of her son. John Jones is not under any legal obligation to make the contribution that he regularly does. When he establishes a short-term reversionary trust for his mother, trust income being paid to her is not being used to discharge his legal obligation. Thus, for the duration of the trust, income and tax on part of his investments can be legally shifted to his mother. Such investment income, taxed in a low bracket to her, will yield more after taxes than that formerly received by the son from such investments.

In only the second of the two preceding examples would shifting of investment income through a short-term reversionary trust produce tax savings sought. However, there are many other family situations where creation of a short-term reversionary trust will not result in use of trust income to discharge a legal obligation. In such cases, the trust will yield income-tax savings and more investment income will be retained within the family unit.

ESTATE TAX SAVINGS CAN BE SECURED

An individual who will leave more than $60,000 at death must consider estate planning during life. For estate tax purposes, one's estate benefits from a $60,000 exemption and certain deductions. However, if the total amount left by an individual in the form of investments, home equity, life insurance payable to survivor, etc., exceeds the $60,000 exemption and any allowable deductions, an estate tax will be incurred. While the Federal estate tax starts at a low 3 per cent rate, it rises to a maximum of 77 per cent.

Previous discussion in this book has been directed at income tax savings within the family unit possible through certain types of transfers. Thus, income tax savings can be secured through a family brokerage account, outright gifts, through the custodian arrangement or tax-favored trust for a minor child, and through the short-term reversionary trust.

Some—but not all—of these transfers could yield future estate tax savings as well as current income tax savings. Dual tax savings—income and estate tax—thus might be secured through outright gifts, custodian arrangements, and tax-favored trust for a minor child.

However, in seeking these dual tax savings, it is essential to secure competent legal advice. For instance, the father might transfer investment property to a custodian or to a tax-favored trust for a minor child. The father can name himself as custodian or trustee. Income-tax savings would not necessarily be lost because the father acted as custodian or trustee. However, for estate tax purposes, it would not be advisable for the father to act in such fiduciary capacity. If the father survived until his child attained twenty-one years of age, estate tax savings would be secured on the father's subsequent death due to earlier transfer of investment property. However, if the father, acting as custodian or trustee, died before his child attained twenty-one, possible estate tax savings would be lost. Even though the child on reaching majority would secure unrestricted ownership of investment property transferred earlier by the father, such investment property would be included in the father's taxable estate.

Where investment property is transferred to a short-term reversionary trust, the primary tax benefit sought is income-tax savings. The grantor of such trust is not surrendering complete ownership of his investment property transferred to the trust. If the grantor should die after such a trust has terminated, his investment property would have reverted to him. It would be included in his taxable estate so the trust would not yield any estate tax saxings. Even if the grantor should die before the trust terminated, investment property in the trust subsequently would revert to his estate. Value of such investment property, reduced only by the value of the outstanding trust income-interest, also would be included in his taxable estate. Thus, the reversionary trust, while it can yield income-tax savings and increase the after-tax yield from investments, will not produce estate tax savings.

However, other trust arrangements can be used to secure estate tax as well as income tax savings.

OTHER TRUST ARRANGEMENTS

In seeking current income-tax savings and future estate-tax savings on death, individuals who will leave taxable estates are making gifts to family members during life. Formerly, most of these gifts were outright in form. An individual would make a direct gift of stocks or other securities from his investment portfolio to a member of his family. However, in recent years, an ever-increasing number of donors are making gifts using trusts. A study based on U.S. Treasury data which covered various levels of individual wealth—considerably under $1 million to more than $10 million—confirms this change in the form of gift. Thus, as a percentage of wealth, outright gifts made by individuals during life range from less than 1 per cent up to 7.8 per cent. On the other hand, lifetime gifts in trust, as a percentage of a donor's wealth, range from a low of 10 per cent up to 24 per cent.

A gift in trust is more complex than an outright gift and involves greater legal complications. For one thing, the donor's legal advisor first must draft a trust agreement and then must carefully check to make certain that it complies with laws covering trusts and taxes, both state and Federal. Moreover, a trustee must be appointed and periodic fiduciary accounting is required. However, in seeking income-tax and estate-tax savings by gift of investment property during life, the trust arrangement offers greater flexibility than the outright gift. And aside from any tax or other legal advantages, use of the trust can preserve investment capital. On an outright gift, the donee-recipient gets full ownership of investment property with no restrictions. After such a gift, the donor could not take any steps to prevent imprudent action by the donee-recipient which might result in loss or dissipation of capital.

SAVINGS FROM TRUST GIFTS

When a donor transfers investment property to a short-term reversionary trust, he retains ownership rights in the property through his reversionary interest. While valuable income-tax savings may be secured for the benefit of the donor's family, the short-term reversionary trust will not yield estate-tax savings. Where a donor transfers investment property to irrevocable, nonreversionary trust, he surrenders ownership to the property transferred. Thus, the donor's family might not only secure current and recurring income-tax savings, but the investment property can be removed from the donor's taxable estate for future estate tax savings. True, both income-tax and estate-tax savings can be secured for the benefit of the donor's family on an outright gift to a family member of investment property. However, the outright gift usually involves a transfer to *one* member of the family. Where a donor makes a gift to an irrevocable trust, multiple beneficiaries can be named. Beneficiaries might include the donor's parents, spouse, children or grandchildren. Moreover, interest of different beneficiaries could be varied. One family member might receive only an interest in the income of the trust, another, only in part of trust capital, perhaps delayed in enjoyment until the trust terminates. A family member might be given an interest in both the income and capital of the trust.

Studies covering the use and advantages of the irrevocable trust, running from short monographs to handbooks hundreds of pages in length, and varying from simple expositions to detailed analyses of complex rules, have been written. In a book dealing with investments, it is impossible to cover in depth the various uses to which such trusts can be put. But this warrants repeating—the trust can be an extremely flexible way to make gifts to family members. Because multiple variations are possible, the trust can be used to secure benefits for the family in a variety of family situations. Consider these examples:

1. A husband creates a trust, all income payable to his wife for her life. On her death, trust principal will be distributed to the children. Presumably, the husband and wife file a joint tax return. This trust, therefore, will not yield income-tax savings. Trust income received by the wife will be taxed on the joint return filed by the couple. However, on this irrevocable transfer, the husband could secure future estate tax savings on his death. He no longer owns the investment property transferred to the trust. On his death, such property will not be included in his taxable estate. Even though the wife continues to get investment income from the trust after her husband's death, trust property will not be included in her estate on her death. She has only an income interest in the trust. Thus, on the deaths of both husband and wife, estate tax is avoided. Trust principal, which the children ultimately receive, is not diluted by estate taxes.
2. A father with substantial investment holdings might use an irrevocable trust to secure income-tax and estate-tax savings for the benefit of his children and grandchildren. During life, he transfers some of his stocks to a trust, income payable to his children for their lives. On their deaths, trust principal is to be distributed to grandchildren. This trust will permit him to shift investment income to children in lower tax brackets. Moreover, principal in the trust will not be subject to estate tax on subsequent deaths of father and children. Trust principal ultimately distributed to grandchildren will not be reduced by estate taxes.

In the preceding example, children get only income interests in the trust. But what if their economic circumstances should change so that in addition to trust income, one or more of the children subsequently has need of trust capital? This possibility can be taken into account. The trustee is authorized to invade trust capital, if needed, for the benefit of the children. Even though this invasion privilege is specifically contained in the trust agreement, income-tax and estate-tax savings possible through the use of this trust are preserved.

By including capital invasion provision in the trust, the father can take a precautionary step for the economic welfare of his children in the event they suffer financial reverses.

WILL THERE BE A GIFT TAX COST?

By outright gift of investment property or gift through the custodian arrangement, the tax-favored trust for a minor, the short-term trust in which the grantor keeps a reversionary interest, and other trusts in which the grantor does not have a reversionary interest, tax savings for the benefit of the family can be secured. However, all of these arrangements require a gift. With the exception of the reversionary trust where the investment property will revert to the owner, all involve a gift of investment capital by the owner to other family members.

On such gifts, the donor may be required to file a gift tax return. However, even where a gift tax return is required, a gift tax may not be due. In minimizing and even eliminating any gift tax, the donor can benefit from certain exclusions, an exemption, and deductions under the tax law. Moreover, even where a particular gift will require payment of a gift tax, the tax savings within the family—both current income and future estate tax—can greatly exceed any gift tax cost.

A donor can benefit from recurring annual exclusions. Thus, a donor can exclude the first $3,000 of each gift to each donee-recipient on gifts made in any year—if the gift qualifies as a "present interest."

An outright gift qualifies as a present interest, allowing $3,000 exclusion to the donor.

A gift to a child using the custodian arrangement also will qualify as a present interest gift. So will a gift through the tax-favored trust. The donor can reduce the value of any gift by annual exclusion on such gift in trust.

On other gifts in trust, exclusion (or exclusions) are allowed for the value of the income interest (or interests) where trust income must be paid to a beneficiary (or beneficiaries). However, with the exception of the tax-favored trust for a minor child, no exclusion (or exclusions) are allowed for trust income interest (or interests) where trust income may be or must be accumulated. Moreover, no exclusion is allowed in reducing the value of trust principal which subsequently will be distributed to beneficiaries when the trust ends.

In addition to annual exclusions available to a donor in reducing value of his gifts for gift tax purposes, the donor is allowed a $30,000 lifetime exemption. Thus, a donor could escape gift tax on gifts in excess of allowable exclusions until such gifts made in one year or over a period of years exceed $30,000.

A gift-splitting provision also is included in the gift tax law. The donor's spouse can "consent" to gifts the donor makes to third parties, e.g., children or other family members. If the donor's spouse consents to the donor's gifts, the donor, in effect, benefits from double exclusion (i.e., increased from $3,000 to $6,000) and the lifetime exemption also is raised from $30,000 to $60,000.

Finally, the donor can benefit from a marital deduction provision on gifts to spouse—if certain tests are met. Where the marital deduction is secured, the donor is allowed to reduce his gift by 50 per cent in computing the amount taken into account for gift tax purposes. Thus, if a husband gave his wife $100,000, in computing any gift tax incurred on such gift he would use a $50,000 amount.

GIFT TAX VALUE ON REVERSIONARY TRUST GIFT

Generally, market value of the property transferred measures the value of any gift for gift tax purposes. Thus, if an investor gave $2,000 in listed securities outright to a member of his family, value for gift tax purposes would be $2,000. Moreover, in this situation, no gift tax return would be required. The outright gift qualifies for the $3,000 exclusion and the gift here would be less than that amount.

On a gift in trust of investment property in which the donor retains no reversionary interest, the market value of the investment property transferred also measures value for gift tax purposes. The donor in such situation has surrendered all ownership rights in the property transferred to the trust.

On the other hand, where a donor transfers investment property to a short-term reversionary trust, he is making a gift of investment income for a period. From a gift tax point of view, this means gift tax reduction even though valuable investment property is transferred to such trust.

In valuing this gift in trust, only the value of the income interest is taken into account for gift tax purposes. For example, according to Treasury Department tables, the value of a gift of income for a period of *ten years* is 44.1 per cent of the value of the investment property transferred to the reversionary trust. Assume a grandfather transferred investment property worth $100,000 to a reversionary trust for his grandson which is to continue for ten years. The value of this gift of income to the grandson is 44.1 per cent of the property ($100,000) transferred to the trust. Thus, in the case of a ten-year reversionary trust, any gift tax incurred by the grandfather is not measured by the value of investment property ($100,000) transferred to the trust, but by the lower $44,100 value (44.1 per cent of $100,000) attributable to the income interest.

If, in the preceding example, the grandfather transferred $100,000 investment property to a reversionary trust for his grandson which was to continue for *twelve rather than ten years*, the value of the income interest would be increased. According to Treasury Department tables, the value of an income interest for twelve years is 50 per cent of the value of the property transferred to reversionary trust. Thus, if the grandfather created a twelve-year reversionary trust, value of his gift of income would be $50,000 (50 percent of $100,000 transferred to the trust.)